難說拒絕

中國人究竟做對了什麼事（中英對照）

博學 博學出版社

王堅 著

難說拒絕
Hard to Say NO

作　　　者　：　王堅　James J. Wang

編　　　輯　：　Annie

封 面 設 計　：　Steve

排　　　版　：　Leo

校 對 監 製　：　Jery

出　　　版　：　博學出版社

地　　　址　：　香港香港中環德輔道中 107-111 號
余崇本行 12 樓 1203 室

出 版 直 線　：　(852) 8114 3294

電　　　話　：　(852) 8114 3292

傳　　　真　：　(852) 3012 1586

網　　　址　：　www.globalcpc.com

電　　　郵　：　info@globalcpc.com

網 上 書 店　：　http://www.hkonline2000.com

發　　　行　：　聯合書刊物流有限公司

印　　　刷　：　博學國際

國 際 書 號　：　978-988-79343-5-6

出 版 日 期　：　2019 年 6 月

定　　　價　：　港幣 $98

Published and Printed in Hong Kong

如有釘裝錯漏問題，請與出版社聯絡更換。

序

今天，中華民族在哲學、文化領域面臨諸多挑戰、疑慮和難解之處，其困難程度絲毫不比中國首創保持連續 40 年國民生產總值 GDP 年平均增長高達 9.5% 以上的世界經濟奇跡，小到哪裡去。

"中國不會成為世界超級大國，因為中國今天出口的是產品，而不是思想觀念。中國的知識體系不能參與世界知識體系的建構，不能成為知識生產的大國。即使中國在快速的經濟崛起，充其量也只能成為一個物質生產大國，但是在精神文化生產和創新乃至輸出上仍然是個無需重視的小國。"（前英國首相柴契爾夫人語）

"20 年後，中國將成為全球最窮的國家"美國前國務卿希拉蕊給出的依據：中國人不瞭解他們作為社會個體應該對國家和社會所承擔的責任和義務；中國人是世界上少數沒有信仰的可怕國家之一，全民上上下下唯一的崇拜就是權力和金錢，自私自利，沒有愛心；中國人所說的政治除了欺騙和背叛沒有其它東西；大多數中國人從來就沒有學到過什麼是體面和尊敬的生活意義；肆無忌憚地對環境的破壞、對資源的掠奪，幾近瘋狂。

"中國對人類文明沒有絲毫貢獻，中國文化影響近乎為零，將來也不會增加"（英國前外交部長伯里斯·詹森語）

"我敢說，你們說不出任何一項創新專案、創新變革以及創新產品是來自中國"，"在一個無法自由呼吸的國家，你將無法進行不同常人的思考；在一個無法挑戰正統的國家，你將無法進行不同常人的思考。因為改變只會從挑戰正統中產生。"（時任美國前副總統拜登語）

"不遠的將來，我們將會發現一個歷史性時刻：自英國喬治三世（1738～1820 年）以來，一個非西方、非民主的國家成為世界上最大的經濟體。倘若這樣的事情發生的話，中國將如何在國際秩序中施展自己的力量？它會接受戰後世界秩序的規範和機構嗎？中國會尋求改變這個秩序嗎？"（澳大利亞前總理陸克文語）

　　"我可以在一個星期內寫一本厚厚的批評中國的書。然而，在有那麼多的不利的困境下，中國的高速增長持續了那麼久，歷史上從來沒有出現過。中國一定是做了非常對的事才產生了我們見到的經濟奇跡。那是什麼呢？這才是真正的問題。"（香港經濟學者張五常語）

　　"這是一個需要理論而且一定能夠產生理論的時代，這是一個需要思想而且一定能夠產生思想的時代。我們不能辜負了這個時代。"（中國國家主席習近平語）

　　正是因為有以上眾多疑惑和不解的問題驅動，以及中國人骨髓裡的不服輸基因驅使，便有了作者的這本思想筆錄彙集。此書專注中國哲學和文化創新與創意，嘗試從一個新的視角切入追根尋源，刨根問底。研究、提煉和總結影響中國哲學和中國文化形成、發展、演化、傳承的最基礎元素。誠然，緣由是創新、創意嘗試之舉，故肯定存在有這樣或那樣的不足。不滿意之處，則當是未來繼續努力探索的原動力，不斷推進。作者本人，只是希冀此書可以精准推送思想觀點的新意，投石問路，拋磚引玉。

作者簡介

我的個人簡歷：水文化研究人 王堅

1965-1971，就讀上海市高安路第一小學

1971-1975，就讀上海市南洋模範中學

1976-1981，就職上海市星火農場 38 連

1981-1985，就讀上海市財經大學貿易經濟系（學士學位）

1985-1989，就職上海市畜產品進出口公司

1989-1990，就讀澳大利亞悉尼大學

1990-1994，就讀美國俄亥俄州 Wright State University 實用經濟專業（碩士學位）

1994-2009，就職美國 Florsheim Asia Pacific Ltd

2009- 至今，就職東隅水文化研究工作室

目錄

第一篇

"水歷史" 研究中的一個重大課題

課題：水的哲學存在和智慧啟示，是中國人文化自信，以及中國式話語體系的理論基礎元素……

水，是影響中國文化形成、發展、演變、進化和傳承最重要的元素之一，且排位元靠前，非常非常的靠前，幾近可以排位第一。

水，天地宇宙間客觀存在的物質，就其自然屬性而言，水本身一氫二氧原子組成一個水分子，它與其他物質一樣普遍和普通，都是宇宙天地中尋常平等的一份子，自然世界中缺了哪一樣物質都難構成一個完整的有機運行體系。然而，就水的社會屬性而論，水卻是特別的不同物質，它賦予了中國文化、中國哲學太多的智慧思考和特殊品質，這與西方文化形成強烈的對比。

研究"水歷史"，中國人不得不提中國的哲學先賢老子，不得不提老子 2000 多年之前所著作的 5000 字《道德經》一書。《道德經》前後共 81 篇，1-37 篇是"道"篇，講述"天之道"即天地宇宙之道，自然之道，或稱作自然規律；38-81 篇是"德"篇，論述"人之道"即人類價值倫理之道，或社會文化之道。

老子《道德經》的本意，是告誡華夏民族的子孫後代"天道"在前，"人道"在後；"天道"在上，"人道"在下；"天道"自然而然，"人道"則非自然之物。"天道"是"人道"的基準和根本，"天道"規範框定"人道"是非曲直標準。"人道"唯有尊重和遵從"天道"之路前行，方能順暢演進和發展。否則，人類任何違背天地自然之舉動，則難逃自然宇宙"天道"的責罰。

天地宇宙的運行之道，乃自然生態系統的規律總體集合。自然規律"道"是自然而然形成、運行，順遂天地自然演化的結果。毋庸置疑，自然生態系統是一個整體的有機系統，即天、地、人（萬事萬物總代表）集合成一體而成。系統之中，水是無可爭辯的中心角色，和最重要核心原素，世間萬事萬物離不開水的浸潤和滋養。沒有水，所有生命體將不復存在。

既然，水在自然生態系統中的地位和作用如此的關鍵重要，那麼高度認識並參學、遵從水的哲學智慧，便成為衡量人類世界聰慧程度的一種基礎標準和尺度。歷史上，中西方在認識世界本源的研究方向上，曾經行走在同一條路徑。西方哲學第一人泰勒斯言"水是最好的東西"；中國哲學先賢老子講"上善若水，水善利萬物而不爭，處眾人之所惡，故幾於道。"

最高的善，就像水那樣。水善於幫助萬物而不與萬物相爭。它停留在眾人所不喜歡的地方，所以接近於道。水"處眾人之所惡，此乃謙下之德也；故江海所以能為百谷王者，以其善下之，則能為百谷王。天下莫柔弱于水，而攻堅強者莫之能勝，此乃柔德也；故柔之勝剛，弱之勝強堅。因其無有，故能入於無間，由此可知不言之教、無為之益也"（老子《道德經》）

水"處下不爭"，是最為謙虛的美德。江海之所以能夠成為一切河流的歸宿，是因為他善於處在下游的位置上，所以成為百谷王。世界上最柔的東西莫過於水，然而它卻能穿透最為堅硬的東西，沒有什麼能超過它，這就是"柔德"所在。所以說弱能勝強，柔可克剛。不見其形的東西，可以進入到沒有縫隙的東西中去，由此知道了"不言"的教導，"無為"的好處。

中國儒家的鼻祖，老子的學生孔子說"智者樂水，仁者樂山"，"眾人處上，水獨處下；眾人處易，水獨處險；眾人處潔，水獨處穢。所處盡人之所惡，夫誰與之爭乎？此所以為上善也"；"夫君者舟也，庶人者水也。水所以載舟，亦可以覆舟。"平民百姓可擁護君主，也能推翻君主。君王好比是船，百姓好比是水，水可以使船行駛，也可以使船淹沒。

"夫水遍與諸生而無為也，似德。其流也，埤下裾拘，必循其理，似義。其洸洸乎不淈盡，似道。若有決行之，其應佚若聲響，其赴百仞之谷不懼，似勇。主量必平，似法。盈不求概，似正。淖約微達，似察。以出以入，以就鮮絜，似善化。其萬折也必東，似志。是故見大水必觀焉。"（《荀子·宥坐》）

水，遍佈天下，給予萬物，並無偏私，有如君子的道德；水性向下，隨物賦形，有如君子的高義；水淺處流動不息，深處淵然不測，有如君子的智慧；水奔赴萬丈深淵，毫不遲疑，有如君子的臨事果決和勇毅；水滲入曲細，無微不達，有如君子的明察秋毫；水蒙受惡名，默不申辯，有如君子包容一切的豁達胸懷；水裝入量器，一定保持水準，有如君子的立身正直；水遇滿則止，並不貪多務得，有如君子的講究分寸；水處事有度，無論怎樣的百折千回，一定要東流入海，有如君子的堅定不移的信念和意志。所以君子見到大水一定要仔細觀察。

中國先聖賢者老子和孔子高度崇拜水品水德，端視具象、顯性的水，幾乎等同於天地宇宙中虛擬、隱性的"道"自然規律。於是，在中國人的普遍認知中，水除了具有獨一無二，不可替代的物理屬性以外，水還有極具深奧智慧的社會倫理和哲學文化屬性。老子和孔子強烈主張人類社會應該參學和模仿水"與世無爭，則天下無人能與之爭"高尚品性。

中國 5000 年的發展歷史，其本身就是一部高度跟進和無限親近水的歷史。中華文明之所以能夠成為世界上唯一的一個延綿 5000 年從沒被中斷過的文明體系，至今仍在持久不斷延續、傳承，向著另一個 5000 年的目標進發，究其根本原因或就在於：中華民族虔誠參學、模仿自然生態系統運行的所有特質，尤其是強化"水"智慧所生成的功效和功能，以此來綜合統籌、架構和組建中國社會的組織形態，以及其相關的治理模式。

中西方文化價值體系中最大的差別和差異，恐怕就在這個似乎極普通的"水"字。可千萬別小看只差一個"水"字，有水或缺水，或根本沒有水，目標和結果卻可能"失之毫釐，差之千里"的遙遠和不同。中西方對於"水"的理解和感悟存在著"天壤之別"的差距，中華文化中，處處彰顯"水"的哲學存在和倫理價值理念，而西方文化裡卻鮮見"水"的痕跡和蹤影。

中華民族的祖輩先賢在思考如何建構一個國家的政治、經濟體制，以及社會組織形式和治理管理方式時，首先想到的是參照、仿學自然生態體系機理，想到是大自然中"水"的絕對核心功能。水能夠串連起天地間所有的生命物質形成一個有機整體系統，並在其中成就"王"者地位。水，並無打算成為王者，但其高尚的品行決定了它就是眾望所歸、心悅誠服的王者，無人能望其項背。

既然確認、肯定了水在自然生態系統中的中心角色，中國人哪有不參照、仿學之理？人類生態系統，之所以配得上稱作人類社會"生態"體系，自然就離不開"水"，水是唯一且無人可以成功替代的統領者。充分並深刻理解這一點，對於認知中國文化，以及中國文化影響下形成的國家發展模式，或發展道路甚為關鍵，甚為重要。一個穩定且有序的系統，須有一個核心或中心，並且是唯一的核心或中心。

仿學自然生態系統的人類社會運行過程，自然而然地需要有一個人、一個家庭、一個家族，或一個現代政黨去充當、扮演水的角色，發揮水的作用。不論東方或西方，任何一個社會的當政者，本就應該責無旁貸地成為全體人民整體利益的代表者和代言人，而非部分人利益的維護力量，成為水功能的執行人，無限貼近、跟進水的要求。這是"人之道"遵從"天之道"的核心要素和基礎要求。

再往細微處講，每一個獨立的水系之下，一定擁有眾多的江河湖泊，以及無數的小溪、細澤和窪地，共同滋養本系統涉及地區的各種各樣生命體—動物和植物，自然而然地形成一個獨立、自主運行的水循環系統。每一條大江或大河，必定存在有一個主要的出海口，由它來承接和統領全流域的地表進出來水，其功效和功能絕非其他次級出海口所能相提並論。從大自然生態系統的整體佈局和機理中，中華民族總是能夠心領神會似地開竅，有所頓悟大自然的組織形式和運行秘訣。

"天道"之下的中國模式

秦朝始皇征服六國，統一中國的 2000 多年以來，中國的"大一統"政治制度和公營私營（國營和私營）並存的混合經濟制度，一以貫之地運作良好。即使有短期的戰亂、分裂衝擊，政經制度也從未發生過本質上的變更。當然，秦朝一統中國之前的幾千年裡，成百成千小國的政體框架基本上與中央集權體制取向一致，多以家庭、家族、氏族社會中的長輩和德高望重的賢者世襲治理、組織和管理，這也可以被視作中央集權"大一統"政治體制的準備時期或雛型階段。

事實上，從黃帝炎帝開始，中國就處在大一統的情形之中，中央集權的政治制度下先是禪讓制，後來因為私利，演變成家天下的帝制。戰國時期，七國都是周天子分封而形成的，七國都自稱華夏或"諸夏"，七國的神話和歷史記憶都是同一個體系，已經擁有和形成了統一的意識。這與周邊的西戎、南蠻、北狄、東夷等其他民族截然不同，管仲提出的"尊王攘夷"主張，就得到諸侯各國的完全肯定和真誠回應。

各諸侯國使用的文字，從甲骨文、金文到篆文，七國一脈相承，基本上是相同和或相似。諸侯各國之間的各類交往，完全不需要翻譯。秦始皇統一韓，趙，魏，楚，燕，齊六國後，實際上就是消滅了地方割據勢力，用郡縣制替代了分封制。秦始皇開創、執行的書同文，車同軌等制度，促使國家文明和制度更加的統一、自主、有序和高效。

這樣一個從一個人，一個家庭，一個家族掌握國家治理權力模版，逐步演變成長，發展到今天中國一個現代政黨代表全體人民的整體利益，主政國家政治、經濟、社會等諸多重大事務的模式。即中國共產黨領導下的多黨合作和政治協商制度。國家的一切權力屬於人民，人民通過各種途徑和形式，管理國家、經濟、文化以及社會事務。決定中國政治和經濟體制的文化、哲學邏輯，在 5000 年歷史進程中始終保持一脈相承。穩定、獨立、自主、可持續是這個政治體制的最顯著特徵。

中國的混合經濟（國營和私營）模式，自古有之。在這個模式裡，國有部門和非國有部門、政府與市場保持適當的平衡。幾千年中，總有一個很強大有力的國有部門存在，國家對關鍵的經濟領域起著直接的干預平衡作用，包括公共基礎設施建設、應付處理各種各樣危機、平衡市場的力量、提供政府公共產品等。凡此種種，在漢代的《鹽鐵論》裡都有專門的論述，歷朝歷代當政者也都實踐著，檢驗著模式的有效性。隨機靈活變化調整，取最大程度的綜合高效和高能，應當是這個經濟體制的最顯著特徵。

今天，中國"社會主義市場經濟"只是一個新的稱謂，新的叫法而已，它只是相對於西方"資本主義市場經濟"而言，且帶有某種意識形態的色彩。但是，其本質依然是中國的混合經濟（國營和私營）模式。世界上許多人誤以為中國的改革開放的目標瞄向西方的經濟模式，中國的轉型經濟，就是從計劃經濟完全轉型到市場經濟，從國有經濟退出轉到私營經濟。這種理解恐怕嚴重偏離中國的真實狀況，完全沒有從中華文明歷史中真正讀懂中國模式的精髓。

在中國，國營經濟成分和私營經濟成分幾千年來一直並存，並相互協調、配合、發展，百分之百的國有化和百分之百的私有化都是中國經濟的"非常態"，混合經濟模式才是中國經濟的"常態"，"看得見的手"和"看不見的手"同時存在，擇時、擇機作用才是中國經濟的正常狀態。簡單地用西方的經濟模式來衡量、解釋中國當前的"改革開放"發展方向，難免碰壁和失望。

中國模式，永遠是中國的政治、經濟的發展模式，絕對不會是西方的多黨票選制＋自由主義市場經濟模式。5000年的時間長河塑造了中國成為人類歷史上除古埃及、古巴比倫、古印度、古希臘之外的第一個，也是最後一個活生生的文明體孤本。從實踐的角度講，它已經可以有充分的理由用來證實中國模式長期存在的合理性和必然性。講到底，中國的政治、經濟模式符合"天道"的要求。

至少對中華民族而言，走適合自己的發展道路符合"天道"常理。不走"老路和邪路"，關乎國家和民族的興盛衰敗前程。選擇走哪一條發展道路，中國人民只會聽從祖輩先聖的教誨和自己內心真誠要求，而不太會多加理睬他人和外人的非份之想。自然界中水循環系統，本身就是一個從不依附任何其他系統存在，而獨立自主發展的自然生態體系，無需顧及他人眼色，相反其他生命體系統卻要嚴重依賴水循環系統才能生存。

中國人參學、仿照大自然水循環系統的架構，一夜之間廢除所有強加給中國人民身上的不平等條約，改變了半殖民地半封建的國家狀態，重新建立起一個具有獨立主權的國家。對外"另起爐灶"、"打掃乾淨屋子再請客"，執行以"和平共處五項原則"為基礎的外交政策，平等待人；對內建立起一整套獨立自主的政治、經濟、軍事、科技、教育、社會、文化等體系。特別令世人讚歎的，是擁有了現今全世界最完整的現代工業製造體系，自力更生發展。

"照抄別國的經驗是要吃虧的，照抄一定會上當的。這是一條重要的國際經驗。"（毛澤東語）"中國人民珍惜同其他國家和人民的友誼和合作，更加珍惜自己經過長期奮鬥而得來的獨立自主權利。任何外國不要指望中國做他們的附庸，不要指望中國會吞下損害我國利益的苦果。"（鄧小平語）

　　"在中國這樣一個有著 5000 多年文明史、13 億多人口的大國推進改革發展，沒有可以奉為金科玉律的教科書，也沒有可以對中國人民頤指氣使的教師爺。什麼是路？就是從沒路的地方踐踏出來的，從只有荊棘的地方開闢出來的。中國特色社會主義道路是當代中國大踏步趕上時代、引領時代發展的康莊大道，必須毫不動搖走下去。"（習近平語）

　　任何時候，中國人民都在堅持自己選擇的發展道路和社會制度，始終把維護國家主權、安全和領土完整放在第一位。同時尊重各國人民自主選擇發展道路的權利，堅持國家不分大小、強弱、貧富一律平等，不干涉別國內政事務，不把自己的意志強加於人；不計較宗教信仰、社會制度和意識形態差別，同世界上所有國家發展相互尊重、平等對待的友好合作關係。

　　即使中國模式滿足"天道"要求，中國人仍然認為"世界上沒有放之四海而皆準的發展模式，各國都需要獨立自主地根據本國的國情來探索符合自己的發展道路。中國堅持走自己的路，既不輸入外國模式，也不輸出中國模式，不會要求別國複製中國的做法。當然，如果有些國家對中國發展的經驗和做法感興趣，我們願意同他們討論，同他們分享，但絕不會強加於人。"（張業遂語）

　　中國人說到做到，言行一致，在自身急需發展的時候，仍然執行對外援助。而對外援助卻始終堅持"不附加任何政治條件"，建國 70 年間援外金額已累計超過 2500 億元人民幣之多，幫助了發展中國家建成 2000 多個成套項目。2000 年以來，中國已先後 9 次宣佈免除重債窮國和最不發達國家對華到期無息貸款債務，切實減輕了有關國家的債務負擔。這與西方人的對外援助"附加政治條件"形成鮮明的對比。

　　中國人向全世界莊嚴承諾：社會主義中國應該用實踐向世界表明，中國反對霸權主義、強權政治，永不稱霸，中國是維護世界和平的堅定力量。中國的發展與進步，不會對任何人構成威脅。將來中國富強起來了，也永遠不稱霸。這是我們矢志不渝的基本國策。外界完全可以從 15 世紀初"鄭和下西洋"的歷史案例中，清晰瞭解和理解到中華民族言而有信，以及其言行舉止背後的文化信仰邏輯。

　　因為，水從來不稱霸，但卻是眾人心目中的"王"者。水從沒有打算過輸出自己的模式，也沒有必要輸出自己的模式，水就是那樣的獨一無二，首屈一指的高尚和尊貴，無人能及；同時，水也不接受他人輸入的模式，緣由根本不存在還有更好的東西，可以替代掉水的位置、功能和榮光品德。水，廣結善緣，當你需要它的時候，水絕對會竭盡全力、不求回報地幫助你，助你一臂之力。中華民族從水品水德中虔誠學習，獲益良多。

"天道"之下的世界治理模式

全球化的今天，中國人不落人後的大踏步走出國門，積極主動融入國際社會。除了向全世界提供中國的產品、服務、市場、遊客、資本和技術等之外，中國人更是智慧地貢獻出了中國思想和中國方案：人類命運共同體。對於整個人類世界，特別是西方世界來講，中國人居然能夠開始向外輸出東方式文化思想了，這簡直就是個晴天劈雷，許多人驚訝、感歎、恐懼、擔心不已。

"人類命運共同體"的理念，與中國傳統文化"天下大同"，"四海之內皆兄弟也"的理念如出一轍，社會普遍鼓勵"人人為公"。"大道之行也，天下為公，選賢與能，講信修睦，故人不獨親其親，不獨子其子，使老有所終，壯有所用，幼有所長，鰥寡孤獨廢疾者皆有所養；男有分，女有歸，貨惡其棄於地也不必藏於己，力惡其不出於身也不必為己，是故謀閉而不興，盜竊亂賊而不作，故外戶而不閉，是謂大同。"（《禮記·禮運》）

大道施行時，天下是人們所共有的，把有賢德、有才能的人選出來，人人講求誠信，崇尚和睦。人們不單奉養自己的父母，不單撫育自己的子女，要使老年人能終其天年，中年人能為社會效力，幼童能順利地成長，使老而無妻的人、老而無夫的人、幼年喪父的孩子、老而無子的人、殘疾人都能得到供養。

男子有職業和事業，女子有婚配家室。百姓大眾收貯被拋棄在地的財物，卻不是為了獨自享用，而是共同享用。同時，憎惡那種在共同勞動中不肯盡力的行為，總要不為私利而勞動。這樣一來，就不會有人搞陰謀，不會有人盜竊財物和興兵作亂，家家戶戶都不用關大門了，這就叫做"大同"社會。中華民族古時的"天下大同"理想既質樸，又具體明確。

沿續"天下大同"的思想，"人類命運共同體"理念率先由中國人提議、推進並踐行，也就成了順理成章的事情。中華民族歷來追求和睦、愛好和平、宣導和諧，"親仁善鄰"、"協和萬邦"。數千年中華文明史造就了獨樹一幟的"和"文化，"和"文化"蘊涵著天人合一的宇宙觀、協和萬邦的國際觀、和而不同的社會觀、人心和善的道德觀"。

"和"與"合"在中國傳統文化價值觀中，佔據著極其重要的核心位置，是中國文化的精髓和第一價值所在。和合，最早出自"商契能和合五教，以保于百姓者也。"（《國語·鄭語》）即商契能和合父義、母慈、兄友、弟恭、子孝"五教"，使百姓安定和諧的相處與生活。和合，講的是和諧、和平、祥和、合作、包容、尊重和融合，強調了化解矛盾事物和諧與協調之中的價值取向。

中國傳統文化中，世代傳承"和"與"合"價值倫理觀。"禮之用，和為貴。"，"君子和而不同，小人同而不和。"（孔子《論語》）；"天時不如地利，地利不如人和。"（《孟子·公孫醜下》）；"天地合而萬物生，陰陽接而變化起，性偽合而天下治"（《荀子·天論》）；"萬物負陰而抱陽，沖氣以為和"（《老子·四十二章》）；"天地者，萬物之父母也。合則成體，散則成始。"（《莊子·達生第十九》）

傳承中華文化歷史，中國國家主席習近平代表中華民族在闡述"人類命運共同體"，以及"和合"理念時講："當今世界，人類生活在不同文化、種族、膚色、宗教和不同社會制度所組成的世界裡"，但是"這個世界，各國相互聯繫、相互依存的程度空前加深，人類生活在同一個地球村裡，生活在歷史和現實交匯的同一個時空裡，越來越成為你中有我、我中有你的命運共同體。"

"人類命運共同體，顧名思義，就是每個民族、每個國家的前途命運都緊緊聯繫在一起，應該風雨同舟，榮辱與共，努力把我們生於斯、長於斯的這個星球建成一個和睦的大家庭，把世界各國人民對美好生活的嚮往變成現實。"既然，人類世界已經跨越了相對隔絕、單打獨鬥的發展階段而成為了一個"地球村"整體，那麼，中國5000年來成功的國家綜合治理模式自然而然地引起全球的關注和熱議，甚至部分被參照、仿學。

中國式國家治理模式的最基本經驗，就是"人道"發展最終要契合"天道"要求，不得逆"天道"而行。人類只有一個地球，各國共處一個世界，面對世界經濟的複雜形勢和全球治理問題，任何國家都不可能置身度外，獨善其身。當前各國家、各民族的未來發展不可能單獨過日子，任何單邊主義強權和霸權行徑也就沒有機會成為全球的主流選項，世界經濟是一個割裂不開的有機整體。

當人類世界被視作一個類似于自然生態系統的有機整體運作時，可持續發展的議題則被嚴肅地擺上議事日程。哪一個國家哪一個民族能夠有資格、有能力在人類社會擔當"水"的王道角色？顯然，西方文化"叢林法則"主導之下的"美國優先"霸權主義不得人心，而中國文化"水法則"引導之下的"合作共贏"平等主張，得到了全世界的強烈共鳴。

簡言之，中國人的價值觀理念，本質上是自然生態崇拜，天地宇宙崇拜，自然規律"道"崇拜，或"水"的崇拜。"水，柔軟親和、剛柔一體、柔中帶剛、剛中懷柔、柔終克剛、變化無窮。"水不僅有剛強堅硬的實力，更具備有柔軟包容的巨大力量，水有剛硬柔和的兩面屬性，剛硬柔和兩性可以互相轉化、交替借力、變化無窮無盡。而且，水最終能夠以柔克剛，以柔懷剛，以柔化剛。

在"人類命運共同體"整體框架之下，中國率先在世界範圍內扮演"水"的核心角色，並且鼓勵其他國家和民族在世界各地方營造更多的水源地，共同給世界輸水，創造財富。中國堅持最大限度的開放本國市場，支持全球多邊貿易體系，更敞開胸懷歡迎各國搭乘中國致富"快車"，共用發展機遇，同世界各國合作共贏。

"一帶一路"，是"人類命運共同體"理念催生之下的具體實踐，已普遍被國際社會成員廣泛的認同和接受，它正在逐步成為推動全球治理體系變革、構建新型國際關係和國際新秩序的共同價值規範和手段方式。"一帶一路"完全是開放性、包容性區域合作倡議，而非排他性、封閉性的中國自家"小圈子"，在"一帶一路"機制中，各國同是平等的參與者、貢獻者，和受益者。

"一帶一路"架構中不斷被強化和推動成型的"五通：政策溝通、設施聯通、貿易暢通、資金融通、民心相通"，似乎可以被想象描述成連接各國和各地區之間類似於自然生態系統中的水道和河道，各個國家以及各個地區都有可能憑藉自身的創新、製造、致富能力，形成水量不同的水源高地，流水相互交匯碰撞，滋潤孕育"一帶一路"沿線國家和地區發展繁榮。

中國模式的世界運用，以及中國經驗的世界實踐，集中體現在中國人聰慧地主張避開宗教信仰、意識形態、文化差異等所有不具備統一共識的範疇，不予涉及和爭執。重點聚焦各國家、民族共同關心的經濟議題入手，展開全球化合作，謀取共贏和多贏。中國式的"全球化"具有鮮明的"和合"特徵和特點：世界經濟的全球一體化，而非世界各國政治、文化、社會、宗教的統一化。

撇開因環境和歷史境遇不同，所形成的各國家、各民族宗教信仰，意識形態，文化習俗等差異分別和無謂紛爭不論，中西雙方一起努力，尋找到人類世界的共同認知和共同價值部分，並持續強化之。中國人貢獻以自然生態頂層大局觀切入論事，以"水"觀點導入論事的創新方法，從悉理上講明白、講請楚"人類命運共同體"的普世性和普惠性。中國人善用智慧構建起東方式話語體系基礎理論框架和內容，解釋人類世界前行方向。

水，具有普世價值；以水論道，自然具有普世的哲學和文化價值。

第二篇

尋找中國人的文化自信

　　講故事，需要語境。講好一個文化故事，更講究挑選個合適的語境。我們講東方中國文化的故事，讓他人理解，特別是讓外國人瞭解、理解中國，很難想像採用西方的概念行得通，能解釋明白中國事情的，西方人的知識智慧解釋不了中國發生的事情，既使是在西方主導全球話語權的今天。否則，事情早早辦妥了。在他人眼裡，中國仍然是一個"謎"樣的國家。

　　可是，中國這邊的情況同樣也不樂觀，依然有那麼一點糟糕和失望，氣氛環境不太盡如人意。中國本土的部分學者專家，知識份子仍是在滿心熱衷地照搬照抄西方的東西，而絕少擔心"洋為中用"過程中的不妥當不合適部分，對西方國家原創性成果研究不足，理解有限知之甚少，缺少起碼的較真精神和態度。同時，他們自己又沒有原創的東西，對於中華文化不能自圓其說，自成一家學術理論。難怪外界他人不願意接受陳詞老調的說教態度和講解方法，更談不上期待形成新型的知識體系。

　　19世紀中葉，西方人達爾文創立了"進化論"。西方知識體系中的"叢林法則"本屬於現代生物學理論範疇。"物競天擇，優勝劣汰，適者生存，弱肉強食"是描述各種生物物種互相進行生存鬥爭，最後由天（自然）來選擇誰留下，誰離去。適應自然變化就存活，不能適應的就滅亡。弱肉強食乃強者之理。萬物生靈，食為天性。不食則不得生，不食則無以續。虎食羊，鷹叼兔，禽啄蟲，畜嚼草；大魚吃小魚，小魚吃蝦蟲，蝦蟲吃泥巴（泥中微生物）。食他物愈強者而己愈強，天下之物能食者則為王矣。

　　"進化論"是一門嚴謹的生物科學，有嚴格的適用對象和範圍界定。人類是生命體，其他動植物也是生命體；人類是高級生命物種，其他動植物卻是低級生命物種；人類物種的生存和發展依賴幾乎所有其他動植物物種，而其他動植物物種的生存和發展只需要依賴一種或幾種階位較低的物種；人類物種具備這樣一種"改天換地"超凡能力，可以決定所有一切生物包括人類自身的生死，甚至擁有影響"天地"環境興衰的能力，而其他低級動植物物種卻沒有這種能力。

　　人類是所有生命體中最聰明、最智慧的高級物種族類，佔據著生物鏈系統中最高的位置，而其他動植物生命物種的聰慧程度遠遠低於人類。拿"進化論"，從低級生物競爭進化中總結出來的普通性知識結論，誤當作是自然界的大智慧，不加區別地簡單套用在人類身上，就未必完全合理，至少是不完全合適。人類或應該勇敢地跳出生物鏈圈向外拓展，更多地從生物鏈系統以外尋找人類大智慧的源泉和靈感。

　　今天，我們國人置疑西方人運用"進化論"，或許用錯了地方，或許擺錯了位置，錯誤地把原本簡單的生物進化學說，硬性轉變、包裝成複雜的現代社會學說公式定理，濫用在人類發展頭上，推行"叢林法則"泛社會化實驗。結果是"物競"的心態，"弱肉強食"的哲理，在人類社會裡播種下多少人間苦果。從種族歧視、殖民地主義、戰爭侵略、顏色革命、政權更疊、以致消滅異族。國與國、民族與民族、宗教與宗教互相爭鬥，互相仇殺，慘絕人寰。全人類急切需要反思西方知識體系中的精華和糟粕，以及西方知識體系的適用範疇。

故此，我們嘗試提出一種新思維和一個新視角，跳出西方話語的老框框，在西方話語體系之外創新、尋找一種全新方法和全新語境，在生物鏈系統之外的水循環系統找尋人類的智慧靈感。水，普遍存在且通俗易懂，既是一種溝通工具，一種理解的中間介質，又是一種具象化式的語言，世界上任何人都能夠清楚明白、理解"水"傳達給外界的資訊含義。參照水的性格和品質，講述中國人故事和中國文化故事。嘗試實踐一種新的知識話語體系，摸索一種既能解釋中國文化自己，又能讓其他人知道並理解的新型知識體系。

中國人是誰？中國人從哪裡來，又到哪裡去？

講老實話，"中國"和"中國人"是一個相當難講清楚，道明白的古老話題。中國人哲學話題，歷史上有許許多多學者專家潛心研究過，可是研究的結果總是那樣千差萬別，莫衷一是。一千個人眼裡的中國，有著一千個不同的中國模樣。碎片化式的中國形象總結，始終置中國身處於一個謎局之中，神迷並且深奧難以讀懂，不容易被外人所理解，甚至國人也未必能夠十分瞭解我們自己。

中國，這樣一個東方國家，是由一群叫做中國人的人群組成的。中國人的性格使然，根本上決定了中國這個國家的國家性格。研究透了中國人的思維方式和群體行為，自然也就瞭解理解了中國。"中國"到底是什麼樣子？西方有過他們的解釋，中國人也有自己的解釋。

絕大多數的中外解釋都只是集中在描述中國現在長成什麼樣子的層面：國人好內鬥不團結；國人不守公德不守規矩；國人自顧自耍小聰明；國人做事隨意不認真；國人缺乏獨立思考隨大流；國人勤勞刻苦，和樂觀忍耐等等。然而，所有研究並沒有再往前深入一步，講解和釋疑中國為什麼會長成這個樣子的。顯然，這樣的觀察結果對全方位理解中國文化和中國人，是遠遠不夠的。

西方人眼中的國人形象

首先，看看西方人是怎麼樣描述中國人的。在西方修士柏朗嘉賓眼裡，中國人都是一些友好的異教徒，十三世紀前後，西方人大都是些虔誠的基督徒，在他們眼裡，中國人雖然享有高度的物質文明，但卻無一例外地都是異教徒，這讓西方人難以理解也難以接受。1245 年，方濟會修士柏朗嘉賓受教皇指派出使韃靼，回國後，他寫出《蒙古行記》。在著述中，他提到一個叫"契丹"的國家，"那裡居住著一個人數眾多的民族。"他發現"他們都是異教徒。他們也聲稱擁有自己的聖人"，他們"信仰永恆的生命，但卻從不舉行任何洗禮。"而那卻偏偏又是一個物質文明非常發達的地方，世上竟有這樣一個民族，他們沒有接受基督的洗禮，但卻在享受著西方人也不曾享受的美味與華服。這讓西方人無以置信，極為震驚。

在門多薩神父眼裡，中國人溫文而有禮。門多薩神父在其《大中華帝國志》中不無悲痛地寫道："最令基督徒傷心的是，在這樣一個富饒美麗的國度裡，聰穎靈巧的人民竟因為不懂上帝的真理而變成愚昧的偶像崇拜者。"他們把一些人尊為聖人，也拜魔鬼，他們可以說沒有什麼宗教信仰。"這不能不使我們感到困惑，甚至陷於深深的沉思而不能自拔。"對中世紀那些虔誠而狂熱的基督徒來說，異教徒就是他們的死敵。

在《大中華帝國志》一書中，門多薩神父敘述了中國人的外貌與秉性，中國人都身體健康、心靈手巧、聰明開化。"他們都是偉大的發明家，勤勞而工巧。"中國人有自己的人生觀，"中國人是心智最高的人種。他們有一套自己關於天地起源，人類誕生的看法。"中國人自足樂觀，"他們是個喜歡宴樂的民族，什麼時候都避免悲傷。"中國人不喜歡戰爭，"中國人有一條法律：既不在自己的國家挑起戰爭，也不侵略別國。"書中詳述了中國的婚禮、喪禮、節慶中的各種禮節。書中也寫到了中國人的酷刑與迷信。

在馬可·波羅眼裡，中國人善良恬靜。與傳教士不同，作為一個商人，馬可·波羅更具世俗色彩。在他所著的《馬可·波羅遊記》裡，通篇都是對中國人的讚美。他寫宋朝的皇帝"性情溫和、行為仁愛"，蘇州人"民性善良怯懦"，機智能幹，具有商業才能。杭州人"性格和平"，"民性恬靜溫文"，品德忠厚，鄰里間友好和睦。友善好客，"那些來這裡經商的異鄉人，也一視同仁，竭誠相待，隨意邀請他們到家中做客，表示友好。"男女間相互敬重，"男人對自己的妻子，表示很大的尊重，沒有妒忌和猜疑。"中國完全是一個世俗的樂園，生活在這個樂園裡的中國人個個都品性良好。

1615年《基督教遠征中國史》（即《利瑪竇中國劄記》）在德國出版問世，利瑪竇先生以其親身經歷詳盡描述了中國人的形象。在他的筆下，中國人勤勞、多才多藝、溫文有禮、尊師重教。同時也指出他所見的中國陋俗，諸如迷信、算命、煉丹，溺嬰鄙女，酷刑枉法以及中國人普遍的多疑與怯懦。

伏爾泰曾經這樣說過："我們對於中國人的優點即使不崇拜得五體投地，至少也得承認他們帝國的治理是世界上前所未有的最優秀的。""歐洲王公和商人們發現東方，追求的只是財富，而哲學家在東方發現了一個新的精神和物質的世界。"在西方一百多年的啟蒙運動中，人們發現中國人的思想竟成為思想家們行進隊伍的一面耀眼的旗幟。孔子的禮制、孟子的仁政，儒家哲學所代表的唯道德主義的中國文明，成為那個時代歐洲的文化理想。

德國最重要的科學家和哲學家萊布尼茨在《中國新事》緒論中寫道："我們從前誰也不相信世界上還有比我們的倫理更美滿、立身處世之道更進步的民族存在，現在東方的中國，給我們以一大覺醒！"他讚美中國有"人類最高度的文化和最發達的技術文明。假使推舉一位智者來裁定哪個民族最傑出，而不是裁定哪個女神最漂亮，那麼他將把金蘋果交給中國人。"

這種認識在另一位元德國偉人歌德那裡得到了延續，他於 1829 年談到中國："中國人在思想、行為和情感方面幾乎和我們一樣，使我們很快就感到他們是我們的同類人，只是在他們那裡，一切都比我們這裡更明朗，更純潔，也更合乎道德。"另一位德國學者克里斯多夫每當"沉浸在對世界各民族的冥思苦索的時候，總是推斷：在上帝創造的這個星球上，中國人是最賢明、最正直、最幸福的一個民族！"

黑格爾則說過，"歷史必須從中國談起"，可中國停留在歷史之外。在中國，個體沒有獨立性和自由。中國民族的性格特徵是："凡是屬於精神的東西，自由的倫理、道德、情感、內在的宗教、科學和真正的藝術，都離它很遠"。

孟德斯鳩說過，氣候使中國人變得懶散、怯懦，中國"是世界上最會欺騙的民族"，"中國人貪利之心極濃"。在孟德斯鳩看來，"中國是一個專制的國家，它的原則是恐怖"。在這樣的國家裡，中國人人性邪惡，沒有榮譽感。中國人懶惰渙散、懦弱順從。他對中國的禮教進行了理性的分析，他認為在中國"禮教構成了國家的一般精神"，推翻了禮教也就推翻了一切。恪守禮教並沒使中國人變得誠實可信，"在中國，欺騙是允許的"，中國是"世界上最會騙人的民族"，中國人"貪利之心極濃。"在那個時代，對中國形象的否定要以孟德斯鳩最甚了。

在美國傳教士雅瑟·亨·史密斯眼中，中國人愛面子，節儉持家，勤勞刻苦，講究禮貌，漠視時間，漠視精確，善於誤解，拐彎抹角，順而不從，思維含混，不緊不慢，輕視外族，缺乏公心，因循守舊，隨遇而安，頑強生存，能忍且韌，知足常樂，孝悌為先，仁愛之心，缺乏同情，社會風波，株連守法，相互猜疑，缺乏誠信，多元信仰，和現實務實。

中國人的形象，在 13 世紀末出現的《馬可·波羅遊記》裡描述得溫文爾雅，道德高尚。到了 19 世紀末亞瑟·史密斯寫作《中國人的性格》時，含有貶義的"中國佬"一詞已根植於西方人的語言之中，"中國人"這一恰當的詞卻被排除在外。西元 793 年，馬戛爾尼使團訪問中國，遭遇"跪禮"之辱，出訪無功而返以後，關於中國人的惡劣印象得到"現實的"證明並迅速在西方傳播開來。西方人對中國人的看法開始變得更壞，更惡劣，更醜陋。

"中華帝國只是一艘破舊不堪的舊船，只是幸運地有了幾位謹慎的船長才使它在近150年期間沒有沉沒。……船將不會立刻沉沒。它將像一個殘骸那樣到處漂流，然後在岸上撞得粉碎，……它將永遠不能修復。"馬嘎爾尼這樣說。孔多塞在其《人類精神進步的歷史畫卷這概述》中認為"中華民族是愚昧、平庸、受屈辱、無能力與勇氣、充滿偏見的民族，如果人們想知道專制政府可以將摧殘人類的機能發展到何種程度，那根本用不著提起那些可怕的迷信，只需要看一看中國就行了。"

德國人赫爾德在《關於人類歷史哲學的思想》中寫道，中國，"這個帝國是一具木乃伊，它周身塗有防腐香料，描畫有象形文字，並且以絲綢包裹起來。它體內血液迴圈已經停止，猶如冬眠的動物一般。所以，它對一切外來事物都採取隔絕、窺測、阻撓的態度。它對外部世界既不瞭解，更不喜愛，終日沉浸在自我比較的自負之中"。"中國人就更荒謬絕倫了！他們把一切儀式都搞得精細繁複，但又都愚蠢透頂。……更有甚者，他們比世界上任何民族都更加冥頑不化，千百年來死守著一些先代留下來的陋俗惡習"，德昆西這樣描述。

法國人盧梭曾經在《新愛洛依絲》裡這樣表述，在中國，"文人、懦夫、偽君子和江湖騙子，整天說個不停，但都是沒有用的空談，他們富有思想但是卻沒有一點才能，徒有虛表，在見解方面匱乏得很。他們有禮貌、會恭維、機智、狡猾和會騙人，把所有應盡的義務掛在口頭上，對所有的道德都裝腔作勢，不知道其他的人性，他們的所謂的人情交往不過是行屈膝禮。"在喬治·安森的《環球旅行記》中，中國人欺詐、貧困、墮落、愚昧無知又冥頑不化。

1840年中英第一次鴉片戰爭，中國一觸即潰、俯首求和的現實，使中國的聲譽一落千丈。此後，許多西方人處處以十足的優越感自居，傲慢地對待中國的一切，隨時隨地都流露出輕蔑的神情。1842年英國海軍軍官在《英軍在華作戰記》中寫道，中國是個長期愚昧而又驕傲自大的國家，是一個沒有自我更新能力和缺乏活力的國家。鴉片戰爭，西洋火炮戰艦戰勝東方大刀長矛的必然結局，"天朝上國"敗於"蠻夷小邦"的現實，引起了中西雙方彼此在認識對方的觀念上發生了根本性逆轉。

19世紀六、七十年代，美國西海岸掀起排華浪潮，"黃禍論"盛極一時。1876年美聯邦國會參眾兩院分別通過決議，派一個特別調查委員會前往三藩市取證。事後集成由100餘人的證詞組成的長達1200餘面的《調查中國移民問題的聯合特別委員會報告書》，其中我們看到人類最可怕的種族歧視與仇恨。

問：從社會方面說，他們是不是一個比非洲種族更優秀的種族？

答：不，先生，他們並不比非洲種族優秀。在我看來，他們比上帝所創造的任何種族都要低劣。

問：據我瞭解，你剛才是說，中國人在上帝所創造的一切有智慧的動物中是最低劣的？

答：我認為，再沒有像中國人這樣低劣的了。在非洲的若干地區，智力的標準比較低，但是道德的標準比較高；就是說，他們是比較誠實的。這些人（中國人）卻已經達到了四千年罪惡的頂點，達到一種文明——這種文明是由於人口過剩產生的罪惡的頂點。

甚至連美國總統希歐多爾·羅斯福，這樣的一國領袖人物，也曾經污蔑說中國人是一個"不道德的、墮落的和不可取的種族。"在那個時代的美國人眼裡，中國人是天生的低等動物、奴隸、乞丐、殘忍的惡棍。那時，西方有關中國的歷險小說總是演繹著同樣的員警與歹徒的故事。惡棍總是中國人，他們兇殘狡詐、無惡不作，總是試圖綁架污辱白人婦女。危急時刻，白人英雄出現了，最後將中國惡棍繩之以法。在十九世紀之後的西方世界裡，正面的中國人形象已蕩然無存。

當中國幾乎被西方人認為是一具"腐朽的木乃伊"，是"停滯和落後"的代名詞的時候，新加坡前總理李光耀卻這樣認為"中國文化鼓勵個人努力奮鬥已達到盡善盡美的地步，無論是為了通過科舉考試，還是成為最好的大米商、最好的木匠、技工或制陶工人。"並認定"中國是這麼一個泱泱大國，有絕對的信心，只要有朝一日回歸正軌，登上世界首席之位是必然趨勢。中國在重振文明之後會有怎麼樣的命運和發展，中國人誰也不會懷疑。這是世界最古老的文明，延續了5000多年不曾間斷的悠久歷史。"

美國蘭德公司（世界第一智庫，美國乃至世界最負盛名的決策諮詢機構）的報告，如是評論中國人和中國文化：

中國人缺乏誠信和社會責任感；

中國人特別強調注重人脈關係；

中國人不懂得體面和尊嚴的生活意義；

中國人自私貪婪，冷酷無情；

中國人沒有勇氣追求他們認為正確的事情；

中國人偏愛接受廉價和免費的物品，總想不勞而獲；

中國人中的絕大多數不懂得優雅的舉止和基本的禮貌；

中國污染極其嚴重，是全世界最不適宜人類居住的國家；

中國人極力避免冒險；

2020 年，中國將會是一個非常貧窮的國家，以我們西方人的標準來判斷。

中國人對於生活的平衡性和意義性並不感興趣，相反他們更執迷於對物質的索取，這點上要遠遠勝於西方人。大多數中國人發現他們不懂得精神靈性、自由信仰以及心智健康這樣的概念，因為他們的思想尚不能達到一個生命（即肉體和靈性的並存）存在的更高層次。他們的思想還停留在專注於動物本能對性和食物貪婪的那點可憐的欲望上。正如亞瑟·史密斯，一位著名的西方傳教士在一個世紀前所指出的，"中國人最缺乏的不是智慧，而是勇氣和正直的純正品性。"

中國人眼中的國人形象

其次，看看中國人是怎麼樣描述本民族自己的。本土人群中，魯迅是個特別的人物。他以一個思想家高度的敏銳感知和探索精神，在塑造孔乙己、阿 Q、祥林嫂等典型形象的同時，也用極為細緻的筆墨細緻地寫出了嚴酷的社會環境，刻畫出了一批麻木愚昧的看客和閒人。"橫眉冷對千夫指"是魯迅創作的宗旨，他用他充滿戰鬥力的筆，無情的批判著那些麻木無情的國民。

魯迅在他的作品中塑造了大量的麻木的看客形象，並對他們加以批判。他的代表作《狂人日記》，就假借"迫害狂"患者的眼光，向滿口仁義道德，心裡卻想著吃人的看客發出控訴。趙貴翁、小孩子、女人、家人都睜了怪眼睛，臉色鐵青，抿著嘴笑，"似乎怕我，似乎想害我"。診病的老頭子滿眼凶光，張著鬼眼睛"從眼鏡橫邊暗暗看我"。甚至魚的眼睛也"白而且硬"，趙家的狗也同謀接洽，"看我兩眼"。他們"都用著疑心極深的眼光"面面相覷，想吃人又怕被吃，一旦被"狂人"戳破，"眼光便兇狠起來"。在這篇文章中，狂人表面上是一個瘋子，但實際上他卻是最清醒的人，他用一雙瘋狂的眼睛看清了這個世界的本質。

魯迅先生借助他的小說寫了一大批渾渾噩噩、不辨是非、麻木不仁的看客，從而深刻形象的表現了愚弱的國民性和他對國民不知覺悟的焦慮。更以一系列的悲劇展示國民靈魂，以"揭出病苦，引起療救的注意"。魯迅說："不在沉默中爆發，就是沉默中滅亡。"他不願同胞們一直軟弱下去，不願中國被叫做"東亞病夫"，雖然現在的中國積貧積弱，但他在激勵同胞們要正視現在的困境，並想辦法衝出困境。

中國臺灣作家柏楊，寫了一本書《醜陋的中國人》，痛斥批判中國人的劣根性。作者以他"恨鐵不成鋼"的態度，指出中國傳統文化有一種濾過性疾病，使子子孫孫受感染，不能痊癒。在文中，柏楊對被保守觀念禁錮的中國人進行了辛辣的嘲諷，大膽剖析中國國民的"劣根性"，自揭家醜，曝露惡習。小到窩裡鬥、髒、亂、吵、不能團結、死不認錯、自私不顧及別人，無秩序，不會講"對不起，謝謝"，喜歡講大話·喜歡講空話，喜歡講假話，喜歡講謊話，更喜歡講惡毒的話，這些國人的不良積習；大到造成中國官場腐敗的科舉，奴性媚骨的宦官制度，愚昧無知的裹腳惡俗等等。

《醜陋的中國人》一書揭示了中華民族"種種醜陋"的性格或心理狀態。通觀全書，柏楊對中華民族及其文化有一個總的看法，那就是：中華民族文化是一個"醬缸"，一個"發酸發臭"的醬缸，而"大多數中國人"就是生活在這個"發酸發臭"的醬缸裡的"醬缸蛆"。"中國人在這個醬缸裡醬得太久，我們的思想和判斷，以及視野都受醬缸的污染，跳不出醬缸的範圍。""在這種長期醬在缸底的情形下，使我們中國人變得自私、猜忌。"以至"落到今天這種醜陋的地步"，故中國人概而言之曰："醜陋的中國人"云云。在柏楊先生眼裡，中國文化傳統應該統統拋棄，因為"中國文化的醬缸發臭，使中國人變得醜陋。"

林語堂著寫《中國人》，舊譯《吾土吾民》一書，他將中國人的性格、心靈、理想、生活、政治、社會、藝術、文化等諸方面，寫得非常幽默，非常美妙，並與西方人的性格、心靈、理想、生活等作了相應的廣泛深入的比較，所以自1935年由美國紐約約翰·戴公司出版以來，在海內外引起了轟動，被美國女作家賽珍珠等名士推崇備至，曾譯成多種文字，在西方廣泛流傳。

"中國是這樣一個偉大的國家，國民生活如此複雜，對她有形形色色的，甚至是互相矛盾的闡釋，都是很自然的事。如果有人持有與我相反的意見，我也隨時準備支援他，並為他提供更多的材料來證明他的正確性。人們能夠獲得真理、體會真理的時刻並不多，只有這些時刻才能永存。"林語堂如是說。

中國人做人處事，圓滑、穩重、內斂，富有耐力，善於察顏觀色，迂回曲折，為人老成世故，講究城府。也就是說非常超脫老猾。中國人為人處事，總體上是比較講究穩妥穩健的。老成溫厚，常常意味著用消極、鎮靜、等待的力量，而不是像年輕人那樣，用青春活力與激情浪漫來處事。中國人每每遇到難題的時候，不是積極地追求進取，從根本上去克服困難，而是用一句"退一步海闊天空"來自我麻醉，有時這樣的做法也叫"丟一卒而勝全域"。

中國人特別善於忍耐，活在中國，要學會忍辱負重，學會屈辱而卑微地活著。"像畜牲一樣活下去"，這就是勝利。忍耐已成為中國人的一大惡習。因為，"中國人已經容忍了許多西方人從來不能容忍的暴政、動盪不安和腐敗的統治。"中國的勝利，常常取決於壽命，看誰有耐心有命去等待。中國人把活著看成人生的最高目的。因此，才有"好死不賴活著"。只要活著，就可以看到你的敵人慢慢死去，然後改變面貌。

中國人非常喜歡消極避世。中國人在得勢的時候非常喜歡儒家，因為，儒家主張"學而優則仕"，那時的心態就是"春風得意馬蹄疾，一日看遍長安花"。但是，由於中國人追求的"學而優則仕"，這個遊戲，具有高度排他性，說到底是一個零和博弈遊戲，因此，人生不如意事常八九。所以，道家的存在是必然的。它為每一個官場失意，賭場失意，情場失意的中國人保留了退路。

中國人喜歡做一個世故的老滑頭。老滑頭的為人處世原則就是：丟一卒而勝全域；三十六計，走為上策；好漢不吃眼前虧；退一步海闊天空。當有人要侮辱你、嘲笑你、藐視你、譭謗你、傷害你、嫌惡你、詭譎你的時候，應該怎麼辦？最好的辦法就是忍受他，依順他，敬他，避他，苦苦耐他，裝聾作啞，漠然置之。冷眼觀之，看他如何結局。其實，在中國，無需要學習什麼中國傳統文化，每個生養在中國這塊古老大地上的人，都是天然的滑頭。滑頭只有老少之分，而沒有"有無"之別。中國的土壤氣候決定了，中國，就是一個必須學得滑頭才能夠活下去的地方。

在中國，所有的問題其實都是飯碗問題，什麼主義都不過是生意，什麼事說到底無非是"升官發財"，再沒有別的事。不管什麼儒家、道家、佛教、基督教、天主教，睡大覺、睡午覺等等，在中國，都是用來"吃"的。因此，吃儒家飯，吃道家飯，吃佛教，吃基督，吃天主教，這些說法在中國是很流行，很普遍的。對精神信仰麻木不仁及採用世俗功利的態度，是中國人的普遍特色。因此，做和尚與做道士也常常與做官一樣，有級別，有肥瘦之分。

"中國人在本性是道家，在文化上是儒家，然而其道家思想卻更甚於儒家思想。"在中國一切都世俗得很。真正的愛情是沒有的。娶妻為了生子，嫁人是為了吃飯。嫁漢嫁漢，穿衣吃飯，現實功利得很。中國人的所謂愛情，都只是在一些神話想像之中，在現實中是從來沒有過的。因為，中國人的家庭本身就是生產單位，就是放高利貸的地方，中國人以"孝道"理念，維繫著一個家庭模式，養兒防老，積穀防饑。一切都是有功利目的的。出來混，遲早是要還的。

中國人的宗教信仰

無論是西方人，還是中國人，講述中國人品性言行故事，基本的套路大致相同或相近，大多都是集中在發掘、描述國人的行為特徵和精神狀態的表層現象，甚少有涉獵、探索關於中國文化深層次主導影響力的部分，難見有深度分析、挖掘中國人如何就長成這個模樣的完整解釋。似乎好像是這樣一種狀況，病人被診斷出一大堆病況和病症，卻並不知道患病的病源和病因，醫生似乎只專注診斷病情，而不開藥方。

這可讓病人如何是好？病人日後如何可以改善、恢復元氣增強體質，如何預防未來不再犯病？

正因此，我們主動來承接任務，潛心努力一把，用心觀察學習、思考總結，嘗試解釋明白中國為什麼能夠長成現在的這個樣子。今天的世界上，還真是比較難找到和中國人有相同經歷，相同思維，或相似性格的民族和國家。

在中國人成長進步的 5000 年歷史長河中，外界中到底有什麼東西能開啟了中國人大智慧的？自然環境中到底有什麼東西，成為影響中國人性格形成的主要因素？找到並理解影響中國文化和中國人性格形成的基礎原素，那怕是部分基礎原素，對於更好、更全面地瞭解中國人助益頗多，解開"中國"之謎便是順理成章，水到渠成的事情。

中國人到底有沒有信仰？中國人的信仰是什麼？一個民族，一個文化不可能沒有自己的信仰，可是中國的確不像西方國家那樣，有一個統一的、有神論宗教信仰。那麼，東方中國的信仰到底是個什麼東西？許多人壓根沒有想明白。當然，按照現存的西方人邏輯思維，習慣定式去想問題找解釋，信仰必須有統一的教堂經書和教義，有一群篤信獻身的牧師傳教士，和一大批虔誠追隨的教徒。

按照此類定義定理和規範解釋，結論自然是中國沒有統一的宗教信仰。中國人什麼都可以相信，或什麼都可以不相信，中國社會缺乏道德倫理標準；中國人缺乏誠信和社會責任感；中國人自私貪婪冷酷無情等說法便流行起來，西方主流話語權者和一部分中國人持有這種觀點。

可是，絕大多數中國人又從內心深處並不認同西方人的這種判斷和看法。中國人的價值觀念不同於西方人的，從來就有自己的崇拜信仰物件。國人並不認為有必要去創造一個存乎于人和自然天地之間的神靈，或宗教來規範、引導人類言論行為，由"天地"直接掌控天底下的所有一切，應該更加合理貼切。

　　萬事萬物中"天地"規律最大,自然"天地"足以擔當起引領世間萬物演變進化之重責。中國是一個信奉"天人合一"的國家,中國人自古以來篤信"天和地",老天爺有眼,天底下最大。"天地人"三位一體,三者結合是一個有機的整體。自然王國中,有天,有地,有萬事萬物。

　　天在上,地在下,萬事萬物位處中間。而在萬事萬物之中,人類始終佔據著頂層的中心位置,是所有生命體物質中最聰慧的一個族類。按照中國人的世界觀理念,天地的有序運行有既定的"道"。所謂道,即是指自然規律。世間萬事萬物的運行,受自然規律的制約,規範和支配。"天地生陰陽",天地之下萬事萬物的生長和消亡,興盛與衰敗都是受"陰陽"變化之規律所影響,無一例外。

　　"陰陽"之道是變化的,是變化之規律。陰陽之間,是一條曲線,而不是一條直線,曲線意味是變動的,是非常靈活的,一直處在運動中的。中國的陰陽理念,陰中有陽,陽中有陰,陰魚有一個白圓點,陽魚有一個黑圓點。從陰到陽,從陽到陰,是不斷變化著的。陰陽雖然是兩個字,然而卻是一氣之消長,一進一退,一消一長。進口處便是陽,退出處便是陰,長處便是陽,消處便是陰;只是這一氣之消長,做出古今天地之間無限的事情來。

　　"陰陽"之道是辯證的,是辯證之規律。陰陽之間,沒有敵我之分,陰是陰,陰也可以是陽;相反,陽是陽,陽也可以是陰,陰陽兩者可以互相轉換變化;陰陽之間,沒有好壞之分,不是說一個是壞的,另一個是好的。好與壞的評價標準,是講究陰陽的整體平衡,和陰陽的整體和諧,陰陽平衡、和諧、適度就是好的,陰陽失衡、過猶不及、極端過度就是不好的。中國人講"工"和"巧",都是在講究合度和適度,要恰如其分恰到好處。樂而不淫,哀而不傷,遜而不諂,寬而不縱,"運用之妙,存乎一心"。

　　"陰陽"之道是對立統一的,是對立統一之規律。陰陽之間,相生相剋。生剋是矛盾的兩個方面,也就是陰陽的兩個方面。相生相剋是事物的普遍規律,是事物內部不可分割的兩個方面。生剋是相對的,沒有生,就無所謂剋;沒有剋,也就無所謂生。有生無剋,事物就會無休止的發展而走向極端,造成物極必反,由好變壞;有剋無生,事物就會因被壓制過分而喪元氣走向衰敗。在生剋這個對立與統一的矛盾中,無論是生的過分還是剋的過分都會因對立而打破相對平衡或統一,事物就會向一方傾斜發展。

　　"陰陽"之道又是循環的,是循環再生之規律。陰陽之間,一靜一動。"無靜不成動,無動不成靜","陰陽只是一氣,陰氣流行即為陽,陽氣凝聚即為陰",氣的流行就是陽動,氣的凝聚就是陰靜。陰陽動靜之間,既有牽制關係,也有輔助關係。動靜相輔相制,兩者互為前提,互為條件,互為結果,循環往復生生不息。"終而始,始而終",荀子這樣說道。

中國人講"道"也好，講規律講陰陽也罷，這些本都是一種無形"懸乎"的東西，現實生活中理解掌握起來相對比較困難。既然"道"無影無蹤，看不見，聽不到，摸不著，觸碰不了感覺不到，但卻又真真實實地存在，無處不在無處不有。那麼，為了更好地理解"道"，具體形象化地感知體會自然規律，普通民眾需要找到一個具象化的參照物，這樣的要求合情合理。

"上善若水，水善利萬物而不爭，處眾人之所惡，故幾於道"（老子《道德經第八章》）。最高境界的善行，就像水的品性一樣，上善至善完美；水善於滋潤萬物而不與萬物相爭名利，停留在眾人都不喜歡的地方。所以，水最接近於"道"。從此，"道"不再是一個虛無的概念幻覺。"水"在中國人的現實生活中，成了"道"，或自然規律的化身。中國哲學先賢老子用"道"形容自然規律，創造性地用有感知的"水"來描述、體認難以感知的"自然規律"，用心何其縝密精細，意義深刻而非同尋常。

水，無色無味，在方而法方，在圓而法圓，無所滯，它以百態存于自然界，于自然無所違也。水為至善至柔；水性綿綿密密，微則無聲，巨則洶湧；與人無爭卻又容納萬物。水有滋養萬物的德行，它使萬物得到它的利益，而不與萬物發生矛盾、衝突。人生之道，莫過於此。中國人從此心悅誠服於"道"，誠服于"水"，尊敬大自然，尊重大自然規律，遵從"天地"自然法則，拜水為老師，從學習、研究、總結水的品德和水的性格中得到智慧靈性靈感，感悟人生道理，開啟人類大智慧。

現實生活中，淺層次感覺中國人什麼都信，什麼又都不完全相信，整個國家沒有單一主流的信仰宗教。在中國，各式各樣教堂和寺廟林林總總數不勝數，畢肩而立。國民百姓很少有難為誰家的習慣，存心跟誰家過不去的，得罪對方。尋常百姓常常是見廟進廟，見佛拜佛。遇教堂進教堂，見神拜神。表面上看，中國人什麼宗教信仰都可以接受。但是，你可千萬別當真，那些只是國人出於禮節，象徵性地禮待一下對方而已，並不真正代表在他們心中"你是唯一"。其實，"尊重"四方周圍萬事萬物，原本就是水品質的優秀基因之一。

在國人心底裡一定有自己始終如一的堅持，虔誠懷揣信仰"水是萬事萬物之源"，"水幾近於道"。水，是中國人的宗教信仰；道，是中國人的宗教信仰；自然天地中的規律集成，才是中國人真實的宗教信仰。所以說，讀懂了水，你便有機會讀懂中國文化，讀懂中國人。道，或自然規律，因為有了水，變得更加直觀和清晰，人類尊重大自然和自然規律，水自然而然地成為了中國人內心誠服、膜拜的對象，並始終追隨5000年，且將再繼續尾追5000年。

西方的知識體系中有一個"叢林法則"。或多或少獲受"進化論"理論的影響，西方文化中一整套關乎"效率"的核心理念概念：自由、民主、法制、人權、競爭、科學、個人主義逐漸整合成型，從深度和廣度上完善了西方的話語體系，促進了西方文化的傳播力度。今天，東方中國的新型知識體系中該不該有一個獨具東方哲學思維的"水法則"作基礎理論架構，構建中國的新型話語體系和知識體系？

"水，柔軟親和、剛柔一體、柔中帶剛、剛中懷柔、柔終克剛、變化無窮。"水不僅有剛強堅硬的實力，更具備有柔軟包容的巨大力量，水有剛硬柔和的兩面屬性，剛硬柔和兩性可以互相轉化、交替借力、變化無窮無盡。而且，水最終能夠以柔克剛，以柔懷剛，以柔化剛。以水為鏡，以史為鏡重新回到中華傳統文化之中，回到中華文化起步的《易經》之中，好好想想祖輩先哲們給我們後代人留存的路標指向，從經典和歷史中尋找本民族的智慧傳承。

找回水，認識水，深度研習水的價值，水的品質，和水的性格特徵。中國古代有自己的文化體系傳承，中間的百多年，經歷過西方文化的衝擊、碰撞和洗禮之後，中國現代社會更需要有自己的新型知識體系和文化體系，講清楚中華文明的起始、發展、未來是怎麼一回事，這不僅為中華民族的復興，而且為世界人類命運共同體的發展，尋找到人類共用的價值觀，和共同的文化價值體系基礎。

第三篇

水，儒釋道同源

講中國文化故事，講中國人故事，其實就是講中國人日常言行舉止，生活規範，和倫理道德的故事。這句話該不該說，怎樣說？那件事該不該做，如何來做？背後實質反映的是國人相信的"好"與"壞"標準。久而久之，益人利己的好事做多了，社會慢慢形成一整套符合本民族百姓思維習慣的禮儀思想和禮儀規範，且其精髓逐漸深入人心，進而內化成中華民族的自覺意識並貫穿于心理與行為活動之中，最終去偽存真，延續累積構成一種文化。

中國的文化有儒家、道家、佛家三大文化體系。通常，講儒釋道，是指以孔子為代表的儒教，以老子為代表的道教，和以禪宗六祖慧能為代表的中國佛教（漢傳佛教）。"釋"講的是古印度太子悉達多·喬達摩，棄皇位而出家追求解脫苦難的安穩，最終在菩提樹下覺悟成聖人後而創立的宗教。因悉達多·喬達摩為釋迦牟尼佛，故又稱釋教，或佛教。這裡需要說明一下，受西方語境的影響，現代漢語中常把"三教"直接等同於三種"宗教"，其實未必準確。中國傳統典籍裡，"三教"之"教"字，僅是"教化"之意，而非現代西方宗教學所說的"宗教"(religion)。

中國的佛教得益於印度佛教東傳。西曆紀元前後，印度佛教開始由印度經西域，沿著絲綢之路傳到中國的，經過長時期傳播，和本土化吸收、消化、發展，而最終形成具有中國本土意識，和民族特色的中國式佛教。佛教起始於印度，發展在中國，又遠傳于日本、韓國和東南亞國家。而佛教在印度本土由於受到印度教及後來傳入印度的伊斯蘭教的排擠，約在西元八、九百年左右，在印度本土逐漸消失消亡。而能保留佛教並發展佛教的中國就自然而然成了當今世界佛教的真正故鄉。

佛教和基督教、天主教、伊斯教、猶太教、印度教、東正教等宗教一樣，是一種外來的文化輸入品。但是，為什麼就只有佛教能順暢地從印度傳入中國，並且被中國主流文化所欣然接受？佛教竟能在異國他鄉的土地上生根、開花、結了果？佛教在中古早期傳入中國，不僅是中國哲學史和宗教史上"最重要的里程碑"（胡適語）。佛教全面影響了中國社會的文化、審美、語言等各個領域和層面，是中國文化中一個不可分割的重要組成部分，且對其他社會領域有著強烈的滲透和廣泛的影響。

佛教對現代的中國人來說，已經是天然的熟悉熟知，甚至幾乎讓人忘記佛教是一個外來的宗教。談中國佛教，就必須從它當初傳入中華疆域的時間議起。禪宗公案中有一個問題曾被反復提及："如何是佛祖西來意？"即佛教因何從西方傳入中土？對於這個問題有許多著名的回答，但卻都不是直接的回答，而是將之視為一個毫無意義的問題。然而，開聊瞎侃或可以如此，可是做學問，追溯歷史源頭卻不能這樣馬虎，草草了事。

英國人湯因比曾提出一個著名的論斷，即宗教的大發展往往尾隨一個帝國的崩潰而來。

佛教在中國的傳播深入，在很大程度上確實得益於兩漢時代儒家文明的政治秩序崩潰之後，持續近四百年的政治分裂和社會危機，這樣一個根基動搖的社會“成為異域思想和制度得以植入的極有希望的溫床”。在這樣一個人們難以預知福禍和未來的災難時刻，佛教恰好踩準時點進入、植入中國，至少在一定程度上給了人們精神上的安寧和指引，讓他們通過對彼岸世界的追求擺脫現實世界中的焦慮痛苦。當然，這應該是強調、解釋時間把握的剛剛好，恰逢合適的機會。

就時機而言，佛教植入中國的時間是恰到好處。然而更重要的是，佛教的核心價值觀理念符合國人的理想願望。如果佛教沒有貼切中國百姓信仰的合適內容，佛教在中國的本土化落地幾乎是不可能的。佛教，和中國本土的儒教和道教一樣，具有一種相似相近，甚至相同的價值觀取向，共同的基因決定了佛教在中國的前途命運。顯然，佛教適合並回應了中華民族的精神要求，並成功地融合進中國主流文化之中，最終成為支撐中國文化的三大支柱之一。

中華文化共同體最初形成，主要是在農耕地區，以孔子、孟子等為代表的齊魯文化，以老子、莊子為代表的荊楚文化，以商鞅、韓非為代表的法家文化，以孫子為代表的兵家文化，以墨子為代表的平民文化等思想智慧交織碰撞，諸家百子經過長時間的磨合，形成了中華文化共同體的基本價值觀念。這個以農耕文化為核心的文化共同體，不斷地融合了一些源於其他族群的文化，特別是漢傳佛教、藏傳佛教，和南傳佛教的文化，組成中華文化的大家庭。

中華文化共同體所有組成部分擁有一個共同的價值信仰，格外尊敬大自然，崇拜大自然規律，膜拜誠服大自然規律“道”的代言者—水，無論儒釋道，還是其他諸子百家，都是在中國土地上真正落了地生了根的，文化上高度認同“水”，水是中華文化的最大公約數。認同“道”，認同“天人合一”，認同“天地人”三位一體，萬事萬物中“天地”規律最大，“天地人”三者結合是一個有機的整體。中華文化共同體最根本的價值觀念，是我們這個民族形成和發展最根本的文化基礎。

水是世間萬物不可或缺的重要組成部分，它以浩瀚、博大的體魄孕育了生命，又以九曲歸一的形態、奔流不息的氣勢啟迪了人類的思想，進而啟迪了人類文化的創造。從古到今，無數人類文化的精華都與水息息相關。“水”及其變化體“雲”、“冰”、“雪”、“霜”、“霧”、“露”、“雹”等共同構成了內涵豐富的“水”文化集成，並與中國傳統文化有著深刻的淵源。“水”文化源遠流長，中國儒釋道三家文化中，便蘊含著豐富的“水”文化基因。

儒家講水

中國古代儒家的代表孔子說："夫水者，啟子比德焉。遍予而無私，似德；所及者生，似仁；其流卑下，句倨皆循其理，似義；淺者流行，深者不測，似智；其赴百仞之穀不疑，似勇；綿弱而微達，似察；受惡不讓，似包；蒙不清以入，鮮潔以出，似善化；至量必平，似正；盈不求概，似度；其萬折必東，似意。是以君子見大水必觀焉爾也。"

孔子認為，水，能夠啟發君子用來比喻自己的德行修養啊。它遍佈天下，給予萬物，並無偏私，有如君子的道德；所到之處，萬物生長，有如君子的仁愛；水性向下，隨物賦形，有如君子的高義；淺處流動不息，深處淵然不測，有如君子的智慧；奔赴萬丈深淵，毫不遲疑，有如君子的臨事果決和勇毅；滲入曲細，無微不達，有如君子的明察秋毫；蒙受惡名，默不申辯，有如君子包容一切的豁達胸懷；泥沙俱下，最後仍然是一泓清水，有如君子的善於改造事物；裝入量器，一定保持水準，有如君子的立身正直；遇滿則止，並不貪多務得，有如君子的講究分寸，處事有度；無論怎樣的百折千回，一定要東流入海，有如君子的堅定不移的信念和意志。所以君子見到大水一定要仔細觀察。

孔子還說："仁者樂山，智者樂水，知者動，仁者靜，知者樂，仁者壽。"仁智者樂山水，仁智者動靜相融，仁智者樂而壽。"智者"的智慧當如水之靈活。若藏於地下則含而不露，若噴湧而上則清而為泉；少則叮咚作樂，多則奔騰豪壯。水處天地之間，或動或靜；動則為澗、為溪、為江河；靜則為池、為潭、為湖海。水遇不同境地，顯各異風采；經沙土則滲流，碰岩石則濺花；遭斷崖則下垂為瀑，遇高山則繞道而行。水，可由滴滴雨水雪水而成涓涓細流，而成滔滔江河，而成茫茫海洋。"智者"的智慧當如"樂水"之靈感。

孔子又說："逝者如斯夫，不舍晝夜。"時光如流水一樣一去不復返，青春終會老去，萬事萬物都將成為流水般的匆匆過客。孔子對消逝的時間、人事與萬物，有如流水般永遠留不住而引發的哲思，它既有因時光流逝、功業未成而導致的深沉感喟，又具有對時間、永恆、變化等物質運動的抽象哲學問題的沉思帶來的哲學感悟。

百姓如江水，為官要慎篤，《孔子家語》云："夫君者舟也，庶人者水也。水所以載舟，亦可以覆舟。"平民百姓可擁護君主，也能推翻君主。君王好比是船，百姓好比是水，水可以使船行駛，也可以使船淹沒。

孔子一生孜孜追求的大同社會，原本就是個充滿仁愛的世界。所以，從某種程度來說，水不僅構成了儒家的思想體系，水也成為了儒家思想核心的象徵。孔子口中的君子仁者身上都閃現出水的靈光。水越是平靜越深不可測，就越像大智若愚的智者。君子無所爭執，正與水"夫唯不爭"相似，"巧言令色，鮮矣仁"，"邦有道，不廢，邦無道，免于刑戮"，不正與水的"言善信，事善能"相符？

儒家的另一個代表人物孟子繼承和發揚孔子"仁"的思想，在對現實社會進行深入思考的基礎上，以性善理論為根據，創造性地提出了"仁政"思想，並認為"不以仁政，不能平治天下"（《孟子·離婁上》）。為了增強其論證的說服力和感染力，善用譬喻的孟子又一次借用"水"的特性和功能，淋漓盡致地闡發了關於"仁政"的思想和主張。

孟子說："民之歸仁也，猶水就下，獸之走壙也。故為淵驅魚者獺也，為叢驅雀者鸇也，為湯武驅民者桀與紂也"（《孟子·離婁上》）。又說："如有不嗜殺人者，則天下之民皆引領而望之矣。誠如是也，民歸之，猶水就下，沛然誰能禦之？"（《孟子·梁惠王上》）

孟子認為，民心歸順仁政，就好像水順流而下，野獸自然向曠野奔跑一樣，這個趨勢是誰也阻擋不了的。他藉此警告統治者，只有施仁政於民眾，以人民的利益為利益，才能使百姓"猶水就下"一樣望仁德而歸附；否則，君王像為淵驅漁的獺、為叢驅雀的鸇一樣，殘民以逞，必然會淪為桀與紂那樣的獨夫民賊，那時，老百姓就會不堪殘暴，揭竿而起，推翻暴君的統治。

在《孟子》一書中，孟子多次舉出大禹治水為民除害造福的業績，盛讚其實行王道的功德。他說："禹思天下有溺者，猶己溺之。"大禹想到天下有遭水淹沒的百姓，就像自己使他們淹沒一般。為了救民於水患災難之中，禹繼承了父親鯀未竟的治水事業，薄衣食，卑宮室，櫛風沐雨，歷盡艱辛，"八年於外，三過其門而不入"。經過十多年的艱苦努力，終於制服了洪水，使人民安居樂業。孟子告誡統治者，只有像大禹治水那樣，以天下為己任，急民眾之所急，憂民眾之所憂，為民造福，才是王者應有的責任和風範。

釋家（佛家）講水

佛教常以水流的流轉不息、易逝難追喻指人生的無常。河水奔騰不息的特徵對宣揚佛教三法印、十二因緣思想是非常恰切的。佛教的基本教義三法印"諸行無常，諸法無我，涅槃寂靜"，意思是世界萬物沒有恆常的存在，一切事物和現象都處在遷流變動中，人的生命也處在永恆不息的生死相續之中。生命短暫無常，無從把握，是一個痛苦煎熬的過程，而生命最大的痛苦莫在於人始終處在生死之流循環往復，永無歇止，這恰如水流瞬間即逝，又無止無休。

《大般涅槃經》曰："是身無常念念不住，猶如電光暴水幻炎，亦如畫水隨畫隨合。"

《大般涅槃經》還將生命的流逝比作瞬間幻滅的水泡："若是行者為生滅法，譬如水泡速起速滅，往來流轉猶如車輪，一切諸行亦複如是。"《雜阿含經》也有水泡之喻："諸比丘，譬如大雨大泡，一起一滅。"人從生到死的過程竟如水泡起滅間短暫脆弱，而在無盡的時間之流裡人也如水泡起起滅滅、無有止歇，世間真如同苦海無邊。人只有努力修行求道才能跳出三界，超出苦海，永斷輪迴而達到涅槃寂靜，這才是真正得到解脫。

佛教把人生命的最終原因歸結為十二因緣，人生就是由無明、行、識、名色、六處、觸、受、愛、取、有、生、老死這十二個環節組成，其中無明是行的因，行是識的緣，一直推演下去直至生是老死的因。這十二個環節形成了一系列流程，眾生就在這生死流轉中不斷迴圈，結束了一個流程，又會開始另一個十二因緣的流程。十二因緣的相續不斷恰如水流不歇，以水流不止比喻生死輪迴是佛教的典型意蘊。

佛教以水的清淨、濕性來喻指佛性、自性的淨潔。《大般涅槃經》云："如水無泥，澄靜清淨。解脫亦爾，澄靜清淨即真解脫。"《大般若波羅蜜多經》言："又如水大性本清潔無垢無濁，甚深般若波羅蜜多亦複如是。"永明延壽的《宗鏡錄》將佛教水喻的意蘊內涵概括為"水喻真心十義"，水喻十義各個不同，卻都圍繞一個中心意蘊：以水喻佛性心性或自性的清淨。佛性（如來藏心）、自性在南朝高僧竺道生的佛性論裡已趨於融合，到禪宗那裡更有了佛性、自性、心性的融合。

《法華經》云："如人渴須水，穿鑿于高原，猶見乾燥土，知去水尚遠，漸見濕土泥，決定知近水。"好像有人在饑渴的時候想要喝水。饑，就是肚子餓；渴，就是想要喝水，非常的乾渴。那麼在這乾渴的期間，想要喝水；這譬喻我們人在凡夫地，想要求佛果；佛果，就是"水"。我們在凡夫的這種境界上，是非常的乾燥，所以就渴，想要喝這個法水、要得成佛果。穿鑿于高原：就在那高的地方，想穿鑿一個井。這穿鑿井，就是修道；你修行，就像開井一樣。

《觀經》日："一一池水，七寶所成。其摩尼水，流注華間。"這個華間，池裡面是蓮花，池的岸邊是寶樹，寶樹需要德水滋養，這個水自然流注樹間，尋樹上下。這水真妙，我們這邊水可以只往下流，不會往上，極樂世界的水可以往上流。可見極樂莊嚴微妙，超逾一切，一切世界裡沒有的，到極樂世界你全看到。

《會疏》日："彼土人天，非水穀身。清淨成就，不須洗濯，何須水耶？唯是為隨意受樂，蕩除心垢故也。"蓮花化身，非依飲水食穀以維身命。本來清淨，何須洗浴？蓋隨意樂而浴，為除心垢耳！心垢消除，自然神開體適。

《淨土大經》日：極樂世界這個池很多，小池十由旬、二十由旬，大池百千由旬，就像大海一樣。在我們這個世界，小池像湖泊，大池像大海。無論是大池、小池，湛然香潔，水都是具有八種功德。一者澄淨。二者清冷。三者甘美。四者輕軟。五者潤澤。六者安和。七者飲時除饑渴等無量過患。八者飲已定能長養諸根四大，增益種種殊勝善根。

禪語日："善心如水"水利萬象萬物，"善心"備焉。水憑滲透性強而滋潤生物；水靠浮力大而可行舟船；水憑流動不息而改善環境，讓地球充滿生機；水可降溫，水可去汙；水可驅動機器，水可以發電生能……水的作用無數，水之善心無邊。

道家講水

中國古代哲學聖賢老子說："上善若水，水善利萬物而不爭，此乃謙下之德也；故江海所以能為百谷王者，以其善下之，則能為百谷王。天下莫柔弱于水，而攻堅強者莫之能勝，此乃柔德；故柔之勝剛，弱之勝強堅。因其無有，故能入於無之間，由此可知不言之教、無為之益也。"

老子認為上善的人，就應該像水一樣。水造福萬物，滋養萬物，卻不與萬物爭高下，這才是最為謙虛的美德。江海之所以能夠成為一切河流的歸宿，是因為他善於處在下游的位置上，所以成為百谷王。世界上最柔的東西莫過於水，然而它卻能穿透最為堅硬的東西，沒有什麼能超過它，例如滴水穿石，這就是"柔德"所在。所以說弱能勝強，柔可克剛。不見其形的東西，可以進入到沒有縫隙的東西中去，由此我們知道了"不言"的教導，"無為"的好處。

老子還說："以其不爭，故天下莫能與之爭，此乃效法水德也。水幾於道；道無所不在，水無所不利，避高趨下，未嘗有所逆，善處地也；空處湛靜，深不可測。善為淵也；損而不竭，施不求報，善為仁也；……。"

"道"是產生天地萬物的總根源，是先於具體事物而存在的東西，也是事物的基本規律及其本源。所以"道"是我們每個人都應該認知與理解的。老子認為，如果你不與任何人相爭利益，所以，天底下沒有人能夠與你比高低，這是效法水的品德。水的德行就是最接近於"道"的，"道"無處不在，因此，水無所不利。它避讓高位趨處下方，因此不會受到任何阻礙。它可以流淌到任何地方，滋養萬物，洗滌污泥。它處於深潭之中，表面清澈而平靜，但卻深不可測。它源源不斷的流淌，去造福於萬物卻不求回報。這樣的德行，乃至仁至善……。

老子對孔子說道：“水幾於道：道無所不在，水無所不利，避高趨下，未嘗有所逆，善處地也；空處湛靜，深不可測，善為淵也；損而不竭，施不求報，善為仁也；圜必旋，方必折，塞必止，決必流，善守信也；洗滌群穢，平准高下，善治物也；以載則浮，以鑒則清，以攻則堅強莫能敵，善用能也；不舍晝夜，盈科後進，善待時也。故聖者隨時而行，賢者應事而變；智者無為而治，達者順天而生。”

水，是最接近于大道的，大道無所不在，而水也有利於一切，不留在高處，卻只往低處去，從來不會逆勢而走，是善於選擇自己的所在。清澈而平靜，深不可測，是善於淵遠深奧，汲取而不會枯竭，付出不求回報，這是善於為仁。遇見圓處所在，必環繞而走，遇見方處所在，必折角而行，塞住必停止，放開就流淌，這是善於守信用。水，能洗去萬般的污穢，能正確地評判高下，這是善於治理萬物。用來載物，可以漂浮其上，用來映照，則清澈如本，用於破壞時沒有什麼能夠阻擋，這是善於使用自己的能力。無論白天黑夜，注滿一處以後便會向前流淌，是善於等待合適的時機。所以，聖人順隨著時機而行動，賢者針對不同的事情而變化，智者不用大動干戈去治理，通達的人順應天時而生存。

莊子是繼老子之後道家最主要的代表人物。莊子和老子一樣，也喜歡從水中感悟和闡發其深邃的“道”理。老子以水論“道”，大多直抒胸臆，是直截了當的斷語；莊子則不然，他往往通過編織奇特的水的寓言故事，來闡發深刻、抽象的哲學道理，其說理方式之奇特、想像之奇幻、運思之深邃、語言之精美，令人歎為觀止。

莊子在《逍遙遊》中，以魚在水中暢遊來比試人在“道”中。江湖浩瀚，魚在其中優哉遊哉，彼此相忘，恩斷情絕。一旦泉源斷絕，河湖乾涸，魚兒們在陸地上共渡危難，共圖生存，只好吐沫相托，呵氣相濕，互相親附，但比之在江湖中逍遙自在的生活，真是天壤之別。“魚相忘乎江湖”，就超越了失水的局限性。由物及人，同樣，人只有徹底擺脫對有限現實的依託，才能擺脫忘卻現實的期待和羈絆，遨遊于無限的自由天地之中，優遊自在，無牽無掛，一任自然。

人類，對水有著天生的偏愛，水中之遊確實充滿了無窮無盡的快意，而莊子更喜歡從游水中體悟他的逍遙遊的境界。同時，莊子更以深廣無際的大海（水）比喻“道”，這和老子喻“道”有一脈相承之處，讓人們感受到“道”的淵深和博大。大海覆蓋了地球表面的十分之七，是地球上最大的物象；大海既博大精深，又包羅萬象，惟有大海，才更能體現老莊之“道”的無限和絕對。

《莊子》曰：“天下之水，莫大于海，萬川歸之，不知何時止而不盈；尾閭泄之，不知何時止而不虛。春秋不變，水旱不知"。大海是天下萬水之源，之歸宿，雖然萬川歸之，並不見海水溢出，雖然尾閭不斷傾瀉，也不見海水乾涸，四季或旱澇的變化也對大海沒有影響，為什麼如此？很簡單，因為海的容量巨大無比。

《莊子》曰："君子之交淡若水，小人之交甘若醴；君子淡以親，小人甘以絕。"君子之間的交情清淡得像水一樣，小人之間的交情甘美得像甜酒一樣，君子不以利相交而以道相合，故清淡親密，小人以利相交故有甜頭，一旦利盡交情就斷絕。

儒釋道同源

"儒釋道"三教的價值觀理念趨同一致，共同以"道"自然規律為尊，以道的代言者"水"為尊。在漫長的文化融合歷程中，"儒釋道"三家思想已然血脈相連，經脈相通，彼此尊重而無相互引奪，自我完善至極而又彼此默契，互相保護又互相支助。"儒釋道"三家的思想內容當然各有側重，表像上看你是你，我是我，你我各具特色各有特質。但是，"儒釋道"三教本質上卻是理念一致，並存相容，多元且相互支撐，你中有我，我中有你，你我同根同源，價值觀理念"水"源遠流長。

中國歷史上能夠形成儒釋道三教會通融合、和而不同的宗教文化體系，在整個人類文明史上也不曾多見。首先，中國的主體民族漢族宗教信仰像"水"那樣的寬容海涵，最大程度開放心胸接受外來文化。其次，由於中國上古時代漢族宗教在創始說和生死說問題上，總是有一些沒說明白的地方，存在這樣或那樣的局限性，儒家需要道家的充實，儒道兩家在論述生死問題上又需要佛教的補養。最後，儒釋道三教心屬同一理趣相通，且各有擅長，以三教的不同功能實現三者和諧共存，終以"以佛修心，以老治身，以儒治世"形成合力，服務中華民族大家庭。

"儒釋道"三教成為一種天然的互補互助關係，既有自我又有容他。三教平等，三教各有長短，功能不同，彼此相輔相成。三教同歸，三教功能卻各有異同，仍然能殊途同歸教化大眾。三教同源"易經"，三教有共同的智慧源頭，源自對大自然規律的臣服，對"水"的膜拜誠服。中國歷史上的儒釋道三教鼎立，並軌融合格局的形成和興盛發展，是我們這個民族貢獻給人類世界治理最棒的禮物之一，宗教信仰是可以共存並立，交相輝映的，"文明衝突"必然趨勢性說法和說辭，未免太過武斷和牽強，恐難完全成立。

"儒釋道"三教虔誠膜拜水，折服水，根本在於透過參學、研究水的品德和行為，中華民族的整體智慧大門逐漸開啟，並且開始明白、知曉文明社會的真實含義。如果人類主動，或被動地被封閉在生物鏈（食物鏈）圈內，只專注參學身邊的動植物生存技巧和技藝，就難言能順利跳出動植物世界那種原始、落後，和愚昧的競鬥狀態之中，根本沒有機會自拔，或提升自我，進而提升人類文明的總體水準和水準。

幸好人類身邊有水世界做榜樣引導，清潔清白、清晰清澈、無色無味、無所他求，而且無私奉獻。它預示並告誡人類，水除了滋養、扶助萬物生長的品德以外，其中還珍藏、隱含有充分體現高度文明特殊品質的兩項元素：公平和廉潔。公平，就是正義公正處事；廉潔，就是清廉自律待人。

人類文明社會是一個生態系統。有人類生態系統，就會伴隨有規則和規律—倫理道德，維持其順暢運轉。人類文明社會是由經濟發展、社會公平和執政廉潔三大支柱互相支撐，保證社會穩定有序。而在這三者當中，執政廉潔尤為重要。因為只有一個廉潔的執政團隊、得到老百姓信任的執政集體，才能夠促進經濟發展，採取各種措施實現社會的公平和公正，和伸張正義。執政廉潔直接關係到執政者地位的合法性和政治穩定，直接關係到執政能力的強弱大小，和維護、增進整個社會的共同利益多寡。

文明社會先進性體現在，廉潔自律不謀私利，全心全意為整體百姓謀福祉，而非為少數個人謀福利。"平出於公，公出於道。"（《呂氏春秋》）社會的公平正義：強化權利公平正義、機會公平正義、規則公平正義諸多訴求，以及社會公平保障體系整體功效。老百姓群體在社會發展的各方面都享有平等的生存和發展權利，實現機會均等。每一位社會成員有機會平等地享有權利，平等地履行義務，平等地承擔責任，平等地受到保護。而非自私自利，只專注為少數權貴服務，只重視為少數富裕人群服務。

"夫水至平而邪者取法，鏡至明而醜者無怨，水鏡之所以能窮物而無怨者，以其無私也。"（《三國志・蜀志・李嚴傳》）水最公平，即便是邪惡不法之徒也會以它作為行為準則；鏡子最明亮，即便是容貌醜陋的人在它面前也沒法抱怨和發怒；水和明鏡，之所以能夠包容天下而讓人心悅誠服，是因為它們最無私。一個文明社會的高度，是其社會公平正義覆蓋百姓群體的寬度和廣度彰顯。

"儒釋道"三教的共同發展，始終沒有把"個人的滿足"看作是首要的追求目標，而堅持認為人的"俗性"有其局限性，不能成為決定人世間重大要務的依據規則。銀河星際之中，除了以"人"為代表的一群動植物生命物種外，仍有大量已知和未知的物質存在，共同影響著周圍世界，故自然規律"道"才是世間第一要務。

明末清初，西方宗教哲學影響逐漸擴及中國疆土，試圖改變中國以"道"自然規律為尊的文化格局，而發展以"人"為尊的西方價值觀，甚至拉攏儒家而直接攻擊釋、道兩教。所幸，儒家並未轉向改弦易幟，踏上西方人的那艘航船甲板，繼續牽手釋道兩家，為中華文化盡心盡力。

在國人的認知中，西方文化強勢有其一定的道理。畢竟，西方文化對人類發展的貢獻，有其積極的一面。西方文化發展以"人"為尊的價值觀，強調"個人主義"人權道德觀理念，強化"效率"提速經濟發展，改善人類物質生活品質，這是值得充分肯定的。

可是，西方社會的"人性"價值觀，一次又一次蠻橫地由其堅船利炮護送，向海外殖民侵略，傳達"人權"的"福音"，西方價值觀的差別"人性"理論和社會"叢林法則"到底能走多遠？能否持久放射"道德"倫理的光芒，仍是一個大疑問，困繞世人。

中國歷史，無論怎樣演繹發展，國人相信"取法其上，得乎其中"的道理，取法於"道"，自然得乎於"人"。國人擅長學習西方的"好"東西，而懂得捨棄其"壞"的東西，儒釋道三家既主張尊重人性，更關注從人性滋長的名利牢籠中將人性徹底解放出來。

中國先哲老子說"域中有四大，而人居其一焉。人法地，地法天，天法道，道法自然。"宇宙中有四個大，而"人"代表的生命物種也佔居其中之一。人遵循與地的法則，地遵循於天的法則，天遵循於道的法則。道遵循自然的法則，造物主是自然法則的主宰。人，再有本事也不可能大過"天地"之道。

"儒釋道"三教聚首合力，用有形的，看得見摸得著的，有感知的"水"，詮釋講解無形的自然規律"道"，源水而來隨水而去，往復循環滋養中華文化 5000 年。祖先賢人"上善若水"的教誨引領，和護佑中國人的言行舉止，生活方式和價值觀取向，功德圓滿。

第四篇

水，中國人高談闊論 5000 年

中國人講"水"議"水"，一講就開講了 5000 年，一聊就深聊了 5000 年。自從有文字記載的中國歷史以來，關於"水"的話題就從來沒有缺席過。相比較於世界其他國家和民族，中國人談"水"的時間最長達 5000 年那麼久；議論"水"參與評論評價的人數最多，人群階層最是廣泛；挖掘總結"水"道德啟示，"水"倫理價值的廣度和深度最是全面，最是濃烈。國人鍾愛"水"的熱情相當獨特，獨一無二舉世罕見。水自然給予回饋我華夏子民，回贈給中華民族的智慧靈感也最是豐碩。

在地球上，有這麼一個民族叫中華民族，他們擁有和使用世界上獨一無二的方塊文字，享有獨特的文化傳統、生活習慣，和禮儀風俗；他們有著不同於世界其他民族獨特的思維習慣和行為方式；他們擁有當今世界最悠久，唯一沒有被中斷的文明歷史；現如今，他們又在全心身投入最強勁復興國家的文明事業，創造著舉世無雙的"中國奇跡"。在這奇跡發生的背後，有一個最最有意思的與眾不同發現或提示：水，這個東西普通且廣泛存在，世界各地到處都有，無人不曉無人不知，但卻只有中國人特別偏愛"水"，愛得那麼深切，那麼虔誠。

一個民族的特質力量首先來自組成這個民族的個體的普遍素質。中國的整體力量，完全是來自組成這個國家的絕大多數中國人所擁有的獨特品質。正是這個國家的人民具有的優秀品質，才造就中華民族得以成為一個偉大的民族，中國成為一個偉大的國家。日本學者桑原隲藏談論中國時稱："無論是一個國家還是一個民族，都是由形形色色、性格各異的人構成的，看似毫無共同之處，但是如果與其他國家或民族比起來，我們就會很容易地發現，這個國家或民族，有許多區別於其他國家或民族所獨有的特徵。"

中國的歷史書藏是一座智慧知識寶庫，是需要耐心才能研讀完的恢弘史詩。千百年來，中國歷史這本皇皇巨作，吸引著無數中外學者、專家前來探秘。他們拄著拐杖，提著竹籃在中國的大山叢林中翻越穿梭，拿著顯微鏡在中國的書庫裡埋頭搜尋，並在不同的時期和地方，從不同的角度提出過各種不同的見解。終於有那麼一天，新的發現呈現在世人眼前，那一大群中國人的性格特點，如同海灘邊粗壯的砂礫般顯而易見，這些性格中美好的方面，更會像寶石般熠熠生輝，即使在陰暗的天空下，也難掩其光芒。

正是這些寶石般閃光的民族性格，使得"中華民族才存續數千年而不衰，面臨數次外族入侵而不亡。"（沙蓮香語）讓我們再一次走進歷史記憶，回到中國的歷史藏書樓庫，尋找出中國人性格特點背後的主要影響原素。明白人或許可以敏銳地意識到：我們正行進在重新認識，重新審視中國文化和中國人自己的路上，文化還是那個熟悉的文化，人群還是那一群熟悉的平民百姓，可時代已經不再是那個從前的時代了。

《易經》說水

古老的《易經》是一部內容博大精深的典籍，其成書年代可能不遲於西周初期。《易經》所涉及的學科門類十分龐雜，如預測學、管理學、醫藥學、控制論、系統論、電腦二進位、武術、氣功等等。綜觀《易經》，可以發現"水"在其中佔有重要地位。《易經》八卦中有乾卦，坤卦，離卦，坎卦，震卦，巽卦，艮卦，和兌卦，其中坎卦代表水。《易經》講"道"，講自然界的規律大道理，講規律變化就像"水"一樣，循環往復變化不止。對於人來講，最重要的是根據變化的情況來調整自己的行動，以適應外界各種變化。"適變"是《易經》諄諄告誡人們的最為重要的一條法則。

《易經》認為；宇宙自然、人類社會之所以會變動不居，乃是因為構成世界的兩種基本因素或者說兩種力：陰與陽（亦即柔與剛）在不斷地發生衝突。《繫辭上傳》說得很明白："剛柔相推而生變化"。這種變化的積極成果則是天地萬物的發生、發展。《易經》認為，事物發展是經過了一個由漸變到突變、由量變到質變的過程的。當事物發展到了它所能容許的最高限度，它就要發生突變，向另一個方向、相反的方向發展，"易，窮則變，變則通，通則久。"（《繫辭·下傳》）

《易經》雖然認為宇宙萬物的變化有自己的規律，不以人的意志為轉移，但《易經》並不認為人在規律面前是完全無能的，它強調人可以認識、掌握這種變化的規律，以變應變，唯變所適。這就非常了不起。承認規律可以認識，可以掌握，這就無異於說，人可以將命運掌握在自己手中。實際上，整個《易經》講的就是人如何掌握自己的命運。變與適變，是《易經》的全部精髓。

《詩經》說水

《詩經》是中國第一部詩歌總集。除了文學、政治、道德意義上的作用外，《詩經》中有大量篇幅描述"水"的部分。《詩經》中有大量關於渭河地區水鄉地貌的描寫。如開篇第一首《關雎》："關關雎鳩，在河之洲。"《毛傳》對"洲"的解釋："水中可居者曰洲。"《詩經》中所涉及的水文就有江、淮、河、漢、沱、汝、淇、涇、渭、溱、洧、汾、汶、漆等20餘條河流。

從《詩經》各篇章中，我們可以瞭解到先秦時期許多河流水量豐沛，河水清澈，水質狀況良好。如《小雅四月》："滔滔江漢，南國之紀。"《毛傳》："滔滔，大水貌。"《小雅鼓鐘》："鼓鐘將將，淮水湯湯。"《魏風伐檀》："河水清且漣猗。"一唱三疊，水清如許！《鄭風溱洧》："溱與洧，瀏其清矣。"《小雅黍苗》："原隰既平，泉流既清。"《毛傳》："土治曰平，水治曰清。"

《詩經》中直接或者間接提到水的篇目約有 40 餘篇，如《周南·關雎》"關關雎鳩，在河之洲，窈窕淑女，君子好求。"《衛風·碩人》中："……河水洋洋，北流活活……。"《衛風·河廣》中："誰謂河廣，一葦杭之……"《魏風·伐檀》更是集"水"之大成："坎坎伐檀兮，置之河之幹兮，河水清且漣猗……坎坎伐輻兮，置之河之側兮，河水清且直猗……坎坎伐輪兮，河水清且淪猗……"。水作為《詩經》中的一個意象，可謂是俯拾即是，信手可得，在《詩經》中，很多詩都與"水"有著直接或間接的聯繫。

《尚書》說水

《尚書》是我國現存最早的記言體史書，是關於上古時代的政事史料彙編。《尚書》也是中國漢民族第一部古典散文集和最早的歷史文獻，《尚書》記錄歷史典籍的同時，向來被文學史家稱為中國最早的散文總集，是和《詩經》並列的一個文體類別。但這些散文，用今天的標準來看，絕大部分應屬於當時官府處理國家大事的公務文書，準確地講，它應是一部體例比較完備的公文總集。

《尚書·洪范》一書中指出"水、火、木、金、土"是世界的本原。"五行，一曰水，二曰火，三曰木，四曰金，五曰土。水曰潤下，火曰炎上，木曰曲直，金曰從革，土爰稼穡。"（《尚書·洪范》）木，具有生髮，條達的特性。火，具有炎熱，向上的特性。土，具有長養、化育的特性。金，具有清靜、收殺的特性。水，具有寒冷、向下的特性。人類很早就開始對水產生了認識，東西方古代樸素的物質觀中都把水視為一種基本的組成元素，水是中國古代五行之一；西方古代的四元素說中也有水。

事物與事物之間存在著一種聯繫，這種聯繫又促進著事物的發展變化。五行之間存在著相生相剋的規律。相生，含有互相滋生，促進助長的意思。相剋，含有互相制約、剋制和抑制的意思。五行相生：木生火，火生土，土生金，金生水，水生木。五行相剋：木剋土，土剋水，水剋火，火剋金，金剋木。相生相剋，像陰陽一樣，是事物不可分割的兩個方面。沒有生，就沒有事物的發生和成長；沒有剋，就不能維持事物的發展和變化中的平衡與協調。沒有相生就沒有相剋，沒有相剋也就沒有相生，這種生中有剋，剋中有生，相反相成，互相為用的關係推動和維持事物的正常生長、發展和變化。

《周禮》《儀禮》《禮記》說水

《周禮》是儒家經典之一，儒家思想發展到戰國後期，融合了道、法、陰陽等家思想，與春秋孔子時思想發生極大變化。《周禮》所涉及之內容極為豐富。大至天下九州，天文曆象；小至溝洫道路，草木蟲魚。凡邦國建制，政法文教，禮樂兵刑，賦稅度支，膳食衣飾，寢廟車馬，農商醫蔔，工藝製作，各種名物、典章、制度，無所不包。堪稱為上古文化史之寶庫。

《周禮》一書與《儀禮》、《禮記》並列，統稱為"三禮"，而且《周禮》還被推為"三禮"之首；它在儒家經典中的地位舉足輕重。《周禮》一書，是自黃帝、顓頊以來的典制，"斟酌損益，因襲積累，以集于文武，其經世大法，鹹粹於是"（《周禮正義序》），是五帝至堯、舜、禹、湯、文、武、周公的經世大法的集粹。所以，《周禮》是中國最早和最完整的官制記錄，也是世界古代一部最完整的官制記錄。

在儒家的傳統理念中，陰、陽是最基本的一對哲學範疇，天下萬物，非陰即陽。《周禮》作者將這一本屬於思想領域的概念，充分運用到了政治機制的層面。《周禮》中的陰陽，幾乎無處不在。《天官‧內小臣》說政令有陽令、陰令；《天官‧內宰》說禮儀有陽禮、陰禮；《地官‧牧人》說祭祀有陽祀、陰祀等等。陰、陽二氣相互摩蕩，產生金、木、水、火、土五行。世間萬事萬物，都得納入以五行作為框架的體系，如東南西北中等五方，宮商角徵羽等五聲，青赤白黑黃等五色，酸苦辛咸甘等五味等等。

《周禮》卷六冬官考工中也記載有："水有時以凝，有時以澤，此天時也"，指出水的旱與澇是隨同氣候的變化而轉變的。《禮記‧月令》裡也記載有"季春之月，令司空日：時而將降，下水將騰，循行國邑，周視原野，修利堤防，道達溝讀……"。《禮記》說："天降時雨，山川出雲。"又認為山川是天地通氣的"孔竅"："天秉陽，垂日星，地秉陰，竅於山川，播五行於四時。"這就是說，山脈具有含藏陰陽之氣的性能，氣揮發出來，即可出雲致雨。

《左傳》《公羊傳》《谷梁傳》說水

《左傳》又稱《春秋左氏傳》或《左氏春秋》，體例是編年記事體，內容大部分是傳注史事，敘述，春秋經文中重要史事的來龍去脈。《左傳》主要記錄了周王室的衰微，諸侯爭霸的歷史。對各類禮儀規範、典章制度、社會風俗、民族關係、道德觀念、天文地理、曆法時令、古代文獻、神話傳說、歌謠言語也都有相關記述和評論。《左傳》與《公羊傳》，《谷梁傳》合秋"春秋三傳"。

源，水源；本，樹根。無源之水，無本之木，比喻沒有基礎的事物。"我在伯父，猶衣服之有冠冕，木水之有本原。"（《左傳‧昭公九年》）。從善如流（《左傳‧成公八年》），也作"從諫如流"。形容聽從正確的意見，就像流水向下那樣迅速自然。"貢之不入，寡君之罪也，敢不共給？昭王之不復，君其問諸水濱。"（《左傳‧僖公四年》）。如果楚國沒有朝貢，那是楚國的罪責，楚國敢不朝貢嗎？昭王南巡溺于漢水，你們還是去問漢水之濱吧。

"曷為以水地？河曲疏矣，河千里而一曲也。"（《公羊傳·文公十二年》）憑藉什麼才能成為水地，河曲疏通了，那麼河一個拐彎就有一千里了。《谷梁傳》曰："高下有水，災曰大水"；《左傳》注："凡平原出水，為大水"。即是說大水是災，或稱為洪災或水災，其標準是"高下有水"或"平原出水"。因為人們多居住在平地或下處，是接水處。

高處出水，不一定是水災，但平地出水或高下同時出水，則無疑是水災了。凡事都有兩面性，古人很早就認識到了這一點，並且一直注意並提倡在相反的兩個方面之間尋求平衡。按照傳統的觀點，失去平衡，偏重一方面，忽視另一方面，事情就會出毛病。陰陽調和，剛柔相濟，事情就會順利發展，興旺發達。執政理當以"寬以濟猛，猛以濟寬"，寬猛相濟的手段治理國家。

《論語》說水

《論語》是中國春秋時期的一部語錄體散文集，主要記錄孔子及其弟子的言行。它較為集中地反映了孔子的思想。由孔子弟子及再傳弟子編纂而成。全書共 20 篇、492 章，首創"語錄體"。南宋時，朱熹將它與《孟子》《大學》《中庸》合稱為"四書"。

水是生命之源，世間萬物都離不開水。而孔子對水的認識，並不是一般意義上的飲用、灌溉、舟楫之水，而是通過對水的觀察、體會和思考，賦予了水的象徵意義和哲學情結。《論語·子罕》中"子在川上曰：逝者如斯夫，不舍晝夜。"從表面上看，這是孔子在河邊對奔騰不息的流水發出的感歎，但孔子感歎的不僅僅是一去不復返的流水，更有稍縱即逝的光陰和瞬息萬變的事物。水之智，教給人們變通與靈活；水之逝，更教會人們珍惜與在意。

《論語·雍也》中，"智者樂水，仁者樂山；智者動，仁者靜；智者樂，仁者壽。"孔子寄情山水最富哲理的話語，智慧的人喜歡水，仁愛的人喜歡山；智者是動態的，仁者是靜態的；智者是快樂的，仁者是長壽的。山、水是世間最普通的自然物，也是最有靈性的東西。山是安定、偉大、豐富的，水是流動、平等、多情的。

孔子觀于東流之水，子貢問於孔子曰："君子之所以見大水必觀焉者，是何？"孔子曰："夫水大，遍與諸生而無為也，似德；其流也埤下，裾拘必循其理，似義；其洸洸乎不淈盡，似道；若有決行之，其應佚若聲響，其赴百仞之谷不懼，似勇；主量必平，似法；盈不求概，似正；淖約微達，似察；以出以入，以就鮮絜，似善化；其萬折也必東，似志。是故君子見大水必觀焉。"（《荀子》）

孔子觀看磅礡東流的一川江水時，學生子貢問他：為什麼君子見了大水就一定要觀看呢？孔子細細分析說：水能遍生萬物而又看似無為，這是德；水的高低流向，在按照規律道理行路，這是義；水那浩浩蕩蕩永不停息的前進法則，這是道；水遇見決口更加聲勢浩大，遇見百仞深谷也無所畏懼，這是勇；水能丈量平面，這是公平的法。

水能注滿容器而不需他物刮平，這是公理的正；水的涓涓細流，能通達所有細微之處，這是纖毫畢現的明察秋毫；水對事物耐心的潤澤滌蕩、對塵埃反復的清潔沖刷，這是春風化雨的教化功能；水雖道路險阻、起伏跌宕但義無反顧地東流，這是目標堅定的志向明確。所以，優秀的人，見到大水磅礡、氣勢非凡，必定駐足觀望。

《爾雅》說水

《爾雅》是辭書之祖。收集了比較豐富的古代漢語詞彙。它不僅是辭書之祖，還是中國古代的典籍——經，《十三經》的一種，是漢族傳統文化的核心組成部分。

《爾雅·釋水》"水中可居者曰洲，小洲曰陼，小陼曰沚，小沚曰坻，人所為為潏。"，"天子造舟，諸侯維舟，大夫方舟，士特舟，庶人乘泭。""逆流而上曰溯洄，順流而下曰溯遊。正絕流曰亂。""江、河、淮、濟為四瀆。四瀆者，發源注海者也。"

《孝經》說水

《孝經》中國古代漢族政治倫理著作。儒家十三經之一。傳說是孔子本人所作。《孝經》，以孝為中心，比較集中地闡述了儒家的倫理思想。它肯定"孝"是上天所定的規範，"夫孝，天之經也，地之義也，人之行也。"指出孝是諸多品德之本，認為"人之行，莫大于孝"，國君可以用"孝"治理國家，臣民能夠用"孝"立身理家。《孝經》首次將"孝"與"忠"聯繫起來，認為"忠"是"孝"的發展和擴大，並把"孝"的社會作用推而廣之，認為"孝悌之至"就能夠"通於神明，光于四海，無所不通"。

"千古興亡多少事，悠悠，不盡長江滾滾流。"數千年封建社會的歷史雖然過去，愛人之心與為人之子的孝敬當是萬世不變的法則。孝，"始於事親，中於事君，終於立身"（《孝經·開宗明義》），"孝道"給今人的啟示是對一切懷有敬畏之心。敬事父母，勤勉工作，立身成仁，至少是我們每個人都可以做到的。茲事體大，然細大不捐，養生送死為孝，端茶送水亦為孝。如果把家庭中的"小事"做好，那麼"大事"自然水到渠成。"齊家"是為了更好地"治國"。

《孝經》講，"在上不驕，高而不危；制節謹度，滿而不溢。高而不危，所以長守貴也；滿而不溢，所以長守富也。富貴不離其身，然後能保其社稷，而和其民人。蓋諸侯之孝也。"雖然身居高官，但能毫無驕傲之心，那麼儘管高高在上，也不會遭到傾覆的危險；如果凡事儉省節約，慎守法度，府庫經費充裕，也不會奢侈浪費。高高在上而沒有傾覆的危險，這樣就能長久地守住尊貴的地位；資財充裕而不奢侈浪費，這樣就能長久地守住財富。能夠緊緊地把握住富與貴，然後才能保住自己的國家，使自己的人民和睦相處。這就是諸侯應盡的孝道。

《詩經》說："戰戰兢兢，如臨深淵，如履薄冰。"凡事必須小心謹慎，戒慎恐懼，就好像走在深潭的旁邊，又好像踏在薄冰的上面。

《孟子》說水

《孟子》"四書"之一。戰國中期孟子及其弟子萬章、公孫醜等著。為孟子、孟子弟子、再傳弟子的記錄。"民為重，社稷次之，君為輕"，是兩千多年前的儒家亞聖孟子提出來的，它的中心重點就是，普天之下人民最為重要，江山社稷尚在其次，而以君王為核心的統治集團的利益更是敬陪末座。

歷代聰明的君王們便有悟出了一些哲理，"水能載舟亦能覆舟"，"民以食為天"，"得民心者得天下，失民心者失天下"。一切統治執政者都必須以老百姓的利益為重，只有老百姓滿意了，江山社稷才會穩定，君王統治集團的利益才能鞏固。這就是古聖先賢的民本思想，它不僅彰顯了古中國賢哲們直面社會真理的勇氣，也進一步告訴了世人中國古文化的厚重和大氣。

"孔子登東山而小魯，登泰山而小天下，故觀於海者難為水，游于聖人之門者難為言。觀水有術，必觀其瀾。……流水之為物者，不盈科不行；君子之志于道也，不成章不達。"（《孟子·盡心上》）登絕頂而一覽眾山小，經滄海則難為水，滄海浩大森森無涯，小江小河小池之水不可與之相提並論。孟子稱讚水具有"不盈科不行"的品性，這種腳踏實地、扎扎實實、循序漸進的風格，正是立志行道的君子所效法的優良德行。

白圭曰："丹之治水也愈于禹。"孟子曰："子過矣。禹之治水，水之道也，是故禹以四海為壑。今吾子以鄰國為壑。水逆付謂之澤水—降水者，洪水也，仁人之所惡也。吾子過矣。"

白圭說："我治理水比大禹還強。"孟子說："你錯了。大禹治理水患，是順著水的本性而疏導，所以使水流注于四海。如今你卻使水流到鄰近的國家去。水逆流而行叫做洚（排泄）水－洚水就是洪水，是仁慈的人厭惡的。你錯了。"

白圭治水"以鄰國為壑"的做法，就是一種損人利己，嫁禍於人的行為，不值得鼓勵和提倡。你知道"以鄰為壑"，人家也同樣知道"以鄰為壑"，結果是人人都成了"鄰"，也成了"壑"，到時候，也就沒有一處乾淨，沒有一處不受災害了。由此看來，"以鄰為壑"的最終結果是害人害己。所以，還是收起這種人人所厭惡的"以鄰為壑"手段，"以鄰為友"，大家和睦相處，互相幫助的為好。

《道德經》說水

《道德經》又稱《老子》，是一部中國古代先秦百家諸子所共仰巨作，是道家哲學思想的重要來源。道德經分上下兩篇，原文上篇《德經》、下篇《道經》，不分章，後改為《道經》37章在前，第38章之後為《德經》，並分為81章。是中國歷史上首部完整的哲學著作。

"上善若水。水善利萬物而不爭，處眾人之所惡，故幾於道。居，善地；心，善淵；與，善仁；言，善信；正，善治；事，善能；動，善時。夫唯不爭，故無尤。"最善的人好像水一樣。水善於滋潤萬物而不與萬物相爭，停留在眾人都不喜歡的地方，所以最接近於"道"。

最善的人，居處最善於選擇地方，心胸善於保持沉靜而深不可測，待人善於真誠、友愛和無私，說話善於恪守信用，為政善於精簡處理，能把國家治理好，處事能夠善於發揮所長，行動善於把握時機。正因為不與他人相爭高低上下，所以就不會有過失，不會有仇家敵手。

老子說："上善若水，水善利萬物而不爭，此乃謙下之德也；故江海所以能為百谷王者，以其善下之，則能為百谷王。天下莫柔弱于水，而攻堅強者莫之能勝，此乃柔德；故柔之勝剛，弱之勝強堅。因其無有，故能入於無之間，由此可知不言之教、無為之益也。"

上善的人，就應該像水一樣。水造福萬物，滋養萬物，卻不與萬物爭高下，這才是最為謙虛的美德。江海之所以能夠成為一切河流的歸宿，是因為他善於處在下游的位置上，所以成為百谷王。世界上最柔的東西莫過於水，然而它卻能穿透最為堅硬的東西，沒有什麼能超過它，例如滴水穿石，這就是"柔德"所在。所以說弱能勝強，柔可克剛。不見其形的東西，可以進入到沒有縫隙的東西中去，由此我們知道了"不言"的教導，"無為"的好處。

佛教緒經說水

《法華經》："如人渴須水，穿鑿于高原，猶見乾燥土，知去水尚遠，漸見濕土泥，決定知近水。"好像有人在饑渴的時候想要喝水。饑，就是肚子餓；渴，就是想要喝水，非常的乾渴。那麼在這乾渴的期間，想要喝水；這譬喻我們人在凡夫地，想要求佛果；佛果，就是"水"。我們在凡夫的這種境界上，是非常的乾燥，所以就渴，想要喝這個法水、要得成佛果。穿鑿于高原：就在那高的地方，想穿鑿一個井。這穿鑿井，就是修道；你修行，就像開井一樣。

《觀經》曰："一一池水，七寶所成。其摩尼水，流注華間。"這個華間，池裡面是蓮花，池的岸邊是寶樹，寶樹需要德水滋養，這個水自然流注樹間，尋樹上下。這水真妙，我們這邊水可以只往下流，不會往上，極樂世界的水可以往上流。可見極樂莊嚴微妙，超逾一切，一切世界裡沒有的，到極樂世界你全看到。

《淨土大經》曰：極樂世界這個池很多，小池十由旬、二十由旬，大池百千由旬，就像大海一樣。在我們這個世界，小池像湖泊，大池像大海。無論是大池、小池，湛然香潔，水都是具有八種功德。一者澄淨。二者清冷。三者甘美。四者輕軟。五者潤澤。六者安和。七者飲時除饑渴等無量過患。八者飲已定能長養諸根四大，增益種種殊勝善根。

《孫子兵法》說水

《孫子兵法》又稱《孫武兵法》，是中國現存最早的兵書，也是世界上最早的軍事著作，被譽為"兵學聖典"。處處表現了道家與兵家的哲學。共有六千字左右，一共十三篇。《孫子兵法》是中國古代漢族軍事文化遺產中的璀璨瑰寶，漢族優秀傳統文化的重要組成部分，其內容博大精深，思想精邃富贍，邏輯縝密嚴謹，是古代漢族軍事思想精華的集中體現。

《孫子兵法》曰："夫兵形象水，水之形，避高而趨下，兵之形，避實而擊虛。水因地而制流，兵因敵而制勝。故兵無常勢，水無常形。能因敵變化而取勝者，謂之神。故五行無常勝，四時無常位，日有短長，月有死生。"

兵的性態就像水一樣，水流動時是避開高處流向低處，用兵取勝的關鍵是避開設防嚴密實力強大的敵人而攻擊其薄弱環節；水根據地勢來決定流向，軍隊根據敵情來採取制勝的方略。所以用兵作戰沒有一成不變的態勢，正如流水沒有固定的形狀和去向。能夠根據敵情的變化而取勝的，就叫做用兵如神。金、木、水、火、土這五行相生相剋，沒有哪一個常勝；四季相繼相代，沒有哪一個固定不移，白天的時間有長有短，月亮有圓也有缺。萬物皆處於流變狀態。

《史記》說水

《史記》，是由漢代的司馬遷編寫的中國歷史上第一部紀傳體通史，記載了從黃帝到漢武帝太初年間三千多年的歷史。《史記》規模巨大，體系完備，全書有本紀十二篇，表十篇，書八篇，世家三十篇，列傳七十篇，共一百三十篇，約五十二萬六千五百字。

《史記》曰："禹抑洪水十三年，過家不入門。陸行載車，水行載舟，泥行橇，山行即橋。以別九州，隨山浚川，任土作貢。通九道，陂九澤，度九山。然河菑衍溢，害中國也尤甚。唯是為務，故道河自積石歷龍門，南到華陰，東下砥柱，及孟津、雒汭，至於大邳。於是禹以為河所從來者高，水湍悍，難以行平地，數為敗，乃廝二渠以引其河。北載之高地[13]，過降水，至於大陸，播為九河，同為逆河，入於勃海。九川既疏，九澤既灑，諸夏艾安，功施於三代。"

《史記》記載：禹治理洪水經歷了十三年，其間路過家門口也不回家看望親人。行陸路時乘車，水路乘船，泥路乘橇，山路坐轎，走遍了所有地方。從而劃分了九州邊界，隨山勢地形，疏浚了淤積的大河川，根據土地物產確定了賦稅等級。使九州道路通暢，築起了九州的澤岸，度量了九州山勢。然而還有黃河氾濫成災，給中國造成很大危害。於是集中力量治理黃河，引導河水自積石山經過龍門，南行到華陰縣，東下經砥柱山和孟津、雒汭，到達大邳山。

禹以為大邳以上黃河流經的地區地勢高，水流湍急，難以在大邳以東的平地經過，否則會時常敗堤破岸，造成水災，於是將黃河分流成二條河以減小水勢，並引水北行，從地勢較高的冀州地區流過，經降水，到大陸澤，以下開九條大河，共同迎受黃河之水，流入勃海。九州河川都已疏通，九州大澤都築了障水堤岸，華夏諸國得到治理而安定，其功績使夏、商、周三代受益不絕。

《史記‧管晏列傳》曰："君子之交淡若水，小人之交甘若醴；君子淡以親，小人甘以絕。"

正人君子之間的交往不帶任務功利色彩，淡的像水一樣；小人之間的交往，都是有所求、有所圖的，為達到私利送給的對方的好處像蜜糖一樣粘稠。君子決不利用職務權勢的優勢為親人謀利益，對待親戚朋友淡的像水；小人則正好相反。

《資治通鑒》說水

　　《資治通鑒》，由北宋司馬光主編的一部多卷本編年體史書，共 294 卷，歷時 19 年完成。在這部書裡，編者總結出許多經驗教訓，供統治者借鑒，宋神宗認為此書"鑒於往事，有資於治道"，即以歷史的得失作為鑒誡來加強統治警示後人，所以定名為《資治通鑒》。

　　《資治通鑒》曰：閏月，辛亥，上（唐太宗）謂侍臣曰："朕自立太子，遇物則悔之，見其飯，則曰：汝知稼穡之艱難，則常有斯飯矣。見其乘馬，則曰：汝知其勞逸，不竭其力，則常得乘之矣。見其乘舟，則曰：水所以載舟，亦可以覆舟，民猶如水也，君猶舟也。見其息於木下，則曰：木以繩則正，後從諫則聖。"

　　閏六月，辛亥（初四），太宗對身邊的大臣說："朕自從立李志為太子，遇見任何事情都親自加以教誨，看見他用飯，就說你知道農民耕種的艱難就能經常吃上這些飯。看見他騎馬，就說你知道馬要勞逸結合，不可耗盡馬的力量，就能常常騎著它。看見他坐船，就說水能夠載船，也能夠翻船，人民就像這水，君主便如同這船。見到他在樹下休息，就說木頭經過墨線處理才能正直，君主能採納意見才為聖君。"

　　臣光曰："夫信者，人君之大寶也。國保於民，民保於信；非信無以使民，非民無以守國。是故古之王者不欺四海，霸者不欺四鄰，善為國者不欺其民，善為家者不欺其親。不善者反之，欺其鄰國，欺其百姓，甚者欺其兄弟，欺其父子。上不信下，下不信上，上下離心，以至於敗。所利不能藥其所傷，所獲不能補其所亡，豈不哀哉！"

　　臣司馬光曰："信譽，是君主至高無上的法寶。國家靠人民來保衛，人民靠信譽來保護；不講信譽無法使人民服從，沒有人民便無法維持國家。所以古代成就王道者不欺騙天下，建立霸業者不欺騙四方鄰國，善於治國者不欺騙人民，善於治家者不欺騙親人。只有蠢人才反其道而行之，欺騙鄰國，欺騙百姓，甚至欺騙兄弟、父子。上不信下，下不信上，上下離心，以至一敗塗地。靠欺騙所佔的一點兒便宜救不了致命之傷，所得到的遠遠少於失去的，這豈不令人痛心！"

中醫藏醫說水

　　中醫，一般指以中國傳統醫學為主的醫學，所以也稱漢醫。是研究人體生理、病理以及疾病的診斷和防治等的一門學科。中醫學以陰陽五行作為理論基礎，將人體看成是氣、形、神的統一體，通過望、聞、問、切，四診合參的方法，探求病因、病性、病位、分析病機及人體內五臟六腑、經絡關節、氣血津液的變化、判斷邪正消長，進而得出病名，歸納出證型，以辨證論治原則，制定"汗、吐、下、和、溫、清、補、消"等治法，使用中藥、針灸、推拿、按摩、拔罐、氣功、食療等多種治療手段，使人體達到陰陽調和而康復。

藏醫藥是祖國醫學寶庫的重要組成部分。藏醫理論認為，人體記憶體在著"隆"（氣）、"赤巴"（火）、"培根"（土和水）三大因素；飲食精微、肉、血、脂肪、骨、骨髓、精七種物質基礎；大便、小便、汗液三種排泄物。三大因素支配七種物質基礎和三種排泄物的運行變化。

中國傳統五行學說即是用木、火、土、金、水五個哲學範疇來概括客觀世界中的不同事物屬性，並用五行相生相剋的動態模式來說明事物間的相互聯繫和轉化規律。五行學說中以五臟配五行即：肝與木、心與火、脾與土、金與肺、水與腎。五臟與五行相生相剋應保持相對平衡和穩定，和諧相處。"木火土金水"這五個符號分別代表"肝心脾肺腎"所統領的五大系統。中醫關注研究人體整體的各個系統之間的關係，並且通過中藥，按摩，針灸，甚至心理作用去調節各個系統之間的平衡，以此保持身體健康。

腎主水，"腎為水髒"，它在調節體內水液平衡方面起極為重要的作用。中醫認為"水"對於維護人體健康有非常重要的作用。飲食物（包括飲用的水）中的"水"進入人體後經脾（脾主運化）、肺（肺主通調水道）、腎（腎主水）、膀胱（氣化）等臟腑的代謝，生成營養物質（化為水穀精微），潤滑臟器或營養全身，其代謝的廢物通過尿液、汗液等方式排出體外。

水穀精微在體內通過各種不同的途徑可以化為"津"、"液"、"血"、"精"等一系列屬於"陰類"的物質。當體內缺水時，從中醫的證候來說，表現為陰虛證，可以是腎陰虛、也可以肺陰虛、胃陰虛、肝陰虛、心陰虛，偶爾還有脾陰虛等。中醫對健康的總體認識是陰陽平衡，當陰陽不平衡時就會導致疾病。體內缺水，出現陰虛證時就會有陰虛內熱的症狀，如潮熱、盜汗、手足心熱、目乾澀、口乾、便乾、心悸、煩躁、腰膝酸軟等。

《黃帝內經》說水

《黃帝內經》是中國最早的醫學典籍，傳統醫學四大經典著作之一，其餘三者為《難經》、《傷寒雜病論》、《神農本草經》。《黃帝內經》在理論上建立了中醫學上的"陰陽五行學說"、"藏象學說"、"病因學說"、"養生學說"、"藥物治療學說"、"經絡治療學說"等學說。從整體觀上來論述醫學，呈現了自然、生物、心理、社會"整體醫學模式"，是中國影響最大的一部醫學著作，被稱為醫之始祖。

《黃帝內經靈樞‧經水》篇運用古代版圖上清、渭、海、湖、汝、澠、淮、漯、江、河、濟、漳十二條河流的大小、深淺、廣狹、長短來比喻人體中十二經脈各自之不同的氣血運行狀況。水，就是大地的血氣；其相對于大地的意義，就像經脈之中流通的氣血相對于人體的意義一樣。十二水，在此主要是以其川流不息的樣子，來比喻經脈受血而周流於人體的狀態，因此稱為"經水"。

"凡此五臟六腑十二經水者，外有源泉而內有所稟，此皆內外相貫，如環無端，人經亦然。故天為陽，地為陰，腰以上為天，腰以下為地。故海以北者為陰，湖以北者為陰中之陰，漳以南者為陽引，河以北至漳者為陽中之陰，漯以南至江者為陽中之太陽，此一隅之陰陽也，所以人與天地相參也。"

凡是五臟六腑相通的十二經脈，其氣血的流行，就像自然界十二條河流之水的流動一樣，既有顯現于外的源泉，又有隱伏在內的歸巢；自然界的河流是內外相互貫通而像環一樣沒有盡頭的，人體經脈之氣血也和它一樣，是內外貫通、迴圈不息的。在上的天，屬陽；在下的地，屬陰。相應的，人體腰部以上的部位，就應於天而屬陽；人體腰部以下的部位，就應於地而屬陰。

根據古法天南地北的陰陽位置，在海水以北的就稱為陰，在湖水以北的就稱為陰中之陰，在漳水以南的就稱為陽，在河水以北到漳水所在之處的就稱為陽中之陰，在漯水以南至江水所在之處的就稱為陽中之太陽。而人體之十二經脈的分佈循行及其相互之間的關係，也與之相對應。以上所述，只反映了自然界部分河流之流行分佈與人體部分經脈循行分佈的陰陽對應關係，但它足以說明人體和自然界是相互對應的。

《毛澤東選集》說水

毛澤東，是中國共產黨、中國人民解放軍和中華人民共和國的主要締造者和領導人，毛澤東思想是一個完整的、內容極其豐富的科學體系。毛澤東是繼承傳頌中國傳統"水"哲學思想的典範，是弘揚發展中國傳統"水"文化的集大成者。縱覽中國歷史上下5000多年，毛澤東留給後人有關"水"的理論文獻最多，最豐富。

同時，他又親身投入實踐"水"，研究掌握的治水實際經驗最多。毛澤東是中國歷史上理解感悟"水"品"水"德的高人賢者，是理論闡述和具體實踐"水"文化當之無愧的第一人，是善學活用"水"哲學思想開天闢地的先行者。

在毛澤東心目中，人民大眾是社會之基礎、國家之基本、江山社稷之基石。毛澤東是中國歷史上第一個執政者，真正把人民群眾的利益放在國家所有事項的第一位，放在最重要至高無上的地位。毛澤東，真正、真誠地賦予人民大眾直接或間接管理國家事務的基本權利。中國人民永遠不會忘記，一九四九年十月一日天安門廣場久久回蕩的"人民萬歲"的聲音。這聲音，已經穿越歷史，穿越時空，沁入中國人民的骨髓。

人民，只有人民，才是創造世界歷史的動力。毛澤東：《論聯合政府》（1945年4月24日），《毛澤東選集》第3卷，人民出版社1991年版，第1031頁

全心全意地為人民服務，一刻也不脫離群眾；一切從人民的利益出發，而不是從個人或小集團的利益出發；向人民負責和向党的領導機關負責的一致性；這些就是我們的出發點。毛澤東：《論聯合政府》（1945年4月24日），《毛澤東選集》第3卷，人民出版社1991年版，第1094—1095頁

黨群關係好比魚水關係。如果黨群關係搞不好，社會主義制度就不可能建成；社會主義制度建成了，也不可能鞏固。毛澤東：《一九五七年夏季的形勢》（1957年7月），《建國以來毛澤東文稿》第6冊，中央文獻出版社1992年版，第547頁

風水論說水

風水術是中國漢民族歷史悠久的一門玄術，學術性的說法叫做堪輿。相傳風水的創始人是九天玄女，完善的風水學問起源于戰國時代。風水的核心思想是人與大自然的和諧。晉代的郭璞在其名著《葬書》中有云："葬者，乘生氣也，氣乘風則散，界水則止，古人聚之使不散，行之使有止，故謂之風水，風水之法，得水為上，藏風次之。"。

古代漢族人民常說："宅以形勢為身體，以泉水為血脈，以土地為皮肉，以草木為毛髮，以舍屋為衣服，以門戶為冠帶。若是如斯，是事儼雅，乃為上吉。"這是把住宅人性化，說明格局搭配得當，對住宅與人都是很重要的。

風水實踐中最主要的是水法，所謂水法就是調整建築物朝向與流水之間的關係，使之處在流水的最佳位置，現代風水中的"水"則泛指一切流動的氣場，如道路，水管等。觀水是風水中一個極重要的方面，水隨山而行，山界水而止，足見山水不可分離，山水影響人居。一個好的風水，必須有滿足山環、水抱、朝向有據、水質甘甜、土地紅黃細膩有光澤、得地還應得時得向的說法。

天文學、地理學和人體科學是中國風水學的三大科學支柱。天、地、人合一是中國風水學的最高原則。中國古代科學家仰觀天文，俯察地理，近取諸身，遠取諸物，經上下五千

年的實踐、研究、歸納和感悟，形成了著稱於世的東方科學—中國風水學。風水理論，實際上就是地球物理學、水文地質學、宇宙星體學、氣象學、環境景觀學、建築學、生態學以及人體生命資訊學等多種學科綜合一體的一門自然科學。風水學既是一門學問，更是一種文化，重申強調人與自然和諧相處的文化。

文人墨客說水

文人墨客泛指文人、文士，類同"文人墨士"。自古以來，文人墨客就與山水結下了不解之緣。也許，是文人墨客與世俗的不屑，隔離，使他們樂於山，醉于水。也許，是山水的魅力，成為文人墨客寄情載道的載體。山水與文人墨客最相愛，最相知，最相融，仿佛是一對情侶。文人墨客與山水，一旦水乳交融，便分不清誰是山，誰是人，誰是水，誰是文墨了。

清朝作家張潮的《幽夢影》中說："有地上之山水，有畫上之山水，有夢中之山水，有胸中之山水。"明代文人袁宏道曾說，"意未嘗一刻不在山水"。的確，在古代文人墨客的精神世界裡，山水可說是他們的宗教。在山水中既可領略"野曠沙岸淨，天高秋月明"的自然美，又能體味"大江東去，亂石穿空，驚濤拍岸，卷起千堆雪"的崇高美，也能感受到"飛流直下三千尺，疑是銀河落九天"的浪漫情懷。

朱自清《荷塘月色》：葉子底下是脈脈的流水，遮住了，不能見一些顏色；而葉子卻更見風致了。月光如流水一般，靜靜地瀉在這一片葉子和花上。薄薄的青霧浮起在荷塘裡。葉子和花仿佛在牛乳中洗過一樣；又像籠罩著輕紗的夢。雖然是滿月，天上卻有一層淡淡的雲，所以不能朗照；但我以為這恰是到了好處，酣眠固不可少，小睡也別有風味的。

月光是隔了樹照過來的，高處叢生的灌木，落下參差的斑駁的黑影，峭楞楞如鬼一般；彎彎的楊柳的稀疏的倩影，卻又像是畫在荷葉上。塘中的月色並不均勻；但光與影有著和諧的旋律，如梵婀玲上奏著的名曲。荷塘的四面，遠遠近近，高高低低都是樹，而楊柳最多。

成語故事說水

"如魚得水"

東漢時期，劉備雖然從漢獻帝劉協那兒弄到一個名正言順的皇叔地位，但是因為並未分得固定的封地，因此投靠了同族劉表，劉表給他送了個新野地區，並經過司馬徽等引薦，劉備三顧茅廬最終將諸葛亮請出，赤壁之戰完勝曹操，為此劉備非常驕傲道若可以得到孔明他就如魚得水了。

"一衣帶水"

南北朝的時候，北方的北周和南方的陳國以長江為界。北周的宰相楊堅，廢了周靜帝，自己當皇帝，建立了隋朝。他決心要滅掉陳國，曾說：我是全國老百姓的父母，難道能因為有一條像衣帶那樣窄的長江隔著，就看著南方百姓受苦而不拯救他們嗎？後來人們就用一衣帶水來比喻只隔了一條狹窄水域的，靠得非常近的兩地。

"山窮水盡"

西元 1167 年，南宋大詩人陸游因力主抗金被免職，回到老家山陰鏡湖旁居住。一次他到附近的山西村遊訪，他即興做詩《遊山西村》："莫笑農家臘酒渾，半年留客足雞豚。山窮水複疑無路，柳暗花明又一村。"來抒發自己懷才不遇的心情。山和水都到了盡頭。比喻無路可走陷入絕境。

水，中國文化的基因

關於"水"的文字記載，在中國的各種歷史書籍中多不勝數，比比皆是。為什麼會是這樣？"書中自有千鐘粟，書中自有黃金屋，書中自有顏如玉"（《勵學篇》），這其中必藏有中國文化這樣或那樣的玄妙之處。什麼是中國人的秘密？這個秘密，使這個星球上最古老的文明，在長達幾千年的漫長時光裡，生生不息綿綿不絕。

世世代代的炎黃子孫，在神州大地上走西口、闖關東、拓墾南荒到處繁衍生息；祖祖輩輩的中國移民走西洋、下南洋、闖東洋，在世界各地落地生根頑強生存，創造著驚人的海外華人奇跡？而且"自紀元前221年以來，幾乎在所有時代，都成為影響半個世界的中心。"（湯因比語）

什麼是中華民族的真正力量？這些力量，幫助這個最最悠遠堅忍的民族，在最嚴酷的自然環境裡求生存圖強，在最嚴苛的生存條件下討生活，在一次次殘酷的自然災害之後重新開荒播種，在一次次血流成河的戰爭之後重新繁衍生息，在一次次十室九空的社會動盪之後再度管弦悠揚，在一次次屍橫遍野的外族入侵之後繼續柳蔭成行，並在經歷了幾十個世紀的腥風血雨之後，在遭受了一百多年的屈辱和痛苦之後，再次挺胸昂頭穩步踏上現代民族復興的偉大征途。

答案，或只有一個簡單的字"水"，以及"水"字背後顯現的哲學智慧。水，生生不息，運動變化，循環往復。"水"的哲學智慧幫助中國人在長達幾千年的漫長道路上，維繫著民族的繁衍、維持著國家的統一、維護著文明的傳承，以及在現代史上再次取得輝煌成就，重新走向復興之路；"水"的哲學智慧使中國人無論是在社會混亂之時，還是在國家衰落之際，總能如籬笆邊那頑強小草，在一次次的浩劫餘燼之後，春風吹又生髮，重喚生機盎然。

水，是區別中華民族和世界其他民族的顯著標識。"中國人摸索出的生活方式已沿襲數千年，若能夠被全世界採納，地球上肯定會比現在有更多的歡樂祥和。若不借鑒一向被我們輕視的東方智慧，我們的文明就沒有指望了。""只要中國人願意，他們可以成為天下最強大的國家。"（羅素《中國問題》）英國歷史學家湯因比也感同身受地說："現在世界各民族中最有充分準備的，是兩千年來培育了獨特思維方式的中華民族"。

水，天地之物，支撐統領整個生態系統的有序迴圈。儘管鬥轉星移，世態變遷，"水"永遠保持著那一份優雅，那一份淡定，和那一份恒久。中國文化深受"水"的品行影響，"水"的高尚品性已深深地植入中國人的血液和骨髓之中。中國人跟隨"水"的指引一路走過5000年，從今往後華夏民族肯定仍將在"水"的恩典感召之下繼續走下去，再走5000年甚至更久遠。水，是中國文化的"根"，是中國文化的"魂"，是中國文化的基因DNA。

第五篇

水，華夏民族圖騰 "龍" 背後的故事

龍，華夏民族的圖騰。龍是中國神話傳說中的神異動物，具有九種動物合而為一，並且具有九不像之形象。《本草綱目爾雅‧翼》云：“龍者鱗蟲之長。王符言其形有九似：頭似牛，角似鹿，眼似蝦，耳似象，項似蛇，腹似蛇，鱗似魚，爪似鳳，掌似虎，是也。其背有八十一鱗，具九九陽數。其聲如戛銅盤。口旁有須髯，頷下有明珠，喉下有逆鱗。頭上有博山，又名尺木，龍無尺木不能升天。呵氣成雲，既能變水，又能變火。”

龍的外在形象是多種動物的融合，歷史上有過多種不同版本的解讀。宋代人郭若虛也提出過“龍有九似”說法，即：角似鹿、頭似駝（馬）、眼似兔（龜）、項似蛇、腹似蜃、鱗似魚、爪似鷹、掌似虎、耳似牛。其實，龍的取材物件遠遠不止這9種，鱷、蜥蜴、豬、馬、熊、鯢、象、狗、羊、蠶、鳥類，以及雲霧、雷電、虹霓、龍捲風、古動物化石等等，都不同程度地參與了龍的融合。

其實，龍作為中國古人對多種動物和天象融合創造的一種神物，實質是祖先對自然力的高度神化和自覺昇華。龍，作為一種圖騰和一般的圖騰不盡相同，它突出反映了中華民族不同於世界其他民族的特殊情懷和品質，背後特別寓意是“和”與“合”的思想。

遠古神話最早的神不是人，而是動物圖騰。原始人很難分清楚人與動物的界限，他們認為某種動物是自己的遠古祖先或保護神，由此形成動物圖騰的概念。圖騰作為氏族部落的標誌，一般是單一的某種動物，氏族部落一旦發生兼併戰爭，勝利者在俘虜對方之後，往往同時會消滅其原有圖騰，新產生的部落氏族擁有的還是單一動物圖騰。

中國的古人體悟到人性與動物禽獸之間有本質上的區別，有意識地揚棄“弱肉強食”的理念和觀念，在“龍”圖騰的形成過程中最大程度地突出、張揚“人性”精神。每一次戰役戰爭定奪以後，新生成的族群出於安定、平穩、發展的考慮，則會采取安撫團結、親近平復那些被吞併氏族和部落人的措施。

在擊敗消滅了某一個氏族或部落之後，並不採用消滅他們精神崇拜和文化寄託圖騰的做法，而是將失敗者的圖騰中的一部分添加在自己的圖騰身上，以示寬宏大度和平定天下。有此可見，龍的形象實質對應一種“和合”團結的氛圍，充分表現中華民族遠古祖先極其寶貴的品質氣度，以及尊重和諧、合作共贏的精神。

中國古代農業耕種，完完全全是靠天地“風調雨順”季節時辰吃飯。“大旱之望雲霓”，“久旱逢甘雨”。風雨來臨之前，往往是先傳來“轟隆轟隆”的沉悶雷鳴之聲。生活中的一切幾乎都指望雨水澆灌的中華先民們，站在播種著全年希望的農田裡，守著萎蔫欲枯的禾苗百無一計之時，當聽到遠方天際邊傳來的隆隆雷電聲，再看到濃雲之中金蛇亂舞，知道甘霖即將到來，這一定是刻骨銘心的時刻。

從此，古代先人對隆隆之聲懷有無限崇敬之意。中國先民們理所當然會抽象出一個有形(閃電)有聲(隆隆)的概念，並用擬聲法將之命名為"隆"，年復一年地盼"隆"望"隆"，期盼"隆隆"之聲送來甘霖。文字出現以後，先民們創造性地採納造就一個大大的"龍"字，專門表示這個概念，並大聲讀作"隆"。

華夏民族有了一個"龍"字，又有了騰雲駕霧，呼風喚雨無所不能"龍"的形象圖騰，並且有意識地借用狂風暴雨前隆隆的雷電轟鳴聲，高聲發音讀"龍"作"隆"聲，我們似乎越來越能夠深切體會華夏民族先人們的智慧情懷，強烈感受到先人們心底裡想要表達的意境，一種與天地大"道"互連相通的意境，一種與自然規律互通相連的意境，一種與"水"相連相生的意境。中國人自古以來就篤信天地，篤信自然規律，篤信"天地人"三位一體，"天人合一"和諧融合。

自然王國中，有天、有地、有萬事萬物。天在上，地在下，萬事萬物位處中間。而在生物鏈萬事萬物之中，人類佔據著頂層位置，是所有生命體物質中最聰慧的一個族類。按照中國人的世界觀理念，天地間有序運行有既定的"道"。所謂道，即是指自然規律。世間萬事萬物的運行，受自然規律的制約，規範和支配。"天地生陰陽"，天地之下萬事萬物的生長和消亡，興盛與衰敗都是受"陰陽"變化之規律所影響。"道"也好陰陽規律也罷，本都是一種無形且相對"懸乎"的東西。

講"懸乎"，是指"道"無影無蹤，看不見，聽不到，摸不著，觸碰不了感覺不到，但卻又真真實實地存在，無處不在，無處不有。那麼具體理解體會自然規律，找到一個具象化的參照物理解"道"，自然就成為十分合理的求知要求和願望。

中國古代哲學聖賢老子說："上善若水，水善利萬物而不爭，處眾人之所惡，故幾於道"。最高境界的善行，就像水的品性一樣，上善至善完美；水善於滋潤萬物而不與萬物相爭名利，停留在眾人都不喜歡的地方。所以，水最接近於"道"，或自然規律。老子早在2000多年以前就告知我們後人如何瞭解掌握"道"。

從此，"道"已不再是一個虛無的概念幻覺。"水"在中國人的現實生活中，成了"道"，或自然規律的化身。老子用"道"形容自然規律，創造性地用有感知的"水"來描述、體認難以感知的"自然規律"。水，無色無味，在方而法方，在圓而法圓，無所滯，它以百態存于自然界，于自然無所違也。

水為至善至柔；水性綿綿密密，微則無聲，巨則洶湧；與人無爭卻又容納萬物。水有滋養萬物的德行，它使萬物得到它的利益，而不與萬物發生矛盾、衝突，和諧和平，包容融合。國人心悅誠服於"道"，誠服于"水"。國人尊敬大自然和大自然規律，遵從"天地"自然法則，拜水為聰慧老師，從學習研究、總結水品行之中得到智慧的靈性和靈感。

雖然，古代的先民們有意識用感知的"水"，體會認知難以感知的"道"或"自然規律"。可是要建立擁有個圖騰，為中國人世代傳承找出一個共同源頭和精神象徵並不是件簡單的事。氏族部落的圖騰本身需要有一定的張揚力、震撼力和號召力，構思創造出一個水樣圖騰似乎有一定難度，不易把握。

華夏民族最終想像創造出"龍"，一種與水相通相連，且反映"和合"精神的多種動物融合體，確定成為炎黃子孫世代傳承的統一圖騰。《說文解字》這樣描述："龍，鱗蟲之長，能幽能明，能細能巨，能短能長，春分而登天，秋分而潛淵。"龍，無所不在，無所不至，無所不能的包容力，即使潛伏也不失其龐大的偉力。

《三國演義》中，羅貫中通過曹操之口，概述了龍的特點："龍，能大能小，能升能隱；大則興雲吐霧，小則隱蔽藏形；升則飛騰於宇宙之間，隱則潛伏于波濤之內。方今春深，龍乘時變"。古代神話傳說中，龍或作為開天闢地的創生神，與盤古齊名；或積極參與了伏羲女媧的婚配，從而繁衍了人類；或幫助黃帝取得了統一戰爭的勝利；或協助夏禹治理洪水，為千秋萬代造福。龍與水相通，龍與水齊名，龍與水並駕齊驅。今天，我們講解龍的故事，實質就是在注釋、講解關乎"水"的故事。

龍的基本神性：喜水、好飛、通天、善變、征瑞、兆禍、示威、威嚴。龍以神的姿態俯視眾生，傳說中總是居於江河湖海之中。龍，喜善變化興雲布雨，是行善利益萬物的神奇動物。古代傳說中，龍能藏能顯能大能小，能飛能行能潛遊，能上九天攬月，能下五洋捉鱉，翻手為雲覆手為雨，呼風喚雨無所不能，造福萬事萬物。

中國文化中，龍象徵著吉祥、權威、高貴和繁榮，中華民族就是"龍的傳人"。龍（Dragon）在中國人民心中是至高無上的吉祥圖騰，我們把自己的國家稱作"東方巨龍"引以為傲。龍是中華民族的代表，也是中國的象徵。

西方人對於龍，有他們自己的一套看法。西方基督教盛行之前，西方龍（Dragon）一直是維京人、塞爾特人和撒克遜人的民族象徵。而在基督教文化中卻認定龍（Dragon）是一種兇殘的動物，邪惡的代表；是一種猙獰的怪獸，惡魔的化身。基督教聖經《新約全書》啟示錄中，龍被描繪為邪惡的"古蛇"、"魔鬼"、"撒旦"。由於中西方民族長期生活在不同的文化背景之下，對同一動物產生不同的理解和聯想，這是客觀存在的事實。

全球化背景下的今天，中國人走出國門去到西方國家，勢必會遇到西方人這樣那樣的置疑和不信，甚至不解和疏離。講好中國故事，用西方人聽得懂的語言講解中國故事。理解中國的方塊文字不容易，理解中文方塊字背後的文化故事就更困難。

相反，全世界所有人觀察和瞭解水則相對容易得多，水在世界各地方都有，是生活的一部分，每個人都可以讀懂它。中國人在理解"龍"背後的"水"故事之後，多傳授些中華文化的常識和知識，特別是"水"智慧給西方人，他們或許能瞭解多一點東方價值理念，比較準確地讀懂中國"龍"，讀懂中國文化。

水，既是一種世界性通用語言，又是中華民族文化智慧的源頭所在。把水當作媒介比喻，講解詮釋中國人的故事，分析剖析中國案例，梳理研究中國模式，準確而有趣，新穎而不失嚴謹。講者興趣盎然，聽者感同身受。因為，水與每個人的生活息息相關，體會貼身真切自然，不說教不做作。凡是自然的東西便會打動人心，講解中國文化故事恰似水潤物無聲，水到渠成，事半功倍。

第六篇

水，與中國神話傳說

水，是影響中國文化形成、發展、演變、進化最重要、最關鍵的因素之一，且排位靠前，非常非常的靠前。

秘密，一個困繞世人多年的關於中國人品性的秘密，或正在被發現，正在被破譯解構。當今時下，整個世界十分渴望瞭解中國文化的博大精深，和其深奧的迷人之處，因為中國人、中國人的思維定式、中國人的行為模式不僅獨特，與眾不同，而且又在實踐中做得明顯好過他人，這更加重了世人強烈的好奇心，破解吃透它。解讀中國，用西方的套路肯定行不通，必須找到一個新的視角重新審視、認識中國文化的獨特品質。

水，天地宇宙間客觀存在的物質，就其自然屬性而言，水本身二氫一氧原子組成一個水分子，無數水分子聚集在一起成水流，水流聚合再成迴圈圈，自主構成一個自然生態體系。就物理生化屬性而言，水與其他物質似乎一樣普通，沒啥特別的，都是天地世界中尋常平等的一份子，缺了哪一樣物質都不成，都難構成一個完整的自然世界。

然而，水卻不簡單，就其社會文化屬性而論，水是特別不同的物質，它賦予中國文化、哲學、價值倫理太多的智慧思考和特殊品質，這與西方文化形成強烈的對比。水，可以去到世界任何一處地方，只要它下決心打算去的地和做的事，誰也攔不住、擋不了水去到它想去的任何一處地方行事。

換一句話講，水有自己的打算和想法，也有自己的能力和辦法，或順勢流淌、或專注滲透、或升騰飛翔，自主克服一切路途上的艱難險阻，百折不撓一路向前。外部環境越是惡劣艱難，水的抗爭烈度越是高亢強大，不屈壓力直至去到它想去的世界任何一個角落或地方。水的字典裡從"沒有克服不了的困難"。

水品水德，深刻影響和造就了中華民族的性格和品質。不論你相信也好，不相信也罷，你會驚訝地發現到中國傳統文化中有許許多多關於中國人不畏艱險困苦，埋頭勤勉，挑戰、超越自我能力的古老神話和傳說。中國人面對自然挑戰不屈服、不怕輸、敢於抗爭，相信用自己的智慧和雙手創造出一個新世界。他們不相信有克服不了的困難，勤勉努力和奮鬥抗爭的精神早已經融入中華民族的血脈骨髓之中。

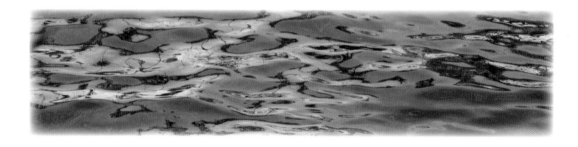

大禹治水

黃河水患，是從堯開始氾濫成災的。當時的黃河流域經常發大水，農田被淹、房屋被毀，百姓流離失所，背井離鄉，生活十分悲苦。堯決心要消滅水患，經過四方部落首領商議，決定派鯀去治水。可是，鯀沒有太多治水的經驗，他只懂得用土埋，建堤築壩，結果治水九年，不但沒有把洪水治服，水災反而頻繁發生，災荒鬧得更凶了。

鯀治水的方法不當，禹接著繼續治理水患。禹首要事是弄清楚黃河水患的來龍去脈，如果採取適當的方法，仍然關不住水，難道就不能用"疏"和"通"的方式，把水給放了；是龍門山堵住了河水的去路，把河道給擠得十分狹窄，才使得河水溢出河道，造成了水災。

造成水災的原因，找到了；治水的新方法也就確定了。大禹治水把整個中國的山山水水當作一個整體來綜合治理，先治理九州：冀州、青州、徐州、兗州、揚州、梁州、豫州、雍州、荊州的土地，該疏通的疏通，該平整的平整，使得大量的地方變成肥沃的土地；然後再治理山脈：岐山、荊山、雷首山、太嶽山、太行山、王擁山、常山、砥柱山、碣石山、太華山、大別山等。

最後，就是要疏通水道，使得水能夠順利往下流去，不至於堵塞水路。龍門山堵住流水河道，就劈開它。大禹率領民眾前後花了 13 年的時間，用開山斧鑿開龍門，並且挖了九條運河，終於把黃河水平穩引入大海。禹採用了"治水須順水性，水性就下，導之入海"，"高處鑿通，低處疏導"的治水思想，成功治水。大禹因降服水患，成為了中國歷史上第一位成功治理黃河的大英雄，被後人尊為"禹神"。

夸父追日

遠古時候，在北方荒野中有座巍峨雄偉、高聳入雲的高山。在山林深處，生活著一群力大無窮的巨人。他們的首領，是幽冥之神"後土"的孫兒，名字叫做夸父。因此這群人就叫夸父族。他們身強力壯，高大魁梧，意志力堅強，氣概非凡。而且還心地善良，勤勞勇敢，過著清苦平靜的日子。

可那個時候，大地荒涼猛獸橫行，人們生活淒苦。夸父為使本部落的人們能夠活下去，每天都率領眾人跟洪水猛獸搏鬥。有一年，天氣非常炎熱，火辣辣的太陽直射在大地上，烤死莊稼，曬焦樹木，河流乾枯。人們熱得難以忍受，夸父族的人紛紛死去。夸父很難過，他仰頭望著太陽，告訴族人："太陽實在是可惡，我要追上太陽，捉住它，讓它聽人的指揮。"族人聽後紛紛勸阻。

但是，夸父心意已決，發誓要捉住太陽，讓太陽聽從人們的吩咐，為大家服務。他看著愁苦不堪的族人說：「為大家的幸福生活，我一定要去。」太陽剛剛從海上升起，夸父告別族人，懷著雄心壯志，從東海邊上向著太陽升起的方向，邁開大步追去，開始他逐日的征程。夸父他穿過一座座大山，跨過一條條河流，終於在太陽落下的地方追上了紅彤彤、熱辣辣的火球。

夸父無比歡欣地張開雙臂，想把太陽抱住。此時的夸父又渴又累，他一口氣喝乾黃河水，又喝乾了渭河水，仍不解渴；夸父又向北跑去，那裡有縱橫千里的大澤，大澤裡的水足夠夸父解渴。但是，沒等夸父跑到大澤邊時，他就在半路上饑渴而死。夸父臨死的時候，心裡充滿牽掛，牽掛著為自己的族人消除困苦。

愚公移山

傳說很早以前，在冀州的南面、河陽的北面有兩座大山，一座叫太行山，一座叫王屋山，山高萬丈，方圓有七百里。在山的北面，住著一位叫愚公的老漢，年紀快九十歲了。他家的大門，正對著這兩座大山，出門辦事得繞著走，很不方便。愚公下定決心要把這兩座大山挖掉。

有一天，他召集了全家老小，對他們說：「這兩座大山，擋住了我們的出路，咱們大家一起努力，把它挖掉，開出一條直通豫州的大道，你們看好不好？」大家都很贊同，只有他的妻子提出了疑問。她說：「像太行、王屋這麼高大的山，挖出來的那些石頭、泥土往哪裡送呢？」大家說：「這好辦，把泥土、石塊扔到渤海邊上就行了！再多也不愁沒地方堆。」

第二天，愚公就帶領全家老小開始挖山。黃河邊上住著一個老漢，這人很精明，人們管他叫智叟。他看到愚公他們一年到頭，辛辛苦苦地挖山運土不止，覺得很可笑，就去勸告愚公：「你這個人可真傻，這麼大歲數了，還能活幾天？用盡你的力氣，也拔不了山上的幾根草，怎麼能搬動這麼大的山呢？」

愚公深深地歎口氣說：「我看你這人自以為聰明，其實是頑固不化，還不如寡婦和小孩呢！不錯，我是老了，活不幾年了。可是，我死了還有兒子，兒子又生孫子，孫子又生兒子；子子孫孫，世世代代，一直傳下去，是無窮無盡的。可是這兩座山卻不會再長高了，我們為什麼不能把它們挖平呢。」聽了這些話，那個自以為聰明的智叟，再也無話可說了。

山神知道了這件事，害怕愚公一直挖下去，就去向上天報告。老愚公的精神把上天感動了，他就派兩個大力神下凡，把兩座大山背走，一座放到朔方東邊，一座放到雍州南邊。從此以後，冀州的南面，漢水的北面，就沒有高山阻擋了。

后羿射日

　　傳說古時候，天空曾有十個太陽。十個太陽就像十個大火團，他們一起放出的熱量烤焦了大地，燒死了許許多多的人和動物。森林著火，河流乾枯，所有的樹木莊稼和房子都被燒成了灰燼。那些在大火中沒有燒死的人和動物，四下奔走，發瘋似地尋找可以躲避災難的地方和能救命的水和食物，祈求上蒼的恩賜。

　　這時，有個年輕英俊的英雄大神叫后羿，他是個神箭手，箭法超群，百發百中。他被天帝召喚去，領受了驅趕太陽的使命。他看到人們生活在火難中，心中十分不忍，便暗下決心射掉那多餘的九個太陽，幫助人們脫離苦海。

　　於是，后羿爬過了九十九座高山，邁過了九十九條大河，穿過了九十九個峽谷，來到了東海邊，登上了一座大山，山腳下就是茫茫的大海。后羿拉開了萬斤力弓弩，搭上千斤重利箭，瞄準天上火辣辣的太陽，嗖地一箭射去，第一太陽被射落了。后羿又拉開弓弩，搭上利箭，嗡地一聲射去，同時射落了兩個太陽。

　　這下，天上還有七個太陽瞪著紅彤彤的眼睛。后羿感到這些太陽仍很焦熱，又狠狠地射出了第三枝箭。這一箭射得很有力，一箭射落了四個太陽。其它的太陽嚇得全身打顫，團團旋轉。就這樣，后羿一枝接一枝地把箭射向太陽，無一虛發，射掉了九個太陽。

　　直到最後剩下一個太陽，它願意按照后羿的吩咐，老老實實地為大地和萬物繼續貢獻光和熱。從此，這個太陽每天從東方的海邊升起，晚上從西邊山上落下，溫暖著人間，保持萬物生存，人們安居樂業。

精衛填海

　　傳說，炎帝有個女兒叫女娃，女娃聰明伶俐，活潑可愛，美麗非凡，炎帝十分喜歡她。一天，她走出小村，找小朋友玩耍，看到一個大孩子把小孩子當馬騎。小孩都累趴下了，大孩子還不肯甘休。女娃走過去，指著大孩子的腦門怒斥道："你這個人太壞了，欺負小孩子算什麼本事，有力氣，去打虎打熊，人們會說你是英雄。"

　　大孩子見女娃是個小姑娘，生得單薄文弱，根本不把她放在眼裡。他從小孩背上跳下來，走到女娃面前說："我是海龍王的兒子，你是什麼人？竟敢來管我。"女娃說："龍王的兒子有什麼了不起，我還是神農的女兒呢，以後你少到陸地上撒野，小心我把你掛到樹上曬乾。"

龍王的兒子說：“我先讓你知道知道我的厲害，往後少管小爺的閒事。”說著動手就打。女娃從小跟著父親上山打獵，手腳十分靈活，力氣也不小，見對方蠻橫無禮，並不示弱，閃身躲開對方的拳頭，飛起一腿，將龍王的兒子踢個嘴啃泥。龍王的兒子站起來，不肯服輸，揮拳又打，被女娃當胸一拳，打個昂面朝天。龍王的兒子見打不過女娃，只好灰溜溜地返回大海。

過些天，女娃到海中游泳，正玩得十分開心，剛巧讓龍王的兒子發現了。他遊過來，對女娃說：“那天在陸地上讓你撿了便宜，今天你跑到我家門前，趕快認個錯，不然我興風作浪淹死你。”女娃倔強地說：“我沒錯，認什麼錯。”龍王的兒子見女娃倔強，根本沒有服輸的意思，立即攪動海水，掀起狂風惡浪，女娃來不及掙扎，就被淹死了，永遠回不來了。

女娃不甘心她的死，她的魂靈變化做了一隻小鳥“精衛”。精衛悲恨無情的海濤毀滅了自己，又想到別人也可能會被奪走年輕的生命，因此不斷地從西山銜來一條條小樹枝、一顆顆小石頭，丟進海裡，想要把大海填平。她無休止地往來飛翔與西山和東海之間。可是那咆哮的大海嘲笑她道：“小鳥兒，算了吧，就算你幹上百萬年，也別想將我填平。”

但是翱翔在高空的精衛堅決地回答說：“就算幹上一千萬年、一萬萬年，幹到世界末日，我也要將你填平。”精衛她飛翔著，嘯叫著，離開大海，又飛回西山去；把西山上的石子和樹枝銜來投進大海。她就這樣往復飛翔，從不休息，直到今天她還在做著填海壯舉。

鑽木取火

在遠古蠻荒時期，人們不知道有火，也不知道用火。到了黑夜，四處一片漆黑，野獸的吼叫聲此起彼伏，人們蜷縮在一起，又冷又怕。由於沒有火，人們只能吃生的食物，經常生病，壽命也很短。

天上有個大神叫伏羲，他看到人間生活得這樣艱難，心裡很難過，他想讓人們知道火的用處。於是伏羲大展神通，在山林中降下一場雷雨。隨著“哢”的一聲，雷電劈在樹木上，樹木燃燒起來，很快就變成了熊熊大火。

大火過後，有個年輕人發現，原來經常在周圍出現的野獸的嚎叫聲沒有了，他想：“難道野獸怕這個發亮的東西嗎？”於是，他勇敢地走到火邊，他發現身上好暖和呀。他興奮地招呼大家：“快來呀，這火一點不可怕，它給我們帶來了光明和溫暖。”人們又發現不遠處燒死的野獸，發出了陣陣香味，人們開始感到了火的可貴之處。

大神伏羲在天上看到了這一切，他來到最先發現火的用處的那個年輕人的夢裡，告訴他：“在遙遠的西方有個遂明國，那裡有火種，你可以去那裡把火種取回來。”年輕人醒了，想起夢裡大神說的話，決心到遂明國去尋找火種。年輕人翻過高山，涉過大河，穿過森林，歷盡艱辛，終於來到了遂明國。

可是，遂明國這裡沒有陽光，不分晝夜，四處一片黑暗，根本沒有火。年輕人非常失望，就坐在一棵叫“遂木”的大樹下休息。突然，年輕人眼前有亮光一閃，又一閃，把周圍照得很明亮。年輕人立刻站起來，四處尋找光源。這時候他發現就在遂木樹上，有幾隻大鳥正在用短而硬的喙啄樹上的蟲子。只要它們一啄，樹上就閃出明亮的火花。

年輕人看到這種情景，腦子裡靈光一閃。他立刻折了一些遂木的樹枝，用小樹枝去鑽大樹枝，樹枝上果然閃出火光，可是卻著不起火來。年輕人不灰心，他找來各種樹枝，耐心地用不同的樹枝進行摩擦。終於，樹枝冒煙了，然後出火了。年輕人為家鄉人們帶回了“鑽木取火”的辦法，人們被這個年輕人的勇氣和智慧折服，推舉他做首領，並稱他為“燧人”，即取火者。

刑天

當炎帝還在統領天下的時候，刑天是炎帝手下的一位大臣。他生平酷愛歌曲，曾為炎帝作樂曲《扶犁》，作詩歌《豐收》，以歌頌當時人民幸福快樂的生活。後來炎帝在阪泉之戰中被黃帝打敗，他的兒子和手下卻不服氣。當蚩尤舉兵反抗黃帝的時候，刑天曾想去參加這場戰爭，只是因為炎帝的堅決阻止沒有成行。

蚩尤和黃帝一戰失敗，蚩尤被殺死，刑天再也按捺不住他那顆憤怒的心，於是偷偷地離開南方天廷，徑直奔向中央天廷，去和黃帝爭個高低。刑天左手握著青銅方盾，右手拿著大斧，直殺到黃帝的宮前。黃帝見刑天殺過來，頓時大怒，拿起寶劍就和刑天搏鬥起來。兩人從宮內殺到宮外，從天庭殺到凡間，直殺到常羊山旁。

黃帝久經沙場，經驗老到。他趁刑天不防，揮劍向刑天的脖子砍去。刑天招架不及，頭顱被斬落下來。刑天感覺到了周圍的變化，知道黃帝已經把自己的頭顱斬下，但是他並沒有氣餒。他站起來，依然右手拿斧，左手持盾，向著天空揮舞。陷入黑暗的刑天以兩個乳頭做眼睛，張開肚臍做嘴，繼續與黃帝搏鬥。刑天雖然失敗了，但是他永不妥協的精神卻永遠激勵著後人。

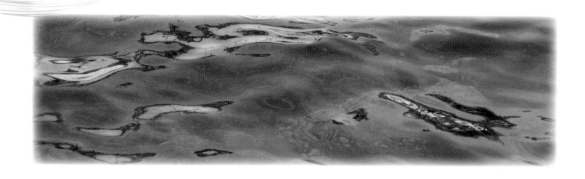

獨特的中國文化魅力

中國的傳統文化中大禹治水、夸父追日、愚公移山、后羿射日、精衛填海、鑽木取火，和刑天等數量眾多的神話傳說傳遞的，是一個共同精神"不屈、抗爭"，明知不可為而為之，明知不可嘗而試之。最後的結果是一回事，抗爭不服輸的態度則是另一回事。有時候，態度、勇氣和精神則更加重要，當遇到了問題、矛盾、困難或災禍時，是去祈求上天賜舍，還是靠自己動手解決克服？中國人從來就有自己的想法和辦法。

西方人則不同，"我們（西方）的神話裡，火是上帝賜予的；希臘神話裡，火是普羅米修士偷來的；而在中國的神話裡，火是他們鑽木取火堅忍不拔摩擦出來的。這就是區別，中國的祖輩用這樣的故事告訴後代，要與自然作鬥爭。""面對末日洪水，我們在諾亞方舟裡躲避，但中國人的神話裡，他們的祖先戰勝了洪水。"

"假如有一座山擋在你的門前，你是選擇搬家還是挖隧道？顯而易見，搬家是最好的選擇。然而在中國的故事裡，他們卻把山搬開了。可惜，這樣的精神內核，我們的神話裡卻不存在，我們的神話是聽從神的安排"（美國大衛·查普曼語）西方人通常是靠等待、靠接濟、靠迴避、靠利用現成的設施和資源來解決問題，度過難關。

比較中西方神話故事，差異和區別就顯露出來了。遇事，遇特別重大事變，中國人往往相對主動積極，迎著困難而上；西方人則相對被動消極，避著困難而走。"中國人聽著這樣的神話故事長大，勇於抗爭的精神已經成為遺傳基因，因此再想到中國人倔強的不服輸精神，就容易理解多了，這是他們屹立至今的原因。"（美國大衛·查普曼語）

對待環境和事件的反應，中西方差異不小。中國人的行為模式，則更貼近水的行為一樣"獨立自主"特質，順勢而為，順流而下；前行路上主動創造財富，積極挑戰外部的艱險和困難，從不相信什麼鬼神救世主，也不可能有什麼鬼神救世主，故棄鬼神不理。"子不語怪力亂神"，中國人只相信依靠人的力量，依靠自己的勤勉和努力、不屈和抗爭求得生存繁衍。"民之所欲，天必從之。"（《書·泰誓上》）民意不可違背，上天都會尊重。

　　"認識你自己"（古希臘哲學家蘇格拉底語）"知人者智，自知者明"國人能夠認識自己，認識中國人自己的品性，並用全世界人聽得懂的語言，講明白中國人的品性非常之重要，而非是假借他人之手、外人之口解釋、傳播中國人形象。坦率講，西方人讀不懂中國人，至多是"知其然"，未必知"其所以然"；他們可以親身體會和瞭解到中國神話傳說呈現的"不屈、抗爭"精神，但未必能夠認知其不服輸精神背後的真正原因和價值支撐。

　　在西方主導全球話語權的今天，曲解中國人和中國文化的人不在少數，許多人說中華民族沒有宗教信仰，沒有敬畏之心，沒有責任之心，缺失社會公德心這樣的說辭到處流行、氾濫。

　　其實，事實並非如西方人講的那樣。現在的問題，有多少人讀懂了中國人和中國文化，包括中國人自己也沒講明白，解釋清楚"中國人到底是誰"這個命題。難道一個沒有宗教信仰的民族，能夠不間斷存續 5000 年？恐怕世人是缺少了一個正確的解釋和答疑而已。

　　中國的確是沒有類似西方社會的"非自然"的人為宗教。然而，中國從來不缺宗教，中國人有自己的"自然"宗教，且唯一的"神靈"自然崇拜。中國人相信天地宇宙，相信天地宇宙中的自然規律"道"，相信水"幾於道"；水幾乎可以是自然規律的同義語，或代名詞。自然規律"道"是隱性的，而水是顯性的，要瞭解、掌握自然規律"道"，則完全可以通過參學、領悟"水"的品性和品德，達致參悟目的。

　　中國的文化價值體系，與西方人的完全不同。中國人是"自然"崇拜，而西方人則是"非自然"崇拜。中國人親近"水"，崇拜"水"，從"水"中參悟、獲取人類大智慧啟迪，西方人卻更願意貼近動植物世界，參學動植物，從中總結供人類生存和生活的知識和常識。人類確實可以從動植物那裡學習、獲取到海量的知識，但絕難學到一丁點人類文明的大智慧：平等、公正和正義。人是萬事萬物之靈，人類"文明"嚮往和追求絕對在動植物之上，不應該也不可能從動植物那裡學到人類文明的大智慧。

　　文化是根，文化是魂，不同的文化具有不同的根系和靈魂。說真的，世界上很難找到一種類似的文化，能像中國文化那樣獨特，特立獨行，鶴立雞群。當然，中國文化再特別，再獨一無二，社會經濟沒有發展起來啥也沒用，沒人會當你中國人一回事，最多也就是把中國視作一個游離在世界大家庭邊緣的"異類"或"怪胎"，沒人會想到中國文明體系居然是領前的那一個，比西方文明要先進和文明的多。

　　只有中國發展了、強大了、復興了、全面領先世界了，西方人才會收起以往的傲慢姿態，專心傾聽由中國人自己講清楚中國文化的來龍去脈和前生今世。講中國故事，講中國的成功故事，讓中國的哲學思想、中國的價值倫理、中國的話語力量像今天"中國製造"魔力一樣走向世界，影響世界。

第七篇

水，中國模式的鮮明特徵

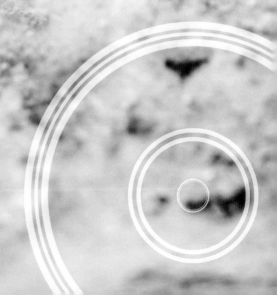

世界範圍之內存在有許多發展模式，有新自由主義主導的“美國模式”、政府導向型的“日本模式”、德國社會市場經濟為代表的“萊茵模式”。各種模式之間既有相同相似的地方，也會有不盡相同、各具特點的地方。理性而言，一個泱泱 5000 年進化發展歷史不曾中斷的文明大國，怎麼也理應有自己叫得響、拿得上檯面的“中國模式”。

對內、對外講清楚自己的社會治理方式和方法，以及社會治理的特徵，予人予己都大有益處，方便世人彼此瞭解溝通。這是一個負責任大國應該給予世界的合理交代，特別是中國準備為世界做出更大貢獻，準備不久以後成為 GDP 世界“第一”的時候，更應該儘早、儘快去做。

什麼叫做模式？模式是可供效仿的模型或範例，是事物發展特點的彙集，是該類事物典型特徵的反映和示範。模式必須具備兩個基本要素：一是該事物在與同類事物的比較中具有自身獨特而鮮明的特點；二是這些特點具有恒定性，能構成穩定成型的體系。

所謂發展模式，是集政治、經濟、文化因素相互作用、共同促進而形成的具有鮮明特徵的經濟社會發展體制。它是國家基本制度在不同的政治文化、歷史傳統和社會框架條件下建立與發展的產物。在經濟發展的過程中，圍繞國家與市場之間、政府與企業之間、國家與社會之間關係的不斷調整，產生了不同的發展體制。

中國模式，是中國政治、經濟、文化因素相互作用、共同促進而形成的具有鮮明特徵的經濟社會發展體制。研究中國模式不同於其他模式的特殊性質，就是試圖要把那些深藏在發展模式中那些恒定不變的結構性因素尋找出來。這些因素或就是中國模式的最核心原素，也是最基本的原素。

從歷史發展的角度考察中國模式，可以清晰地體察其合理長存的理據，以及文明先進的素質。儘管中國模式表現在林林總總不同方面，但其核心關鍵是中國特有的政治模式和經濟模式，這兩個方面互相關聯，互相依存，互相強化支撐。毋庸置疑，古代中國一直是排名世界最先進行列的國家，並持續保有千年之久。只是從明朝萬曆年間開始，中國經濟逐步走下坡路；清末鴉片戰爭時期前後，中國經濟更是一落千丈，衰敗落後進一步加速。

新中國建立以後的一段時間裡中國的 GDP 一直徘徊在世界前十名開外。然而，從 20 世紀末期中國經濟重新又開始發力，並持續躍進。在短短的 10 來年內連續超過了加拿大、義大利、法國、英國和德國，站穩世界“第三”位置；2010 年，中國更進一步取代日本成為世界第二大經濟體；順利發展的話，2035 年前後中國就將可望超過美國，重新回到世界“第一”的寶座。

　　這是人類歷史發展史上的一個罕見的奇跡。從 1979 年到 2011 年的三十二年間，中國的 GDP 連續四次每八年翻一番。從近代歷史上看，一國 GDP 翻一番的時間，英國用了 58 年 (從 1780 年起)，美國用了 47 年 (從 1839 年起)，日本用了 33 年 (從 19 世紀 80 年代起)，而印尼用了 17 年，韓國用了 11 年。而且，很少有國家能夠做到 GDP 連續翻番，中國不僅做到且繼續進行著創新歷程。

　　一個國家從歷史發展的峰頂，跌落衰敗到幾乎亡國滅族的谷底，再從谷底頑強爬起站立起來，重新集結起來衝擊峰頂。這個世界上，還真難見到除中國以外的第二個國家能夠做到達成這一奇跡的，只有中國人"敢為天下先"開天闢地重新走上復興之路。中國人是怎麼做到的？而其他民族卻不能或幾乎不可能。道理秘笈就在中國的傳統文化之中。

　　中國模式具備一以貫之的哲學基礎，即中國的 5000 年國家治理模式建立在始終如一，一以貫之的哲學理論基礎。國人的哲學倫理取向，自古以來就是相信天地自然規律，相信"道法自然"，相信"天人合一"和諧融合。虛心向大自然求教，不容有失。中國模式師從於天地自然規律"道"，師從於"水"，具備獨特而鮮明的基本特徵：恒久！持久 5000 年或更長時間段的恒定性，持續性和可靠性，構成一個穩定成型的社會治理和社會發展綜合體系。

　　自然王國中，有天地自然規律"道"，可是"道"卻無影無蹤，看不見聽不到摸不著，觸碰不了感覺不到，但又真真實實地存在，無處不在無處不有。中國古代哲學先賢老子講解說："上善若水，水善利萬物而不爭，處眾人之所惡，故幾於道"。最高境界的善行，就像水的品性一樣，上善至善完美；水善於滋潤萬物而不與萬物相爭名利，停留在眾人都不喜歡的地方。所以，水最接近於"道"，或自然規律。

　　自此，"水"在中國人的現實生活中，成為自然規律"道"的同義語或代名詞，成為了自然規律"道"的化身。老子用"道"形容自然規律，創造性地用有感知的"水"來描述、體認難以感知的自然規律，直白簡單，扼要明確。中國人心悅誠服於"道"，誠服于水，拜水為老師。無論歷史如何演繹變化，中國人有自己的傳統信仰，有自己的哲學堅持，國家治理模式就常反映出中國式哲學思考的特殊品質和性格。

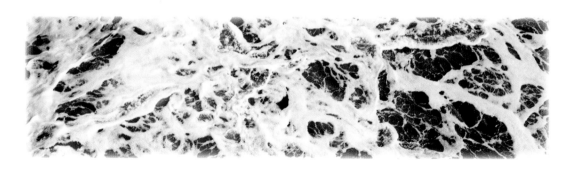

中國模式特徵

1. 生態性

　　自然界中的水循環系統是一個運動不止，生生不息的綠色生態體系。水永遠不停地流動，循環運動不止。在太陽輻射和地球引力的推動下，水在海陸間形成循環圈，太陽熱量蒸發海洋表面的水至天空，空氣中水汽形成雲霧，雲霧隨大氣環流運動，又形成雨雪冰雹降水地面，降水落到地面後轉化為地下水、土壤水和地表徑流，地表徑流（大江大河）最終經過一個出海口，又流回到海洋，由此形成水的動態循環體系。各種各類生命體，在水的循環系統滋潤滋養下茁壯蓬勃成長。

　　中國人學習水循環系統知識，感悟體認到國家治理體系原型，類似或相似于水的循環再生系統，講究整體系統的統一性和可持續性，循環往復生生不息。自古以來，中國人就高度認可"大一統"的國家治理體系，並堅守其幾千年之久，自秦始皇統一中國起始，中華民族一直沿用"大一統"的國家治理體系至今沒有任何改變和動搖，儘管世界其他國家被"折分"無數次。

　　我們的祖輩父輩們有自己的理想模樣，他們的堅持和執著有自己的理由，有傳統智慧的引領和真實踐行的護佑。否則，"大一統"的國家治理體系早就被歷史潮流所淘汰，其中的道理不言自明。華夏民族祖先前輩們的認知和堅守更貼近自然天成和原始生態狀況，符合天地之"道"，而非人為想像臆造。

　　中國現行的國家治理體系，也是沿續中華民族 5000 年的歷史傳承、文化傳統、經濟社會發展基礎上長期發展、漸進改進、內生性演化的結果，不是哪個人哪個政黨憑空臆想出來，或隨隨便便可以任意更改的。總體來講，國家的政治穩定、經濟發展、社會和諧和民族團結，是最終決定"大一統"國家治理體系存續保留，完善發展的最根本理由。

　　西方人有一種傳統觀點"政府是必要的惡"，而中國人並不這樣認知，他們視"政府是必要的善"，政府應該是人民集體意願的代言者和承載人，是國家的首席治理實踐者。中國人有強烈的"家國情懷"，史書萬卷字裡行間都是"家國"二字。《大學》有云："古之欲明明德於天下者，先治其國；欲治其國者，先齊其家；欲齊其家者，先修其身。""修齊治平"，由個人而家庭，由家庭而社會，由社會而國家，由國家而天下是中國人特有的社會倫理價值邏輯。

　　"未有我之先，家國已在焉；沒有我之後，家國仍永存。多少滄桑付流水，常念家國在心懷。""家國同構，家國一體"，家是縮小的國，國是放大的家。"一玉口中國，一瓦頂成家，都說國很大，其實一個家"，每個人的生命體驗都與家國緊緊相連。"家天下"是中華民族傳統的一個最本質特徵。愛國如愛家，危難時舍小家為大家，這種觀念深入人心。民族危亡關頭，忠孝不能兩全之際，相比盡孝奉親，為國臨危赴難更具備傳世英名，因為國是一個大家，國之不存，家將焉附？

2. 穩定性

自然界中的水循環系統是一個極其"穩定"的生命運動體系。自然界中的水，通過蒸發，包括植物蒸騰，水汽輸送、降水、下滲、地表徑流和地下水徑流等一系列過程和環節，把大氣圈、水圈、岩石圈和生物圈有機地聯繫起來，構成一個龐大的水循環系統。

無論水的形式如何發生變化，常溫液態，零度固態，百度氣態，其水的總量永遠恒定不變。中國古代哲學聖賢老子說："天長地久，天地所以能長且久者，以其不自生，故能長生。"天，之所以長，是它不為自己而存在；地，之所以久，是它不為自己而生存！天長地久的那般穩定，是根植在每個中國人靈魂中的渴望。

中國人做事謀略，特別關注營造一個穩定的內外部生存發展環境。沒有穩定，中國的"改革開放"就成了一個不切邊際的空想；沒有穩定，中國的發展就是一個遙不可及的奢望。"摸著石頭過河"，是中國民間一句歇後語，較為直白地說，一個人想過一條不熟悉的河，在沒有前人給出經驗，沒有船，也沒有橋等情況下，如何分清這條河哪個地方水深，哪個地方水淺，水深的地方有可能淹死人，而水淺的地方人能夠淌水過。在事先不知道這條河詳細情況下，就只能以身試水摸索著河裡的石頭，以較為保守的甚至原始的方法，逐步摸清情況並想辦法安全涉水。

中國的"改革"走的是一條穩妥推進逐步深化之路，採納的是東方"漸進式改革"的轉型路徑，捨棄西方外科手術式的"休克療法"改革方法。改革，是在基本社會體制框架（特別是政治制度）和主導性意識形態不發生變化的前提下所進行的改革，特別強調是在堅持國家基本制度和原則基礎上的自我完善，逐步調整公有制和私有制混合比重，堅守國家主體經濟為先，經濟制度改革是漸進式的，是逐步進行的過程。

中國的改革，實行的是"從體制外到體制內"的改革戰略，具體地講，中國改革採取了一種不首先釘住國有部門這個舊體制的主幹部門打攻堅戰圍剿戰，而是避開其主力鋒芒，先在"體制外"展開的戰略攻堅。通過農村改革、實行對外開放、某些地區發展非國有經濟，和從區域來擴展市場這幾項政策使得改革的先行地區、主要是沿海地區經濟迅速發展，積累改革經驗和資本。這樣就給我們的改革找到經濟上和政治上的支撐力量，改革的時間和空間有更大更寬的迴旋餘地。

中國的改革，採取的是"逐項的、部分的、增量的，先點後面"的改革試點，常常是先確定幾個點，給予預定目標進行試驗，取得經驗後再逐步推廣至全面。改革採取的路徑是從下到上先易後難；先經濟後政治；先對增量部分進行改革，然後用增量的改革成果帶動存量改革。中國式的從下到上漸進式改革方式，社會震盪小，試錯求真成本低，成果績效顯著。

改革的特別之處，在於"穩定"的前置前導，中國沒有進行全面大規模的私有化，避免社會極端分化和動盪。改革過程事先並沒有完善的理論指導，更沒有預先設計的改革路徑藍圖。然而，中國人上上下下卻心領神會"摸著石頭過河"之道，摸索走出了一條獨具特色的中國式發展道路，取得了很大的成功。

3. 開放性

自然界中的水循環系統是開放式體系，嵌於"天地人"系統之中，具有整體獨立、開放動態、生態循環等特徵。水在其循環過程之中，從不封閉自我，敞開心扉地與所有遇見的生物，包括植物和動物，進行自由平等的交流，滋養萬物。水從來不拒絕外界交流物件，能走多遠走多遠，能飛多高飛多高，不論是誰只要你願意，水絕對會尊重你，與你交朋友幫助你成就你。"欲致魚者先通水，欲致鳥者先樹木，水積而魚聚，木茂而鳥集。"

中國人對"開放"和"封閉"兩種格局所帶來的結果有刻骨銘心的感受和體會，對國家自我怛封閉"落後挨打"的結局有切膚之痛。中國歷史上的輝煌朝代傲立世界民族之林·從秦漢，唐宋，元明，直至清朝前期，以及今天的"改革開放40年"無一不是開放強大的朝代。

滿清後期，政府把自己完全封閉起來，排斥外來文化和文明。清朝政府實行了更加嚴厲的海禁。康熙年間，清廷與羅馬教廷發生禮儀之爭，不僅西洋人在中國傳教受到嚴格限制，對外貿易態度也發生根本變化。清朝實行閉關政策，妄自尊大，使中國自絕於世界大潮之外，嚴重阻礙了中國的社會經濟發展。

"對內改革，對外開放"的戰略決策，是新中國成立以來第一個以開放為主題的重大國策。這一政策改變了中國長久以來對外封閉的局面，使中國對外敞開國門實施自由貿易。改革開放的影響是顯著的，其中成就是巨大的。從1978年至2018年，中華人民共和國由一個尚有6.8億人生活在貧困線下，與世隔絕的國家，變成了一個經濟繁榮，有著活躍市場的強大經濟體，並減少了全世界近1/4的貧困人口數。

人民生活也伴隨著"改革開放"日新月異，物質精神生活不斷豐富。據官方資料表明，中國自1978年改革開放到2018年，人均國民生產總值由225美元上升到9000多美元。2018年，中國的外匯儲備達到3萬多億美元，成為美國最大的債權國家。2018年，中國國內生產總值（GDP）13多萬億美元遠超過日本近3倍，成為世界第二大經濟體。

今天的中國，更加開放，更加自信，更加忘我工作。中國正在努力奮鬥，早日重新回到"冠軍國家"行列之首，再一次恢復世界國家編排序列的正常狀態。

4. 整體性

自然界中的水，分成氣態、固態和液態三種不同的形態。三種不同形態的水，互相獨立聯繫轉換，並形成一個統一有序的整體。水，不斷運動變化，通過太陽蒸騰作用，液體水汽化升空，水汽冷卻以後形成雲成雨，降雨落下形成規模，河水、冰川水、土壤水、湖泊水、地下水體組成地表徑流，地下徑流重新回到海洋，完成循環圈。各個獨立水體之間的關聯緊密，具有水源的相互補給關係，在能量、品質、數量上都息息相關環環相扣，缺失任何一環都不行。個體離不開整體，整體不能缺失個體，兩者相輔相成。

中國，是人類歷史上最為古老的文明古國之一，她雖歷經數千年風雨激蕩，卻一直生生不息；古代中國雖屢經分裂，遭受多少回分分合合的頓挫與磨難，但國家始終沒有瓦解，相反，它不斷走向統一，並一度成為世界古代文明中最為強盛的國家。

當代英國著名學者湯因比論及中國歷史文化時，曾有這樣的感歎："幾千年來，中國人比世界任何民族都成功地把幾億民眾從政治文化上團結起來，顯示出這種政治上文化上統一的本領，具有無與倫比的成功經驗。"中國文化中的一個鮮明"傳統"，即歷史悠久的愛國主義傳統，和集體主義傳統。

中國人有一個傳統，叫作從"整體"出發的傳統，西方則是強調從"個體"出發的傳統。中國人學習"水"的整體架構和總體意識，將宏觀世界和微觀世界統一起來，整體對待。照顧個體和兼顧整體並重，側重有度整體統籌。要自由要民主，也要有統一有集中；個體傾向自由民主，集體則要側重統一和集中；先自由後統一，先民主後集中。

典型的2008年北京奧林匹克運動會開幕式，給予全世界一個直觀的中國式"集體主義"展示。中國的發展不僅要通過個體的方式取得，更需要通過集體主義的方式取得。成千上萬的中國舞者就像一個人一樣行動，像一個人一樣擊鼓，像一個人一樣起舞，按照精確的編隊疾走而不會絆倒或者衝撞。"集體主義"力量和技巧充分呈現，向世人公示傳遞中國奇跡般的發展和復興。

社會中，每一個體是基礎，個體意志人格理應得到尊重，而集體又是個體的充分集合，是眾多個體的集體代表者。個體的自由民主在前，集體的統一集中殿後，如此前後呼應相輔相成，整體有序運行。在強調提倡"集體主義"的時候，絕不是說可以不注意個人利益，不注意局部利益，不注意暫時利益。

相反卻是強調說個人利益和集體利益，暫時利益和長遠利益是統一的。"個人主義"不應該為了一己私利而罔顧公益、甚至傷害他人的"自私自利"，而是強調所有的個人都具有相同和平等的權利和責任，社會不會允許任何個人以任何理由踐踏任何其他個人的權利，或犧牲他人的利益以成就自己的私利。

5. 包容性

大自然中，水對絕大多數物質具有親和性，水分子能與其他物質分子形成水合粒子。水分子，是兩個氫原子和一個氧原子鍵合在一起，而形成的無機物質，水分子帶有極性。因此，水自身具備成為生命源泉的基本條件。大自然中的水，不是以單一水分子的形式存在，而是由若干水分子通過氫鍵作用而聚合在一起，形成水分子集群，不停歇地運動構成水循環圈。

正因為水分子中的氧原子上，有一對孤對電子具有路易士鹼性，多數電解質物質能夠溶解于水。所以，液態水能溶合溶解論許許多多的其他物質，並能夠提供各個物質相互碰撞和反應的最佳介質。水是萬能溶劑，是任何其他物質完全無法與之相比較的最好溶解物。

中國治理模式中充分展現"水"的溶解融合特點和功能。國人傳統上沒有強烈的宗教意識，中國人的人生態度"適中"，不落於"禁"與"縱"的兩個極端偏向，不失于生命應有的和諧。對待外來異族宗教。不固執不偏執，堅守開明通達、恰當適中、學以致用的立場，留用有利於我民族發展的一切有益精華，棄用不利於我民族發展的所有糟粕。國家大政方略上秉持尊重開放、相容並蓄，和諧融合的態度，對待所有外來異族宗教。

福建泉州是世俗和眾神共浴的聖地，有"世界宗教博物館"之譽。朱熹的"此地古稱佛國，滿街都是聖人"，說的是佛教和儒教。事實上，在泉州全盛時期，佛教、道教、基督教、天主教、伊斯蘭教、印度教、日本教和睦共處。

在泉州古城核心區西街，佛教古刹開元寺紫雲大殿後回廊中央，有兩根古印度教石柱，雕刻內容都與印度著名史詩《摩訶婆羅多》和《羅摩衍那》有關。開元寺不遠處，是泉西基督教堂，古大厝門前還立有道教信眾認為可以避邪的"石敢當"。一條老街上，數種宗教信仰和諧共存，其開化包容程度堪稱世界一絕。

中華民族是一個嚴于律己，愛好和平的民族，主張"己所不欲勿施於人"。百姓生活中的矛盾，常是被"大事化小，小事化了"處理，相互的包容性特別強，不會因為你的信仰，習俗而採取敵對態度。而且，中國人十分好客，很容易跟其他國家的人和平共處。但是，中國人卻又很自主，不喜歡強加給別人觀念，同時也不接受別人強加給自己的觀念。這種獨特的理性的力量，相容並蓄，和諧又合理，往往能同化各種外來的"非我族類"的東西。這確實是一種強大的文化感召力量。

中華民族獨特的理性力量和文化力量，多少次感化、漢化各種各樣外來的"非我族類"。今日的中國境內，基督教、天主教、伊斯蘭教、猶太教、東正教、佛教、道教和儒教和諧共處共生共榮；舊日的外敵契丹族、匈奴、鮮卑、拓跋、羌族、氐族、羯族、女真族、金人、蒙古族、滿清族入我中華以後，其命運就同大漢民族緊緊地捆綁在一起，成為中華民族大家庭中不可或缺的一員，融洽相處共同進退。華夏民族強大的感化、同化異族宗教的文化力量，護佑中華民族綿延至今，亘古流長。

6. 和諧性

自然界中的水循環系統，是整個生態系統和各子系統的協調監控體系。水，串聯起生物鏈上每一個環節中的生命物體，平衡每一個獨立物種的均衡發展，致使整個生態系統得以遵循天地之間既有規律，有序和睦地運行。生態系統中，一種生物以另一種生物為食物來源，而另一種生物又以第三種生物為食物來源，由此在多種生物之間，形成一個以食物關係聯接起來的連鎖關係。食物鏈中的綠色植物，利用陽光的"光合作用"，把無機物製造成有機物，把光能轉變成儲存於有機物中的化學能。

各種動物直接或間接依賴綠色植物製造出的有機物生存，食草動物依賴植物為生，食肉動物依賴食草動物為生，雜食動物依賴植物和動物為生。細菌和真菌等營腐微生物，把動植物的屍體、排泄物、和殘落物等所含的複雜有機物，分解成簡單的無機物，歸還到無機環境中，再重新被綠色植物利用來製造有機物。生態系統中，水扮演獨一無二的，極其關鍵的協調角色，承擔起能量流動、物質遷移和轉化的全部功能。

中國人崇尚"和諧"哲理。上古時期，伏羲氏創著的《易經》裡包含著"天人合一"、"和諧共處"、"對立統一"等哲學思想。軒轅黃帝、儒家和道家一以貫之地尊崇"天人合一"學說。天人合一觀是人與自然和諧、社會和諧、世界和諧的基礎，也是"和諧"這一概念的最初源頭。孔子在2000多年前也提出"和諧"理念，《中庸》第一章：中也者，天下之大本也。和也者，天下之達道也。即和諧是適中，不走極端，才能達道，符合事物發展規律。

水在生態循環系統中擔當的協調和諧功能，正是中國人參學的理想對象。中國模式中的治國方略和治理方式，廣泛得益于水的智慧啟發。國人努力在人類社會中扮演類似"水"的功能角色，有機合理協調各方利益，促進和諧包容性增長。對內構建"和諧"社會，對外力促"和平"世界。

60 多年來，新中國共向世界 166 個國家和國際組織提供了近 4000 億元人民幣援助，派遣 60 多萬援助人員，其中 700 多名中國援外工作者為他國發展獻出了寶貴生命。中國先後 7 次宣佈無條件免除重債窮國和最不發達國家對華到期政府無息貸款債務。

2020 年前，中國還將向發展中國家提供 "6 個 100" 的專案支援，包括 100 個減貧項目、100 個農業合作專案、100 個促貿援助專案、100 個生態保護和應對氣候變化專案、100 所醫院和診所、100 所學校和職業培訓中心；向發展中國家提供 12 萬個來華培訓和 15 萬個獎學金名額，為發展中國家培養 50 萬名職業技術人員，設立南南合作與發展學院。

回望中國國內扶貧減貧開發事業，從 1978-2018 的短短 40 餘年間，共計 6.8 億人快速擺脫貧困，被譽為世界人類歷史的 "中國奇跡"。貧窮，是文明社會的頑疾。消除貧窮，是中國執政黨義不容辭的責任與使命。與國外民間的、小規模的生活救濟不同，中國政府是舉全國之力，有計劃、有組織、大規模地進行扶貧。"政府主導" 型的扶貧模式，是中國實現快速減貧的基本前提條件。"政府主導，社會參與，以人為本，自力更生，開發扶貧" 的扶貧方略，以及符合中國國情的扶貧開發道路，是人類減貧史上的一大創舉。

"和諧" 永遠在路上，所做的努力沒有最好，只有更好和更高、更遠。中國歷史上首創的 "科舉" 制度和中國今天的 "高考" 制度，為普通平民晉升提升進入國家知識和管理階層鋪平道路；"耕者有其田"、"井田制"、"大同社會"、"打土豪分田地"、"人類共同命運體"、"中國夢"、"一路一帶"、"亞投行"、"上海合作組織"、"金磚國家組織"、"金磚銀行"、"中美新型大國關係"、"親誠惠容的周邊外交"、"10+1 中國 - 東盟組織"、"10+3 中日韓 - 東盟組織"、"中日韓自由貿易區"、"減免農業稅賦"、"治理環境污染"、"吏治 + 反貪污腐敗" 老虎蒼蠅一起打。

"習馬會"、"軍隊改革"、"聯合國維和"、"博鰲亞洲論壇"、"香山論壇"、"中國 - 亞歐經濟發展合作論壇"、"中歐合作論壇"、"中非合作論壇"、"中阿合作論壇"、"中國 - 小島國經濟發展合作論壇"、"全民醫療保障體系"、"全民社會保障體系" 國家政府高度關注民生，努力構建涵蓋城鄉居民就業、養老、醫療、救助、住房、教育、公共文體服務、環境保護、公共安全、權益保障等十大民生保障體系。"和諧" 努力作為不止步，不停歇，奔跑不息。

小議小結

現在全世界人，包括中國人自己都在苦苦尋問，許多人不清楚，或在爭論不休到底有沒有一個中國模式的存在？回答當然是肯定的、明確的。中國一直就有一個適合自身發展的國家治理模式，而且持續、穩定、運作了 5000 年，成效業績卓著。今天的中國執政者，仍在傳承、堅守、沿續著祖輩們開創的，一以貫之的中國模式。

既然中國傳統的國家治理模式合理存在了 5000 年，而且完全有能力、有成效地保證中華民族的不斷繁衍成長，以及國家的長治久安。那麼，哪有什麼理由不去全面深入地總結、從理論的高度講解清楚中國模式。講明白中國模式內外在含義，對中國自身的發展，對世界其他國家和民族的啟發，以及對提升中國發展影響力益處頗多。

中國歷史上所有的執政者，無論是古代的皇帝、皇權家族、或是任何現代政黨都堅持一個基本的原則鐵律：代表 "天下" 行事替天行 "道"，即代表天底下所有人的利益做事。而不是像西方人那樣，政黨體系中只有代表個別集團利益的政黨，而沒有代表全體民眾利益的政黨。中國任何一個朝代的執政者都宣誓代表 "全民" 利益，它與西方代表 "集團" 利益的政黨相比，根本就不是一回事，且有著最本質的區別，執政的成效也相差甚遠。

對待國家掌權統治者的優劣評價和去留更替，中國社會有自己 "中國式" 的民主程序和做法。執政權的更替，通常是以一個 "朝代" 改朝換代來界定和實施執行，而不是像西方現代社會那樣多個政黨之間競爭上崗，輪流執政，每四年或若干年選舉投票產生國家執政領袖。

中國人一旦相信一個執政者或執政者團隊，選擇其成為全民利益的代表人替國家民族操辦事情，一般都會給予最大的熱忱和最大的耐心支援。執政者團隊內部的人事升遷變動，一般交由執政當權者自行選擇處理。社會分工中，每一個人幹自己最擅長的事，政府執政者專注打理國家民族發展的大事，其他的各民主黨派專責監督，百姓專注獨立發展個人的各種專項事業，政府和百姓各司所職，各行其事，相輔相成相得益彰。

政治模式上，自公元前 221 年秦始皇統一中國，毅然拋棄了周朝的封建制，而在全國範圍內實行郡縣制，開中央集權政制制度之先河。兩千多年來，儘管改朝換代世道沉浮，但中國人就從來沒有改變過自己的政制治理模式。中國歷史上一個 "朝代" 週期跨度平均是兩三百年，這是個規律事實。

中國式國家治理模式中有關 "民主程序" 的執行安排，與西方國家的相比較而言，更多的還是反映出中國人的哲學思考，遵從天地自然規律 "道"，遵從 "水" 的品性，更多的還是考慮社會繁盛發展，需要恒久、穩定、持續、和諧的外部環境，且在現實操作中盡最大努力探求和實踐。

經濟模式上，中國自古代"春秋戰國"時期起始就實行公營和私營混和經濟模式，一直保持至今。據史書記載，最早提出"鹽鐵專營"的是齊國丞相管仲，而真正將"鹽鐵專營"形成國家政策的是漢武帝。公營，或國營企業參與國家經濟體系運作距今已實施2000多年，中國實行典型的混合經濟模式，國營部門和非國營部門、政府與市場要保持適當平衡。

世界上基本找不到像中國這樣的經濟治理模式，在2000多年的歷史時期裡，總有一個很強大的國有部門，國家對關鍵經濟領域起著直接的指導作用。從歷史上看，私有經濟或者民營經濟在中國是一直存在，中國絕對不可能走到像西方那種私有經濟佔國民經濟主導地位的地步。

全面的國有化和全面的私有化都不可能是中國經濟的常態，混合經濟模式才是中國經濟的正常狀態。通常情況下，國營經濟和私營經濟的成分比例在不同的時間段適時地被調整被變動，有時"國進民退"，有時"國退民進"以適應當時的國家經濟整體發展需要。變化和調整，對于中國人來講是再正常不過的事。

基於具有原創精神的"中國模式"不是別的什麼東西，它是中國人民親身實踐幾千年走出來的一條生存道路，是中國人民用勤勞和智慧創造出來的一條發展道路。中國模式的探索創新，毫無疑問是人類歷史上最偉大的實踐、最輝煌的社會系統創新工程，國人正在運用其政治智慧成就、完善一個全新的社會治理體系，為人類世界打造新型的社會治理範本，中國模式無疑是人類文明的一種嶄新形態。

堅守、傳承、執行傳統的中國式國家治理模式，是中國歷史發展的選擇，不是哪一個人或哪一個執政黨人可以隨隨便便改變得了的，人民是這個國家的真正"主人"，他們的選擇和決定是第一位的。"天下大勢，浩浩蕩蕩，順之者昌，逆之者亡。"

歷史的前進發展始終有一個慣性的推動力量，一旦形成便會組織成一個強大的"勢"持久、持續地推動下去，這種大潮大勢是很難阻擋和改變，中間或會有小股倒流逆流，或會有短時間相反方向的浪花，但絕對沒有可能改變潮流"勢"的方向。除非，中國治理模式與現實脫節，與中國人民的理想要求脫節，中國的歷史已經，並將繼續給出屬於中國人的答案。

第八篇

水，讀懂中國人的訣竅之處

今天的世界，渴望瞭解理解透中國文化的人越來越多，包括西方人和中國人自己，緣由是今天中國的影響力與日俱增，全世界越來越重視中國的存在，對中國模式產生了前所未有的興趣，也意識到瞭解中國的重要性和急迫性。中國的快速發展，中國的國家綜合實力直逼全球"老大"美國，大有近期內趕上、超越美國，並取而代之成為世界經濟首席國家。

近現代的中國人向西方拜師取經，在學習西方的過程中逐漸長大成熟。可是，西方現存流行的、通用的所有知識和智慧儲備，適合西方社會運作的理論和規律卻都已經難以有效地解釋中國的發展故事。同時世界範圍之內，更是少見有能在文化層面上講清楚中國現象和中國人言行舉的。

中國人是誰，他們到底在想什麼？這事可真是有點讓人犯難犯暈，如果沒人能夠解答清楚這個基本疑問，整個世界都會擔心中國人一旦成為世界政治經濟的領頭人，將會把人類社會帶往何處去？不可否認，以美國為代表的西方社會將會第一個站起來，激烈反對中國掌舵，替換掉西方人現有的統治權地位，中國人憑什麼就能扛起領導人類世界的大旗？這恐怕是今天滿世界"中國威脅論""中國崩潰論"嚷嚷聲到處流行，並且還大有人群相信、追隨的基本原因。

"中國威脅論""中國崩潰論"，更是和"文明衝突論"糾結在一起向世界廣泛擴散傳播。不同文明之間必然發生衝突，一種處於強盛時期的文明必然殖民、擴張、稱霸，輸出自己的文化，用自己的文化來消滅、代替異己的文化。如亨廷頓說："文化幾乎總是追隨著權力。歷史上，一個文明權力的擴張通常是同時伴隨著其文化的繁榮，而這一文明幾乎總是運用它的這種權力向其他社會推行其價值觀、實踐和體制。"西方人真的非常恐懼、害怕未來的前途在他們這一代人手中失控。

西方人被驚嚇得不輕，中國人這樣成長下去，那還了得。西方人有一條自己曾經走過的發展路徑，他們認為依據自己歷史和文化知識可以解釋清楚中國，可以講明白其他歷史、文化、地域、思維方式不同的人群，和他們的行為模式。他們主觀上試圖把中國的變革和發展納入到西方曾經經歷過的"發展階段"中去，以西方人的經驗智慧論證中國崛起、復興後必然會像他們自己過去那樣殖民、擴張和稱霸。

西方人在用自己的思維方式來判定所有的"文明"形態和演進路徑，人類文明就只能是一種發展道路，也就是西方人已經走過的那條道路。西方人的判斷確實過於簡單，就只有那麼一點知識，還特別固執己見，拒絕接觸接受新知識，孤芳自賞活在西方人自己思想的小圈子裡。外人想要指望西方人講明白中國故事，恐怕是一個極難實現的奢望，西方的知識和智慧或許真的太粗淺、太簡單，太稀少，不夠用了。

馬可‧波羅的《馬可波羅遊記》、門多薩的《大中華帝國志》、金尼閣的《基督教遠征中國史》、李明的《中國現狀新志》、安遜的《世界旅行記》、杜赫德的《中華帝國通志》、松本一男的《中國人與日本人》、利瑪竇的《利瑪竇中國劄記》、亞瑟‧史密斯的《中國人的性格》都從不同側面、不同程度剖析過中國人，涉及過一些中國文化的表層現象，但從沒有講明白中國人言行舉止背後的思維邏輯和哲學依據。

當然，中國人自己也應該面壁自省，也會著急上火，至今沒有中國人站出來講明白中國文化的獨特性特徵和特點。中國本土學者中嚴複、林語堂、魯迅、柏楊、金紫千等人也曾經努力過描述中國人的國民性格，可是外界的疑慮始終存在，世界仍然不理解中國，或者說不夠理解中國。

世界對中國的"不理解"並不一定都是負面的"誤解"，而是說，對中國的"負面誤讀"依然長時期存在，但更普遍的現象是，目前世界仍然缺乏對中國全面正確的認識。世界沒有多少人看懂、看透中國，中國人也會置疑自己有何德、何能去領導人類世界，除非你講清楚、闡述得讓人明白，讓人心服口服。

講清楚中國人的思維模式和群體行為，是一個巨大的挑戰。說句公道話，準確地講解、釋疑中國人從來就不是一件容易的事情，想要完全地理解中國文化更是困難重重。從前，沒人講或沒人講明白中國人，問題還不是很嚴重，畢竟中國人自己被地理環境圈圍起來生活，走出去迎進來都不容易。對外即使有聯系，也不太多，規模和範圍影響有限。

千百年來，中國人自己過日子沒事，你只要照本宣科循規蹈矩，按照前人足跡前行，在相對封閉的自然環境中自我發展便心滿意足，倒也相安無事。但是，當今全球化情形之下，假若再沒有人講，或再沒人講明白中國人，問題就會很突出、很麻煩，甚至有些衝突加劇、升級，因為全世界許多人不知道、不清楚，疑慮人類未來的合理預期。

現如今，西方人對於中國認知的最大誤區，是主觀上認定中國沒有統一的國家宗教，這對他們西方人來說太可怕了。環顧世界其他國家，絕大多數國家都有一種主流宗教。歐美國家信奉基督教、猶太教或天主教；中亞、西亞、北非國家普遍信仰伊斯蘭教。

泰國、緬甸、斯里蘭卡等一些東南亞、南亞國家信仰佛教；日本多數國民信仰神道教；唯有中國人信什麼教的都有，遇到誰相信誰，什麼都信等同於什麼都不相信。如果一個民族沒有自己的宗教信仰，這個民族的靈魂就會不受宗教戒律的約束，容易走火入魔，做出難以想象的惡劣行為，最終釀成人禍。

俗話講"山外有山，樓外有樓"，西方人可是欠少見識，多慮而已。其實中國人從來就不缺失宗教信仰，只是信仰崇拜的與西方人不太一樣。西方人從來就沒有真正走入中國人的心裡，讀懂中國文化，從來也沒有意識到中國人求學大自然，參學大自然中的具體對象群完全不同於西方。

人類生存在地球之上，生態圈系統中有許多知識和智慧來源地，其中包括生物鏈（食物鏈）系統，水循環系統，波循環系統，光循環系統，磁場能量系統。面對眾多參學模仿對象，中國人主要傾向于從水循環系統中學習知識，獲取本民族傳統文化的智慧靈感，提取哲學倫理精華；同時，也從動植物那裡學習生存繁衍知識，和提升效率的各種技術手段。

中國人講水，拜水為師，做學問是認真的。中國哲學聖賢老子在講述自然規律"道"時，這樣描述說："上善若水，水善利萬物而不爭，處眾人之所惡，故幾於道"（老子《道德經第八章》）。最高境界的善行，就像水的品性一樣，上善至善完美；水善於滋潤萬物而不與萬物相爭名利，停留在眾人都不喜歡的地方。所以，水最接近於"道"。

中國人的認知中，自然規律"道"早已不再是一個虛無的概念幻覺。"水"在中國人的現實生活中，成了大"道"，或自然規律的化身。老子用"道"形容自然規律，又創造性地用有感知的"水"來描述、體認難以感知的自然規律。全世界所有人要明白一個事實，在中國人心底裡始終有他們自己一以貫之的堅持，虔誠懷揣信仰"水是萬事萬物之源"，"水幾近於道"。

水，是中國人的宗教信仰；道，是中國人的宗教信仰；自然天地中的所有規律集成，才是中國人真實的宗教信仰。中國人心悅誠服於"道"，誠服于"水"，尊敬大自然，尊重大自然規律，遵從天地自然法則，拜水為老師，從學習、研究、探求水的品德和水的性格之中得到啟發，中華民族世代持久模仿水，參學水，實踐水5000年不斷，是師從"水"教導成長起來的民族。

國人群體行為

1. 像水那樣游走四方，中國人滿世界安家落户。

中國人天生就是這樣一群人，愛好闖蕩江湖，愛好結交朋友，愛好體驗生活，樂意走遍天底下所有地方，四海為家。今天，你可以發現在尼羅河，愛琴海，阿爾卑斯山，亞馬遜河，大堡礁，挪威峽灣，中央洛磯山脈，以及南極洲和北極點，到處都是中國人的身影。你只要能夠在外面的世界立足腳根，事業和家庭有成，都是好樣的，值得全族家人讚許，大可以風風光光，衣錦還鄉，光宗耀祖。

2004 年的夏季，我的一位記者朋友李先生，與另二位新華社記者一起，跟隨中國"雪龍號"科考船考查南極洲，航行途中路經巴西亞遜第二大城市克阿裡。按照職業習慣，記者們相約一起上岸尋找網吧發稿。

在當地熱心人的指引下，他們終於找到了一家小網吧。這是一個讓人頭疼的網吧，網速慢得驚人，時不時斷線，就在他們上網的時候，出現了一個壯碩的亞洲男人面孔，徑直來到一台機器前安靜地上網。李先生隨口說，"來了一個日本人"，沒想到那人抬起頭說"是中國人"，是熟悉的中國話。

這位鄧先生來自臺灣，來克阿裡 10 個月了，之前在聖保羅。他們一家很早從臺灣來巴西謀生，一家子都是醫生。10 個月前，鄧先生和妻子還有兩個孩子來到克阿裡，在一家公立醫院做外科醫生。他介紹，這個城市只有 5 個亞洲人，除了他們一家四口，還有一個日本人。

記者三人好生驚奇，和鄧先生聊了好久，紛紛感歎中國人的開拓、生存能力，因為亞馬遜沿途很多土著人都因為受不了自然條件的惡劣和蚊蟲的叮咬，已經紛紛搬到城市裡去了，而中國人依然向縱深內陸挺進。鄧先生他很喜歡克阿裡的寧靜和純樸民風，以及生活工作現狀。分手告別時，大家互道珍重。真是應了那句老話，有人的地方就有中國人，沒想到在這麼偏僻的地方還能遇見故鄉人。

自然界中，水可以想去任何一個地方，水也可以去到任何一個地方，水更可以滲透到任何它想要去的地方。全世界有了這樣的驚奇發現：有水的地方就有中國人，滿世界見到中國人安家落戶的蹤影足跡。

2. 像水那樣滋養萬物，中國人熱衷賺錢。

中國人天生就是這樣一群人，本能地喜歡財富，拼命賺錢，熱愛攢錢。無論生存環境、生活環境優劣好壞如何，始終認為賺取錢財是人生最基本的第一要事，他們永遠把掙錢養家放在生活的第一位置，其他東西可以暫時擱置一旁，甚至不問不理。擁有錢財的絕對重要性超過其他一切事項。5000 年來，中國人憑藉吃苦耐勞，親力親為和勤奮努力的幹勁，用自己的雙手辛勤勞作，創造財富，積累財富，世代傳承財富。

2009 年 11 月，新加坡內閣資政李光耀參加亞太經合組織工商領導人峰會，李光耀在與美國《時代》週刊國際版編輯邁克爾·伊里亞德交流時，談及西方指責中國"它不是民主體制"時，他埋怨西方根本不懂東方中國，說中國人希望更好的生活，而不是選票，中國也許沒有民主制度，但中國人目前對提高生活水準比對選票和言論自由更感興趣。

李光耀示說：「中國人對民主體制不感興趣。」他解釋，在中國人努力追趕世界的過程中，他們主要關心的是實現他們在亞洲更發達的經濟體看到的生活水準。他進一步說：「你有你們的民主活動人士，但中國人擔心自己的投票權和言論自由嗎？他們想過上在香港、新加坡和金融危機之前的臺灣看到的生活。」

中國領導層的遠見也同樣讓李光耀印象深刻。在被問及是否贊同美國國家經濟委員會負責人拉裡·薩默斯所謂中國正在規劃 20 年以後的事情時，李光耀說：「比 20 年更遠。他們正在為下一代規劃。」他指出，中國已經有了下一代領導人的人選，「這不是依據選民一時興致隨意做出的選擇，而是在他們稱之為中紀委的機構的嚴格監督之下形成的。

這是一個令人印象深刻的制度。」李光耀先生所言真實貼切，他的潛臺詞是：中國人最關心賺錢，而不是其他。他們正在專心孜孜地規劃長期，超長期經濟發展大計，加速財富積累。中國人什麼活都可以幹，只要能賺錢。沒有錢掙的活，中國人是最不願意搭理的。絕大多數的中國人沒日沒夜忙於拼命賺錢，目的只有一個，都是為了獲取一個更富足的物質生活基礎。

大自然中，萬物生長不能沒有水，人類生活中，時時刻刻離不開金銀錢財的陪伴支撐。人世間財富的功能，就如同自然界水的功能一樣，重要且不可或缺。全世界有了這樣一個奇妙發現：中國人特別喜歡錢，能賺錢，愛攢錢。

3. 像水那樣循環往返，中國人特別想家戀鄉。

世界上，每個民族每個人都愛戀自己的家鄉和國家。但是，沒有一個民族，可以像中國人那樣戀家，思戀自己的出生地、所屬國如此深情狂熱。中國人天生就是這樣一群人，窮盡一生一世戀家思鄉。「遊子思歸、落葉歸根、衣錦還鄉」，是我們中國人骨子裡最深切、最濃郁、最真摯的一種情結。正是這種戀家的情結，魂牽著一代又一代異客遊子思鄉的神經。

1956 年 4 月，中華民國前副總統李宗仁先生面對毛澤東的直言勸誡「愛國一家、愛國不分先後，以誠相見，來去自由」，以及「四可」意見：「李先生可以回來在祖國定居；可以回來，也可以再去美國；可以在歐洲暫住一個時期再定行止；回來以後可以再出去，如果還願意回來，可以再回來。總之，來去自由，沒有約束。」後斷然表示說：「我們不能再像斷了線的風箏似地，浮萍浪跡，飄泊西東。樹高千尺，葉落歸根。我是中國人，一定要回中國去，在祖國的土地上尋找我最後的歸宿。」

「我總不能把這把老骨頭拋在異國他鄉啊。人到晚年，更加思念父母之邦。蔣介石那個所謂的中國，是與我無緣的。我如今悔之太晚。我最大的錯誤，就是與蔣介石決裂得太晚。

一時猶疑，錯失良機，釀成千古之恨。宗仁老矣，但我還要回去，回到祖國去，現在亡羊補牢，還尚有殘年。"1965 年 7 月 18 日零點 30 分，一架波音 707 客機從巴基斯坦卡拉奇起飛，衝破漫漫黑夜，搭載著李宗仁拳拳愛國之心，飛向祖國。

1969 年 1 月 30 日午夜 12 時，李宗仁在生命彌留之際，堅持口述了一封給毛澤東和周恩來的信："我在 1965 年毅然從海外回到祖國，所走的這一條路是走對了。在這個偉大的時代，我深深地感到能成為中國人民的一分子是一個無比的光榮。在我快要離開人世的最後一刻，我還深以留在臺灣和海外的國民黨人和一切愛國的知識份子的前途為念。他們目前只有一條路，就是同我一樣回到祖國懷抱。"

水，不論流經多遠飄流多久飛離多高，走再遠的路也要義無反顧地回到它的起始點，回到它的老家出發地，然後再重新集合開拔，開始一輪新的循環。現實中，中國人愛水愛得深沉，愛得迷戀，他們離鄉之痛、思鄉之苦、戀家之切的感情往往比其他國家族裔來得更加深遠綿長。全世界有了這樣的驚奇發現：中國人就是特別的思鄉、特別的戀家，和特別的熱愛自己的國家。

4. 像水那樣謙卑無爭，中國人愛好低調。

中國人天生就是這樣一群人，從小就受教於長輩們的諄諄訓導："夾著尾巴做人，人怕出名豬怕壯，槍打出頭鳥"；做人做事要低調，隱忍不張揚。山不解釋自己的高度，並不影響它的聳立雲端；海不解釋自己的深度，並不影響它容納百川；地不解釋自己的厚度，並沒有誰能取代她作為承載萬物的地位；人不吹捧自己的天賦，並不影響人類處於生物鏈頂端的現實尊貴。

針對全球熱議美國未來學家約翰・奈斯比特 2009 年出版的《中國大趨勢》，以及英國學者馬丁・雅克 2010 年出版《當中國統治世界》現象時，中國時任外交部長李肇星先生冷靜地評論說："不必總談大國崛起，還是應該低調做事。"意在提醒中國人既要看到我們發展的成就，更要正視我們所處的現狀；既要堅定自信，又不能盲目自大。

關於"中國崛起"話題，我們無法阻止別人說好話，關鍵在於我們如何對待和評價自己。一個不太妙的現象是，聽了國外這些吹捧，國內某些人真患上了天真爛漫的幼稚病，自高自傲起來。就是我國崛起了，也不足以自大驕傲。經濟上是這樣，軍事上也是如此。如果我們自己同自己比，經濟、國防、科技力量確已有了長足的發展，但與發達資本主義國家，特別是與美國比，尚有一大段差距。

倘若我們真正崛起到強盛之地，周邊一些國家甚至小國就不敢強佔我領土和島嶼，就不會依恃某個超級大國在我家門口窮兵黷武。中國人民應時刻保持清醒的頭腦，居安思危，加快發展，使我們在維護世界和平，捍衛領土完整，推進祖國統一大業上實現真正的"大國崛起"和"民族復興"。李肇星的一席話，道出了中國國人的心聲。

水，處下不爭。水有滋養萬物的品行，水從容地澤惠萬物，幫助萬物生靈茁壯成長，卻從來不去爭名奪利，不計回報，默默無私地奉獻心力，低調付出是"水"的至高品行。全世界有了這樣的新奇發現，中國人特別感佩和推崇低調做人。

5. 像水那樣拒絕常形，中國人欣賞變化。

中國人天生就是這樣一群人，面對變化從來不懼怕，坦然直面變化，欣然接受變化，巧妙把握變化於股掌之中。兵無常勢，水無常形。以靜制動，以動制靜，以此動靜制衡彼動靜。"上有政策下有對策"，"走一步看一步"，"兵來將擋，水來土掩。"不管外界發生什麼樣的情況變化，對方使用什麼樣的手段變化，中國人總會找到相適應的對付方法，解決問題。

人稱"何伯"的香港煙草公司董事長、著名慈善家何英傑先生一生低調神秘，其廬山真面目，一向鮮為人知。祖籍江蘇無錫的何伯，少年時代的他對機械產生濃厚興趣，9歲入學，但14歲時輟學，進入家族的印刷廠當學徒。他憑著年輕人的幹勁，在短短兩年間，學會了畫石、拼版、印刷等整套工藝技術，16歲時已擔任家族印刷廠的經理了。

勤奮好學，是他走向成功的基礎。他18歲結婚，20歲以2000元自立門戶，創立了上海新亞印刷廠。抗日戰爭中人們大都逃難去了，工人及技術人員大量缺乏，他卻在堅守，使新亞印刷廠成為那時上海唯一開門營業的印刷廠，經營利潤也相對提高了10倍。何伯在短短一年時間，僅經營紙張就賺了數十萬元。這時，他已有自己的投資策略，有意開辦香煙廠。

1942年，何伯在上海創立香煙廠，第一個牌子"高樂"十分暢銷，於是他不斷擴大投資規模和其它的業務領域。第二次世界大戰結束後，36歲的他，親赴英國訂購先進的捲煙機，1949年運抵香港，正式創立了他的香港煙草公司。半個世紀以來，，何伯的事業由印刷至紙張，由紙張至香煙、由香煙又發展至金融投資業務，其範圍遍佈香港和美加地區。

自然界中的水，是最善於變化的物質。"逝者如斯夫，不舍晝夜。"水最善於隨勢而動、順勢而為，適應外在環境的變化。水之靈動善變，或藏於地下含而不露，或噴湧而上清澈為泉，水少則叮咚自樂，水多則奔騰豪邁。

水處天地之間，動靜皆宜，進入山間成澗、成溪、成江河，匯入窪地成池成潭、成湖成海。水，柔軟親和，剛柔相濟、以柔克剛，變化無常。全世界有了這樣的特別發現：中國人特別的擅長變化，愉快研習並適應世界的千變萬化。

6. 像水那樣知恩感恩，中國人竭力踐行忠孝。

中國人天生就是這樣一群人，對國家盡忠職守，對家庭盡孝幫扶。忠孝思想主宰了中國人幾千年，它是維繫國家和家庭不可或缺的紐帶，是中華民族獨具的智慧生存方式。在中國文化思維中，人與人不僅具有同類的血脈親緣關係，也具有從天道秉承而來的道德親緣關係，這是彼此能夠仁愛忠誠而和諧相處的哲學基礎。"忠孝"基礎上擴展而來的仁愛、忠義價值觀，構建起中國"大一統"社會超穩定機制的道德框架。

每年，中國有一個重要節日—清明節。清明節是中華民族生命精神集中體現的日子，表現著炎黃子孫崇敬先人、仰慕古賢的民族精神。清明節讓我們每一個人都意識到：我們有共同的祖先，我們的血管裡流著相同的血。

清明節大約始于周代，至今已有 2500 多年歷史，自唐德宗年間（西元 790 年）開始，清明節就有放假祭拜的制度，呈現官民共度的盛況。清明節日體現飲水思源、凝聚族群、迎春健身及關愛自然的意義。其內容主要包括：墓祭、食青團、楊柳插棗、踏青植樹、戴柳賞花、放風箏、蕩秋千、農事、寫詩賦文等。

清明節，中國人不辭辛苦地返鄉祭奠祖先、緬懷先人，在莊嚴肅穆的祭祀活動中，生命血緣的鏈條依次由活著的個體生命、家庭生命聯上已故去的家族、氏族生命，形成了中華民族認祖歸宗的紐帶，沉澱為個人道德涵育，家庭、家族團結，國家統一的重要基礎。所以，清明節是中國人通過祭祀先人，叩拜先賢，緬懷先烈而折射出另一個生命主題：追思感恩。

"清明時節雨紛紛，路上行人欲斷魂。借問酒家何處有？牧童遙指杏花村。"唐代詩人杜牧的《七絕·清明》詩，勾畫出了一幅美麗的水墨畫，春雨、牧童、酒家，詩人匆匆的步履牽引著清明節的詩情。今天的清明節，依然在人們的日常生活中佔有著重要的位置。感恩前輩，紀念先人，慎終追遠，展望未來。

大自然的水，有來有去運動不息，循環不止輪迴永恆。它是自然界中忠於職守，履行"忠孝"的模範典型。無論水處在世界任何一個地方，或者以任何一種形式存在，它最終總是不忘以降水的形式回到大地，回到它無私奉獻心力的地方，滋潤大地養育萬物，從來沒有一句怨言，從來不敢有半點懈怠。全世界有了這樣的獨特發現：中國人特別推崇、堅持奉行忠孝。

7. 像水那樣結伴同行，中國人喜歡聚集紮堆熱鬧。

中國人天生就是這樣一群人，特別喜歡熱鬧，特別喜歡聚集在一起，歡天喜地無拘無束地鬧騰。通常，中國人參加各種宴會、活動、或外出旅行，總是偏愛結伴，尋找熟知的同伴，並迅速紮堆組成一個小團體，這樣他們才有安全感，才可談吐自如談笑風生。相反，中國人則會感覺到絲絲緊張、孤獨、無聊和不自在。

王竹傑，1984年移民加拿大，在那裡蹲了六年"移民監"，"刑滿釋放"就去了香港，後來又搬回到北京，然後就徹底沒有再回過加拿大。說起在北京的"重生"經歷，老王眉飛色舞地搶詞申述，中國人是個群居的民族，喜歡熱鬧紮堆，注重家庭和人情往來，崇尚四世同堂、兒女繞膝。

西方人特立獨行，各過各的，似乎少了中國人那樣的人情味，咱爺們從來就不習慣。在北京，有多少親朋好友，每週都要有幾次聚餐，或請客，或被人請，吃吃喝喝，熱熱鬧鬧，家長里短，談笑風生。中國人總是喜歡找個理由要請客吃飯，或者找個理由讓別人請客吃飯，總是在動腦子找樂子盤算、琢磨誰又欠了誰的一頓飯，或一次約會，索要一個聚在一起的機會。

吃，在中國是一大文化現象，中國人的這種集體吃喝的民族嗜好，已經不單純是為了滿足口腹之欲，而就是創造一個大家聚在一起說笑的機會，而邊吃邊侃是最有興致的人生趣事之一。中國人不僅喜歡聚餐，串門也比西方人多。今晚你來我家串門，明天我找個理由回訪。這就是中國人，有閑就串門、聚會、嘮嗑、熱鬧，聯絡和增加彼此感情。

西方人則比較注重個人獨處，他們寧可在家讀書、上網、冥想、看電視，也不會出門和人吃喝、侃大山的。中國人就是一個喜歡群居，喜歡熱鬧的民族，幾千年的留下的習慣活法，本性難改，當然也沒必要去更改。

自然界中的水，自從以降水的形式降落地面以後，本就以獨立形態，自由散居於大地任何一個角落，愉快滋養萬物。但是，水從來不滿足現狀，它要做更多的事情，水聚集在一起形成規模，才可能做大事。

水分佈散落四方各處，卻永遠聚焦同一個目標，結伴成千上萬細流，彙集湧入江河湖泊，向東直奔大海。一路做大、做強形成規模效能。全世界有這樣的發現：中國人特別維護"集聚"，從內心深處喜歡"集體主義"。

8. 像水那樣不偏不倚，中國人信奉中庸之道。

中國人天生就是這樣一群人，喜歡佔據中間位置。無論上下左右前後，東西南北，居中的位置最可靠、最安全、最靈活，去到哪個方向距離都最短，攻守兼備進退有據，可以全面合理地把握掌控大局和事業進程。

中國人堅守中庸之道，持中而有度，防止"過"與"不及"兩種非理想狀態。中庸之道，就是要避免"過"與"不及"兩種極端，將"不及"者補之，將"過"者去之，從而使事物不偏不倚，恰到好處。中庸之道強調事物平和的性質、處事方法的適度，以及運用這種方法時所必須具備的靈活性。

有一天，孔子的弟子子夏問老師："顏回這人怎麼樣啊？"孔子說："顏回呀，他在誠信上超過我。"子夏又問："子貢這人怎麼樣啊？"孔子回答說："子貢在敏捷上超過我。"子夏又問："子路這人怎麼樣啊？"孔子回答說："子路在勇敢上超過我。"子夏又問："子張這人怎麼樣啊？"孔子回答說："子張在莊重上超過我。"子夏站起身，問孔子說："那麼這四位為什麼都拜您作老師呢？"

孔子說："坐下吧，我告訴你。顏回雖然誠信，卻不知道還有不能講誠信的時候；子貢雖然敏捷，卻不知道還有說話不能太伶牙俐齒的時候；子路雖然勇敢，卻不知道還有應該害怕的時候；子張雖然莊重，卻不知道還有應該詼諧親密的時候。所以，他們才認我作老師啊！"

所以，避走極端路，堅守中道是正道。

自然界中的水在運動循環過程中，秉承公平、持中、守正原則，從不偏袒、不偏幫自然界中任何一方，始終居中對待世間萬物，養育滋潤萬物成長。零度或零度以下，水結成固體冰，是水的一種極端；百度或百度以上，水蒸發成氣體，是水的另一種極端；0-100度之間，水呈常態液體，是水的居中守正位置。

水處常溫，居中維持液體狀態，最大限度的無私滋潤大地，養育世間萬物。全世界有了這樣的獨特發現：中國人特別擅長"中庸之道"，不偏不倚不左不右，折衷調和避走極端。

9. 像水那樣無眠無休，中國人熱愛辛勤工作。

中國人天生就是這樣一群人，酷愛勞動喜歡工作。國人辛勤工作的熱情程度，絕非其他民族可以想像，可以比較高低的。不誇張地說，中國人最勤奮節儉，最具有吃苦精神。而勤勞致富精神，是當今世界最值得廣泛尊敬的美德之一。

"中國員工是勤勞的世界冠軍"。據德國媒體報導,著名市場調研機構 GfK 曾經對德國和其他 7 個國家的 8000 名員工進行了一項名為"哪個國家的員工最勤勞"的問卷調查,結果顯示,中國員工公認為最勤勞"。"你們中國人真勤勞!"一個外國友人說。"何以見得?"中國人好奇地反問。老外認真地說:"我觀察過了,大街上 5、6 點鐘就有人忙活了,可你們還嫌不夠早,連每天的早餐場所,都要樹立標牌,拼命催人趕吃早點。"

雖是一句調侃的話,但中國人的勤勞並不是自吹自誇的。"業精於勤""百種弊病,皆從懶生"時刻警醒提示國人,不得偷懶偷生。勤勞,已經是中國人有別于他人的醒目標籤,甚至是融入中國人血液之中的"基因"。中國人的勤勞可謂有目共睹,舉世聞名。

中國人似乎是為勤奮而生,為工作而樂的一個族群。中國人的勤勞,是一種最古老的"植物",不僅隨著時光的流逝,從遙遠的古代傳承至今,散發奇異的芳香;也伴著華人的腳步,從中華大地流轉世界各地,在異國他鄉綻放出神奇的光芒。世界上任何一個民族都是勤勞的,但中華民族的勤勞無疑是超越於其他各民族之上的。

世界上很多種族都是勤奮的,但中國人的勤奮無論在強度,還是在長度;無論在地域分佈,還是在世代傳承都是無可比擬的。全世界一致地認為,無與倫比的堅韌和無可比擬的勤勞,是中國人獨具的高尚品德。

自然界中,水循環是一個永不停息的動態運動系統,在太陽的作用下,海洋表面的水,蒸發到大氣中形成水汽,水汽隨大氣環流運動,一部分進入陸地上空,在一定條件下形成雨雪降落;大氣降水到達地面後,再轉化為地下水、土壤水和地表徑流。地下徑流和地表徑流最終又回流到海洋,由此形成淡水的動態循環,周而復始循環不止,日夜不停歇地奔流運作。

10. 像水那樣平等處世,中國人主張尊重彼此。

中國人天生就是這樣一群人,傾心於彼此禮讓,彼此尊重。"己所不欲,勿施於人"是國人千百年來的自覺主張和自我要求。自己不願做的事,不想做的事,不能做的事,以及做了也做不成的事,就別指望或打算強迫別人去做。做任何事,都要推己及人,將心比心,不要強人所難,更不要給別人造成傷害。人與人之間的交往應該堅持尊重他人,平等待人。

和平共處五項原則是由中國政府提出,並與印度和緬甸政府共同宣導的在建立各國間正常關係及進行交流合作時應遵循的基本原則。

1954 年 6 月 25 日,中國的周恩來總理對印度和緬甸進行了訪問。訪問印度期間,他同印度總理尼赫魯舉行了會談,兩國總理發表聯合聲明,重申了兩國簽訂的《關於中國西藏地方和印度之間的通商和交通協定》中所規定的兩國之間關係的五項原則：互相尊重領土主權；互不侵犯；互不干涉內政；平等互利；和平共處。聲明指出，這些原則不僅適用于中印兩國之間的關係，而且也適用於一般的國際關係問題。兩國總理特別希望運用這些原則來解決印度支那問題。

6月28日至29日，周恩來訪問緬甸，同緬甸聯邦總理吳努舉行了會談，並發表聯合聲明，同意和平共處五項原則也是指導中緬關係的原則。中印和中緬總理的歷史性會談和聯合聲明的發表，得到了亞洲和世界各國人民的讚揚。

全世界每個民族和國家都有這樣一個共識和期許，尊重和被尊重，理解和被理解。國家和國家之間，民族和民族之間不能以大小、強弱、貧富區別對待，應該平等相待互相尊重。故此，全世界發現中國人不遺餘力地主張"尊重彼此"，維護和推進世界文化的多樣性。

自然界中的水，謙卑平和知性隨意，不擺架子不鬧脾氣。雖然，水是所有生命體的源頭，締造了這個世界，創造出了世間萬千生物。然而，水卻從來沒有打算居功自傲，從來沒有打算針對誰去指手劃腳，也從來沒有準備呼風喚雨狂傲自大。水，永遠懷揣謙卑和感恩之心，一視同仁善待所有生命物質，服務世界上的所有一切生物。

11. 像水那樣剛柔並濟，中國人主張軟硬並舉。

中國人天生就是這樣一群人，採取"中庸"的同時，從沒有忘記有軟硬兩手，軟硬兼施剛柔並濟。軟硬兩手應該一起抓，不能一手軟一手硬。有時則軟的更軟，硬的更硬，軟硬兩手擇時用力，時硬時軟，時軟時硬，軟中帶硬，硬中帶軟，軟硬兩手交替互助，恰到好處運用軟硬兩手技法，謀取理想的"中庸"效果，相當的靈驗。

越南為在南海問題上對抗中國，斥鉅資採購了戰機和潛艇等先進武器。越南自認為，在南海之爭中的優勢是在家門口作戰。越南裝備導彈的艦艇和潛艇攻擊之後就能退回基地，遠途而來的中國艦隊則可能進退失據。越南不必跟中國軍艦一對一地比拼，而可將其越戰中應用自如的遊擊戰術拿到海上，有可能在潛在對華衝突中佔據優勢。

現代戰爭是立體的戰爭，若中越之間爆發南海戰爭，怎麼會是遊擊戰那般小打小鬧。戰爭初始，越南的機場、港口、水力、電力和軍事基地將不保，遭到來自對方空中和海上的飽和打擊，徹底癱瘓越南的空軍和海軍。再者，奪取越南非法開採的大批油井，一舉收回其非法霸佔的29個南海島嶼。越南打算在南海玩"硬"耍流氓，中國就以更加強硬的一手回應。

中國人參學水的軟硬兩種特質，模仿吸收靈活應用。軟有軟的功效，硬有硬的特點。

實施軟和硬，要根據不同的時間、不同的環境，和不同的情形，針對具體情況採取相適應的手段解決問題。沒有固化的對錯舉措，最終結果則必須合乎目標要求。全世界發現中國人沒事不惹事，有事真不怕事；中國人不好戰，也不懼戰；中國人強勢，但不強硬，主張建立高壓強勢"不戰而屈人之兵"。

水，是剛柔兩性的結合體，剛強與柔軟同存於一個物體之中。以零度為界限，零度之上，水呈現出柔軟親和的一面，熱情歡愉友好；零度之下，水呈現出剛毅堅強的另外一面，冷靜果斷決然。水，亦柔亦剛，剛中有柔，柔中有剛，剛柔並濟，柔終克剛，剛柔互動轉化，變化無窮。

12. 像水那樣天然本色，中國人喜好純粹純真。

中國人天生就是這樣一群人，喜歡原始本色和簡單真在的東西，最愛土地和房屋。一件物品，原來長什麼樣就該是什麼樣，喜歡也就喜歡那種天然原始的模樣。既然是天然渾成的本色物品，就有其存在的合適理由，沒有必要試圖去阻止或改變，惟有積極去適應順應並尊重珍惜。原始本色從來就是一種簡單，一種真實，和一種現實存在。

西方人一般很難理解中國買家對房子的熱情。在中國人的觀念裡，有房子才有根，而且凡事都講究擁有。香港恒基地產主席李兆基曾用"女人買手袋"來比喻中國內地客人到香港買樓的心態："豪爽客買樓不貴不買，不靚不買，不是名牌不買，就好像女人買手袋，要買幾十萬元一個的才高興，幾百元的根本看不上眼！"

根據跨國房地產及資本管理公司仲量聯行的統計數字顯示，目前香港 1000 萬港元豪宅的 20% 被內地有錢人買走，2000 萬港元豪華大宅中內地買家約佔 30%，5000 萬港元豪宅佔 40%，一億港元以上的豪宅 70% 被內地富人買走。香港地產仲介公司中原集團老闆施永青慨歎說"香港樓市已不是 700 萬人的市場，而是全國 13 億人口的市場。"

中國人的衣服，最好是要純毛的、純麻的、純絲的、純棉的、純絨的；房子，最好是自家擁有的；黃金白銀要 100% 成色的。中國人還喜歡完整原本的形象，上桌食品講究個"全"字，全羊全豬、全魚全蝦、全雞全鴨全鵝，有頭有尾有始有終。

更有甚者，中國人還對天然的，有點份量的器件物品懷有好感，他們熱衷收藏金銀、玉石、沉香、甲骨、紅木、翡翠、樹根、瓷器、甚至文玩核桃，世代相傳，樂此不疲。全世界終於明白國人對原始的、本真的、純天然的東西有一種與生俱來的好感。

自然界中的水分子，結構小而簡單。兩個氫原子加一個氧原子，鍵合粘在一起形成一個水分子，簡單到不能再簡單。然而，水的原始本色作用卻不簡單，實用萬能、多元複雜且不可替代。

水是地球和我們體內最豐富的物質，一個成年人體內的 70% 是水，而嬰兒體重的 90% 是水。對於人體而言，水參與生命的運動，排除體內有害毒素，幫助新陳代謝，維持有氧呼吸，保持體內溫度。水的作用與功能是最原始，最基本的，獨一無二的物質。

13. 像水那樣前呼後擁，中國人採納跟隨前行。

中國人天生就是一群注重規避風險的人，一般比較保守，不喜歡高調冒頭，情願採取跟跑前行的策略，山寨模仿他人，不願創新探險。在一個集體中，個人被要求與集體保持一致，如果出現不一致，個人則被要求調整個體的行為，以配合服從整體的意志和利益。因此，集體總是用統一標準要求其所有成員。

據說在馬德里市中心 TIRSO DE MOLINA 市場中，以一家華人店鋪為中心，半徑 20 米內，至少有五家以上同類型的商鋪。如果說，商品分門別類之後能有所區別，生意還是有的做的，但問題就是商品雷同、經營模式雷同，甚至擺設都雷同，千篇一律造成了大家都慘淡經營的現狀。從前跟風紮堆是為了抱團賺錢，現在紮堆是為了搶生意。都賣一樣的貨，市場越來越小。

在 TIRSO DE MOLINA 開餐館的一位華人老闆說，"現在這條華人批發街沒有競爭力了，根基不深的商家差不多都撤出這個地區，能堅持下來的大多是有實力有資本的華商。TIRSO DE MOLINA 華人批發街早就失去往日的繁榮，從門庭若市到如今門可羅雀，真是慘淡經營"。

中國人特別喜歡借力使力，水到渠成。根據力學的原理，領跑者承受的阻力，要遠遠大於緊跟在領跑者身後的跟跑者，跟跑者明顯佔領跑者的便宜。跟隨潮流而動相對省時省力。"長江後浪推前浪，前浪死在沙灘上。"

大多數中國人寧願跟跑而非領跑，寧做鳳尾不做雞頭。況且，相關數字表明，原始創新成功率是 26%，而模仿創新成功率則是 90%，這就是中國人潛意識中的後發優勢。採納跟隨跟進策略，既可以最大限度保障生命安全，又可以輕鬆獲取跟隨紅利，何樂而不為？全世界終於明白，中國人特別喜歡跟隨跟進，後發而動穩獲收益。

自然界中的水，在上游的水源地自由自在，愜意輕鬆獨立歡愉。一旦準備出發參加長途旅行時，它便自覺自願放棄自我，結伴拉伙投入大河大江的懷抱，從上游出發，一路向下緊隨前行，河水沿途不斷吸引新的加入者，自由奔流前呼後擁，逐浪奔流千百里直至匯入大海，跟從隨從不用費多大的勁。

14. 像水那樣川流不息，中國人重視長期計畫。

中國人天生就是這樣一群人，喜歡從長計議。國人發現和解決問題，有其非常成熟老道的一套方法。凡事遵守祖宗誡言"兵者，國之大事，死生之地，存亡之道，不可不察也。"小心處理行事。謹慎穩妥，當心一著不慎滿盤皆輸。中國人遇事，傾向制定個長期計畫解決問題，他們更樂意耐心穩妥地努力，一點一滴扎實推動，他們更善於謀略和從長計議，做長遠計畫並將其付諸實施到底。

中國現正在著手制定導彈擊潰外敵海軍來犯的長期計畫，重在防範域外大國在本地區的潛在破壞威脅，挑拔是非無端生事渾水摸魚。中國並不具備能力在航母戰鬥群、驅逐艦、戰鬥機方面，直接與西方大國比試數量優勢，但卻在認真琢磨計畫，擁有數百枚、數千枚遠端彈道導彈和反艦巡航導彈，對在距中國海岸線約 1000 公里內執行任務的外敵水面艦艇構成的直接阻遏。

同時，中國正在試圖建立了一個日益複雜的雷達、聲呐和偵察衛星網路，用來跟蹤外國海軍部隊，限制他們在西太平洋的行動能力。避短揚長，你打你的，我打我的，打得贏就打，打不贏就走，變換打法纏鬥對手。中國人民解放軍在沒有完全取勝把握的情況下，不準備謀求在航母、艦艇或飛機品質上與強國較量，而是謹慎地將資源集中於導彈發展和採購，以在西太平洋獲得對敵國海空軍部隊的獨特優勢。待時機成熟，再爭取軍事的全面性壓倒優勢。

自然界中的水流，從高山峻嶺中流向山間，在山間夾縫處彙集成小溪，成百成千條小溪再集合成大江大河，沖下平原奔湧向海，連綿不斷川流不息，源源不絕源遠流長。水循環系統自身有一套監管監查機制，跟隨季節變化，適時補充水源地水量供應，形成長期有效機制，供給淡水資源給大地，滋養生物靈動生命。

中國人從水循環機制體系中獲取靈感。一旦確立方向認准目標，明確一條貫穿全盤進退的主要路線之後，便落實制定一個可執行的中長期行動計畫。隨後，就是持之以恆地貫徹執行，必要時修正以後再重新執行，直至成果收穫。全世界終於發現，中國人鍾情制定長期計畫，穩妥操作，穩步進取。

15. 像水那樣明鏡映月，中國人酷愛臉門面子。

中國人天生就是這樣一群人，喜歡講究面子。愛面子，是中國人重要的心理特徵之一。人有臉，樹有皮；人活一張臉，樹活一張皮。坐奔馳車比坐奧迪有面子、坐奧迪車比坐桑塔納車有面子；住山水別墅比住都市公寓有面子、住都市公寓比住大雜院有面子；打高爾夫球比打乒乓球有面子。人活在世上，就是圖給人留個"高大尚"的印象，讓人看得起、記得住。

隋朝大業六年元宵節，為了接待西域各國酋長和商人，充分展示大隋朝的盛威，"於（東都洛陽）端門街盛陳百戲，執絲竹者萬八千人，聲聞數十裡，自昏至旦，燈火光燭天地，終月而罷，所費巨萬。"

朝廷又有下令裝點市容，要求簷宇統一，珍貨充積，店設帷帳，人穿華服，賣菜的地方要鋪上用龍鬚草編的席子，街道兩邊的樹上也要披綢掛緞，裝扮得五彩繽紛。客人經過，酒店老闆要邀入進餐，"酒飽而散，不取其值"。還要謊稱："中國豐饒，酒席例不取值"。

史書上說，農曆正月正值北方千里冰封的時節，隋煬帝便命人用絹帛纏樹，給不明真相的客人說這是"仙晨帝所"。隋朝的中國，當時已經足夠強大富裕，根本就不用裝點門面也比潘邦小國好得多，但是卻與隋煬帝想展示給外邦人的面貌有出入，於是有了隋煬帝的"面子"工程。

中國人特別愛"面子"，"家醜不可外揚，打腫臉充胖子，打人不打臉揭人不揭短。"然而，面子這個東西，卻又無法向外國人譯解明白，無法為之準確下個定義。它似乎像是榮譽，又不完全是榮譽；它像是財富，又不準確是財富，但它比任何世俗的財產都來得寶貴。

有時，面子比命運和恩惠還要有力量，它堪比法律戒規還要受人尊敬。中國人正是相信這種門面虛榮的東西，支撐生活的方方面面，講究"面子"一生不疲。全世界終於發現，中國人如此癡情迷戀關係，人情，和臉面。

水，無色無味清澈潔靜，恰似一面映照人間自然的明鏡。一彎湖水，四周青山環抱楊柳依依，綠意盈盈翠竹吻波，湖畔岸邊群峰靜立，倒映在水中。此時此景，山是水的傍依水是山的解讀，永不停息的水景映射最是綺麗奪人，淋漓酣暢地演繹了水的靜態和動態之美感。也正是有了水，周圍的一切都為之變得靈動起來鮮活起來，美得一片迷離沉醉，讓人歎為觀止。

16. 像水那樣居後不爭，中國人信守後發制人。

中國人天生就是這樣一群人，習慣於防守在前，先禮後兵，出其不意，後發制人。智者生存需要有高超的大智慧，在運用智謀的時候，別人從小處入手，我則從大處著眼；別人從近處看，我則從遠處望；別人越是躁動紛亂，我則冷靜沉著，而事態反而能夠複歸正常；別人遇事束手無策，我則處理問題得心應手。

中國出拳回擊越南在南海無端生事。越南執意通過海洋法，企圖強化對中國西沙和南沙群島的法理聲索，越南挑釁在前。作為回應，中國民政部宣佈國務院批准設立地級三沙市以強化對西沙群島、中沙群島和南沙群島的島礁及其海域的行政管理和開發建設。

中國海洋石油總公司宣佈在靠近"九段線"的南海地區對外開放九個海上區塊供與外國公司合作勘探開發，海南省還宣佈將西沙群島的四個區域劃定為文化遺產保護區。中國海監船和漁政船組成的編隊適時起航赴南海我國主張管轄海域維權執法，常態化巡航更加有力。

同時，中國與東盟國家進一步加強高層往來和友好合作，與有關國家一道妥善處理分歧，分化、瓦解個別國家利用柬埔寨東盟系列會議、香格里拉對話會等國際場合炒作南海問題、干擾中國與東盟合作大局的企圖。

中國後發制人出拳，真正體現了有理有利有節，化被動為主動，既為維權也為維穩。中國出拳是寄希望于南海各方有所警醒，回到對話與合作的正確軌道上來，不要一味侵權，把中國的克制、忍讓誤讀為軟弱和退讓。中國並不追求在南海問題上比試誰的拳頭更硬，中國追求的是一個和平穩定的周邊環境，一個地區各國能夠集中精力發展合作的大環境。

自然界中的水，一向以禮讓謙和的姿態示人，"夫唯不爭，故天下莫能與之爭。"水，不爭利不爭功，不貪名不貪祿，惟一做的是默默奉獻；水，永遠居在最下處，永遠停留在別人不願呆的地方，全心全意地成全他人，故此受到廣泛的尊重，世界上沒有一樣東西能夠與之相比較相匹配，沒有一樣東西能夠和水相爭"上善"的地位。

中國人先禮後兵，後發制人，遇到難以調和的對立和衝突，不首先發難，不恣意挑鬥，不首先打第一槍，做到講理知禮在前，仁至義盡，後發制人，進退有道。如果"禮"不奏效，然後再起"兵"。用兵之目的，不是要武力暴力征服他人，而是要徹底制止和消除紛爭和衝突。從此，全世界終於明白，中國人固守先禮後兵，後發制人的傳統智慧。

17. 像水那樣見縫就鑽，中國人缺乏邊界意識。

中國人就是這樣一群人，缺乏公共邊界概念，難守公共規矩，缺失規則意識。在公眾場合，他們不太知道自己應該怎麼做，他們不太知道自己應該為公共事物盡哪些個人義務和責任，只顧自己方便，而不管他人有什麼樣的感受。

身在異鄉，尊重當地的風土人情，既能夠有效融入其中，為旅行帶來便利，也能夠避免摩擦省去不必要的麻煩，但部分中國人遊客似乎並不懂這些道理。在中東國家埃及，當地人抱怨一些衣著超短裙、吊帶裝的中國女遊客"穿得太少了"。對於信仰伊斯蘭教的穆斯林來說，女性在公共場合的著裝應端莊，且儘量避免裸露過多皮膚。外國朋友希望遊客們能儘量尊重當地習俗，不要穿著超短裙、超短褲，尤其是遊覽清真寺。

部分中國人遊客在去教堂、宮殿、博物館、劇院等地參觀時，著裝太過隨意，甚至還出現邊參觀邊打電話的現象，這些都是對他國文化藝術的極不尊重，很容易引起當地人的反感。但是，面對他人異樣的目光，中國遊客似乎無所察覺，仍然我行我素，這些無視所在國家風俗習慣的不禮貌行為往往會成為“文明衝突”的藉口和導火索。

水在海洋與陸地之間運行轉移，水在運動過程之中呈現出多種多樣的形式，時而原地凝固，時而流動位移。有時向上蒸騰，有時向下滲透，更多的是平行飄流。水，可以同時沿上下、前後、左右任意的方向，全方位地運行移動，水流運動沒有明確固定的界限可言，走到哪裡算哪裡，難有規則可以遵守遵循。

中國人特別隨意，習慣于無規則運動狀態，遇見縫隙就鑽，天生缺乏邊界意識。中國人少有公共邊界意識，少有社會規則意識，更加缺乏公眾秩序的理念和規範。中國人天不怕地不怕，什麼都敢說什麼都敢做，什麼都敢為天下先。全世界認識到中國人真是太特別，太小眾扎眼，他們心裡有一套外人未必瞭解的，只屬於他們自己的遊戲規則，容易引起他人側目和不悅。

18. 像水那樣深藏不露，中國人習慣若隱若現。

中國人天生就是這樣一群人，視“深藏不露”為美德，不主張把情緒、情感向外表露，內斂含蓄，喜怒不形於色。深藏不露是一種本事。深藏不露應該是胸有成竹、謙虛謹慎的一面，更有城府深沉之意。

中國人主張“難得糊塗”，寧可顯得愚笨一些，也不可顯得太過聰明；寧可約束一下，也不可太鋒芒畢露；寧可隨和一點，也不可趾高氣揚；寧可謙讓一點，也不可太過激進。鼓勵處事妥當圓通，因為圓的壓力最小，可張力最大，可塑性最強，所以最是安全可靠。

中國的國防力量究竟有多大呢？美國國防部就這一問題給出的答案很有意思，“沒有人知道中國真正的國防力量有多大，很可怕”。美國國防部在其 2012 版《國防授權法》中這樣寫道：中國不僅在致力於開發尖端武器，還在對宇宙戰鬥力進行廣泛投資。

報告書還首次提到了中國最新型反艦導彈“東風 -21D”的實戰配置。被稱為“航母殺手”的東風 -21D 射程長達 1500 公里，被認為是美國在西太平洋地區作戰的一大威脅。美國軍事專家們還普遍認為，東風 -21D 有能力攻擊在本地區活動的美國核動力航母“喬治·華盛頓號”。

報告書中還記載了很多美國無法馬上做出回答的疑問。也就是說，由於中國在軍事領域非常強調內部保密問題，因此美國無法對中國的軍事情況進行精確的分析。"中國不僅在隱藏自己的軍事能力，還在隱瞞本國的戰略目標與決策過程，正在成為造成區內國家不安原因"。中國的軍事力量會越來越強，非常可怕。

自然界中落到陸地表面的那一部分降水，除了凝結在高山上的冰雪、人類和動植物攝取用水、和地表徑流水以外，有絕大部分的降水深藏在地下，形成地下水和地下徑流。通常，地下徑流的流量、流速、以及地下水所處深度位置沒有人準確知曉掌握。水，往往深藏不露。瞭解和掌握大自然規律的忽明忽暗，若隱若現狀態，懂得深藏不露，藏巧於拙。

什麼都在那裡明擺著，什麼都是陽謀，沒有陰謀。透明不透明取決你有多大的本事，你看得懂就好，看不懂也別指望別人告訴你全部真相，因為。這個世界本來就不是完全透明的，模糊不清是一種常態，一種正常狀態。全世界開始逐漸明白，中國人是這樣玩轉"韜光養晦"，深藏不露，厚積薄發的。

19. 像水那樣同質共處，中國人互相不買帳。

中國人似乎天生就是一群不善團結，內鬥不斷的人，他們講究"陰陽"學理，天是陽，地是陰；上是陽，下是陰；男是陽，女是陰；單是陽，雙是陰。陰陽互通互聯，互為獨立又互相轉化變化。

陰就是陽，陽就是陰，永遠可以正著說，也可以反著說，誰也說服不了誰。最後，沒有對錯，沒有結論，永遠是平手收場。凡中國人紮堆的地方都免不了內鬥。中國的成語裡有一山不容二虎，同室操戈，相互傾軋，勾心鬥角，兄弟倪牆，反目成仇，文人相輕，同行是冤家。而且，凡是變着法子修理中國人最厲害的，不是外國人，恐怕是中國人自己。

中國人的好鬥，就是限於內鬥，窩裡鬥。二十世紀20年代，蔣介石率部討伐北方的軍閥，路過山東時，遭到日本人滋事挑釁，老蔣怕引起摩擦，不敢對外吱聲，還是繼續北上專打中國人。1931年918事變，東北20萬軍隊不予抵抗，失去東三省。老蔣不做正面應對，並且壓制百姓抗日。然而，面對強敵，步步退卻的蔣介石對幾個連鹽都吃不上的紅軍兄弟卻多次圍剿，寧殺一千，不漏一人，欲置其於死地而後快。

美其名為"攘外必先安內"，實際上是是耗子扛槍窩裡橫。如果沒有蘇聯紅軍進攻東北，沒有美國投擲的兩顆核彈，蔣介石他大概還得在重慶的防空洞裡多躲藏幾年。老蔣內鬥都紅了眼，昏了頭，與慈禧的"寧與友邦，不與家奴"如出一轍，置日本侵略者於不顧，一門心思屠殺本族兄弟。

地球上的水分子，由兩個氫原子，一個氧原子共同組成，簡單且實用。水分子極其容易分開和分離，又極其容易重新組合結合在一起。而且，水分子是一種萬能溶劑，除了油之外，幾乎可以與其他所有物質相溶相合，生成一種新的物質。水分子與水分子之間，同質同性，互不相欠，互不影響，你可以離開我，我也可以離開你，你我價值完全一樣，地位平等功能類同。

中國人無論走出去，或請進來，十分擅長與外族異域打交道，廣泛結交朋友；甚至中國人有足夠的勇氣和韌力，多次同化漢化外族入侵者，化敵為友。可是國人內部之間，卻屢見"國人相輕"，你看不起我，我看不起你，人人互不買帳互不服氣，挖坑使絆內鬥不休。

一個中國人是條龍，三個中國人是條蟲，"一個和尚挑水吃，兩個和尚抬水吃，三個和尚沒水吃"，"一盤散沙"成為中國人的顯著印記。全世界似乎認識到中國人之間不團結，"窩裡鬥"是平常事。

20. 像水那樣逆來順受，中國人素來隱忍耐受。

中國人天生就是這樣一群人，逆來順受，忍辱負重。中華民族這種無可比擬的忍耐力一定是用來完成一種崇高使命的，忍受委曲、誤解，甚至被壓榨成疾，砍頭槍殺奪去生命，也得忍耐承受。

但是，真的有那麼一天，中國人被逼到牆角，到了忍無可忍、退無可退之時，也必然在沉默中猛然爆發，以其排山倒海之勢反擊，掀你個人仰馬翻，拼你個魚死網破，決戰生死存亡。

有一天，記者採訪日本老兵，一些老兵講的是方言，記者聽不懂，無奈，只能去找自己的日本朋友翻譯，那位日本朋友開始時翻譯的很溜，但是後來聽到這些老兵講述怎樣怎樣毆打中國百姓、殘殺中國百姓，越聽越殘忍，那個日本朋友就越來越痛苦。

第二天，記者一早接到了那位日本朋友的電話，他想了一晚上，覺得必須打這個電話。他接着說，現在中日之間關係挺好的，請記者為中日兩國之間的友誼考慮，不要把這些事實向中國民眾公佈，不要影響兩國關係，中國人如果知道了日軍曾經做了什麼，絕對是會仇恨日本的。

記者拿著電話，良久良久，說不出話來，最後，記者說：你知道嗎？全世界都知道這段歷史，不知道的只是你們日本人而已！日本朋友聽後，吃驚的不得了，說：啊，你們中國人都知道啊！你們知道，還能這樣對待日本，真是寬容大量至極。

在順命、信命的中國人群中，幾千年來，殘暴的帝王、貪婪的官僚、殘忍的酷吏、沉重的兵役、繁重的勞役、嚴酷的法律、嚴明的體制、嚴格的禮教、森嚴的等級、豪強的侵奪、土匪的搶掠、流氓的騷擾、宗族的威壓、長輩的威權、長官的意志、強者的打壓、弱者的攻擊、同行的妒忌、同門的冷箭、同志的反戈、老人的猜忌、男人的蠻橫、女人的醋意等等這些都是在千錘鍛煉中國人"隱忍"功夫。

大自然中的水，跟隨環境的變化而變化，逆來順受，順來順往，從來不曾計較、投訴過待遇不公。水放在杯中，它就是杯子的形狀；水放在水池裡，它就是水池的形狀；水流淌翻滾在江河之內，它就隨境所型，千變萬化千姿百態。然而，就水的本質而言，功能和作用依舊保持不變，絲毫不會因外界環境變化所為而受到任何影響。

水，沒有恒定的狀態，沒有固定的形體，卻可以適應任何環境。全世界驚奇地發現，中國人獨具不同凡響的艱忍耐力，冠絕全球。

21. 像水那樣獨立中立，中國人傾向自顧自家。

中國人天生就是這樣一群人，滿腦子的"人倫"觀念，中國傳統文化講究的是，君臣、父子、夫妻、兄弟、朋友之間的關係。簡單講，就是以自己的生活為圓心，向外擴張劃一個半徑，一圈一圈地推出去。做每一件事情，常常要先看這件事和自己關係的遠近親疏，再決定該不該做，怎麼做。中國人多是先關心自己血緣親族，然後再是其他人。有時，對其他人的苦難則表現出不同尋常的自私與冷漠，對公眾事務普遍缺乏關愛。

元旦前夜，我與一幫朋友去北京三里屯參加一個聚會。正當我們歡快地享受著新年前夜的美好時刻時，一件突如其來的事情讓我們的笑聲戛然而止。我與我的美國小伙傑克走在其他朋友前面100米左右。我倆最先看到大概二、三十個人聚集在路邊，一個正在抽搐的年輕姑娘躺在地上，全身顫動，腦袋隨著身體的抖動而不斷撞擊水泥地面。

離她最近的人與她只有大概兩米的距離，然而沒有一個人主動伸出手來幫助她，大家完全沒有行動。根據她周圍旁觀者人數估算，這個女孩應該已經躺在地上至少三分多鐘。我與傑克脫口而出："醫生！醫生！"但無人回應，人們只是沉默地看著我們，氣氛糟糕透頂。

中國人凡事習慣自己照顧自己，事不關己高高掛起；傾心于"小而全大而全"的生活方式，遇事不求人，少求人，有求於人不如多要求自己；主張管好份內事，不喜歡挑頭出頭，不喜歡結盟。久而久之，給世界留下"各人自掃門前雪，不管他人瓦上霜"的印象。全世界發現中國人喜歡自顧自家"兩耳不聞窗外事，一心只讀聖賢書"，頗有些"獨善其身"的味道。

大自然中水循環系統，是一個獨立運行的中立體系。講獨立性，就是說水系統本身不必依附於其他生態系統的支持和配合，而能夠獨立地循環運行，自成一體完成往返輪迴。中立性則是說，水系統從不強行結盟他人，中立不偏邪地處事待物。

22. 像水那樣任人拆分，中國人內心缺乏安全感。

中國人天生就是這樣一群人，內心總有著一種莫名難言的焦慮和煩惱，且煩躁和不安，迷惘和彷徨與日俱增。現如今，全社會普遍傾向掙快錢，金錢財富的多寡似乎成為了成功與否的唯一價值標杆。窮人掙錢為翻身，富人掙錢圖傳代。掙不到錢的跳腳，掙錢少的煩惱，掙大錢的更著急上火，有錢傍身更要用心費力保值增值錢財。錢多錢少的故事沒有個盡頭，內心深處哪來的平靜、快樂和安全。

你在中國乘坐公車，就像是參加一場肉搏戰。每當公車駛來，從來不會是排好隊有秩序而上，而是個個爭先恐後唯恐不及。車門一打開，乘客們蜂擁而上，人人都用盡九牛二虎之力，只為擠進車廂佔位，惟恐成為留在站臺上的最後那個。

乘火車，每次進站，都像是重溫一遍喪權辱國中國近代史。候車室還沒剪票，就黑壓壓的一大群人擠在前面，寧可伸長頭頸張望，前推後擠的卡位，待到工作人員開始剪票，人群便騷動起來，裡三層外三層的圍了上去，擠得個水泄不通，只想從鐵柵門爭先而出。

你偶然也會有好運氣，碰到排隊的狀況，可是隨時有可能插隊的人，他們對早已成列的隊伍視而不見，毫不在意先來後到的社會秩序，把老少皆知的社會公德踩在腳下，帶著一股不達目的誓不甘休的霸氣，昂首挺胸地挺進，施展著渾身招數見縫插針的迂迴繞進，受指責而不讓，遇挫折而不退。

水，寧靜而平實，誠實而歉卑。你需要它的時候，水隨時隨地精心侍侯著；你不需要它的時候，水靜靜地呆在低窪處隨時恭侯準備著。你把水放進杯子裡，水成杯樣；你把水放進盆裡，水成盆樣；你把水放進桶裡，水成水桶樣；你把水放進池子裡，水成水池樣；水，從來沒有怨言，從來不曾投拆控告過。公平的講，水任由他人擺弄戲弄，哪有"安全"保障可言。

中國人內心深處往往藏有一種天然的不安全感。社會環境中存在大量的不確定性，任何不確定性導致非穩定狀態，而非穩定狀態往往給人們帶去的，是諸多的非安全衝擊。在急劇變化的時代，人們很容易被外界力量所裹挾，稍有不慎應對失誤便會掉隊，安全感則趨向於弱化。

23. 像水那樣規模流動，中國人擅長群眾運動。

中國人天生就是這樣一群人，對群眾運動有特別的好感，通曉人海戰術。國人歷來主張辦大事，就要"集中優勢"力量突破困難和阻礙，"傷其十指不如斷其一指"各個擊破。中國人熱愛"群眾運動"，擅長"群眾運動"，且擁有一種非凡的組織動員能力。在中國人的記憶裡，人民群眾直接參與規模宏大、聲勢浩大的"群眾運動"屢見不鮮，有成功的歡欣喜悅，也有失敗的經驗教訓。

張藝謀，2008 北京奧運會開幕式總導演，在閒話聊起開幕式設計思路時這樣描述，"這是中國人最偉大的節日，我們要讓全世界的人感受到中國人的激情、浪漫。"開幕式運用了很多高科技術，"我也絕對沒有忽略人的本性。如果傳統的人海戰術是老觀念的話，我們是用人海戰術和新媒體的結合，這個一加一絕對不是簡單等於二，是一種新力量。"

外國朋友對奧運會開幕式好評如潮。《紐約時報》評價："如果說這個驚人的開幕式表達了對中華古老文明的至高敬意，試圖激發一個古老民族的驕傲，那它同時也對充滿疑慮的外國傳遞了這樣的信號：別害怕，我們沒有惡意。"《衛報》評論道："張藝謀全力掃清了所有障礙，讓這場演出和周圍的一切相匹配，並很好地詮釋出，中國是在古老文明基礎上崛起的一個現代國家這個意圖。"

大自然中水氣，在空中遇冷降落到陸地以後，便會朝一個地點集聚，向一個特定的方向流動。向下，一路向下流動，水在向下聚集流動的過程中，逐級逐次形成規模效應，最終構成強大的水勢和水能。水從高處向下流動聚集，含蓋流經的面積愈大，水的規模愈大，功效貢獻也就愈大。

中國人歷來熟悉"舉國體制"，運用群眾運動。群眾運動是中國人克敵致勝的傳家法寶，憑藉這個法寶打遍天下無敵手。眾人群策群力，有錢的出線，有力的出力；眾人抬柴火焰高；人心齊，泰山移。舉全國之力，率全國民眾規模運作，集中優勢力量各個擊破。全世界終於明白，中國人如此熱衷"群眾運動"，成效卓著。

24. 像水那樣持續流動，中國人實踐持久戰。

中國人天生就是這樣一群人，從小便知曉"持久"的魔力。"水滴石穿"，高處的水滴溫柔地撲向磐石蒼涼的胸膛，親吻潤濕了粗糙的石體，就這樣在歲月輪迴不知不覺之間，終於有一日，一滴水親破石之肌骨，洞穿而過。水石二角色在天長地久中演繹了一個哲理：當一種運動軌跡以義無反顧的方式持久出現後，哪怕是以最柔弱的力量前行，全世界最終都要給它讓路。

1938 年 5 月，毛澤東寫下了《論持久戰》一文。毛澤東主席把他的整個抗日戰爭的計畫都明明白白地公佈天下，結果中國的抗日戰爭就是這樣展開和結束的。交戰國日本都必須在看了這個計畫的情況下忠實地遵守這個計畫。

毛澤東主席的《論持久戰》就是預先寫好了的一段歷史。這是人類歷史上唯一的把戰爭計畫公開發表出來，而且還按照這個計畫執行，敵人對手也不得不配合，結果實現了這個計畫的三個階段"戰略防禦、戰略相持和戰略反攻"的結果。

日本是一個小國，它地少、物少、人少、兵少，經不起長期的戰爭。再者，在國際上，敵人是失道寡助，而我們呢，卻是地大、物多、人多，而且是得道多助。這是由戰爭的性質所決定的。這些特點，規定了雙方一切政治上的政策和軍事上的戰略戰術，決定了戰爭的持久性和最後勝利是屬於中國，而不是日本。

地球自轉，並且圍繞太陽公轉。水，始終是在運動的狀態之中。持久不斷流動運動是一種常態，是一種常規，是一種符合自然規律的活動形式。然而，視覺感知上的靜止或停頓，只是因為參照物的相對靜止，而產生的一種錯覺而已。活水，流動的水，滋養大地萬千生物，生生不息枝繁葉茂。

戰國時荀子在《勸學》一文中說："故不積跬步，無以致千里；不積小流，無以成江海。騏驥一躍，不能十步，駑馬十駕，功在不舍。"說的也就是這個道理。恒久堅持不懈，便能成就事業宏圖。全世界驚奇地發現，中國人有能耐持久耐心的處理事務，以柔克剛，以弱勝強，積小勝為大勝，以時間換取發展進步的空間。

25. 像水那樣隨意流淌，中國人得過且過。

中國人天生就是這樣一群人，做事一向隨意馬虎，大多數人養成了安於現狀不思進取的習性，"做一天和尚撞一天鐘"混日子。做事不太講認真，不多求精確，差不多就行。這點就像胡適先生當年寫的《差不多先生傳》一樣：中國人大部分是差不多先生的子孫，對待是非曲直，向來只要差不多就行。

王秉剛，國家科技部 863 計畫電動汽車重大科技專項特聘專家，前幾天去了一趟長城汽車廠，仔細瞭解了他們自主研發的缸內直噴渦輪增壓 2 升汽油機的情況。他發現被集成到長城這款發動機裡的許多關鍵零部件都是外國公司的產品：電控噴射系統是德爾福的，增壓器和鏈條是柏格華納的，變氣門機構 VVT 是依納的，這些也無可厚非。

可是，連一些簡單附件都是從外國買進來：氣門是伊頓的，氣門座是帝伯格茨的，活塞與軸瓦是輝門的，活塞環是 ATG 的，水泵皮帶是蓋茨的，火花塞是博世的，皮帶張緊器是萊頓的，增壓壓力控制閥是皮爾柏格的，就連汽缸蓋罩蓋也是一家叫勃樂尼的外國公司供應的。中國人怎麼可以這樣不思進取，躺在外國人的技術上得過且過。

大自然中的水流動前行的目的地，只有最低洼處。只要有可能，什麼也阻止不了水向更低的洼地流進。水，要做個真正的自己，爭脫束縛衝破羈絆，肆意奔向原野，隨性放縱無拘無束，頑強執著卻又精靈聰慧，前行奔湧途中有勇猛，有謀略，不糾纏瑣事，不浪費時間，過得去就好，過得去就行。

在中國，有位"差不多"先生。提起此人，人人皆知處處留名，你肯定遇見過他，認識他，一定聽過別人閒聊起他。差不多先生的大名，天天掛在中國人的口中"凡事只要差不多，就好了"世界上怕就怕"認真"二字，中國人就是最難講認真，全世界終於知道，中國人一直有做事馬虎隨便，對付將就，湊合差不多的壞毛病。

26. 像水那樣滿山遍野，中國人主張地盤優勢。

中國人天生就是這樣一群人，喜歡擁有地盤，以人心贏取掌控地盤疆域。"普天之下，莫非王土，率土之濱，莫非王臣。"雖然中國人認為擁有佔領地盤固然重要，但是以謀勢贏取人心更是重要，失去了人心，原有的你家領土屬地也會輕易丟失掉，反之亦然。故贏得人心，則沒有必要去征服"蠻夷之地"，而以爭取籠絡外族異教人心歸屬為上上策。

1962 年十月的一個夜晚，毛澤東在中南海召見了他的政治軍事將領們。在西部萬里之外的喜馬拉雅山腳下，中印兩國軍隊正在刺骨嚴寒中對峙。爭執發生在一條有爭議的邊界線上，印度堅持英國殖民者劃下的麥克馬洪線，而中國只承認大清前朝的國界。爭論地區在喜馬拉雅山麓下的一條由所謂的麥克馬洪線所界定的地區，它有 125,000 平方公里，相當於美國的整個賓夕法尼亞州。

毛澤東決定說，這次要"敲打"印度一下，讓他們回到談判桌上來。但是，我們要克制，教訓教訓印度人就可以了。軍事部署按照毛澤東的思路佈置下去，幾個星期後，中國軍隊給予印軍沉重的毀滅性打擊。但是，中國卻在勝利後退回了以前的實際控制區，甚至連繳獲印軍的重武器也全部歸還。

中國是一個傳奇的國家，它幾千年延綿不斷的文化裡面蘊藏著豐富的戰略和治國之策。中國人注重地盤領土，卻又強調不爭一城一地之得失，既拿得起又放得下，主張慢慢積蓄力量，以勢取勝，讓對手服服貼貼歸順平復。

大自然中的水，滿山遍野隨處可見，是天地間分佈最廣的物質之一。水，自從天上降落在地面以後，便首先打主意滲入地下，成為地下水、和地下徑流的一部分，熱衷安營紮寨，分佈佔據陸地的每一個角落，形成絕對優勢。除非大地飽和勸退離開，水樂意隨時流走，退而求處其他地域，或者聚集成地上徑流，朝向大海奔流而下，繼續參與下一輪循環。

人到那裡，影響自然帶到那裡。中國人歷來喜歡圈地、圍地佔領實地，建立地形優勢。他們是實力策略的忠實執行者，佔地為先，先佔先得，然後形成一圈，地上地下聯成一片，耐心耕耘積累相對優勢，廣泛佔領擁有地盤往往就能爭取到有形的實質利益，積小勝成大勝。中國人迷戀水的魅力，托水啟示所賜，懂得以"勢"取勝，掌握高超的智慧和謀略，實施有效戰略包圍，搶佔實地。

中國人憑藉把控水能和水勢的靈性技巧，熟練發揮"戰略包圍"藝術，運動戰中常常採用迂迴包抄的策略，分割包圍對手，持久耐心地與對方周旋，靈活機動地應對變化，盡可能調動對手四處出擊，致其顧此失彼前後失據，最大限度消耗對手的有生力量，迫使其退卻，讓出其所佔領土地，爭取人心"不戰而屈人之兵"，最終完勝敵手于無形之中。全世界終於開始開竅，慢慢明白中國人是怎樣贏取天下人心，攻城掠地的。

27. 像水那樣公平處事，中國人追求大同世界！

中國人天生就是這樣一群人，無論是興盛還是衰落，是富強還是貧弱，他們始終在追逐夢想，不懈地追求"中國夢"，不斷地追求"天下為公"、"世界大同"的夢想。當今世界 239 個國家和地區、幾千個民族、70 億人口共生一個地球，共處一個天下，是人類的命運共同體。"大同世界"不僅是中國人民自身的需求和夢想，也是世界各國人民共同的願望和夢想。

孔子理想中的社會："大道之行也，天下為公，選賢與能，講信修睦。故人不獨親其親，不獨子其子。使老有所終，壯有所用，幼有所長，矜寡孤獨廢疾者皆有所養。男有分，女有歸。貨，惡其棄於地也，不必藏於己；力，惡其不出於身也，不必為己。是故謀閉而不興，盜竊亂賊而不作。故外戶而不閉。是謂大同"。

大道通達的年代，天下是民眾共有的。選舉賢能的人，把領袖的位置傳給他，人們講信用重和睦。因此人們不只是愛自己的親人，不只是把自己的孩子當孩子。要使老人得以安享天年，成人有用武之地，兒童可以健康成長，鰥寡孤獨的人及殘廢、有病的人都能得到供養。男人有合適的職業，女人能適時地婚嫁。人們反對浪費財物，但也不會據為己有；人們討厭偷懶的人，但也不會讓別人只為自己出力。所以陰謀都得不到施展，盜賊也不會發生，外出時都不用關門，這就是大同社會呵。

《太公六韜》中借姜太公之口有過一個解釋："天下非一人之天下，乃天下人之天下也。"（《太公六韜》）孟子在談到君王的地位時說："使之主祭而百神享之，是天受之；使之主事而事治，百姓安之，是民受之也。"即讓他主持祭祀，所有神明來享用了，說明天授予他了；讓他主持政務，政務得以治理，百姓非常滿意，說明民眾授予他了。

"大同世界"應該是一個在政治上實行人民治理，經濟上實行共有共用的社會，在大同世界裡，人性發展到了圓滿的境界，不但和諧地共用社會的物資，而且都能過著有人性尊嚴的生活，彼此互尊互重，所以大同世界的景象便是"天下為公"。中國人心中的"大同世界"的理想，不是以武力來統治全世界。

中國人的"大同世界"理想也決非領土的擴張，"和平"才是中國歷代政治所追求的理想。中國人的"盛世"，西漢的"文景之治"，唐代的"貞觀之治"，清朝的"康乾盛世"，無一不是和平安樂國民富足的時代。中國領土自夏朝代以來不斷地擴張，依靠的是和平的文化融和力，而不是戰爭的軍事征服。

大自然中的水，對於公平公正公開原則要求，從來就不曾含糊，並且嚴格認真執行。水，無論遇見誰對待誰，強大或弱小，富有或貧窮，都是一律平等相待，公平公正有加。水，絕對沒有一丁點的偏見或好惡，偏袒欺負任何其他生命物質。水不平則溢，人不平則鳴。水，保持不了平衡、平穩，就停不住、站不穩、留不住，就會下瀉滿溢。

中國人歷來嚮往追逐大同世界、天下為公，提倡"君子和而不同"。"吾疾貧富不均，今為汝均之"，國人可以忍受生活不"富"，但絕對不接受不"均"的社會現狀。處事公平公正似水，待人公正廉潔如冰。全世界終於有所知，有所懂，中國人世代追逐"世界大同"的緣由。

28. 像水那樣親和萬物，中國人主張和平和順！

中國人天生就是這樣一群人，歷來主張人心和善、家庭和睦、人際和順、社會和諧、人間和美、世界和平。中國的文化從始至終就是以"和"為終極的價值追求。"和"被廣泛地應用到家庭、國家、天下世界。孔子提出"和為貴"，從治理國家的角度肯定"和"的作用。

孔子還提出"和而不同"，認為"和"的本質在於統一和協調多種因素的差異。荀子提出"和則一，一則多力"，認為在一個組織內部人們和諧相處，就能取得一致，取得一致力量就會增大。孟子提出"天時不如地利，地利不如人和"，認為只要內部和諧，上下齊心合力，就能無往而不勝。

兩千多年前，中國人就已經通過海陸兩條絲綢之路，與世界各國開展商貿往來。從2100多年前張騫出使西域到600多年前鄭和下西洋，海陸兩條絲綢之路把中國的絲綢、茶葉、瓷器等等輸往沿途各國，帶去了文明和友好，贏得了各國人民的讚譽和喜愛。

現如今，"一帶一路"海陸並舉，南北呼應，是中國向世界貢獻的"中國智慧"和"中國方案"，習近平代表中國在2013年9月和10月分別提出建設"新絲綢之路經濟帶"和"21世紀海上絲綢之路"的頂層戰略構想，強調相關各國打造互利共贏的"利益共同體"和共同發展繁榮的"命運共同體"。

"一帶一路"，這條世界上跨度最長的經濟大走廊發端於中國，貫通中亞、東南亞、南亞、西亞乃至歐洲部分區域，東牽亞太經濟圈，西系歐洲經濟圈。它是世界上最具發展潛力的經濟帶，沿線各國的前途命運，從未像今天這樣緊密相連、休戚與共。跨越時空的"一帶一路"宏偉構想，從歷史深處走來，融通古今、連接中外，順應和平、發展、合作、共贏的時代潮流，承載著絲綢之路沿途各國發展繁榮的夢想，賦予古老絲綢之路以嶄新的時代內涵。

大自然中的水，平等對待世界一切生命和一切事物物件。水，不心滿于富貴，不埋怨於貧窮，不管置於陶碗還是金碗之中，均一視同仁親和平順待物。水還是水，不以接觸物件的改變而變化相處態度。器歪水不歪，物斜水不斜。故此，水便有了"水準"之雅號，對誰都親和修睦。倘如遇見欺壓弱勢、坑蒙拐騙不公平的惡行，水便奔騰咆哮，所謂"不平則鳴"。

中國人深知武力、體力、物力，都不能征服人心，能征服人心者，是公平之道，是和合、和平之勢。由水的公平引申出"善行"，與人交往，對強者與弱者都要心存友善，對強者要尊重，對弱者要理解和幫扶。你以怎麼樣的態度對待別人，別人也會以同樣的態度回敬對待你；對強弱者一視同仁不偏不依，就可得眾人之力，無所不成，無往不勝。

中國人持有"水"一樣的平和、親合品質，凡事以"和為貴"，憑借柔情似水的親和、潤物細無聲的奉獻、溶物的和睦平順、相容的融合大度的秉性，與世界相處。中華民族堅持走一條有別於西方大國依靠戰爭完成發展的和平崛起之路。全世界終於開始理解，中國人是如此癡迷"和順和平"，以及"和為貴"。

小議"中國人到底是誰？"

回答"中國人到底是誰？"命題，我們嘗試著梳理出一部分國人的群體行為，當然這僅僅是一小部分，以及這些群體行為模式背後反映的思維邏輯、哲學思考，和文化脈絡。毋庸置疑，國人的群體行為與自然界中"水"之間存在明顯清晰的"正相關"關係。這或是了解和理解中國文化和中國人的新視角。

既使憑藉手中的這一組中國人群體行為作範本，世人或也足以準確地判斷出國人的所思所想，言行舉止，待人接物特質，以及生活方式、倫理道德、價值觀取向完全不同於世界上其他國家和民族，中國的文化和中國人的終極信仰有其自身的高度和寬度，獨一無二，獨樹一幟。

中國文學家魯迅曾經說過："中國在道教根深。如果一個人想要瞭解中國的歷史和文化，一個人必須理解道教第一。"中國文化大家林語堂如是說："中國人在本性是道家，在文化上是儒家，然而其道家思想卻更甚於儒家思想。"

中國哲學聖賢，道家的開山鼻祖老子說："道生一，一生二，二生三，三生萬物"（《道德經》第四十二章）道生一，一是太極；一生二，二是陰陽；二生三，三是陰陽配合；三生萬物，萬物是萬事萬物。道即自然規律，是獨一無二的，道本身包含陰陽二氣，陰陽二氣相交而形成一種適勻的狀態—和氣，萬物在這種狀態"和氣"中產生。萬物背陰而向陽，並且在陰陽二氣的互相激蕩而成新的和諧體—萬事萬物。

中國人的信仰崇拜對象，與西方人的有本質不同。西方人信仰追隨人類主觀意識下臆造出來的一個宗教，宗教設置一個擁有強大權力、力量、道德地位的神或神權系統，逼促人們敬畏，逼促人們依靠，逼促人們不敢違抗背叛，甚至逼促人對這個絕對的權威不敢有任何思考和質疑。

信宗教者，上天堂得永生；不信宗教者，入地獄且不得永生。高壓威嚴下的宗教神權，往往有一套哲學理論系統，給人以精神以及實際操作上的指引，解釋得了的歸上帝，解釋不了的也統統歸上帝，簡單、高壓、強勢。

相比較西方宗教，中國人的宗教觀則寬鬆自然了許多，崇拜信仰者自然而然地由心生發，隨和自由。老子說"域中有四大，而人居其一焉。人法地，地法天，天法道，道法自然。"宇宙中有四個大，而"人"代表的生命物種也佔居其中之一。人遵循與地的法則，地遵循於天的法則，天遵循於道的法則。

道遵循自然的法則，而自然法則是萬事萬物的主宰。你信與不信或信什麼，是你的自由，天地自然不會干涉你、阻礙你，做你想做的事，信你想信仰的任何對象，上天堂入地獄也是你個人的選擇，唯有天地之意絕難違背，自然規律絕難違抗抵擋，人再有本事也不可能大過自然天地之道，順從自然規律是正道。

自然規律"道"無影無蹤，看不見，聽不到摸不著，觸碰不了感覺不到，但卻又真真實實地存在，無處不在，無處不有。而自然現象卻是顯而易見的，看得見，聽得到摸得著，觸碰得了感覺得到。所以，自然界中的各種事物和現象便成為觀察、理解道的合理途徑，從自然現象入手觀察"道"，深究觸及自然規律"道"的精髓部分，核心部分和本質部分。

自然世界中有天、有地，有自然規律"道"。天在上，地在下，而"水"則代表著自然規律統領其他一切物質，水是萬事萬物之源，眾生之本。同樣是取自然界對象作為參學、模仿範本，中西方的取捨有着巨大的差異，最終形成的哲學理念南轅北轍，各不相同。

西方人專注在生物鏈（食物鏈）圈內尋找、挖掘學習對象，側重關注效率，物質和金錢多寡，更多的是從低於人類聰慧程度的動植物那裡學習知識獲取智慧；而中國人的興趣關注點則廣泛、寬泛許多，更擅長在生物鏈圈和水循環圈兩個系統中找尋、挖掘學習參照對象，在生物鏈圈中學習、獲取人類生存發展技術和技巧的同時，又從高於人類聰慧程度的水循環圈中拜師求知，獲取人類倫理道德和哲學智慧靈感。

聰慧的中國人充分認知人類物種的有限和短處，而將自身的境界眼光努力向上向外處拓展，面向圈外更遠更深處求知求學，謙卑地向水循環系統討教博學知識和人類大智慧，而非像西方人那樣，只埋頭在生物鏈圈內向下向裡尋找參學對象。中國文化的獨特之處就在於其站立的位置，遠高於西方；中國哲學的層級遠在西方之上。

英國的歷史學家湯恩比認為：如果這個世界有未來，未來的世界要靠中國，為什麼？他認為中國是唯一具有天下情懷的一個國家。自達爾文主義盛行以後，"弱肉強食"，"優勝劣汰"，"叢林主義"、"國家民族主義"等觀念已經席捲了整個歐洲，他們只有"小我"的民族國家，而中國人卻是懷抱"平天下"的博大胸懷，這是一種容納天下的情懷。

德國科學家和哲學家萊布尼茨在《中國新事》緒論中這樣寫道："我們從前誰也不相信世界上還有比我們的倫理更美滿、立身處世之道更進步的民族存在，現在東方的中國，給我們以一大覺醒。"他高度讚美中國有"人類最高度的文化和最發達的技術文明。假使推舉一位智者來裁定哪個民族最傑出，而不是裁定哪個女神最漂亮，那麼他將把金蘋果交給中國人。"

400多年前，義大利傳教士利瑪竇不遠萬里來到中國。帶著"為什麼強大的中華帝國卻沒有殖民周邊弱小民族"的疑問，他開始潛心研究中華文明。他發現一個與西方全然不同的歷史文化傳統，發現了一個不是黷武而是和平主義的國家。於是利瑪竇在他著名的《中國答記》中發出由衷感歎："中國雖有裝備精良的軍隊，但他的人民卻從未想過要發動侵略戰爭，從未有過征服的野心"和諧理念早已深深地蘊藏于中華民族的文化傳統與民族性格之中，紮根於中華民族千百年的歷史實踐之中。

偉大的思想家羅素認為"中華民族是我所遇見的世界上最優秀的民族之一。"對於這樣一個美好的國家"卻遭到如此的虐待,我要對世界上每一個強國發出更嚴重的聲討。"他深刻地認識到中國的重要性:"中國問題,即使對於中國以外的任何人都不發生影響,也具有深遠的重要性,因為中國人口大約佔人類總人口的四分之一。然而,實際上,全世界都將受到中國事務進展的重大影響,無論好壞,在今後兩個世紀內,中國事務的進展將是一個決定性的因素。"

羅素睿智地看到中華文明的價值:"中國傳統文化注入新的來自西方的優秀元素,將來所產生的新文明或許比西方曾經產生過的各種文明更好。"一個西方人尚能意識到中華文化的價值所在,中國人自己就更應該了解和明白東方中華文化的獨特本質和精髓之處。

宇宙生態系統中,自然規律最大,"水"最大,不論你相信或不相信,喜歡或不喜歡,有神論者或無神論者,中國人或西方人皆難以違背天地之命,難以抗拒自然之運。人類世界範圍之內,中國人學"水"5000年不停腳步,往後5000年仍將繼續參學"水",實踐"水"不斷前行。

中華民族定位自己在人類社會中演繹"水"的角色地位,像水那樣待人接物,與其他國家和民族和睦相處,共同繁榮。中國新型話語權強烈倡導尊重包容、平等相待、互商互諒,互幫互助、互惠互利、合作共贏、和諧和平,以"水利萬物而不爭"的品行規範世界引領者風範,中國人以"不爭"的姿態言行舉止,待人接物,有所作為,有所建樹。

水性中國,水性中國哲學文化,水性中國倫理道德價值觀,水性中國人的言行舉止。

第九篇

讀後思考要點

中華民族是一個有宗教信仰的，信仰自然宇宙和自然規律"道"，信仰天地自然是唯一神靈的民族，他們是純粹、完全的"有神論"者，並不是像從前外界普遍認知的所謂"無神論"者；

中華民族被外界冠以"無神論"者的稱謂，只是因為中國人的"自然"宗教信仰並不符合西方世界的"非自然"宗教信仰標準說辭，故被外界誤認為是獨特的"無神論"者；

中西方的世界觀和價值觀差異極大，基本上是呈現相反方向的運行軌跡和存在狀態，東方欣賞"集體主義"，西方主張"個人主義"；東方堅持兼顧的"自由集中、民主統一"，西方強調絕對的"自由、民主"；東方人視政府是問題解決者，西方歸罪政府是問題製造者；

中華民族基於信仰自然規律"道"，信仰"幾近於道"的水，言行舉止和倫理道德體系參學、模仿水。那西方人又是參學、模仿什麼成長起來的？又或是完全自主、獨立封閉地成長起來？有一點可以確信，西方文化和哲學裡難見水的影響力；

上善若水，水的智慧至高無上。5000年一路參學、模仿水品水德成長起來的中華民族哲學和文化水準，理論上講不可能，也不應該落後於包括西方世界在內的任何人。中華民族理應有一套獨具東方智慧的話語體系；

水善利萬物而不爭，一個虔誠參學、模仿水言行舉止的中華民族，即使未發展起來，或已經發展和強大起來，也本能地遠離霸權和強權。哪來的"中國危險論"、"中國崩潰論"和"修昔底德陷阱"說教？理論上講不通，實踐上也難找到証據；

中華民族花了整整5000年時間，堅持不懈、全神貫注地在幹同一件事情：為普天下的最大多數百姓，創新、締造一個更加公平、和諧、正義、文明的社會組織形態。中國人的創新點，著眼並落實在遵循、仿學水循環的自然機理，基於"人道"契合"天道"要求，構建人類社會；

讀懂了水，全世界所有人，包括中國人自己有機會近距離看清楚，弄明白中國文化和中國哲學的本質特徵，中國已不再是一個謎一樣的國家，中國人也不再是離群寡居的"異類"。然而，中國文化依然是那樣博大精深，源遠流長，亮點頻生；

中國缺少朋友夥伴國家？試問這個世界有多少國家和民族像中華民族那樣親近、崇拜水。隨著世界上越來越多的國家和民族體悟到水的智慧之處，中國的朋友國家順理成章地遍佈天下；

水，普遍存在於世界各地，各國家、民族對水的物理屬性和物質功能認知大致相同，但對水折射的社會和文化屬性，或精神世界理解不盡相同。然而，這並不代表水喪失了普世價值，只是反映了不同人群對水的認知和感悟水平差異而已。水具有獨一無二、至高無上的"普世價值"。

Hard To Say

NO

What Chinese People Just Do It Right

定價：港幣$98

ISBN:978-988-79343-5-6

Chinese English parallel texts

By James J. Wang

Hard to Say NO

by James J. Wang

Copyright © Global Publication Company 2019
ISBN 978-988-79343-5-6

Edited by Annie
Front cover design by Steve
Book design by Leo
Proofreading by Jery
Printed by Global Learning

First printing edition June 2019

Published and Printed in Hong Kong

Price: HKD$98

Global Publication Company
RM. 1203, Yu Sung Boon Bldg,
107-111 Des Voeux Rd C.,
Central, Hong Kong

Tel: (852) 81143294
Fax: (852) 3012 1586
Email: info@globalcpc.com
website: www.globalcpc.com

online store: http://www.hkonline2000.com

Prologue

◇◇◇◇◇◇◇◇◇◇◇◇◇◇◇◇

Today, the Chinese people are facing many challenges, doubts, and problems in philosophy and culture. The difficulty in overcoming them is on par with the difficulty in maintaining an annual GDP growth rate of over 9.5% for 40 consecutive years. Yet China became the first country in the world to achieve the latter, a world economy miracle.

"China will not become a global superpower, because China is exporting products instead of thoughts today. China's knowledge system cannot contribute to the building of the world's knowledge system and China will not become a major country in knowledge production. Despite China's rapid economic growth, it will only become a major country in manufacturing. In terms of cultural production, creativity, and exports, China remains a small country that needs no major attention." (according to Margaret Thatcher, former Prime Minister of the United Kingdom)

"After 20 years, China will become the poorest country in the world," said Hillary Clinton, the former Secretary of State of the United States. She provides the following reasons for her claim: The Chinese people do not understand their responsibilities and obligations for the country and society as individuals in society. China is one of the few horrible countries in the world where people do not have faith. The only things the entire country worships are power and money. People there are selfish and unsympathetic. The politics that Chinese people refer to are nothing but lies and betrayal. Most Chinese people have never learned the significance of a decent and respectable lifestyle. Their unscrupulous acts of environmental destruction and resource exploitation have almost reached a level of craziness.

China has made no contribution to human civilization. The impact of Chinese culture is close to zero, and it will not increase in the future." (according to Boris Johnson, former Secretary of State for Foreign and Commonwealth Affairs of the United Kingdom)

"I dare say that you cannot name any innovative case, innovate change or innovate product that comes from China. In a country where people cannot breathe freely, you will not be able to think differently. In a country where people cannot challenge the authority, you will not be able to think differently, because change only comes from challenging the authority." (according to Joe Biden, the then former Vice President of the United States)

"In the near future, we will witness a historic moment: A Non-Western, non-democratic country will become the world's biggest economy since the reign of George III of the United Kingdom (1738-1820). If such thing happens, how will China give play to its strengths under the world order? Will it accept the standards and institutions under the postwar world order? Will China seek to change such order?" (according to Kevin Rudd, former Prime Minister of Australia)

"I could write a thick book criticizing China within a week. Despite many difficulties and obstacles, China has maintained such a long period of rapid growth that was unprecedented in history. China must have done something really right to make this economic miracle happen. And what is that? That is the real issue." (said Steven Ng-Sheong Cheung, a Hong-Kong-born American economist)

"This is an era where theories are needed and will be produced. This is also an era where thoughts are needed and will be produced. We must live up to the expectations of this era." (said Xi Jinping, President of the People's Republic of China)

This book, a collection of the author's thoughts, is inspired by the aforementioned doubts and problems about China as well as the unyielding spirit in the genes of the Chinese people. With a focus on Chinese philosophy and creative culture, this book tries to trace the source and get to the bottom of things from a new perspective by studying, extracting, and summarizing the most basic elements that influence the formation, development, evolution, and inheritance of Chinese philosophy and culture. Granted, the creative attempts in this book may have many shortcomings. The shortcomings will be the motivation of the author's ongoing endeavors and discoveries in the future. The author hopes this book presents creative ideas accurately, and serves as a trial to start further discussion on the book's subject.

About the Author

Resume: Researcher of Water Culture James J. Wang

1965-1971	Study at Shanghai No.1 Gaoan Road Primary School
1971-1975	Study at Shanghai Nanyang Model High School
1976-1981	Work at Company 38 of Shanghai Xinghuo Farm
1981-1985	Study at Department of Trade Economy, Shanghai University of Finance and Economics (Bachelor's Degree)
1985-1989	Work at Shanghai Animal By-products Import-Export Co., Ltd.
1989-1990	Study at the University of Sydney, Australia
1990-1994	Study at Wright State University, State of Ohio, USA (Master's Degree in Applied Economics)
1994-2009	Work at Florsheim Asia Pacific Ltd., USA
2009-Present	Work at East Water Culture Research Office

CONTENT

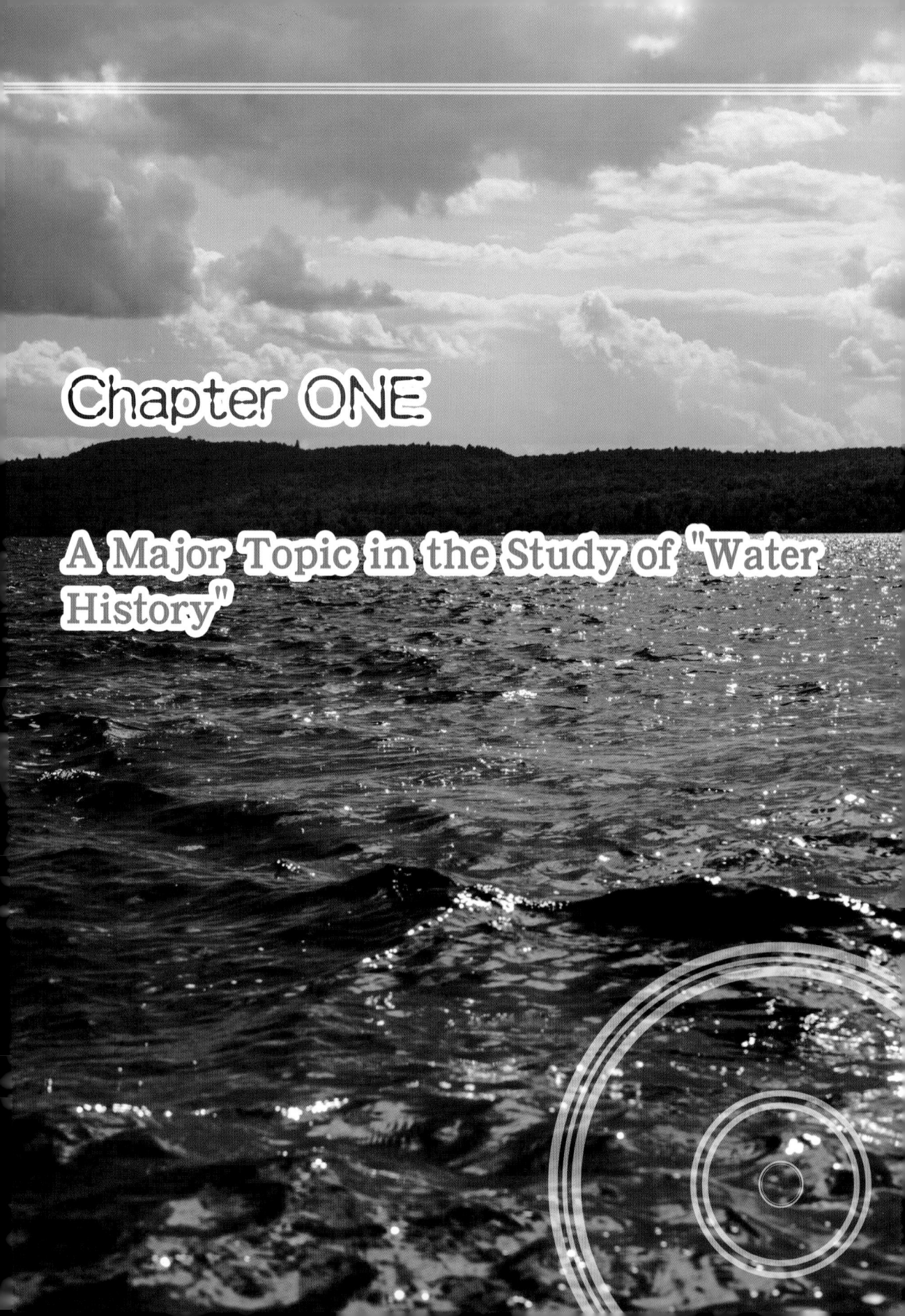

Chapter ONE

A Major Topic in the Study of "Water History"

Topic: The existence of philosophy of water and its revelation of wisdom are the fundamental elements of Chinese people's cultural confidence and the Chinese discourse system...

Water is one of the most significant factors affecting the formation, development, evolution, and inheritance of the Chinese culture. It can almost be regarded as the most decisive factor.

Water is a substance of objective existence in the world. From the perspective of nature, the water molecule is composed of two hydrogen atoms, each linked by a single chemical bond to an oxygen atom. Water is as common and ordinary as other natural substances. They are all equal and regular members of the universe. The world of nature cannot function as an integrate, organic operating system without any of them. However, water is unique and different from a social perspective. It inspires many thoughts of wisdom and special qualities in Chinese culture and philosophy, which stands in great contract with Western culture.

To study the history of water, the Chinese people have to talk about ancient Chinese philosopher Laozi and his 5,000-character classic text *Tao TeChing (The Book of the Way)* written more than 2,000 years ago. With a total of 81 chapters, the first 37 chapters of *The Book of the Way* are Tao Ching, while the remaining chapters are TeChing. The former discusses the way the world, universe, and nature work, namely the natural law, and the latter revolves around human values and ethics, as well as social and cultural norms.

In *The Book of the Way*, Laozi aims to tell the descendants of ancient Chinese people that "the Way of nature" precedes and remains on top of "the Way of Human," and that former is natural while the latter is not. The former is the base and foundation of latter, and the former makes rules about the rights and wrongs of latter. The latter can only evolve and develop smoothly by respecting and following the former. If human beings break any rules of nature and the world, they will be punished by "the Way of nature."

The way the world and universe work is a collection of how the ecological system operates. The "way" of nature, or laws of nature, are the natural result of formation, operation, and evolution on the earth. There is no doubt that the ecological system is an integrated, organic system where heaven, earth and man (representing everything) come together as a whole. Within the system, water indisputably plays the central role and serves as the most crucial element. Nothing in the world can exist without the nurture of water. Without water, all beings will cease to exist.

Since water plays such a key role in the ecological system, fully understanding and respecting the philosophical wisdom regarding water has become a standard for human intelligence. In history, China and the West used to be on the same team when it comes to understanding the origins of the world. The first Western philosopher Thales argues that "water is the first principle of everything,"

while Laozi said, "The highest excellence is like water. Water is good at benefiting everything without vying for any fame or gain. Water is in a place which is despised by the public, but it is the place where one is closest to truth."

The best form of benevolence is just like water. Water is good at helping everything, without competing with any of them. It remains in places where people do not like, thus getting closer and closer to Tao. "By putting itself in places where people do not like, water shows its modesty. The reason why ocean can become the king of all rivers is that it places itself in the lower reach. Nothing in the world is softer and gentler than water, and nothing can beat it in terms of tackling tough problems. This is the virtue of gentleness. Therefore, softness and gentleness can win over toughness and hardness. Invisible things can penetrate something without a crack. This is 'silent' instruction and the benefit of 'inaction'". (*The Book of the Way* by Laozi)

By remaining at lower places and avoiding competing with others, water has shown the most modest virtue. The reason why ocean can work as the destination of all rivers is that it stays in the lower reach. Nothing in the world is softer than water, but water is the best in penetrating the hardest thing. This is the virtue of softness. Therefore, the weak can beat the strong, and the soft can win over the hard. Something invisible can enter something without a crack. This reveals what is "silent" instruction and the benefit of "inaction".

Confucius, a student of Laozi, once said, "The wise find pleasure in water; the benevolent find pleasure in hills." He also said the following about water, "When everyone else stays above, water is the only one to stay below; when everyone else chooses to be comfortable, water is the only one to put itself at risk; when everyone else prefers cleanliness, water is the only one that embraces dirty things. Water stays at all places where people loathe – who can compete with that? This is the highest excellence." Confucius also compared water to ordinary people, "The ruler is like a boat, while the ordinary people are like water." Water can either carry a boat or overturn it." The ordinary people can either support or overthrow the throne. The ruler is like a boat, and the people are like water. A boat can either sail on or sink in the water.

"Water is everywhere and gives itself to all beings without being partial. It is like a gentleman's virtue. Water flows downwards and takes shape of its containers, just like the noble characters of a gentleman. Water flows endlessly in shallow places and unpredictably in deep areas, resembling the wisdom of a gentleman. Water will rush forward into the deepest valley without hesitation, resembling the determination and bravery of a gentleman. When water is filled into a container, its surface is always flat, which resembles the sense of justice in a gentleman. Water stops filling the container when it is full, like the integrity of a gentleman. Water can reach every little corner, like a gentleman being observant. Water can clean all kinds of things with repeated washing inside out, resembling a gentleman's positive influence. Despite all difficulties, water must find itself into the sea in the east, just like the firm belief and strong perseverance of a gentleman. Therefore, when a gentleman sees a massive flow of water, he must observe it carefully." (*You Zuo, Xunzi*)

"Water is everywhere and gives itself to all beings without being partial. It is like a gentleman's virtue. Water flows downwards and takes shape of its containers, just like the noble characters of a gentleman. Water flows endlessly in shallow places and unpredictably in deep areas, resembling the wisdom of a gentleman. Water will rush forward into the deepest valley without hesitation, resembling the determination and bravery of a gentleman. It does not argue for itself when framed, just like the tolerance of a true gentleman. When water is filled into a container, its surface is always flat, which resembles the sense of justice in a gentleman. Water stops filling the container when it is full; its lack of greediness resembles the integrity of a gentleman. Water has its own rules of doing things: Despite all difficulties, it must find itself into the sea in the east, just like the firm belief and strong perseverance of a gentleman. Therefore, when a gentleman sees a massive flow of water, he must observe it carefully.

Chinese philosophers Laozi and Confucius highly worship the qualities and virtues of water. Looking at the physical water is almost like examining the virtual, invisible laws (or "Tao") of nature and universe. Therefore, in the minds of most Chinese people, water is not only a unique and irreplaceable physical entity, but also the embodiment of social ethics, philosophy, and culture with ultimate wisdom. Laozi and Confucius strongly suggest the human society follow the paradigm of the philosophy of water -- to be in harmony with the rest of the world and thus to be incomparable.

The five-thousand-year history of China is that of following and being intimate of water. The Chinese civilization is the world's only civilization that lasts for 5,000 years without any interruption. It continues to thrive, aimed at lasting another consecutive 5,000 years. The reason for the Chinese civilization's longevity may be: The Chinese people have been modestly learning and imitating all characteristics in the operation of the ecological system. By focusing on the functions and effects of "the wisdom of water," the Chinese people have coordinated, organized, and built many forms of organization and related governance models in the Chinese society.

The biggest difference between Chinese and Western cultures and values probably lies in "water". The importance of "water" can never be underestimated. As the saying goes, a miss is as good as a mile. Targets and outcomes can vary tremendously due to the presence or absence of "water". China and the West have totally different understanding and perception of "water". The philosophy and ethical values of "water" are embodied in the Chinese culture, which are rarely seen in the Western culture.

When Chinese ancestors thought about how to establish a country's political and economic systems, social organization, and governance method, the first thing that came to mind was to refer to and imitate the natural ecosystem and the absolutely core function of "water". Water connects all the living things on earth to form an organic and whole system. Water dominates the world. Though with no intention to do so, water is worthy of the throne due to its noble conduct. It is invincible.

As the central role of water in the natural ecosystem is acknowledged and recognized by Chinese people, the Chinese people must refer to and imitate it. The human ecosystem is naturally

inseparable from "water". Water is the only and irreplaceable leader. Fully grasping this point is vital to see the national development model and path of China, influenced by the Chinese culture. A stable and ordered system must have a sole core or center.

In the human society that imitates the natural ecosystem, a person, a family, or a modern political party is expected to play the role of water. Regardless of the East or the West, the ruling party of any society has no excuse to shirk the responsibility of being the representative and spokesperson of all, rather than some, people. This is the core element and basic requirement for "the Way of human" to follow "the Way of nature".

Specifically, under each independent water system, there must be numerous rivers and lakes, as well as countless streams and ponds. They nourish all the animals and plants in the system and form the independent water system with autonomous circulation. Every large river has a main estuary for water inlet and outlet. There's no comparison between the main estuary and other estuaries, in terms of function. The Chinese nation is always inspired by the pattern and mechanism of the natural ecosystem. It perceives the secrets of organization and operation of the nature.

Chinese model under "the Way of nature"

For over 2,000 years since the First Emperor of Qin conquered the six states and unified China, the "Great Unity" political system and the system for public-private (state-owned and private) mixed economy in China have been working well consistently. Despite the short-term wars and splitting shocks, the political and economic system has never changed in essence. As it should be, the polity frameworks of hundreds of small states were basically in line with the centralization system, most of which were hereditary governance, organization, and management by the elders in the family and clan society and the highly respected sage. This can also be regarded as the preparation period or the prototype stage of the centralized political system of "Great Unity."

In fact, from the beginning of the Yellow Emperor and Yan Emperor, China was already in the statue of the Great Unity. The political system of centralization was the abdication system at the very beginning and evolved into the hereditary monarchy due to self-interest. During the Warring States period, the seven states were formed by enfeoffment of Emperor of Zhou Dynasty and they all claimed to be Huaxia or "Zhuxia." The myths and historical memories of the seven states all belong to the same system, and they already possessed and formed a unified consciousness. This is completely different from Xirong, Nanman, Beidi, Dongyi and other ethnic groups. Guan Zhong's proposition of "revering the king and expelling the barbarians" has been fully affirmed and sincerely responded by the vassal states.

The texts used by all vassal states, from scripts on oracle bones, inscription on bronze to seal script, are the same and similar, which can be traced to the same origin among the seven states. There is no translation needed for all kinds of communication among the vassal states at all. After the First Emperor of Qin unified six states of Han, Zhao, Wei, Chu, Yan, and Qi, it eliminated the local

separatist forces and replaced the enfeoffment system with the county system. The unified writing and the unified transportation system that the First Emperor of Qin pioneered and implemented promoted the unity, autonomy, orderliness and efficiency of the national civilization and system.

Such model as one person, one family, one clan held the power of state governance gradually evolved into one that a political party in China represents the overall interests of all the people and administrates the political, economic, social and other major issues of the country, namely, the system of multi-party cooperation and political consultation under the leadership of the Communist Party of China. All power of the nation belongs to the people, and the people manage the national, economic, cultural and social affairs through various channels and forms. The cultural and philosophical logic that determines China's political and economic system has always been in the same line in the five-thousand-year history. Stability, independence, autonomy, and sustainability are the most prominent features of this political system.

China's mixed economy (state-owned and private) model has existed since ancient times. In this model, the state sector and the non-state sector, the government and the market maintain appropriate balance. For thousands of years, there has always been a strong and powerful state-owned sector. The state has played a direct role in balancing the key economic sectors, including constructing public infrastructure, coping with various crises, balancing market forces, and providing governmental public goods. All of these have been specifically discussed in the *Discourses on Salt and Iron* of the Han Dynasty, and the past dynasties have also practiced and tested the validity of the model. The adjustment of random and flexible changes and taking the maximum degree of comprehensive efficiency and high energy should be the most prominent featur

Today, China's "socialist market economy" is only a new title, which is only a relative to the Western "capitalist market economy" with some ideology. However, its essence remains China's mixed economy (state-owned and private) model. Many people in the world mistakenly believe that the goal of China's reform and opening up is the Western economic model and its transitional economy is a complete transition from planned economy to market economy, and a transition from state-owned economy to private economy. This kind of understanding may be seriously deviated from the real situation of China, and there is absolutely no quintessence in understanding the Chinese model from the history of Chinese civilization.

In China, the state-owned economic component and the private economic component have coexisted for thousands of years, and they have coordinated and developed. 100% nationalization and 100% privatization are the "abnormalcy" of the Chinese economy while the mixed economic model is the "normalcy" of it. The "visible hand" and the "invisible hand" coexist and the effect of timing and opportunity choice is the normal state of the Chinese economy instead. Simply measuring and explaining the development orientation of China's current "reform and opening up" with the Western economic mode will inevitably meet with refusal and cause disappointment.

The Chinese model will always be China's political and economic development model, and it definitely won't be the multi-party voting system plus the liberalism market economy of the Western countries. In the past 5,000 years, China has become the first and also the last living unique civilization in the history of mankind besides ancient Egypt, ancient Babylon, ancient India, and ancient Greece. From a practical point of view, there are already sufficient reasons to prove the rationality and inevitability of the long-term existence of the Chinese model. In essence, China's political and economic model conforms to the requirements of "the Way of nature."

At least for the Chinese nation, it is compliant with the common sense of "the Way of nature" to follow the development path that fits. Not taking the "old and evil path" is related to the prosperity of the country and the nation. In choosing the development path, the Chinese people will only listen to the instructions from ancestors and sages, and follow their sincere demands in mind instead of caring more about the inordinate ambitions from others and outsiders. The water circulation system in nature is itself a natural ecosystem that doesn't depend on any other existing system. The eyes from others do not need to be taken into account but other living systems must rely heavily on the water circulation system to survive on the contrary.

Referring to and modelling after the structure of the natural water circulation system, the Chinese people abolished all the unequal treaties imposed on them overnight, changed the status of the semi-colonial and semi-feudal country, and re-established a country with independent sovereignty, externally, "starting another stove" (meaning: Starting all over again from the beginning), "cleaning the house before treating guests" (meaning: Eliminating the remnants and privileges of imperialism in China first, and then establishing diplomatic relations with Western countries), implementing the diplomatic policy based on the "five principles of peaceful coexistence" and equally treating others; internally, establishing a set of independent political, economic, military, scientific, educational, social, cultural and other systems. What is especially fascinating to the world is that it has the most complete modern industrial manufacturing system in the world today and it is self-reliant during development.

"There is a truth that a country will suffer losses if it copies the experience of other countries." (said by Chairman Mao) "The Chinese people cherish the friendship and cooperation with other countries and their people, and cherish their right of independence and self-determination of their own after long-term struggling. Any foreign country should not expect China to be their vassal, nor expect China to undertake the painful result that harms our interests" (Deng Xiaoping).

"In such a big country with more than 5,000 years of civilization and more than 1.3 billion population to advance the reform and development, there is no textbook that can be regarded as a golden rule nor a teacher who can give strict orders to the Chinese people. Then what is the road? It is trampled out from where there is no way and opened up from where only thorns are created. The road of socialism with Chinese characteristics is a broad road for contemporary China to catch up with the times and lead the development of the times, and we must go unswervingly." (Xi Jinping)

At any time, the Chinese people are insisting on the development path and social system they have chosen, and always put the maintenance of national sovereignty, security, and territorial integrity as top priority. At the same time, they respect the right of people of all countries to choose their own development path. They insist that all countries are equal despite the difference in size, strength, and wealth. They do not interfere in other countries' domestic affairs or impose their own will on others. Regardless of the difference in religious beliefs, social systems, and ideology, they develop friendly and cooperative relations of mutual respect and equal treatment with all countries in the world.

Even if the Chinese model meets the requirements of "the Way of nature", the Chinese people still believe that "there is no universal development model in the world. All countries need to independently explore their own development path according to their national conditions. China insists on its own path without importing foreign models or exporting the Chinese model, or requiring other countries to copy China's practices. However, we are willing to discuss and share our development experience and practices with them if they are interested, but we absolutely won't impose our experience on them." (Zhang Yesui)

The Chinese people have done as what they have said, and continue to assist foreign countries when in urgent need of development. In supporting other countries, China has always insisted on "no political conditions attached," and the amount of foreign assistance in the 70 years since the foundation of the People's Republic of China has accumulated more than RMB250 billion, helping developing countries to build more than 2,000 complete sets of projects. Since 2000, China has announced nine times to exempt the heavily indebted poor countries and the least developed countries from expired interest-free loans from China, effectively reducing the debt burden of the countries concerned, which is in stark contrast to the "additional political conditions" of the foreign assistance from westerners.

The Chinese people solemnly promise to the world that socialist China will show the world with practice that China opposes hegemonism and power politics, and will never seek hegemony. China is the staunch force for safeguarding world peace. China's development and progress will not pose a threat to anyone. In the future when China is rich and strong, it will never seek hegemony, which is its basic national policy that it will never abandon. From the historical case of "Zheng He's voyages" in the early 15th century, the outsiders can clearly know that the Chinese nation is faithful in word and understand the cultural belief and logic behind its words and deeds.

Water never dominates, but it is the "king" of everyone. Water has never planned to export its own mode, nor does it need to do so. Water is that unique, noble and can't be surpassed. At the same time, water does not accept the mode input by others as there is nothing better to replace its position, function, and glory. Water has made many good friends by performing good deeds. When you need it, water will definitely do its best to help you without asking for return. The Chinese nation has learned a lot from the pledge of water.

The world governance model under "the Way of nature"

In today's globalized world, the Chinese people have made great strides to open up and actively participate in the international community. Apart from providing China's products, services, markets, tourists, capital, and technology to the world, the Chinese people have also intelligently proposed the Chinese thought and the Chinese plan: A Community of Shared Future for Mankind. For the human world, especially the Western world, it is almost a thunderclap that the Chinese people are able to export Eastern culture and thoughts. Many people feel surprised, frightened, and worried.

The concept of "a Community of Shared Future for Mankind" is exactly the same as that of the traditional Chinese culture – "Great Harmony" and "People around the world are all brothers and sisters". The society generally encourages "everyone to work for society." "When the Grand course was pursued, a public and common spirit ruled all under the sky; they chose men of talents, virtue, and ability; their words were sincere, and what they cultivated was harmony. Thus, men did not love their parents only, nor treat as children only their own sons. A competent provision was secured for the aged till their death, employment for the able-bodied, and the means of growing up to the young. They showed kindness and compassion to widows, orphans, childless men, and those who were disabled by disease, so that they were all sufficiently maintained. Males had their proper work, and females had their homes. (They accumulated) articles (of value), disliking that they should be thrown away upon the ground, but not wishing to keep them for their own gratification. (They labored) with their strength, disliking that it should not be exerted, but not exerting it (only) with a view to their own advantage. In this way (selfish) schemings were repressed and found no development. Robbers, filchers, and rebellious traitors did not show themselves, and hence the outer doors remained open, and were not shut. This was (the period of) what we call the Grand Union. " (*Li Yun, The Book of Rites*)

When the Grand course is implemented, the world is shared by all people. People with good morals and talent will be selected. Everyone is honest and respectful and advocates harmony. People will not only support their own parents and children, but also enable the elderly to live a peaceful life in old age, and facilitate the middle-aged people to work for society and young children grow up smoothly. This will support the widowers and widows, children who lost their parents, the elderly without a child, and the disabled.

Men have occupations and careers, and women have marriages and families. People pick up the abandoned property on the ground for sharing, not enjoying it alone. At the same time, people hate the kind of behavior when one refuses to do the best in the joint labor, and always seek no personal gain in work. In this way, no one will engage in conspiracy, and no one will steal property or arouse the war. Every household will not have to close the gate. This is a society of Great Harmony. The ideal of "Great Harmony" in ancient China is both qualitative and specific.

Following the idea of "Great Harmony", the concept of "a Community of Shared Future for Mankind" was first proposed, promoted, and practiced by the Chinese people, and it became a matter of course. The Chinese nation has always pursued concord, loves peace and promotes harmony. They

are always "good friends and neighbors" and "chase coexistence of all nations in harmony." The long-lasting history of Chinese civilization has created a unique "harmony" culture. The "harmony" culture contains the cosmology of combination of universe and human, the international view of all nations' peaceful coexistence, the harmonious but different social views, and the moral view of kindness among people."

"Harmony" and "combination" occupy a crucial and core position in the values of the traditional Chinese culture, and are the essence and first value of Chinese culture. "Harmony" and "combination" were originally derived from " Shang Qi combined five teachings in harmony in order to protect the people" (*Discourses of the States – Zheng*). It means that Shang Qi combined the "Five Cardinal Moral Codes" – the righteousness of a father, compassion of a mother, fraternal kindness of an older sibling, respect of a younger sibling, and filial piety of a child in harmony, so that people can get along and live in peace and harmony. Harmony and combination refer to harmony, peace, civility, cooperation, tolerance, respect, and integration. It emphasizes the value orientation of resolving the harmony and coordination of contradictions.

In traditional Chinese culture, the value of "harmony" and "combination" has been passed down from generation to generation. "In practicing the rules of propriety, it is harmony that is prized." "The superior man is affable, but not adulatory; the mean man is adulatory, but not affable" (*Analects* by Confucian). "Opportunities of time vouchsafed by heaven are not equal to advantages of situation afforded by the earth, and advantages of situation afforded by the earth are not equal to the union arising from the accord of men" (*Gongsun Chou II, Mencius*). "Heaven and earth are combined to produce all things, yin and yang change, and sex and falsehood combine to govern the world" (*Tianlun, Xunzi*). "All things leave behind them the obscurity (out of which they have come) and go forward to embrace the brightness (into which they have emerged), while they are harmonized by the breath of vacancy." (*Chapter 42, Laozi*). "Heaven and earth are the parents of all things. Life starts when they are combined and death comes when they are separated" (*Dasheng XIX, Zhuangzi*).

Inheriting the history of Chinese culture, Chinese President Xi Jinping expounded the concept of "a Community of Shared Future for Mankind" and "harmony and combination" on behalf of the Chinese nation, "In today's world, human beings live in a world composed of different cultures, races, skin colors, religions, and social systems." However, "in this world, the degree of mutual connection and interdependence among countries has deepened unprecedentedly. Human beings live in the same global village, in the same time and space where history and reality meet, and increasingly become a community of destiny where you have me and I have you."

"A Community of Shared Future for Mankind, as its name implies, means that the future and destiny of each nation and each country are closely linked. We should share weal and woe through thick and thin, strive to build the planet where we were born and grew up into a harmonious family, and turn the aspiration of the people of all countries for a better life into reality." Since the human world has crossed the stage of relative isolation and independent development and has become a

"global village" as a whole, China's five-thousand-year-old successful model of comprehensive national governance has naturally attracted worldwide attention and heated discussion, and has even been partially referenced and imitated.

The most basic experience of Chinese-style national governance lies in that "the Way of human" must conform to rather than run counter to "the Way of nature." Human beings have only one home – the earth, shared by all countries in the world. No country can stand out the complex and global economic and governance issues. Nowadays, no country is an island. Unilateralism and hegemony cannot find any way to become mainstream. The world economy is an organic and indiscerptible whole.

When the human society is considered as an organic whole that resembles the natural ecosystem, the issue of sustainable development is seriously placed on the agenda. Which country or nation is capable of playing the role of "water" in the human society? Obviously, "America First" hegemony dominated by the law of the jungle in the Western culture is contrary to the will of the people. Comparatively, the propositions of "win-win cooperation" and equality guided by "the law of water" in the Chinese culture enjoys immense popular support.

In short, Chinese values, essentially, worship the nature, the earth, natural law, and "water". "Water is soft, tender, yet strong with countless changes." Water not only has strong strength, but also tolerance. It is both soft and strong. The two-sided attributes are interconvertible with countless changes. Moreover, water can ultimately conquer the strong with the soft.

Under the overall framework of "a Community of Shared Future for Mankind", China takes the lead to play the central role of "water" and encourages other countries and nations to create more water sources in various parts of the world to jointly deliver water to the world and create wealth. China adheres to opening its domestic market to the maximum extent. China supports the global system of multilateral trade, and welcomes countries to ride on the Chinese "express" to become prosperous through win-win cooperation.

"The Belt and Road Initiative" is a specific practice derived from the concept of "a Community of Shared Future for Mankind", widely recognized and accepted by members of the international community. It is gradually becoming a common value norm and means to drive the reform of the global governance system and create new international relations and order. "The Belt and Road Initiative" is an entirely open and inclusive initiative of regional cooperation, rather than an exclusive, closed, and "small circle" of China. All countries are equal participants, contributors, and beneficiaries in the mechanism of "the Belt and Road Initiative".

"Five Types of Connectivity" driven and enhanced by "the Belt and Road Initiative": Policy coordination, facilities connectivity, unimpeded trade, financial integration, and people-to-people bonds. The "Five Types of Connectivity" can be regarded as waterways and rivers connecting countries and regions. Leveraging their own innovation, all countries and regions and acquire

wealth and create highlands of water sources which can drive the prosperity of countries and regions participating in the "the Belt and Road Initiative".

The application of Chinese model and experience to the world demonstrates that, Chinese intelligently advocate to avoid the areas with no unified consensus, such as religious beliefs, ideologies, and cultural differences. We are supposed to focus on economic issues concerned by all countries and nations, conduct global cooperation, and seek to achieve win-win and all-win situations. The Chinese-style "globalization" has the distinct characteristic of "harmony": It supports the global integration of the world economy rather than the unification of politics, cultures, societies, and religions of all countries in the world.

Regardless of differences in and disputes over religious beliefs, ideologies, and cultural practices of various countries and ethnic groups caused by varied environments and histories, China and the West should work together to identify and constantly enhance common understanding and values of the human world. Chinese people consider things from the viewpoint of the natural ecology, introduce the innovative perspective of "water", and interpret the universality and inclusiveness of "a Community of Shared Future for Mankind." Chinese people construct the basic theory of Eastern-style discourse system and explain the direction of the human world.

Water has universal value. The way of water has universal philosophical and cultural values.

Chapter TWO

Search for the Cultural Confidence of the Chinese People

Storytelling requires context. A good cultural storyteller pays more attention to choosing a suitable context. If we want to tell the story of oriental Chinese culture and let people, especially foreigners to understand it, it is hard to imagine that Chinese stories can be clearly and precisely explained via Western concepts. What is happening in China cannot be explained via the knowledge of the western people, even if they are dominating the global discourse in today's world. Otherwise, things can be much easier. In other people's eyes, China is still a "mysterious" country.

However, the situation in China is not very pleasant. It is a little bit terrible and disappointing. The atmosphere and environment in China are not very satisfactory. Some Chinese scholars, experts, and intellectuals are still enthusiastically copying things from the west, but seldom worry about the inappropriateness that may happen in this process. They lack sufficient research on the original research achievements from the west. With a limited understanding, they do not have a serious spirit or attitude. Meanwhile, they do not have anything original and cannot provide a satisfactory explanation of Chinese culture, so they formed a new academic theory. No wonder why the outsiders are reluctant to accept the teaching and explanation of platitudes and have no expectation for the new knowledge system.

In the middle of the 19th century, Darwin created the "evolution theory" in the west. Originally, the "law of the jungle" belongs to the category of modern biological theory in the Western knowledge system. "It is not the strongest of the species that survive, but the one most responsive to the change." It describes that various species compete with each other in order to survive, and nature will finally choose who will stay and who will leave. Species who can adapt to natural changes can survive. If not, they will die out and extinct. The weak serving as a prey to the strong is the law of the jungle. Eating is the nature of every species. People cannot live or survive without eating. Tigers eat sheep; eagles eat rabbits; birds eat insects and livestock eat grass. Big fish eats small fish; small fish eats shrimp and shrimp eats the microorganisms in the mud. The more food you can have, the stronger you are. The species who can eat everything on earth will be the king.

"Evolution" is a rigorous biological science with strict application objects and scope. Humans are living beings, so as other animals and plants. Humans are the high-level living species, while other animals and plants are low-level. Human survival and development depend on almost all other animals, plants, and species, while the survival and development of other species only rely on one or few lower-level species. Human beings have such an extraordinary power that can determine all species' life and death, including humans themselves. They even have the power of changing the natural environment that other lower animals and plants do not have.

Human beings are the most intelligent and advanced race of species, occupying the highest position in the biological chain. Other animals and plant life species are far less intelligent than human beings. Taking the "evolution theory" as an example, it might not be completely reasonable or at least not completely suitable to take the general knowledge conclusions that are summed up from the evolution of low-level biological competition as the great wisdom of nature, and indiscriminately

apply them to human beings. Humans should bravely jump out of the biological chain to expand outward, and find more source and inspirations of human wisdom beyond the biological chain.

Today, we doubt that westerners may apply the "evolution theory" at the wrong place or position. They might have mistakenly changed and packaged the originally simple biological evolution theory into a complex formula of modern social theory, misused it on the human development, and carried out the "jungle law" pan-social experiment. These result in the mentality of "material competition" and the philosophy of "the law of jungle", which made countless human beings suffer from it. From racism, colonialism, wars and invasion, color revolution, regime change, and even the elimination of other aliens, tragedies happen among countries, nations, and religions and they fight and kill each other. All mankind urgently needs to reflect the essence and dross of Western knowledge systems, as well as their application scope.

Therefore, we try to propose a new thought and a new perspective, jumping out of the old frame of Western discourse, innovating and looking for a new method and context outside of the Western discourse. We will also be looking for human wisdom and inspirations in the water circulation system rather than the biological chain system. Water, ubiquitous and easily understandable, is not only a communication tool, an intermediate medium of understanding, but also a figurative language. Everyone in the world can clearly understand the meaning of the information that "water" conveys to the outside world. We should tell the story of Chinese and Chinese culture with reference to the character and quality of water. We should also try to practice and explore a new system of knowledge discourse that can explain the Chinese culture and let others know and understand it.

Who are the Chinese people? Where do they come from and where will they go?

To be honest, what is "China" and "Chinese" is an old topic that is quite difficult to explain and understand. The philosophy topic of China has been studied by many scholars and experts in history, but the results are always very different. In the eyes of a thousand people, China has a thousand different appearances. The fragmented image of China has always put it in a mystery maze. It is fascinating and esoteric, but difficult to understand. It then becomes harder for outsiders to understand, even the Chinese people may not be able to completely understand ourselves.

China, such an oriental nation, is made up of a group of people called Chinese. The character of the Chinese people has fundamentally determined the national character of China. A thorough research on the way of thinking and group behavior of the Chinese people can help understand China. What is "China" like? The Westerners have had their explanations, and the Chinese people have their own explanations.

The vast majority of the above explanations are only focused on the description of the current Chinese characteristics: The Chinese people are marked by frequent internal strife and disunity; they do not obey the public rules or morals and are not well-disciplined; they are clever in trivial matters; they are not serious in their work; they easily follow the general trend and lack the ability of independent

thinking; they are diligent, hardworking, optimistic, and tolerant. However, all the researches have not gone one step further to explain why China has become such a nation. Obviously, such observations are not deep enough for a comprehensive understanding of Chinese culture and the Chinese people.

The image of the Chinese people in the western world

First of all, let's see how some Westerners describe the Chinese people. In the eyes of Western monk John of Plano Carpini, the Chinese people were friendly pagans. Around the thirteenth century, most Westerners were devout Christians. In their eyes, it was hard to understand and accept that the Chinese people were pagans although they boasted of high-degree material civilization. In 1245, a Franciscan monk named John of Plano Carpini was sent as an envoy of Pope to the land of the Tartars. After he returned, he wrote *Ystoria Mongalorum*. In the book, he mentioned a dynasty built by "Khitan" people. "There lived a people composed of a large number of inhabitants." He found that "they were all pagans. They also claimed that they had their own sages." They "believed in everlasting life but they were never baptized." And it was exactly a place with well-developed material civilization. It was an unexpected fact that there were such a people who were never baptized but enjoyed delicacies and finery the Westerners had never enjoyed. This shocked the Westerners.

In the eyes of the priest Juan Gonzales de Mendoza, the Chinese people are gentle and polite. In the book *The History of the Great and Mighty Kingdom of China and the Situation Thereof*, the priest Mendoza wrote sadly, "The saddest thing for Christians is that clever and deft Chinese people in such a beautiful and wealthy country finally become fatuous idolater due to their ignorance of the truth of God." They acknowledged some people as the sages and worshiped ghosts. It could be said that they had no religious belief. "This made us confused and dropped into thought." For those devout and crazy Christians in the Middle Ages, pagans were their mortal enemy.

In the book *The History of the Great and Mighty Kingdom of China and the Situation Thereof*, the priest Mendoza described the appearance and disposition of the Chinese people. They are healthy, ingenious, clever, and civilized. "They are great inventors. They are diligent and skillful." They have their own outlook on life. "The Chinese is a people with the highest mental level. They have their own views on the origin of heaven and earth as well as the birth of mankind." The Chinese people are self-sufficient and optimistic. "They are a nation that loves parties and having fun, always avoiding sorrow." They do not like wars. "The Chinese people have a law: Do not provoke wars within their own country or invade other countries." The book details the Chinese weddings, funerals, as well as various customs and rules for festivals. It also gives an account of the Chinese brutal corporal punishment and superstitions.

In the eyes of Marco Polo, the Chinese people are kindhearted and peaceful. Different from missionaries, Marco Polo who is a businessman introduces China in a more secular way. In his book *The Travels of Marco Polo*, he is always praising the Chinese people. He describes the emperor of the Song Dynasty as a "temperate and merciful" man. The Suzhou people are "kindhearted, timid, and overcautious." They are wise and capable persons and are good at business. The Hangzhou people are

"peaceful and gentle." They are sincere and kindly and get along well with neighbors. The Hangzhou people are very kind and hospitable. "Those who come from other places and come here for business are treated equally and sincerely. The Hangzhou people invite them home to show a friendly attitude." Men and women respect each other. "Men respect their own wife, without any jealousy or suspicion." China is an absolutely mundane paradise. The Chinese living in this paradise are all kind and friendly.

In 1615, the book *De Christiana expeditione apud sinas suscepta ab Societate Jesu* (also called "*Commentarj della Cina*") was published in Germany. Matteo Ricci detailed the image of the Chinese people with his experiences. In his works, the Chinese people are hard-working, versatile, gentle, and courteous. They show respect to teachers and attach great importance to education. Meanwhile, he points out China's undesirable customs, such as superstition, fortunetelling, concocting pills of immortality, drowning of infants, preference of boys to girls, brutal corporal punishment, perverting the law and pervading suspicion and cowardice.

Voltaire once said, "Even if we don't admire too much the advantages of the Chinese people, we must at least admit that their empire's governance is the unprecedentedly best in the world." "European princes, dukes, and merchants explore the East just for wealth, while European philosophers have discovered a new spiritual and physical world in the East." In the Enlightenment of more than one hundred years in the West, it was discovered that the thoughts of the Chinese people have become a dazzling banner for thinkers going forward. Confucius's ritual system, Mencius's thoughts on benevolent governance, and the moralism-oriented Chinese civilization represented by Confucian philosophy, became the cultural ideals of Europe in that era.

Leibniz, Germany's most important scientist and philosopher, wrote in the introduction to *Das Neueste von China*, "We never believed in the existence of a nation that is more advanced than our ethics and more progressive in our ways of conducting oneself in society. Now China in the East gives us a big awakening!" He praised China for "the highest level of human culture and the most advanced technical civilization. If a wise man is elected to decide which nation is the most outstanding, rather than deciding which goddess is the most beautiful, then he will hand over the golden apple to the Chinese."

This kind of cognition was extended by another great German Goethe. He talked about China in 1829, "The Chinese people are almost similar to us in terms of thoughts, behaviors, and emotions, so that we soon feel that the Chinese and Germans are the same kind. The difference is that everything there is clearer, purer, and more ethical than ours." "When German scholar Christopher is immersed in the meditation on the nations of the world, he always infers that on the planet created by God, the Chinese people are the sagest, the most righteous, and the happiest nation!"

Hegel said, "History must be talked about from China." But China stayed outside history. In China, individuals had no independence or freedom. The character of the Chinese nation is, "Everything that belongs to the spirit, such as moral principles and emotions free from constraints, inner religion and science as well as true art, are far away from them."

Montesquieu said that the climate had made the Chinese people indolent and coward. China was "the most deceptive nation in the world" and "the Chinese people were very greedy for benefits." According to Montesquieu, "China is an authoritarian country and its principle is terror." In such a country, the Chinese people were evil in human nature and had no sense of humor. The Chinese people were indolent, lazy, coward, and obedient. He made a rational analysis of the Chinese feudal code of ethics. He believed that the "feudal code of ethics constituted the general spirit of the nation" in China. As a result, overthrowing ethics can overthrow everything. Adherence to the feudal code of ethics did not make the Chinese people become honest and trustworthy. "In China, deception is allowed." China is "the most deceptive nation in the world." The Chinese are "very greedy for benefits." In that era, Montesquieu negated the image of China in the strongest way.

In the eyes of American missionary Arthur Henry Smith, the Chinese people are sensitive about their own reputation and manage the household industriously and thriftily. They are diligent, hardworking, and polite. They tend to disregard time and precision. They are inclined to misunderstand others and talk in a roundabout way. They are obedient in mind but do not act in such an obedient way. Their thinking is ambiguous. They are unhurried. The Chinese belittle other nations and lack public interests, fettered by old conventions. Resigned to the situation, they live tenaciously. They are tolerant and easy to feel content. They give priority to filial piety and fraternal duty and benevolence. They lack sympathy and integrity, and always generate mutual suspicions. There are multiple religious beliefs and the Chinese people deal with concrete matters relating to work.

The image of the Chinese people, described in the book *The Travels of Marco Polo* that appeared at the end of the 13th century, is gentle and morally noble. At the end of the 19th century when Arthur Smith wrote *Chinese Characteristics*, the word "Chinaman" with derogatory meaning was rooted in the language of Westerners, and the proper word "Chinese" was excluded. In 793, the George Macartney diplomatic corps visited China and was ordered to kneel to the Emperor, which they regarded as an insult. With no diplomatic progress, the diplomatic corps returned to Britain. Then, the bad impressions about the Chinese people were confirmed and quickly spread in the West. Westerners' perceptions of the Chinese people began to get worse and uglier.

"The Empire of China is just a dilapidated old ship. It is just because there are a few cautious captains that the ship has not sunk for nearly 150 years fortunately. The ship will not sink immediately. It will drift like a wreck and then run into a bank, broken into pieces... It will be beyond repair." George Macartney said. In the book *Sketch for a Historical Picture of the Progress of the Human Spirit*, Condorcet believes that "the Chinese nation is an ignorant, mediocre, and humiliated nation, full of prejudice and with no abilities or courage. If people want to know how an authoritarian government can destroy human functions, there is no need to mention those terrible superstitions. China is a typical example."

German Herder wrote in *Ideas on the Philosophy of the History of Mankind* that "China is a mummy. It is coated with antiseptic spices, painted with hieroglyphics, and wrapped in silk. Its blood circulation has stopped, like a hibernating animal. Therefore, it takes an attitude of isolation and

obstruction for all foreign things. It doesn't know about the outside world and doesn't like the outside world, either. It is immersed in the self-conceited and has a sense of superiority." "The Chinese people are even more ridiculous! They complicate all the rites which are foolish. ... Some Chinese people are even more stubborn than any other nation in the world and for thousands of years they have been obsessed with some vulgar customs and habits left by their ancestors." De Quincey described.

The Frenchman Rousseau once said in *La Nouvelle Héloïse* that in China, "literati, cowards, hypocrites, and swindlers have been talking too much every day, but what they have said are useless. They are thoughtful but incapable, lacking unique views. They just appear better than they are. They are polite, witty, tricky and deceiving and flatter others. They always talk about the obligations and morals and do not know other human natures. Their so-called human relationship is just curtsy." In George Anson's *Voyage Round the World in the Years MDCCXL, I, II, III, IV*, the Chinese are deceitful, impoverished, degraded, ignorant, and incorrigibly obstinate.

During the first Sino-British Opium War in 1840, China's immediate collapse and kneeling for humiliating peace severely defamed China. Since then, many Westerners have treated China with full superiority and arrogance, showing contempt at anytime and anywhere. In 1842, British naval officers wrote in *The Operations of the British Army in China* that China is a country reigned by ignorance and arrogance for a long time, a country without self-renewal ability and vitality. In the Opium War, the inevitable victory of the Western artillery and warships over the Eastern spears and swords, and the fact that the "heavenly empire" was defeated by the "small barbarian states", caused a fundamental reversal in the understanding of each other between China and the West.

From the 1860s and 1870s, the West Coast of the United States was swept across by waves of anti-Chinese activities, and the "Asian Peril" theory flourished for a time. In 1876, the Senate and House of Representatives of the United States passed resolutions respectively, dispatching a special investigation commission to San Francisco to collect evidence. Following the investigation, a 1,200-page *Joint Special Committee Report on the Investigation of Chinese Immigration* consisting of testimony from over 100 people was compiled, from which we can see the most terrible racial discrimination and hatred of mankind.

Q: From a social point of view, are they a better race than the African race?

A: No, sir, they are no better than Africans. In my opinion, they are inferior to any race created by God.

Q: As far as I know, what you just said is that the Chinese are the worst among all the wise animals created by God?

A: I don't think there is any race inferior to the Chinese. In some parts of Africa, intellectual standards are relatively low, but moral standards are relatively high; that is, they are more honest. These people (the Chinese) have reached the culmination of evil of the past 4,000 years, a civilization that is the culmination of evil caused by overpopulation.

Even the US President Theodore Roosevelt then, the leader of a country, once slandered the Chinese is an "immoral, vile, and undesirable race." In the eyes of Americans of that epoch, the Chinese were inborn animals, slaves, beggars, and cruel villains. At that time, the Western adventure stories about China always presented the same story of police officers and gangsters. The villains were invariably Chinese who were fierce, cunning and wicked and always attempted to kidnap and rape white women. At the critical moment, the white hero appeared and finally brought the Chinese villains to justice. In the Western World after the nineteenth century, the positive image of the Chinese had disappeared.

While China was regarded by Westerners as a "decayed mummy" and a synonym for "stagnation and backwardness", Lee Kuan Yew, ex-Prime Minister of Singapore, argued that "the Chinese culture is so encouraging that every individual influenced by it will strive for perfection; people intending to pass the imperial examination or to become the best rice merchant, carpenter, craftsman or potter will try their best." He added that China is such a big country that it entertains absolute confidence in the inevitable trend to be the world leader as soon as it returns to the right track one day. No one in China doubts the fate and development China will experience after the revitalization of civilization, in that this is the oldest civilization in the world, which has a long history of more than 5000 years without interruption."

According to a report of Rand Corporation (the world's top think tank, the most prestigious decision-making advisory body in the United States and even the world), the Chinese people and Chinese culture feature as follows:

Chinese people lack honesty and social responsibility.

Chinese people attach great importance to personal relations.

Chinese people do not understand the decent and dignified life.

Chinese people are selfish, greedy, and ruthless.

The Chinese have no courage to pursue what they think is right.

Chinese people prefer cheap and free goods and always want to get something from nothing.

The vast majority of Chinese do not understand elegant manners and basic courtesy.

China is extremely polluted and the most unlivable country in the world.

The Chinese try their best to avoid taking risks.

By 2020, China will be a very poor country, judging from the standards of Westerners.

Chinese people are not interested in the balance and significance of life. On the contrary, they

are way more obsessed with material acquisition than Westerners. Most Chinese people find that they do not understand such concepts as spirituality, free belief, and mental health, because their mentality has not reached a higher level at which the life should be (that is, the coexistence of body and spirit). Their mentality remains focused on the miserable instinctive desire of animals for sex and food. Arthur Smith, a famous Western missionary, pointed out a century ago that "What the Chinese lack most is not wisdom, but courage and integrity."

Image of Chinese in the eyes of the Chinese people

Secondly, let us see how the Chinese describe their own nation. Among native Chinese, Lu Xun was a special figure. With a thinker's keen perception and exploratory spirit, he not only created typical images of Kong Yiji, Ah Q and Mrs. Xianglin, but also depicted the harsh social environment with his pen and ink, bringing a group of numb and ignorant stand-bys and idlers to life. "Pointed at by the whole world, I remain determined and sober." This is what sustained Lu Xun's literature. He used his powerful pen to criticize those numb and emotionless Chinese people severely.

Lu Xun created a large number of numb stand-bys in his works and criticized them. His masterpiece *The Madman's Diary* is a complaint of a paranoid against a cannibalistic stand-by who pretended to be benevolent and righteous. The weird eyes of Uncle Zhao, children, women, and family members all protruded on their fearful face, and they grinned saying, "They seem to be afraid of me and want to hurt me." The sick old man looked fiercely at me with his ghost-like eyes open, "peeking at me from the lens of his glasses." Even the eyes of fish were "white and hard", and the dog of Zhao conspired, "looking at me when I passed." They all looked at each other with suspicious eyes. They wanted to eat others and were afraid of being consumed. Once what they thought was unveiled by the madman, their eyes became fierce. The madman in this book appears to be a maniac, but in fact he is the soberest person. He sees what the world actually is with his crazy eyes.

Lu Xun depicted a large number of idle, indifferent and extorted visitors in his novels, thus profoundly expressing the weakness that permeated the whole nation and his anxiety about the common unconsciousness. His novels were also a series of tragedies showing the soul of Chinese people to "unveil the suffering and arouse the attention to treatment." Lu Xun said, "We either rise up in silence or perish in silence." He did not want his compatriots to remain weak and to be called the "sick men of East Asia." Although China was poor and weak then, he was encouraging his compatriots to face up to the plight and find ways to get out of it.

Bo Yang, a Taiwanese writer, wrote a book entitled the *Ugly Chinese*, which criticized the vile nature of the Chinese people. The writer was extremely sad to see China unable to be prosperous. He pointed out that a disease was infecting the traditional Chinese culture so that the children and grandchildren were also infected and incurable. In his book, Bo Yang mocked the Chinese people bitterly who were shackled by conservatism, boldly analyzed the "bad root" of the Chinese people, and exposed the ugliness and improper habits of his family. People would fight with each other in

their own families, and they were dirty, chaotic, noisy, selfish, stubborn, unable to say "sorry" or "thank you"; they liked to talk meaningless and fake things, lie and speak malicious words. These were some of the bad habits of the Chinese; bad habits also existed nationwide, such as the corrupted imperial examination system, slavish and flattering eunuch system, and the ignorant tradition of foot-binding.

The *Ugly Chinese* reveals the "ugly" character or psychological state of the Chinese nation. Bo Yang has a general view of the Chinese nation and its culture, that is, Chinese culture is a "jar", a "sour and stinky" jar, and "most Chinese" are maggots living in this "sour and stinky" jar. "Have been confined to this jar for too long, what the Chinese thought, judged and viewed were polluted by it and could not escape out of it." "As a result, we Chinese became so selfish and suspicious that we came to be so ugly today." In a word, the ugly Chinese. In Bo Yang's eyes, the traditional Chinese culture should be abandoned thoroughly, because "the sauce jar of Chinese culture stinks and makes the Chinese ugly."

The *Chinese* (previously translated as *My Country and My People*) was written by Lin Yutang, who presented the characters, mind, ideals, life, politics, society, art, and culture of the Chinese people in a humorous and marvelous way. He also compared the above-mentioned elements with those in the Western in an in-depth manner. This is why this book made a splash from home and abroad after it was published by John Day in New York in 1935, highly praised by American female writer Pearl Buck and other celebrities and translated into multiple languages that widely circulated in the West.

"China is such a great country and its national life is so complex that diverse and even contradictory interpretations of this country are natural. If someone holds an opinion contrary to mine, I am ready to support him and provide him with more materials to prove he is correct. Moments when people can acquire and experience the truth are rare, but only these moments can remain forever." observed Lin Yutang.

Chinese people are smooth, prudent, preserved, enduring and opportune. They are so sophisticated that they do not speak their mind. That is to say, they are experienced and even cunning. Chinese people are generally prudent when they get along with others. Being mature and meek often means that they prefer to resort to the power of negativity, calmness and waiting, rather than the youthful vigor and passionate romance owned by the young. Whenever the Chinese encounter difficulties, they do not actively pursue progress to overcome difficulties fundamentally, but they uphold the philosophy of "one step back to see the spacious sea and vast sky" to comfort themselves. Sometimes this philosophy is also called "the death of a soldier in exchange for the whole territory."

Chinese people are particularly enduring. When living in China, a person should learn to bear humiliation and live humbly. "Live like an animal." That's victory. Tolerance has become a great vice of the Chinese people because "the Chinese have tolerated tyranny, turbulence, and corruption that many Westerners have never tolerated." China's victory often depends on its longevity. He who is patient and lives long enough will win finally. Chinese people regard staying alive as the supreme

purpose of life. Therefore, as an old saying goes, "Decent death is no better than a decayed life." As long as you are alive, you can see your enemies decease and gain the ultimate victory.

Chinese people like to seclude from the outside world passively. When going uphill, Chinese people are very fond of Confucianism that advocates that "people with excellent academic performance should step in the political world." At that time, people were so satisfied as if they could appreciate all flowers in Chang'an (an ancient capital of China) ridding a galloping horse in the spring breeze. However, the philosophy that "people with excellent academic performance should step in the political world" is a highly exclusive game that is essentially a zero-sum game. As life is often unsatisfactory, Taoism inevitably exists to provide a way out for every Chinese who is frustrated in the officialdom, casino, and romance.

Chinese people like to be a cunning old man who lives in this world upholding the philosophy of "the death of a soldier in exchange for the whole territory"; the best way is to stay away from risk; a good man should not be put in a disadvantageous position; one step back to see the spacious sea and vast sky. What should you do when people want to insult, mock, despise, slander, hurt, hate, and trick you? The best way is to endure, obey, respect, stay away from him and even surrender yourself to the suffering when necessary, pretend to be deaf and dumb and show indifference to see how it ends up. In fact, with no need to learn any traditional Chinese culture, everyone who lives in the ancient land of China was born to be cunning, ranging from the old to the young. No one in China is immune to cunning. The soil and climate of China determine that China is a place where you cannot survive until you learn how to be cunning.

In China, all the problems are actually about income. All doctrines are nothing more than business. What really matters is nothing more than "promotion and prosperity." Doctrines and religions such as Confucianism, Taoism, Buddhism, Christianity, and Catholicism, or even trivial things like napping are edible in China. Therefore, eating Confucian food, Taoist food, Buddhist food, Christ food and Catholic food are very popular and common in China. The indifference to spiritual beliefs and the secular utilitarianism are the common characteristics of the Chinese people. Therefore, to be a Buddhist monk or a Taoist monk is often the same as to be an official, which is categorized by ranking and income.

"The Chinese are Taoist in nature and Confucian in culture, but their Taoist thought is more than Confucian thought." Everything in China is very secular. There is no real love. The marriage is for the sake of reproduction and survival. The reality requires a person to be utilitarian. The so-called love of the Chinese people only exists in mythology and imagination but never in reality, because the Chinese family itself is a production unit, that is, a place where loans are granted. The Chinese people use the concept of "filial piety" to maintain the family model, believing that raising children is to have someone to depend on when parents are old, and grain should be stored in case of famine. Everything in China has a utilitarian purpose. You reap what you saw.

Religious belief of Chinese people

Both Westerners and Chinese tend to adopt the same or a similar model to tell stories about the personalities and conducts of Chinese people. Most of them explore and describe the behavioral features and mentality of Chinese people, and only a few probe into the dominant influence of the Chinese culture. Therefore, it is rare to see a complete explanation for how Chinese people have developed into what they are today. It is something like this: A patient is diagnosed of a series of diseases and symptoms but does not know the causes; a doctor tends to focus on diagnosis alone, without giving a prescription.

What should the patient do with it? How should the patient do to recover and improve his/her health and prevent the diseases from a relapse?

Against such a backdrop, we decided to shoulder the mission and tried to explain what has made China what it is today through careful observation, diligent study, active thinking and meticulous summarization. It is indeed hard to find a nation in the world which share the same experiences, thinking and personality with the Chinese nation.

In the 5,000-year history of China's development, what external factors enlightened the great wisdom of Chinese people? What natural factors were the main ones that shaped the personality of Chinese people? Seeking and understanding all the fundamental factors, even if some of them, that influenced the Chinese culture and the personality of Chinese people will provide a deeper insight into Chinese people and help uncover the mysteries about China.

Do Chinese people have any belief? What is the belief of Chinese people? It is impossible to find a nation or a culture which does have any belief. But China is different from a Western country which has a standard theistic religious belief. Then, what is the belief of the Oriental China? It is a question that has confused many people. According to the logical thinking of Westerners, belief must involve standard church classics and doctrines, a group of devoted priests and missionaries, a large quantity of pious believers.

If belief is defined this way, it is natural for us to come to the conclusion that China does not have a standard religious belief. As a result, such sayings as "Chinese people can have belief in everything or in nothing, and the Chinese society lacks moral and ethnic standards", "Chinese people is dishonest and lack a sense of social responsibility" and "Chinese people are selfish, greedy and indifferent" have gone virus among Westerners who have mainstream discourse power and among some Chinese people.

Nevertheless, the majority of Chinese people don't really agree with such evaluation and sayings. The Chinese values are different from the Western ones, and Chinese people have always had something to revere. Chinese people don't think it necessary to create a god between human and nature or a religion to standardize and direct what human says and does. For them, it is more appropriate to have everything dominated by the "universe."

The rules of the universe plays the most important role in everything. Therefore, the "universe" is mighty enough to lead the evolution of everything in the world. China is a country which advocates the principle of "combination of universe and human." Since the ancient times, Chinese people have had a strong belief on "heaven and earth" and believed that the universe is the mightiest in the word. The integration of "heaven", "earth" and "man" has led to a dynamic entity. In the kingdom of nature, there are heaven, earth and everything.

Heaven is high above, and earth is right under, and everything stays between the two. Human has always held a central position on the earth and is the most intelligent group among all living creatures. According to Chinese people's view on the world, the orderly development of the universe follows designated "truth." The "truth" refers to natural rules. Everything in the world is restricted, standardized and dominated by natural rules. "The universe gives birth to Yin and Yang." The growth and death or the prosperity and decline of everything in the universe are all influenced by the rules for the change to Yin and Yang.

The rules of Yin and Yang are changing, and they are the rules of change. There is a curve rather than a straight line between Yin and Yang. A curve indicates changing and high elasticity and implies "in motion." According to the Chinese Yin-Yang theory, Yin and Yang are integrated. There is a white dot in Yin Fish, while there is a black dot in Yang Fish. The mutual conversion between Yin and Yang is changing all the time. Despite that Yin and Yang are two Chinese characters, they serve as the two opposite forces of Qi (literally means "energy"). If an entrance is Yang, then the exit will be Yin; if the increase is Yang, then the decrease will be Yin. These two opposite forces have contributed to infinite things in the universe since the ancient times.

The truth of Yin and Yang is dialectic. It is rules of dialectics. There is not a clear boundary between Yin and Yang. The two can be mutually converted. There is not justice between the two, either. Hence, it is inappropriate to say that one is bad while the other is good. The evaluation criterion for good and bad lies in the overall balance and harmony between Yin and Yang. If there is balance, harmony and appropriateness between Yin and Yang, it is regarded as "good"; otherwise, it is deemed as "bad." Chinese people pay attention to "work" and "skill." This indicates that they value fitness and appropriateness and seek for "proper." Do not be unduly joyous; do not be overwhelmingly sad; be modest rather than flattery; be tolerant but not let everything out of control. "The skillful utilization of these principles depends on mind."

Yin and Yang are a unity of opposites. The truth of Yin and Yang is the truth about unity of opposites. Yin and Yang can supplement each other, but they can also offset each other. Supplement and offsetting are the two sides of contradiction as well as two aspects of Yin and Yang. Mutual supplement and offsetting are a universal rule for everything and are two indispensable parts of everything. Supplement and offsetting are relative. Without supplement, there will not be offsetting; without offsetting, there will not be supplement. If there is only supplement, everything will develop endless into an extreme situation which will turn "good" into "bad"; if there is only offsetting, everything will be overly restrained and then disappear. In the unity of opposition between

supplement and offsetting, excessive supplement or offsetting would break the relative balance or unity and everything will deviate from the balanced track.

The truth of Yin and Yang is also the rule of cycle. The relationship between Yin and Yang is also the relationship between "dynamic" and "static." "Dynamic would not exist without static, and static will perish if dynamic disappears." "Yin and Yang take the form of Qi. Yin Qi disperse to generate Yang, while Yang Qi is condensed to form Yin." The dispersing of Qi is dynamic Yang, and the condensation of Qi is static Yin. The relationship between Yin and Yang and between dynamic and static is a restraint and supplementary one. Dynamic and static are mutually supplementary and restraint and serve as a prerequisite, condition and result for each other. This cycle is infinitely repeated. As Xunzi put it, "Ending is followed by beginning, and beginning leads to ending."

The "truth" or Yin and Yang theory that is valued by Chinese people is actually something invisible and "magical", so it is difficult to understand it in daily life. "Truth" cannot be traced. They cannot be seen, heard, touched or felt, but they exist and are universal. To have a better understanding of "truth", it is natural for ordinary people to find a concrete reference object to feel natural rules in a specific way.

"The highest excellence is like water. Water is good at benefiting everything without vying for any fame or gain. Water is in a place which is despised by the public, but it is the place where one is closest to truth." (*Chapter VIII of The Book of the Way* by Laozi) The supreme goodness is like water in pursuit of perfection; water is good at nourishing all things without competing with them for fame and wealth, stays in undesirable places. Hence, water is closest to "truth." It can be seen here that "truth" is not an intangible concept or illusion. "Water" has become "truth" in the daily life of Chinese people or an incarnation of natural rules. Laozi, the renowned Chinese philosopher, used "truth" to explain natural rules and creatively compared "natural rules", which are hard to describe and perceive, to "water." Revealing his great commitment, this was highly significant and extraordinary.

Water is colorless and tasteless. It can take the shape of a square or a circle according to situation. It is fluid and can be any shape in nature and reach any place. Water is of extremely excellence and softness. Sometimes, it flows silently; sometimes, it runs turbulently. It is free from any competition, but at the same time it is inclusive to all. Water can moisten everything. It benefits everything but never contradicts with any of them. This is exactly the truth of life. Therefore, Chinese people admire "truth" and "water", showing respect to nature, natural rules and the principles of the universe. Learning from water, they study and summarize the quality of water and obtain wisdom and inspiration from water. Water conveys the truth of life and serves as the source of human wisdom.

In reality, it seems that Chinese people have a faith in everything but do not show full belief in everything and that there is not a mainstream religious belief that is upheld across the country. In China, there are numerous churches and temples of different kinds. It is rare for Chinese people to purposely provoke a fight or quarrel with others. Usually, ordinary people would show their pilgrimage to any temple or Buddha sculpture they come across. They would also enter a church

if they encounter one, showing respect to God. Seemingly, Chinese people can accept all kinds of religious belief. But don't take it seriously, because they just do it out of politeness. Such a conduct should not be interpreted as that a religious belief is something unique in their mind. In fact, showing respect to everything around is one of excellent attributes of water.

It is sure that each Chinese person has something to persist in. With piety, some of them believe that "water is the origin of everything" and "water is closest to truth." Water is a religious belief for Chinese people, so is truth. In fact, the natural rules are what Chines people really have a faith in. Therefore, if you have a deep understanding of water, you will gain much knowledge of the Chinese culture and people. Thanks to water, truth or natural rules have become more understandable. Human respects nature and follows natural rules; hence, water has served as something that wins admiration from Chinese people. Water has been revered by Chinese people for 5,000 years and will continue to be respected for 5000 years to come.

In the Western knowledge system, there is a law called "the law of the jungle." More or less under the influence of the theory of evolution, a set of "efficiency"-related core concepts gradually took shape in the Western culture, including freedom, democracy, rule of law, human right, competition, science and individualism. This has reinforced the Western discourse system in depth and width and expanded the coverage of the Western culture. Is it necessary for us to develop a "law of water" featuring the Oriental thinking in the new Chinese knowledge system, which can be used as a basic theoretical framework to establish new Chinese discourse and knowledge systems?

Water not only has strong strength, but also tolerance. It is both soft and strong. The two-sided attributes are interconvertible with countless changes. Moreover, water can ultimately conquer the strong with the soft. We should take water and history as a mirror to reflect on our present-day life. We should turn to the traditional Chinese culture and *I-Ching*, the beginning of the Chinese culture, to think about the road signs that our ancestors left for us. We should seek the wisdom heritage of the Chinese nation from classics and history.

We need to regain and understand water and probe into its value, quality and attributes. In the ancient times, China inherited its own cultural system for hundreds of years. Facing the impacts from and the interaction with the Western culture, it is more urgent for China to develop a new knowledge and cultural systems to introduce the origin, development and future of the Chinese civilization. This will not only make contribution to the revitalization of the Chinese nation but boost the development of a Community of Shared Future for Mankind, the pursuit of shared values for human, and the establishment of a shared cultural and value system.

Chapter THREE

Water, the Same Origin of Confucianism, Buddhism, and Taoism

Telling stories of Chinese culture and Chinese people is actually about their daily behavior, living standards, and ethics. Should this be said and how to say it? Should that be done and how to do it? This, in fact, reflects the standards of "goodness" and "badness" that people believe. As good conducts that benefit both the doer and others are accumulated, the society has gradually formed a set of ideas and norms regarding good manners that are in line with the thought of the nation, and its essence has gradually penetrated the mind of the people and then been internalized into the consciousness of the Chinese nation. After presenting itself in people's mind and activities, the false is removed and the correct is preserved to create a culture.

There are three major cultural systems in Chinese culture: Confucianism, Taoism, and Buddhism, specifically the Confucius-led Confucianism, Laozi-led Taoism, and Chinese Buddhism represented by Huineng, the six ancestors of Zen Buddhism (Han Buddhism). The Chinese character " 释 " refers to the religion founded by Siddhartha Gautama, the ancient Indian prince who abandoned the throne and secluded himself from the secular world in pursuit of peace and stability and eventually became a saint under the Bodhi tree. The religion created by Siddhartha Gautama is also called Buddhism. We also need to point out here that influenced by the Western context, modern Chinese often equates the concept of " 三 教 " in Chinese with "three religions", which is not necessarily accurate, given that in Chinese traditional books, the character " 教 " merely means "enlightenment" instead of "religion" defined by modern Western religion.

The Chinese Buddhism came into being thanks to the eastward spread of Indian Buddhism. Coinciding with the beginning of Gregorian Calendar, Indian Buddhism began to spread from India to China along the Silk Road. After a long period of dissemination, and localization, absorption, digestion and development, the Chinese Buddhism with local Chinese consciousness and national characteristics was created. Buddhism originated in India, developed in China, and spread as far as to Japan, Korea and Southeast Asia. However, due to the exclusion fueled by Hinduism and Islam that was introduced into India later, Buddhism gradually disappeared in India in the eighth and nineteenth centuries A.D. China, in which Buddhism was preserved and developed, has naturally become the real home of Buddhism in the world today.

Buddhism, like Christianity, Catholicism, Islam, Judaism, Hinduism, and Orthodox, is a foreign cultural import. But why was Buddhism the sole religion that was smoothly introduced into China from India and accepted by the mainstream Chinese culture? Why can Buddhism take root, blossom and bear fruit in foreign lands? The introduction of Buddhism into China in the early ancient times marked the "most important milestone" in the history of Chinese philosophy and religion (observed Hu Shi). Beyond that, Buddhism has a comprehensive impact on the culture, aesthetics and language of Chinese society, becoming an indispensable part of Chinese culture and exerting extensive impact on the society.

Buddhism is so naturally familiar to modern Chinese people that they almost forget that Buddhism is a foreign religion. When we talk about Chinese Buddhism, we must start from the time when it was first introduced into the territory of China. One question in the Chan case has been

repeatedly mentioned, "What does Buddha come from West for?" That is, why was Buddhism spread westward to China? There have been many famous but indirect answers to this question, which is regarded as being meaningless. Nevertheless, learning and tracing back to the source of history should be more meticulous and patient.

Englishman Toynbee once made a famous conclusion that the great development of religion often followed the collapse of an empire. The spread of Buddhism in China was largely attributed to the political splitting and social crisis that had lasted for nearly 400 years after the collapse of the political order advocated by Confucianism in the Han Dynasty. The society whose foundation was being shaken became a breeding ground where foreign ideas and systems could find their places. At this critical moment when people could hardly predict the blessings and calamities, Buddhism entered China opportunely, at least to a certain extent, granting people spiritual tranquility and guidance that enabled them to get rid of anguish and suffering in the real world by pursuing the world on the other side. Of course, what is emphasized here is the opportune moment of Buddhism stepping in China.

The time when Buddhism was introduced into China was opportune. More importantly, however, the core values of Buddhism conform to what the Chinese people desire for. If Buddhism had not fitted in the beliefs of the Chinese people, it would have been almost impossible to localize in China. Buddhism, like native Chinese religions such as Confucianism and Taoism, has a similar or even identical value. Such common gene determines the future and destiny of Buddhism in China. Obviously, Buddhism adapted to and responded to what the Chinese nation wanted spiritually, and integrated into the mainstream Chinese culture so successfully that it eventually becomes one of the three pillars supporting Chinese culture.

The Chinese cultural community was firstly created in farmland areas. The Qilu culture represented by Confucius and Mencius, Jingchu culture represented by Laozi and Zhuangzi, Legalist culture represented by Shang Yang and Han Fei, Military culture represented by Sun Tzu, and mass culture represented by Mozi. After a long period of integration, the various schools formed the basic values of the Chinese cultural community. This cultural community, with farming culture as its core, constantly integrates cultures originating from other ethnic groups, especially those of Buddhism spreading to China, Buddhism spreading to Tibet and Buddhism spreading southward. All these cultures are part of the large family of Chinese culture.

All components of the Chinese cultural community have a common value: The particular respect of nature that encourages people to obey the law of nature and worship the water, the representative of the law of nature ("Tao"). Cultures that take root and flourish in China, such as Confucianism, Buddhism, Taoism and other schools of thought, give high recognition to "water" culturally, which is the largest convention of Chinese culture. The recognition of "Tao", the "combination of universe and human", the "trinity of nature, earth and mankind", the primacy of nature and earth in all things, and the combination of nature, earth and mankind as an organic whole. The most fundamental values of the Chinese cultural community are the most fundamental cultural basis for the formation and development of our nation.

Water is indispensable to everything in the world, breeding life with its vastness, enlightening mankind with its ceaseless momentum, and facilitating the creation of human culture. From the ancient times to today, there have been countless human cultures that shine because of water. "Water" and its variants, such as "cloud", "ice", "snow", "frost", "fog", "dew" and "hail", constitute a diverse water-themed cultural integration, and can be stretched back to the traditional Chinese culture. The "Water" culture has such a long history that three major cultures in China, Confucianism, Buddhism and Taoism, all contain noticeable cultural gene of "water".

Water in the eyes of Confucianism

Confucius said, "Water can inspire a gentleman to use it as a metaphor for his virtue cultivation. It spreads all over the world and contributes to all things without partiality, just like a gentleman's morality; wherever it goes, all things grow like a gentleman's benevolence; water flows downward, and things are shaped like a gentleman's nobility; water flow unceasingly in shallow places, and unexpectedly in deep places, like a gentleman's wisdom; water rushes to the abyss without hesitation, like a gentleman's decisiveness and courage; water infiltrates into even the smallest holes without subtlety, like a gentleman's insight; despite groundless accusation, water remains silent and open-minded, like a gentleman's inclusive mind; carrying all the mud and sand, it remains clear at last, like a gentleman's capability of transformation; when loaded with measuring instruments, water will keep itself at a certain level, like a gentleman's integrity; water will not seek additional interest when it is full, like a gentleman's meticulous and proper manner; regardless of the difficulty and obstacles, water flow eastward into the sea, like a gentleman's unswerving faith and will. Therefore, when a gentleman sees a flood, he must observe it carefully."

Confucius believed that water could inspire a benevolent man to cultivate his morality. "Water is everywhere and gives itself to all beings without being partial. It is like a gentleman's virtue. Wherever it goes, all flourish like a gentleman's benevolence. Water flows downwards and takes shape of its containers, just like the noble characters of a gentleman. Water flows endlessly in shallow places and unpredictably in deep areas, resembling the wisdom of a gentleman. Water will rush forward into the deepest valley without hesitation, resembling the determination and bravery of a gentleman. It does not argue for itself when framed, just like the tolerance of a true gentleman. Absorbing mud and sand all the way, water comes out crystal clean ultimately, like a gentleman's extraordinary ability to transform things. When water is filled into a container, its surface is always flat, which resembles the sense of justice in a gentleman. Water stops filling the container when it is full; its lack of greediness resembles the integrity of a gentleman. Water has its own rules of doing things: In spite of all difficulties, it must find itself into the sea in the east, just like the firm belief and strong perseverance of a gentleman. Therefore, when a gentleman sees a massive flow of water, he must observe it carefully.

Confucius also said, "The benevolent find pleasure in hills, and the wise find pleasure in water; the knowledgeable are dynamic, the benevolent are quiet, the knowledgeable are happy, and the

benevolent enjoy longevity." A man of benevolence and wisdom likes mountains and rivers and strikes a good balance between dynamism and peace, which explains their joy and the consequent longevity. The wisdom of "the wise" should be as flexible as water, which does not reveal itself if hidden underground and remains clean when springing out. When the amount of water is little, it is tinkling for pleasure; when the amount of water is huge, it is galloping proudly. Water is either dynamic or static between heaven and earth. When dynamic, it is converted to streams and rivers; when static, it becomes pools, lakes and ocean. The charm of water varies from one scenario to another. It trickles through sandy soil, splashes when lapping rocks; plummets into waterfalls when encountering cliffs, and detours when blocked by mountains. Drops of rain and melted snow can integrate into thin flows and converge to be a torrential river and vast ocean. The wisdom of "the wise" should be inspired by the "fondness of water".

Confucius also said, "Water flows by in both day and night." Time is irrecoverable. Youth will wither and everything will become a hasty passer-by like running water. Confucius's philosophical thoughts on the lost time, people, and things are like flowing water. They are the deep sigh for the unachieved cause because of the lost time, and also the philosophical introspection sparked by the contemplation on abstract philosophical questions such as time, eternity, and change.

The mass is like rivers that deserve the caution of officials. In *Words of Confucius*, it is said that, "The ruler is like a boat, while the ordinary people are like water. Water can either carry a boat or overturn it." The ordinary people can either support or overthrow the throne. The ruler is like a boat, and the people are like water. A boat can either sail on or sink in the water.

The harmoniously society pursued by Confucius throughout his life was supposed to be a world of benevolence. Therefore, to some extent, water not only constitutes the Confucian ideological system, but also symbolizes the core of Confucianism. The gentle and benevolent described by Confucius were inspired by water. The more tranquil the water, the more unpredictable it is, which resembles a wise man who hides his considerable wisdom under the foolish appearance. Gentlemen argue for nothing, similar to the water that will do everything except arguing. "Clever words and sharp observation are bestowed on the benevolent". "A state governed by Tao will flourish, while a state deprived of Tao will perish." This is exactly what water presents, "living up to promise and delivering good results".

Mencius, another representative of Confucianism, carried forward and developed Confucius' thought of "benevolence". Contemplating what was occurring in the society and proceeding from the theory of man born with good nature, he proposed the creative thought of "benevolent governance", and believed that "a government without benevolence is unlikely to rule peacefully" (*Mencius, Lilou, I*). To make what he advocated more persuasive and popular, Mencius who was good at metaphors once again resorted to the characteristics and functions of "water", through which he expounded his ideas and propositions on "benevolent governance".

Mencius said, "People accepting benevolence is like water flowing down and beasts going wild.

Therefore, it was the ordinary people who overthrew tyrants Jie and Zhou (*Mencius, Lilou, I*). He also said, "A man resisting the temptation of slaughter will be expected by the state to reign. It is true that people accepting benevolence is like water flowing down. Who can resist it? (*Mencius, King Hui of Liang State, I*)

Mencius believed that people's acceptance of benevolent governance is like water flowing down and beasts going wild, which is an irresistible trend. He warned the rulers that only when benevolence was bestowed on the people and the interests of the people were taken into account, could the people be benevolent and virtuous like water flowing down. Otherwise, the ruler would inevitably degenerate to kings like Jie, who lost the popular support ultimately and got toppled as a result of the previous cruelty inflicted on his people. When such cruelty happened, the people who could not tolerate would rise to overthrow the tyranny.

In Mencius, Mencius repeatedly cited Dayu's achievement in flood control for the benefit of the people and praised his virtues in the practice of kingship. He said, "The idea that people could drown evoked empathy in Dayu's mind." When realizing that people could drown, Dayu felt like as if he had been the main culprit. In order to save the people from flood, Yu inherited his father's undone cause of water control. He cut the amount of clothes and food for himself, moved to palaces of simple decoration, weathered the storm on his own, and underwent a series of hardship. "Dayu spent eight years on flood control and even passed by his own house for three times without entering." After arduous work of over a decade, the flood was finally controlled so that people lived and worked in peace and contentment. Mencius warned that rulers fulfilled obligation only when they took the interest of the people as their duty, rose to what the people urged for, shared the people's worries and benefited the people as Dayu did.

Buddhist interpretation of water

Buddhism often compares the ever-running and hard-to-catch water to a changeable life. The persistent running of river water can serve as an efficient tool to popularize the Dharma Seals and the Twelve Links in the Chain of Causation in Buddhism. As a basic Buddhist doctrine, the Dharma Seals is quoted as "Constant change to everything in Nirvana silence". This means that nothing in the world would stay unchanged and human life is repeated in a life-death cycle with constant change. Life is short, unpredictable and uncontrollable. It is a process full of pain and suffering. The greatest pain about life is that people always repeat the life-death cycle without any interruption. This is the same with running water which is short-lived but infinite.

As is recorded in *Mahayana Mahaparinirvana Sutra*, "Life is always changing. It is like lightening, rainfall and fire; it is also like the painting of water, which is highly random." Besides, it compares death to a bubble that bursts in an instant, "The birth and death of a person is like the rapid formation and burst of a bubble. It develops like a wheel and is constantly repeated." A similar metaphor can also be found in *Samyuktagama Sutra*, "Life is like a bubble in a rain, appearing and

then disappearing." The life cycle of a person is like a bubble which lasts for a short time and is highly fragile. In the ever-running time, human lives and dies like a bubble and the cycle is repeated ceaselessly. The world is like a boundless ocean of sufferings. Only by endeavoring to cultivate oneself and seeking truth will a person be able to separate himself/herself from the three divisions of the universe, free himself/herself from the ocean of sufferings, permanently break the cycle to achieve the nirvana silence. This is a liberation in a true sense.

In Buddhism, the ultimate causes for human life are summarized as "Twelve Links in the Chain of Causation". According to it, human life consists of twelve links, including "ignorance", "conduct", "recognition", "designation", "six divisions", "touch", "acceptance", "love", "take", "possess", "live" and "die of aging". "Ignorance" is the cause of "conduct" which is the cause of "recognition". The deduction proceeds this way until "live" is the cause of "die of aging". These twelve links form a procedure, and all creatures follow this life-death cycle constantly. Once a procedure ends, another one starts. The continuity of the twelve links in the chain of causation is like the continuous running of water. Comparing the continuous running of water to the ever-lasting life-death cycle is a typical meaning of Buddhism.

In Buddhism, the cleanness and moisture of water indicate the purity of Buddhist nature and self-nature. As is recorded in *Mahayana Mahaparinirvana Sutra*, "It is clean and clear, like water without any mud. Disengagement goes the same way. Cleanness and clarity are disengagement in a true sense." According to *Mahayana Prajnaparamita Sutra*, "It is also like water which is naturally clear and clear and even as deep as prajnaparamita." *Soul Mirror Record* by Yung-ming Yen-shou, interprets the implication of the Buddhist water metaphor as "Water is a metaphor of the ten meanings of a sincere soul." The ten meanings are different from each other, but they center around a core meaning: water is compared to the disposition of Buddha or the tranquility of self-nature. Nature of Buddha (Tathagata-garbha heart) and self-nature had been integrated in the theory on nature of Buddha by Zhu Daosheng, a monk in the Southern Dynasties (420-589). Then, Zen Buddhism combined nature of Buddha with self-nature and disposition.

According to *Lotus Sutra*, "It is like someone is thirsty and wants to drink water during a journey on a plateau. If he/she sees that the soil is dry, he/she would know that water is still in distance. If the soil is moistened, he/she would be sure that there is water nearby." It is like a situation where one is hungry and thirsty and thus needs to drink water. Hunger indicates wanting to eat something, while thirsty implies wanting to drink water. During the period of thirsty, one desires to drink water. It is like ordinary people want to seek Buddhist fruit in the earthly world. The Buddhist fruit is "water". The world for ordinary people is very dry, for which the people feel thirsty and want to drink the magic water or eat the Buddhist fruit. Traveling through a plateau: ones wants to dig a well in a place of a high altitude. Digging a well is a process of self-cultivation.

As is recorded in *Read Sutra*, "A pool consists of seven valuable things. Buddhist water runs in it." In this pool are lotuses, and there are value trees on the banks. The trees need water to grow, so the water runs through the trees. The water here is wonderful. In the early world, water can only run

downwards, but on the Pure Land it can run upwards. This shows the solemnness and wonder of the heaven. What cannot be found in the earthly world can be seen on the Pure Land.

According to *Hui Shu*, "Those on the Pure Land don't live on water or grains. They cultivate themselves in a pure environment and don't need cleaning. Therefore, they don't need water. For that reason, they can freely achieve happiness and eradicate spiritual dirt". As a lotus incarnation, they don't rely on water or grains to maintain livelihood. They are born clear and thus don't need bathing. Therefore, they can freely take a happy bath just to erase spiritual dirt. After spiritual dirt is wipe off, they would be in a good mood and feel physically healthy.

According to *Pure Land Sutra*, there are many pools on the Pure Land. A small pool is about 100 to 200 miles long, and a big one is about hundreds of thousands of miles long. All these pools make the Pure Land a vast ocean. In the earthly world, a small pool is like a lake, and a big one is like an ocean. Both small and big pools are clean and fragrant. Water has eight attributes. First, it is clean. Second, it is cool. Third, it is sweet. Fourth, it is gentle and soft. Fifth, it is moistening. Sixth, it is peaceful. Seventh, it quenches thirst and hunger. Eighth, it nurtures the four basic elements of the world and strengthens the root of everything.

As Zen indicates, "kindness is like water." Water facilitates everything and thus it has "kindness". Water can penetrate almost everything and thus can moisten all living creatures. With a strong buoyant force, water can drive ships. Running water can improve environment and fills the earth with vitality. Water can lower temperature, remove stains, drive machines and generate power and energy. Water has numerous functions, and its kindness is boundless.

Taoist interpretation of water

Laozi, the ancient Chinese philosopher, was quoted as saying, "The highest excellence is like water. Water is good at benefiting everything without vying for any fame or gain. This shows the modesty of water. The reason why ocean can become the king of all rivers is that it places itself in the lower reach. Nothing in the world is softer and gentler than water, and nothing can beat it in terms of tackling tough problems. This is the virtue of gentleness. Therefore, softness and gentleness can win over toughness and hardness. Invisible things can penetrate something without a crack. This is 'silent' instruction and the benefit of 'inaction'".

According to Laozi, an extremely kind person is like water. Water can benefit and nurture everything but does not compete with them. This is the virtue of modesty. The reason why ocean can work as the destination of all rivers is that it stays in the lower reach. Nothing in the world is softer than water, but water is the best in penetrating the hardest thing like stone. This is the virtue of softness. Therefore, the weak can beat the strong, and the soft can win over the hard. Something invisible can enter something without a crack. This reveals what is "silent" instruction and the benefit of "inaction".

Laozi also said, "If you don't want to compete, nothing in the world will win over you. This is an example of the virtue of water. Water is close to truth. Truth is universal, and water can reach anywhere. Water runs from a high place to a low one without reversing its route and well adapts itself to any place. It is quiet in an empty place and is unfathomable. It is as deep as an abyss. It can be absorbed but will not run out. It offers help without seeking any reward. It is a good example of benevolence..."

"Truth" is the origin of everything in the world. It came into being before anything tangible and is the fundamental rule and source of objects. Therefore, "truth" is something that every person should recognize and understand. According to Laozi, if you don't compete with others for benefits, you will be the winner in the world. This conduct exemplifies the virtue of water. The virtue of water is closest to "truth". "Truth can be found everywhere, so water can reach wherever it wants. It avoids a high place and run towards a low place, for which it will not encounter any obstacles. It can flow to any place, nurture everything and wash away all stains. It is in a deep pool which looks clean and quiet but is unfathomable. It runs continuously to benefit everything without longing for reward. These conducts are extremely benevolent.

Laozi told Confucius, "Water is close to truth. Truth is universal, and water can reach anywhere. Water runs from a high place to a low one without reversing its route and well adapts itself to any place. It is quiet in an empty place and is unfathomable. It is as deep as an abyss. It can be absorbed but will not run out. It offers help without seeking any reward. It is a good example of benevolence. It takes another route when it comes across a circular place, and it bends its way when it encounters a squared place. If it is blocked, it will stop; if it is released, it will flow. This shows that it keeps its words. Water can wash away all stains and make a correct assessment. This demonstrates that it is good at governance. It can carry things with its buoyant force and can be taken as a mirror. It can damage anything tough. This indicates that it can make good use of its strengths. In the daytime and at night, it fills a place with water and then moves on to the next place. This manifests that it can wait for a good chance. Therefore, sages take action according to chance; virtuous people change their strategies according to situation; wise people govern through inaction; reasonable people survive according to times."

Water is closest to truth. Truth is universal, and water can reach anywhere. Water runs from a high place to a low one without reversing its route and well adapts itself to any place. It is clean, quiet and unfathomable. It is as deep as an abyss. It can be absorbed but will not run out. It offers help without seeking any reward. It is a good example of benevolence. It takes another route when it comes across a circular place, and it bends its way when it encounters a squared place. If it is blocked, it will stop; if it is released, it will flow. This shows that it keeps its words. Water can wash away all stains and make a correct assessment. This demonstrates that it is good at governance. It can carry things with its buoyant force and can be taken as a mirror. It can damage anything tough. This indicates that it can make good use of its strengths. In the daytime and at night, it fills a place with water and then moves on to the next place. This manifests that it can wait for a good chance. Therefore, sages

act according to chance; virtuous people change their strategies according to situation; wise people govern through inaction; reasonable people survive according to times.

Zhuangzi is the most important representative of Taoism after Laozi. Like Laozi, Zhuangzi enjoys feeling and exploring the profound "truth" of water. When using water to discuss "truth", Laozi expressed his opinions in a direct way and made straightforward statements in most cases. But Zhuangzi tended to made up a serious of fables about water to interpret profound and abstract philosophical truth. His interpretation features a special form, amazing imagination, deep thoughts and exquisite wording.

In his *Enjoyment in Untroubled Ease*, Zhuangzi compared fish swimming freely in water to people living in "truth". In the wide rivers and lakes, fishes are swimming to their heart's content. They don't miss each other and show little concern for others. Once the source of springs is blocked and the rivers and lakes go dry, they weather through the crisis on land together. With no choice, they have to help each other by exhaling bubbles to sustain each other. This is a scene totally different from their care-free life in the rivers and lakes. In this case, "Fishes forget one another in the rivers and lakes" exceeds the limitation of water shortage. Likewise, only by getting rid of the support from limited reality will human be able to forget the expectation and restriction of reality and freely live in the universe, without being bothered by anything.

Human shows an inherently affection to water. It is true that swimming in water is full of infinite enjoyment. But Zhuangzi preferred to feel his untroubled ease from swimming in water. Meanwhile, he compared the vast ocean (water) to "truth", preserving the spirit of Laozi who compared "truth" to water. By doing so, he revealed the vastness and extensiveness of "truth". Ocean accounts for 70% of the surface of the earth and is the biggest object on the earth. It is vast and deep and tolerant to everything. The infinity and absoluteness of Laozi's "truth" can be embodied in nothing than ocean.

According to *Zhuangzi*, "Of all the waters under heaven there are none so great as the sea. A myriad streams flow into it without ceasing, and yet it is not filled; and afterwards it discharges them (also) without ceasing, and yet it is not emptied. In spring and in autumn it undergoes no change; it takes no notice of floods or of drought. Sea is the source and destination of all waters in the world. Despite that tens of thousands of rivers flow into it, it will never overflow; although these rivers constantly flow out of it, it will never become dry. The changes caused by seasons, draught and floods have little impact on it. Why? The reason is simple: sea has a tremendous capacity.

As is recorded in *Zhuangzi*, "The intercourse of superior men is tasteless as water, while that of mean men is sweet as new wine. But the tastelessness of the superior men leads on to affection, and the sweetness of the mean men to aversion."

The Same Origin of Confucianism, Buddhism, and Taoism

Confucianism, Buddhism and Taoism share the same values and respect the primacy of the natural law of Tao and its spokesman, water. In the long process of cultural integration, the three schools of thought have been linked profoundly with each other, featuring mutual respect, understanding, protection, and support without contention. Confucianism, Buddhism, and Taoism naturally have their own ideological focus and seem to be drastically different from each other. However, these three schools are conceptually identical advocating coexistence, compatibility, pluralism, and mutual support. Sharing the common value of "water", the three schools have thrived for a long history.

The integration of Confucianism, Buddhism, and Taoism in the Chinese history to form a religious and cultural system of harmony and difference was rarely seen in human civilization. First of all, the religious beliefs of the Han ethnic group, the main one in China, are as tolerant and open-minded as water to accept foreign cultures. Secondly, given the ambiguity on the issues of religious creation and life and death in ancient China, the Confucianism had such inevitable limitations that required the diversity brought by Taoism, and Confucianism and Taoism needed the supplement of Buddhism when the issue of life and death was discussed. Finally, Confucianism, Buddhism, and Taoism share the same philosophy and interests, and each has its own advantages, so that they co-exist with different functions in harmony. Ultimately these three serve the Chinese nation by encouraging people to "develop the mind with Buddhism, cultivate a person with Taoism and govern the state with Confucianism".

The natural complementary and supportive relationship of Confucianism, Buddhism, and Taoism retains their respective features and tolerates differences. The three schools are equal with their own functions and strengths and weaknesses so that they complement each other. The three schools share the goal of instructing the mass but the functions of the three are not totally identical. The three schools share the origin of wisdom, the Book of Changes. Such origin lies in the obedience to the laws of nature and the worship of water. The integration and flourishment of Confucianism, Buddhism, and Taoism in Chinese history is one of the best gifts that our nation has contributed to the world governance. Religious beliefs can coexist and shine upon each other. The proposition of inevitable clash of civilizations is too arbitrary and far-fetched to be fully established.

Confucianism, Buddhism, and Taoism worship water piously and obey it. The fundamental is to study the virtue and conducts of water to open the door of wisdom of the Chinese nation and understand what a civilized society is. If mankind is actively or passively enclosed in the biological chain (food chain) and only concentrates on learning the living skills and techniques of animals and plants around them, it is difficult to shatter the shackle of the primitive, backward and ignorant contention of the natural world, and thus humans will have no chance to improve themselves and create splendid human civilization.

Fortunately, the water around us, which is crystal clear, colorless, tasteless, and selfless, serves

as an example to guide us. It foretells and warns human beings. Apart from nourishing and supporting the growth of all, water also contains two elements which fully reflect the special quality of advanced civilization: Fairness and honesty. Fairness means justice and honesty means self-discipline.

A civilized human society is an ecosystem accompanied by laws and rules - ethics to keep the society running smoothly. The civilized human society is supported by three pillars of economic development, social justice, and ruling integrity so that the society is stable and orderly. Among these three, the ruling integrity is particularly important because only there is a clean ruling team trusted by the people can the government promote economy, achieve social fairness and uphold justice. Ruling integrity is directly related to the legitimacy, political stability and ruling ability of the ruling party, thus influencing the common interests of the society.

The advanced nature of a civilized society dwells on the fact that the government is so honest and self-disciplined that it works wholeheartedly for the welfare of the people, rather than for the welfare of few individuals. "Justice derives from fairness, and fairness derives from Tao" (*Lü's Spring and Autumn Annals*). The social equity and justice are embodied in rights, opportunities, and rules as well as the overall effectiveness of the social security system. The ordinary people are endowed with the equal rights to exist and develop in all aspects and are given equal opportunities. Every member of society has the equal opportunity to enjoy rights, perform obligations, assume responsibilities and be protected equally. The government should not be selfish and only focus on serving a few people of power and wealth.

"If water is evenly distributed, the vile will obey the law; if the mirror is clear, the ugly will have no anger. Water and mirror can suppress complaint in that they are selfless." (*Romance of Three Kingdoms, Romance of Shu State, Li Yan*) Water is the fairest yardstick that is taken even by the evil as a code of conduct; mirror is the brightest object in front of which even the ugly have no way to complain or get angry. Water and mirror tolerate the world and convince people because they are the most selfless. The height of a civilized society is revealed by the breadth and width of its social fairness and justice that cover the common people.

The hand-in-hand development of Confucianism, Buddhism, and Taoism has never regarded "personal satisfaction" as the primary goal of pursuit, but insisted that the "vulgarity" of human beings has such limitations that it cannot be the basis for determining what is important of the world. In the galaxy interstellar, a large number of known and unknown substances apart from the species represented by "human", which affect the surrounding world together. Thus, the law of nature, that is "Tao", is the top priority in the world.

In the late Ming and early Qing Dynasties, the influence of Western religious philosophy gradually extended to China in an attempt to change the cultural pattern of China which regarded "Tao" as the natural law, and develop the Western values which respected "human". To this end, Westerners even tried to work with Confucianism to attack Buddhism and Taoism directly. Fortunately, the Confucianists did not change their minds or surrender themselves to the Western

provocation. They continued to work hand in hand with Buddhism and Taoism to contribute to Chinese culture.

As far as the Chinese people are concerned, the dominance of Western culture can be justified to some extent. After all, the contribution of Western culture to human development is positive. The Western culture deserves full recognition for its human-oriented values, the emphasis on "individualism", human rights and morality, the stress on "efficiency" to speed up economic development and improve the quality of human material life.

However, in the name of the "human-oriented" values, the Westerners, relying on their advanced weaponry, have invaded and colonized overseas territories to convey the "gospel" of "human rights". It remains a huge doubt that haunts the world whether the discriminative human-centered theory and the "law of the jungle" of the Western values can sustain, and whether the glory of "ethics" can be preserved.

No matter how the Chinese history develops, the Chinese people have faith in "resorting to and benefiting from law". Naturally the faith in "Tao" will benefit "man". Chinese people are good learners of what is good in the West while knowing what should be discarded. Confucianism, Buddhism, and Taoism advocate respecting human nature and liberating human nature from the cage of fame and wealth upon which human nature grows.

Lao Tzu, a Chinese philosopher, once said, "There are four major domains and mankind is one of them. Man governed by earth, earth governed by heaven, heaven governed by Tao, and Tao governed by nature." Man follows the law of the earth, earth follows the law of the heaven, heaven follows the law of Tao, and Tao follows the law of nature, which is dominated by the Creator. Man, no matter how capable he is, cannot be greater than the laws of "heaven and earth".

The synergy of Confucianism, Buddhism, and Taoism explains the invisible natural law of Tao with visible, tangible and perceptible "water". Tao derives from water and flows along with it to nourish the Chinese culture for 5,000 years. The instructions of the saint ancestors of "the highest excellence is like water" guide and bless what Chinese people say and act, their way of life and values. This is an extraordinary accomplishment.

Chapter FOUR

Water, in Heated Discussion by Chinese People for Five Thousand Years

The Chinese people have talked about "water" for 5,000 years in an in-depth manner. Since the written history of China, the topic of "water" has never been absent. Compared with other countries and nationalities around the world, Chinese people have talked about water for as long as 5,000 years; the number of people who have talked about water is the largest, and this topic covers the most extensive social groups; Chinese people are also the best ethnic group in exploring and summarizing the ethical value of water. Chinese people's passion for "water" is so unique that it is even rare in the world. Naturally water gives back to Chinese people the most insightful wisdom and inspiration.

On the earth, there is such a nation called the Chinese, who is the only ethnic group that owns and uses square scripts and maintains unique cultural traditions, living habits, and custom; they have unique ways of thinking and behavior different from other nations in the world; they boast the longest civilized history, also the only uninterrupted one, in the current world; now, they are committed wholeheartedly to the most vigorous cause of rejuvenating the country and creating the unparalleled "Chinese miracle". Behind this miracle, there is an interesting and unique hint: Water, which is so commonplace and widespread that it exists everywhere in the world and is known to everyone. However, only the Chinese people have a special preference for "water" and even deep and pious love for it.

The special strength of a nation comes primarily from the general quality of the individuals who make up the nation. China's overall strength derives entirely from the unique quality possessed by the vast majority of the Chinese people who make up the country. It is the excellence of the people of this country that makes the Chinese nation and China great. When talking about China, Japanese scholar Sakahara Sakuhara said, "Either a country or a nation is made up of people of different backgrounds and personalities, who seem to have nothing in common, but if they are compared with other countries or nationalities, we can easily find that this country or nation has many unique characteristics that other countries or nationalities do not own."

China's history book collection is a treasure house of knowledge and a magnificent epic that requires patience to read. For thousands of years, the magnificent work of Chinese history has attracted numerous scholars and experts from home and abroad. With crutches in hands and bamboo baskets on the back, they trudged through the mountains and jungles in China, searched for the mystery hidden in books with their microscopes, and proposed different opinions at different times and places. Finally, one day when new discoveries were shown to the world, the characteristics of numerous Chinese people were as clear as day. The beauty of these characteristics will shine like jewels, even breaking the dark sky.

It is these shining national characteristics that "sustain the Chinese nation for thousands of years without going downhill and prevent the Asian country from perishing after countless foreign invasions" (by Sha Lianxiang). Let's go back to the Chinese history to find out the main influencing factors of the Chinese characteristics. Insightful people may be keenly aware that we are on the way of re-understanding and reviewing Chinese culture and the Chinese people. The culture and the people remain what they were, but the context is no longer what it was.

Water in the *I-Ching*

The ancient *I-Ching* is an extensive and profound classic, which might be compiled in as early as the Western Zhou Dynasty. The *I-Ching* embraced a wide range of subjects, such as forecasting, management, medicine, cybernetics, system theory, computer binary system, Chinese Kung Fu and Qigong. In this magnificent book, "water" plays an important role. The *I-Ching* includes Eight Diagrams, namely the Gan, Kun, Li, Kan, Zhen, Su, Gen and Dui, among which Kan represents water. The *I-Ching* advocates Tao, the laws and principles of nature, indicating that the change of laws is like water in constantly changing cycles. The most important to people is to adjust their actions on the basis of the changing circumstances to adapt to diverse changes in the outside world. "Adaptability" is the most important rule that the *I-Ching* exhorts people.

According to the *I-Ching*, nature, universe and human society are constantly changing in that two basic factors or two forces that constitute the world are in constant conflict: Yin and Yang (i.e., flexibility and solidity). According to *Legend of Xi Dictionary I*, "Flexibility and solidity push and pull resulting in changes." The positive outcome of such change is the occurrence and development of all things in the world. According to the *I-Ching*, things are developed from gradual change to sudden change or from quantitative change to qualitative change. When things develop to the maximum tolerable extent, they will change abruptly and develop to the opposite direction. "Poverty triggers changes, changes break a new path that lead to eternity." (*Legend of Xi Dictionary II*)

Although the *I-Ching* holds that the changes of all things in the universe have their own laws and do not hinge on the will of human beings, it does not consider that human beings are entirely powerless in the face of laws. It emphasizes that human beings can understand and master the laws of such changes in order to adapt themselves to changes. That is extraordinary. The Book recognizes that the law can be understood and mastered, meaning that people can hold their destiny in their hands. In fact, the *I-Ching* is about how people control their own destiny. Change and adaptation are the essence of the *I-Ching*.

Water in *The Book of Songs*

The Book of Songs is the first poetry collection in China. Playing a role in literature, politics and morality, *The Book of Songs* spends a large part in describing "water". *The Book of Songs* contains descriptions about the water landscape in Weihe area. For example, as *Guan Ju*, the first poem of the collection goes: "Doves sing on the river island." *The Legend of Mao* explains the Chinese character "洲" as follows: "Somewhere livable in the water is called 洲." *The Book of Songs* includes more than 20 rivers such as Jiang, Huai, He, Han, Tuo, Ru, Qi, Jing, Wei, Qin, Fan, Fen, Wen and Qi.

The Book of Songs tells us the abundant and crystal-clear water of many rivers in the pre-Qin period. For example, in one of the poems *Xiaoya April*: "Han and Jiang Rivers flow with momentum, the signature of the South"; in *The Legend of Mao*: "Rivers run with momentum." In *Xiaoya Drum*

Bell: "Drum bells ring, Huai River runs"; in *Wei Feng Fatan*: "The river is clear and ripple." After sing three songs, the water remains as clear as it was! In *Zhengfeng Qin Fang*: "Qin and Qi Rivers feature cleanness." In *Xiaoya Shumiao*: "The land is plain, the spring is clear." Another excerpt of *The Legend of Mao*: "The plain land is good, so is the clean water."

There are over 40 articles directly or indirectly referring to water in *The Book of Songs*, such as *Zhounan Guanju*, "Doves sing on the river island. A fair lady earns the affection of a gentleman"; in *Weifeng Shuoren*: "... Rivers of vitality gallop northward..."; in *Weifeng Heguang*, "A boat sails on a wide river...". "Wei Feng Fatan" is a poetry collection of "water": "Water is clean and ripple..." As an image of *The Book of Songs*, water can be said to be found everywhere in it. A large number of poems in *The Book of Songs* are directly or indirectly related to water.

Water in *The Book of History*

The Book of History is the earliest recorded historical book in China, which is a compilation of political and historical materials in ancient times. *The Book of History* is also the first classical prose collection and the earliest historical document of the Han nationality in China. As a record of historical classics, the Book is called the earliest prose collection in China by literary historians, and is a literary genre parallel to *The Book of History*. However, in the eyes of modern literature, most of these essays are actually official documents regarding state affairs at that time. To be precise, they should be a complete collection of documents.

The Book of History Hongfan points out that "water, fire, wood, gold and earth" are the origin of the world. "Five elements of the world include water, fire, wood, gold and earth. Water moistens, fire burns, wood erects, gold dazzles and earth nourishes crops (*The Book of History Hongfan*). Wood is characterized by germination and strictness. Fire is hot and upward. Earth supports cultivation and nourishment. Gold is tranquil and calm. Water is cold and downward. The mankind has long been aware of water, which is regarded as a basic element in the simple material outlook of ancient East and West. Water is one of the five elements in ancient China, and one of the four elements in the theory of ancient West.

There is a connection among things, which promotes the development and change of things. There is a law of mutual generation and restraint among the five elements that breed and promote each other, while constraining and inhibiting each other. In terms of mutual generation, wood for fire, fire for earth, earth for gold, gold for water, and water for wood. With respect to mutual restraint, wood against earth, earth against water, water against fire, fire against gold, gold against wood. The mutual generation and restraint are like Yin and Yang, the two indivisible aspects of things. Without generation, there would be no occurrence and growth of things; without restraint, there would be no balance and coordination in the development and change of things. The mutual generation does not exist without mutual restraint. This interdependent relationship promotes and maintains the normal growth, development and change of things.

Water in *Rites of Zhou, Ritual* and *The Book of Rites*

Rites of Zhou is one of the Confucian classics. In the late Warring States Period, Confucianism integrated Taoism, Law, Yin and Yang, which was greatly different from that in the Spring and Autumn Period. *Rites of Zhou* is information-intensive, ranging from astronomy, traffic to animals. Specifically the book includes the follows: state system, politics, law, culture, education, rite, music, military, taxation, food and clothing, temple, traffic, agricultural, commerce, agriculture, medicine, craftsmanship and classic works. It is deemed as the treasure house of ancient cultural history.

Rites of Zhou, Ritual and *The Book of Rites* are called "Three Rites", among which *Rites of Zhou* takes the primacy. It plays an important role in Confucian classics. *Rites of Zhou* is a classic since the Yellow Emperor and Zhuanxu. "This book considers pros and cons, follows tradition and incorporates the expertise of literature and martial arts (*Rites of Zhou, Preface of Justice*). *Rites of Zhou* is the collection of classic works since the period of Five Emperors to Yao, Shun, Yu, Tang, Wen, Wu and Zhou Gong. Therefore, *Rites of Zhou* is the earliest and most complete official record in China and even in the ancient world.

In the traditional Confucian philosophy, Yin and Yang are the most fundamental pair of philosophical categories. Everything in the world is either Yin or Yang. The author of *Rites of Zhou* has fully applied this ideological concept to political mechanism. Yin and Yang in *Rites of Zhou* are ubiquitous. According to a book entitled *Tianguan Internal Official*, the government decrees are either Yang or Yin; the book *Tianguan Premier* said that rites are either Yang or Yin; in the book *Diguan Shepherd*, sacrifice rites are also either Yang or Yin. Yin and Yang are conflicting against each other to generate five elements of gold, wood, water, fire and earth. Everything in the world has to be incorporated into the system of five elements, such as the five directions and the middle, five kinds of sound, five colors of green, red, white, black and yellow, and five tastes of sour, bitter, salty, sweet and pleasant.

According to the Volume VI of *Rites of Zhou*, "Sometimes water is condensed and sometimes water is saturated. The form of water depends on the time". It is pointed out that the drought and flood are determined by climate. According to the *Moon of The Book of Rites*, "the months of spring feature sunshine; in case of occasional torrential rain, the government is obliged to make regular inspection in the field to build dams and ditches..." According to *The Book of Rites*, "When it rains, mountains and rivers are reigned by cloud." It is also believed that mountains and rivers are the interconnection between heaven and earth. "The sun and stars dwell on the sky, and mountains and rivers sow five elements in four seasons." That is to say, mountain ranges are capable of containing the Qi of Yin and Yang. When Qi evaporates, cloud and rain follow.

Water in *The Commentary of Zuo, Gongyang Zhuan* and *Guliang Zhuan*

The Commentary of Zuo is a historical chronicle, most of which are biographies, narratives, and the origin and development of important historical events in the classics of Spring and Autumn Period.

The Commentary of Zuo mainly records the decline of the Zhou royal family and the history of the warlords fighting for hegemony. All kinds of ritual norms, rules and regulations, social custom, ethnic relations, moral concepts, astronomy and geography, calendar and chronology, ancient documents, mythology and legends, ballads and speeches are also recorded and addressed. *The Commentary of Zuo, Gongyang Zhuan* and *Guliang Zhuan* are the "Three Annals of Spring and Autumn".

The water without source and the wood without root are metaphors for groundless things. "My whole life is like clothes with crown, wood with root and water with source." (*The Commentary of Zuo Ninth Year of Zhaogong*). Like flowing water, a man should be benevolent and open-minded (*The Commentary of Zuo Eighth Year of Chenggong*), meaning that following the right ideas is as quickly and naturally as water flowing down. According to *The Commentary of Zuo Fourth Year of Xigong*, "It is the fault of Chu State if it does not contribute. Chu must contribute, shouldn't it? King Zhao got drowned in Han River while he was visiting the South. Just ask Han River why this happened."

"What makes a water field? When a river flows smoothly, it will be one thousand miles when the river turns" (*Gongyang Zhuan Twelfth Year of Wengong*). In *Guliang Zhuan* (noted in *The Commentary of Zuo*), flood is disaster that is caused by an excessive amount of water flowing downwards or "plains inundated with water" which people mostly inhabited.

Flood does not necessarily occur when excessive water flows downwards, but it is definitely a disaster when water outflows in both plain and high places. Every coin has two sides, which is realized by ancients who sought a balance between the opposite two sides. According to the traditional points of view, things will go wrong if the due balance is lost, with focus on mere one side and neglection of the other. The harmony between Yin and Yang, and the balance between flexibility and solidity lead things to progress and flourish. Therefore, governance is supposed to blend tolerance and strictness.

Water in *The Analects of Confucius*

The Analects of Confucius is a collection of quotation prose in the Spring and Autumn Period of China, which mainly records the words and deeds of Confucius and his disciples. It is the best reflection of Confucius' thoughts. Compiled by Confucius' disciples and their reincarnated disciples, the book consists of 20 volumes and 492 chapters, which is the first book of "quotation style". In the Southern Song Dynasty, Zhu Xi rated it as one of the "Four Books" together with *Mencius*, the *Great Learning* and the *Doctrine of the Mean*.

Water is the source of life, without which nothing in the world could exist. Confucius' understanding of water is not confined to drinking, irrigation and sailing in the general sense. Instead he bestowed the symbolic meaning and philosophical complex on water through the observation, experience and reflection of water. In *The Analects of Confucius, Zi Han*, "Confucius said on the river that water flows in both day and night." This seemed to be Confucius' sigh on the flowing water, but what Confucius sighed for was not only the flowing water that never returned, but also the valuable

time that elapsed in an instance and the things in constant changes. The wisdom of water teaches people flexibility and adaptability, and the flowing water reminds people to cherish and care.

In *The Analects of Confucius, Yong Ye*, "The wise find pleasure in water, and the benevolent find pleasure in hills; the wise are dynamic, the benevolent are quiet; the wise are happy, the benevolent enjoy longevity." This marks the most philosophical utterance by Confucius who place his sentiments in mountains and rivers. Mountains and waters are the most common natural things in the world, and they are also the most spiritual ones. Mountains are stable, great and rich, while water is dynamic, equal and sentimental.

Observing the water flowing eastwards, Confucius was asked by Zigong, "Why must a gentleman observe water when he sees it?" Confucius answered, "Water flows everywhere to nourish all things without asking for return, a sign of virtue; water follows the law of nature by flowing downwards, a sign of righteousness; water flows in an endless stream, a sign of Tao; if the water is determined to flow to a valley of extreme danger, it will advance without a shade of fear or hesitation, a sign of courage; water is a fair yardstick, a sign of law; water devotes without seeking reward, a sign of righteousness; water flows into even a tiny hole of the soil, a sign of insight; water is also a mirror of kindness; despite winding and twisting, water flows eastwards relentlessly, a sign of determination. This is why a gentleman must observe water when seeing it (*Xunzi*).

When staring at the vast river flowing eastwards, Confucius was asked by Zigong: Why must a gentleman observe water when he sees it? Confucius added that water can give birth to all things without going against the law of nature, which is a sign of virtue; water flows in accordance with the law of nature, which is a sign of righteousness; the vast water advances relentlessly, which is a sign of Tao; water is emboldened when a breach is ahead and passes a valley of extreme danger fearlessly, which is a sign of courage; water is a fair yardstick, which is a sign of law.

Water can fill containers without scraping the surface flat, which is a sign of justice; water trickles to the tiniest places into which it can penetrate, which is a sign of good observation; water can moisten things patiently and wash away the dust repeatedly, which is a sign of enlightenment; water flows eastwards despite the tortuous and dangerous way ahead, which is a sign of determination. Therefore, excellent people, when they see the magnificent water and its extraordinary momentum, must stop to watch.

Water in *Erya*

Erya was the first dictionary-style book incorporating a wide range of ancient Chinese vocabulary. Besides, it was also one of the classics of ancient China – one of the Thirteen Classics, which are the core component of the traditional culture of the Han nationality.

In *Erya Interpretation of Water*, "The Chosen One builds a boat, the vassals navigate the boat, the officials protect the boat, and the common people support the boat." "This boat either goes

upstream or downstream. It causes disorder to travel through the water directly by stopping It from flowing." "There are four grand rivers in China, the Yangtze River, Yellow River, Huaihe River and Jishui River. "Rivers and lakes flow to the sea."

Water in *The Classic of Filial Piety*

The Classic of Filial Piety is a political and ethical work of the Han nationality in ancient China, one of the thirteen Confucian classics allegedly written by Confucius. *The Classic of Filial Piety* centers on filiality and focuses on the Confucianist ethical thoughts. It affirms that "filiality" is the norm prescribed by the God. "Being filial is a natural norm that everyone in this world should observe." It points out that filiality is the foundation of virtues, and holds that filiality should top all virtues". Rulers can govern the country with filiality, and subjects can manage their families with filiality. *The Classic of Filial Piety* was the first book that linked filiality with loyalty, believing that loyalty is the development and expansion of filiality. The book also extends the social role of filiality by saying that filiality can be "connected with gods, enlightening four seas and accessible to everything".

"The rise and fall of the history are dwarfed by the Yangtze River that keeps flowing." Although the feudalism for thousands of years has been past, affection and filiality remain the eternal rule. Filiality means that "a person should love his families, stay loyal to the ruler and maintain self-integrity." (*The Classic of Filial Piety, Preface*). What the "filial piety" illustrates people today is the reverence for all. That is, to respect our parents, to work diligently and to show benevolence should be the bottom line for a person. Filiality is detected in both small and big deeds. The considerate care of parents or a small cup of tea for parents should both be deemed as filiality. If the "small things" in a family are well done, then the "big things" will come naturally. The purpose of "sustaining a harmonious family" is to better "govern the country".

The Classic of Filial Piety says, "Be not arrogant at the top, be fearless at the height; be restrained and prudent, like a bowl full of water without overflowing. This is why fortune and nobility can accompany a person invariably. Being rich and noble, they can protect their communities and their people. This should be attributed to the filiality of vassals. High-ranking officials who reject arrogance will not be subjected to the risk of being overthrown; if a person is thrifty, law-abiding, and does not lavish when the treasury house is in good conditions, he is also immune to the danger of being overthrown. In doing so a person can maintain nobility for a long time; the possession of huge wealth without extravagance and waste enables a person to obtain lasting fortune. Only a person who clings to fortune and nobility can preserve his country and keep people in harmony. This is the filial duty of vassals.

In *The Book of Songs*, "Discretion is like a man who is confronting the deep valley or walking on the thin ice." That is to say, discretion is a quality necessary for everything so that a man can act without conservatism or fear.

Water in *Mencius*

Mencius is one of the Four Classic Books that was written by Mencius and his disciples Wan Zhang and Gongsun Chou in the Mid-Warring States Period and was recorded by Mencius, his disciples and their reincarnated disciples. "The people are the most important, the society is the second, and the ruler is the least", a concept put forward by Mencius, another Confucian saint over two thousand years ago who believed that the people are the most important in the whole world, while the society is the second most important, and the interests of the king-led ruling class should be the least priority.

The wise emperors of the past dynasties have come to realize some philosophies, such as "Water can either carry a boat or sink a boat", "Food is the center of the people", "Those who are popular with the people win the state, those who are loathed by the people lose the state." All rulers must focus on the interests of the common people. Only when the common people are satisfied, can the society be stable and the interests of the king-led ruling class be consolidated. This is the people-centered thought of ancient sages, which not only shows the courage of ancient Chinese sages to face the reality, but also further tells the world the magnitude and generosity of ancient Chinese culture.

"Confucius stands atop Mount Taishan overlooking the whole Shandong, and stands atop Mount Tai overlooking the whole world. Thus it is difficult to focus on water if you are used to ocean, and it is difficult to utter a word after staying long with the saint. If you are observing water, you will definitely see the wave it sparks.... Water could not flow without flexibility, and a gentleman cannot be righteous without devotion to Tao (*Mencius Dedicated to the Heart I*). The view atop the mountain dwarfs anything else, and it is difficult to focus on water if you are used to ocean. The sea is so vast and boundless that small rivers and pools are not comparable with it. Mencius praised water for its "doing nothing against the law of nature". Being down-to-earth and step-by-step is precisely the virtue a gentleman aspires to.

Bai Gui said, "Dan was better at water control than Yu." Mencius said, "Not exactly. How Yu controlled water was in line with the law of water, in that he deemed everywhere of the world as his neighbor. Today we have neighboring states. If rivers are diverted, there will be excessive precipitation that leads to flood, which is detested by benevolent people. What you have said is not proper."

Bai Gui retorted, "I am better at harnessing water than Dayu." Mencius said, "You are wrong. Dayu harnessed the flood as is guided by the nature of water, so that the water flowed into the sea. Now you are sending water to neighboring countries. Water running against the current is called "gu" (drainage) - Gu means flood, which is detested by benevolent people. You're wrong."

Bai Gui's "beggar-thy-neighbour" approach to water management is an act of benefiting oneself by harming others, which is not encouraged and advocated. You know "beggar-thy-neighbour", so do others. As a result, everyone takes this approach. By then, everywhere is filthy and haunted by disasters. From this point of view, the ultimate result of "beggar-thy-neighbour" is to harm oneself. Therefore, it is better to abandon the "beggar-thy-neighbour" approach detested by everyone, and "friend-thy-neighbour", so that everyone can live in harmony and help each other.

Interpretation of water in *The Book of the Way*

The Book of the Way, also called *Laozi*, is a masterpiece that was revered by the 100 philosophical schools before the Qin Dynasty in China and serves as an important source of Taoist philosophical ideas. It is divided into two volumes. In its original version, Volume I is *De Jing*, and Volume II is *Dao Jing*. Neither of the two volumes was subdivided into chapters. Later, it was changed, with the first 37 chapters included in *Dao Jing*, and the remaining 38 chapters included in *De Jing* and classified into 81 chapters. It is the first complete philosophical masterpiece in the Chinese history.

"The highest excellence is like water. Water is good at benefiting everything without vying for any fame or gain. Water is in a place which is despised by the public, but it is the place where one is closest to truth. The excellence of a residence is in the suitability of the place; that of the mind is in abysmal stillness; that of associations is in their being with the virtuous; that of words is in their trustworthiness; that of government is in its securing good order; that of the conduct of affairs is in its ability; and that of the initiation of any movement is in its timeliness. And when one with the highest excellence does not wrangle about his low position, no one finds fault with him." A person with the highest excellence is like water. The excellence of water appears in its benefiting all things, and in its occupying, without striving (to the contrary), the low place which all men dislike. Hence (its way) is near to (that of) the Dao.

The most benevolent person stays in a well-selected place where he/she keeps a peaceful mind and profound thoughts. He/she communicate with others with sincerity, friendly and selfless. He/she keeps his/her words, excels in national governance, gives full play to potentials and grasps a ripe time. As he/she does not compete with others, he/she will not face any losses, nor will he/she have any enemy.

Laozi was quoted as saying, "The highest excellence is like water. Water is good at benefiting everything without vying for any fame or gain. This shows the modesty of water. The reason why ocean can become the king of all rivers is that it places itself in the lower reach. Nothing in the world is softer and gentler than water, and nothing can beat it in terms of tackling tough problems. This is the virtue of gentleness. Therefore, softness and gentleness can win over toughness and hardness. Invisible things can penetrate something without a crack. This is 'silent' instruction and the benefit of 'inaction'".

A person with the highest excellence is like water. Water can benefit and nurture everything but does not compete with them. This is the virtue of modesty. The reason why ocean can work as the destination of all rivers is that it stays in the lower reach. Nothing in the world is softer than water, but water is the best in penetrating the hardest thing like stone. This is the virtue of softness. Therefore, the weak can beat the strong, and the soft can win over the hard. Something invisible can enter something without a crack. This reveals what is "silent" instruction and the benefit of "inaction".

Interpretation of water in Buddhist classics

According to *Lotus Sutra*, "It is like someone is thirsty and wants to drink water during a journey on a plateau. If he/she sees that the soil is dry, he/she would know that water is still in distance. If the soil is moistened, he/she would be sure that there is water nearby." It is like a situation where one is hungry and thirsty and thus needs to drink water. Hunger indicates wanting to eat something, while thirsty implies wanting to drink water. During the period of thirsty, one desires to drink water. It is like ordinary people want to seek Buddhist fruit in the earthly world. The Buddhist fruit is "water". The world for ordinary people is very dry, for which the people feel thirsty and want to drink the magic water or eat the Buddhist fruit. Traveling through a plateau: ones wants to dig a well in a place of a high altitude. Digging a well is a process of self-cultivation.

As is recorded in *Read Sutra*, "A pool consists of seven valuable things. Buddhist water runs in it." In this pool are lotuses, and there are value trees on the banks. The trees need water to grow, so the water runs through the trees. The water here is wonderful. In the early world, water can only run downwards, but on the Pure Land it can run upwards. This shows the solemnness and wonder of the heaven. What cannot be found in the earthly world can be seen on the Pure Land.

According to *Pure Land Sutra*, there are many pools on the Pure Land. A small pool is about 100 to 200 miles long, and a big one is about hundreds of thousands of miles long. All these pools make the Pure Land a vast ocean. In the earthly world, a small pool is like a lake, and a big one is like an ocean. Both small and big pools are clean and fragrant. Water has eight attributes. First, it is clean. Second, it is cool. Third, it is sweet. Fourth, it is gentle and soft. Fifth, it is moistening. Sixth, it is peaceful. Seventh, it quenches thirst and hunger. Eighth, it nurtures the four basic elements of the world and strengthens the root of everything.

Water in *The Art of War*

The Art of War, also known as *Sun Wu's Art of War*, is the earliest existing military book in China and the world. It earns the reputation of the "Code of Military Science". The philosophy of Taoism and military strategies permeates the book. Containing 13 chapters of 6,000 words, *The Art of War* is a brilliant treasure in the military cultural heritage of the ancient Han nationality in China. It is an important part of the excellent traditional culture of the Han nationality. Its content is extensive and profound, its thought is exquisite and rich, and its logic is rigorous and precise. It can be regarded as a mirror of the essence of the ancient Han military thought.

According to *The Art of War*, "The image of army resembles water, which avoids going upwards and is inclined to going downwards. The army will stay away from the strongest of enemies and attack the weakest part. Water flows according to the terrain, while victorious army adapt its strategies that vary from one enemy to another. Therefore, the army is dynamic strategically while the water has no fixed shape. Winners are those who change their strategies on the basis of their enemies. Therefore,

none of the five elements is invincible and the four seasons do not remain at the same position. The time of seeing the sun or the moon also varies within a year."

The nature of army is like water, which flows from high to low. The key to victory is to bypass the fortress of enemies and attack the weakest part. Water flows according to the terrain, and the army adopts the winning strategy according to the enemy. So there is no unchangeable situation in military operations, just as flowing water has no fixed shape and direction. Those of remarkable military ability change military strategies on the basis of enemies. The five elements of gold, wood, water, fire and earth are mutually reinforcing and constraining, none of which is invincible; the four seasons are successive, none of which remains without being replaced; daytime and the shape of moon also vary. Everything is in constant changes.

Water in *The Records of the Grand Historian*

Written by Sima Qian in the Han Dynasty, *The Records of the Grand Historian* is the first general history of biography in Chinese history. It records the history of over 3000 years from the Yellow Emperor to the beginning of Emperor Wudi's reign in the Han Dynasty. *The Records of the Grand Historian* is a large-scale and well-organized work with twelve chapters, ten tables, eight books, thirty family chapters and seventy biographies, totaling 130 chapters of approximately 526,500 words.

According to *The Records of the Grand Historian*, "Yu spent thirteen years harnessing water without returning home. Carriages ran on land, boats sail on water, bridges established among mountains. People inhabiting islands travelled afar to make contribution to the Central. Even if there were roads connecting mountains, rivers and lakes, the overflow of rivers victimized China. Deeming water control as his own mission, Yu thought that rivers flows downwards turbulent, so it was difficult to control it on plain land. Despite the fruitless effort, Yu constructed two channels to divert the river. Rainfall in the highland in the north converted to water that flowed downward across the plain land, where the river diverged into nine smaller ones before entering the Bohai Sea. Such diversion solved the flood disaster and benefited the future generations substantially."

According to *The Records of the Grand Historian*: Yu spent totally 13 years combatting flood without even paying a visit to his families. He took a carriage on roads, sailed on water and trudged across the mud, travelling throughout the whole country. After that, he prescribed the boundary of Jiuzhou Island. Taking the terrain into account, he smoothed the river and determined taxation level based on the land and speciality. To build better roads, he constructed dams on the coast of Jiuzhou Island and measured the terrain of Jiuzhou Island. However, considering the flood of the Yellow River that remained to jeopardize China, Dayu focused on harnessing the Yellow River by diverting the river southwards from Jishi Mountain to Huayin County through Longmen, and eastwards through Dizhu Mountain, Mengjin and Luorui to Dapi Mountain.

Yu thought that where the Yellow River flowed before reaching Da Pi was high and turbulent,

which made it difficult to pass on the flat land in the east of Da Pi. Such turbulent water would often shatter river banks and cause floods. Therefore, he diverted the Yellow River into two rivers to reduce the water potential and diverted water northward. After the diversion, the river flowed through Jizhou area of high terrain to big lakes after absorbing rainfall. There would be nine rivers incorporating the flood of the Yellow River and flowing into the Bohai Sea. In doing so the rivers of Jiuzhou Island had been dredged. All lakes on Jiuzhou Island had been dammed and all vassals of China were governed and stabilized. Such achievement benefited the three generations of Xia, Shang and Zhou.

According to *The Records of the Grand Historian, Biographies of Guan and Yan*, "The intercourse of superior men is tasteless as water, while that of mean men is sweet as new wine. But the tastelessness of the superior men leads on to affection, and the sweetness of the mean men to aversion;

the gentle become more intimate despite the lightness, while the vile find no way to sustain despite the initial sweet". The contacts between the gentle are not utilitarian, as light as water; the contacts between the vile are for the sake of interests, so they are as sticky as honey to each other in order to achieve self-interest. Gentlemen never take advantage of their position and power to seek benefits for their families or friends and treat them as light as water; what the vile do is just the opposite.

Water in *Comprehensive Mirror in Aid of Governance*

Comprehensive Mirror in Aid of Governance (History as a Mirror in modern Chinese) is a 294-volume chronological history book compiled by Sima Guang in the Northern Song Dynasty, who spent 19 years compiling the book. In this book, the editor summarized numerous experiences and lessons for the rulers. Emperor Shenzong of the Song Dynasty believed that this book was "in view of the past, for the good of governance". That is, to strengthen the rule by reviewing the gain and loss of history. Thus the book was entitled *Comprehensive Mirror in Aid of Governance*.

According to *Comprehensive Mirror in Aid of Governance*, in the leap month of the Year of Xinhai, the Lord (Emperor Taizong of the Tang Dynasty) said, "Ever since I decided on the prince that will succeed to throne, I have been reminding him of what the origin is all the time. When having meals, I say: You know how hard it is to harvest crops, so you are not allowed to waste food. When riding a horse, I say: "If you know this horse spares no effort when running, you should preserve its strength so that it can serve you long". When seeing him in a boat, I say: Water can either carry a boat or overturn it; people are like water and rulers are like a boat. When the prince takes a break in the shade, Taizong said, "Wood is upright with a rope and you should take the good advice of others to be a good ruler."

According to *Comprehensive Mirror in Aid of Governance*, in the leap month of the Year of Xinhai, the Lord (Emperor Taizong of the Tang Dynasty) said, "Ever since I decided on the prince that will succeed to throne, I have been reminding him of what the origin is all the time. When having meals, I say: You know how hard it is to harvest crops, so you are not allowed to waste food. When riding a horse, I say: "If you know this horse spares no effort when running, you should preserve its strength so

that it can serve you long". When seeing him in a boat, I say: Water either carries a boat or sink the boat; people are like water and rulers are like a boat. When the prince takes a break in the shade, Taizong said, "Wood is upright with a rope and you should take the good advice of others to be a good ruler."

The minister Sima Guang said, "Credit is the supreme treasure of the emperor. The state is safeguarded by the people, and the people is protected by credit; without credibility, the people will not follow, and without the people a country would be impossible. Therefore, in ancient times, those who achieved kingship did not deceive the state, those who established hegemony did not deceive the neighboring countries, those good rulers did not deceive the people, and those who were good at managing the family did not deceive their relatives. Only fools did the opposite, deceiving neighbors, people and even brothers, fathers and sons. No confidence was found from top to bottom or vice versa, and it was doomed to utter failure. The advantages obtained by deception is far from healing a fatal wound. What you get is far less than what you lose. This is such great sorrow, isn't this?

The minister Sima Guang said, "Credit is the supreme treasure of the emperor. The state is safeguarded by the people, and the people is protected by credit; without credibility, the people will not follow, and without the people a country would be impossible. Therefore, in ancient times, those who achieved kingship did not deceive the state, those who established hegemony did not deceive the neighboring countries, those good rulers did not deceive the people, and those who were good at managing the family did not deceive their relatives. Only fools did the opposite, deceiving neighbors, people and even brothers, fathers and sons. No confidence was found from top to bottom or vice versa, and it was doomed to utter failure. The advantages obtained by deception is far from healing a fatal wound. What you get is far less than what you lose. This is such great sorrow, isn't this?

Water in Traditional Chinese Medicine and Tibetan Medicine

The Chinese medicine generally refers to the traditional Chinese medicine (TCM), so it is also known as Han medicine. It is a subject that studies human physiology, pathology, disease diagnosis and prevention. Based on the theory of Yin-Yang and Five Elements, TCM regards the human body as the unity of Qi, shape and essence. Through the diagnostic methods of looking, hearing, asking and cutting, it explores the etiology, pathogenicity, location, analysis of pathogenesis and the changes in organs, meridians and collaterals to identify diseases, sums up the syndrome types and determine the treatment principles. Treatment methods include "Sweat, vomiting, descending, harmony, warming, clearing, tonifying and eliminating", and traditional Chinese medicine, acupuncture, massage, cupping, Qigong and diet therapy, so that the human body realizes the Yin-Yang harmony for recovery.

Tibetan medicine is an important part of the TCM treasury. According to the theory of Tibetan medicine, there are three main factors in human body: Long (qi), Chiba (fire) and Peigeng (earth and water); seven material bases of diet including meat, blood, fat, bone, bone marrow and sperm; and three excretions of stool, urine and sweat. Three major factors govern the movement of seven material bases and three types of excreta.

The traditional Chinese theory of five elements generalizes the attributes of different things in the objective world with the five philosophical categories of wood, fire, earth, gold and water, and illustrates the law of interrelation and transformation of things with the dynamic model of five elements that generate and constrain each other. The five elements correspond to five organs respectively: liver and wood, heart and fire, spleen and earth, gold and lung, water and kidney. Five organs and five elements should keep relative balance and stability to live in harmony. The five symbols of "wood, fire, earth, gold and water" respectively represent the five systems governed by "liver, heart, spleen, lung and kidney". TCM highlights the study of the relationship between the systems of human body, and regulates the balance between these systems through traditional Chinese medicine, massage, acupuncture, and even psychological effect to sustain health.

Kidney is the organ corresponding to water, playing an extremely important role in regulating the water-liquid balance in the body. Chinese medicine believes that "water" plays a vital role in maintaining human health. The "water" in diet (including drinking water) enters the human body and is metabolized by spleen (of transmission), lung (of water channel), kidney (of water), bladder (of gasification) and other viscera to produce nutrients (essence of food), lubricate organs or nourish the whole body. The metabolic waste is discharged through channels like urine and sweat.

The essence of food can be transformed into a series of "Yin" substances such as "Jin", "liquid", "blood" and "sperm" in the body. When water deficiency occurs in the body, the syndrome diagnosed by TCM should be the Yin deficiency that can occur in lung, stomach, liver, heart, and occasionally in spleen. The overall understanding of health in traditional Chinese medicine is the Yin-Yang balance, the loss of which will incur diseases. Water deficiency in the body causes symptoms featuring Yin deficiency and internal heat, such as hot flashes, night sweats, dry eyes, dry mouth, dry stool, palpitation, irritability and lumbar and knee soreness.

Water in the *Inner Canon of the Yellow Emperor*

The *Inner Canon of the Yellow Emperor* is the earliest medical classics in China, one of the four classics of traditional medicine along with *Classic of Complicated Diseases, Treatise on Febrile Diseases and Miscellaneous Diseases* and *Classic of Shennong Herbal Medicine*. The *Inner Canon of the Yellow Emperor* establishes such theories as "Yin-Yang Five Elements Theory", "Tibetan Phenomenon Theory", "Etiology Theory", "Health-preserving Theory", "Drug Treatment Theory" and "Meridian Therapy Theory" in TCM. Discussing medicine from a holistic point of view, the book presents the "holistic medical model" of nature, biology, psychology and society. It is one of the most influential medical works in China and is known as the ancestor of medicine.

Inner Canon of the Yellow Emperor, Water Through Meridians uses the ancient maps of twelve rivers, Qing, Wei, Hai, Hu, Ru, Mian, Huai, Luo, Jiang, He, Ji and Zhang, to describe the different operation of Qi and blood in the twelve channels of the human body. Water is the blood of the earth; water is to the earth what blood circulating in the meridians is to the human body. The twelve rivers

flowing in an endless stream resembles the meridians and blood flowing around the human body, thereby known as "water through meridians".

"All the five organs, six viscera and twelve meridians are endowed with internal and external sources, which are interlinked as the ring without end. This is true of the human body. The Heaven represents Yang while the earth represents Yin, so what is above the waist is Heaven and what is below the waist is earth. Therefore, the sea located in the north is Yin, the lake located in the north is Yin of Yin, the lake located in the south is Yang, the part between the north of the river to the lake is Yin in Yang, the part from the south of Luo to the river is Yang in Yang. This is how Yin and Yang distribute in a water ecosystem, in which the mankind and the Heaven are involved.

The Qi and blood in the twelve meridians connecting five organs and six viscera flow like the water of the twelve rivers in nature, which are endowed with both external sources and hidden internal destinations. The rivers in nature run through each other resembling a ring with no end, and so do the Qi and blood of human meridians that circulate continuously both inside and outside. The Heaven above belongs to Yang and the earth below belongs to Yin. Correspondingly, the part above the human waist should belong to the Heaven (Yang); the part below the human waist should belong to Earth (Yin).

According to the positions of Yin and Yang in the ancient calendar, the sea located in the north is Yin, the part in the north of a lake is Yin in Yin, the river located in the south is Yang, the part between the north of a river to the lake is Yin in Yang, and between the south of Luo to the river is Yang in Yang. This corresponds to how the twelve meridians of the human body distribute and interact with each other. What has been mentioned here only reflects the corresponding relationship between the geographic distribution of some rivers in nature and the distribution of Yin and Yang along some meridians in human body, but this analogy can show that human body corresponds to nature.

Water in the *Selected Works of Mao Tse-tung*

Mao Zedong is the main founder and leader of the Communist Party of China, the People's Liberation Army and the People's Republic of China. Mao Zedong Thought is a complete and extensive ideological system. Mao Zedong is a model of inheriting and promoting the traditional Chinese philosophy of "water", and a master of carrying forward and developing the traditional Chinese culture of "water". Throughout the last 5000 years of Chinese history, Mao Zedong contributed the most diversified theoretical literature on "water" to the future generations.

He was also engaged in the practice of "water", accumulating extensive experience of water control. Mao Zedong is an outstanding figure in Chinese history who contemplates and understands the virtue of "water". No one in Chinese history has done better than Mao in elaborating and practicing the "water" culture in theory. He is also a pioneer who is good at learning and applying the philosophy of "water" to break a new path.

In Mao's mind, the people are the foundation of a society and country. The first people-centered leader in Chinese history, Mao prioritized the interests of the people in state governance. He genuinely and sincerely granted the people the basic right to be directly or indirectly engaged in state affairs. The Chinese people will never forget the utterance of "Long Live the People" echoed in Tian'Anmen Square on October 1, 1949. These words have been carved in history and the mind of Chinese people.

The people, and only the people, are the driving force to create the world history. Mao Zedong: *On the United Government*(April 24, 1945). *Selected Works of Mao Tse-tung*, Volume 3, People's Publishing House, 1991, P. 1031

Scrving the people wholeheartedly and never abandoning the masses; keeping the interests of the people in mind rather than the interests of individuals or minor groups; the consistency of responsibility to the people and to the leading organs of the Party. These are our starting points. Mao Zedong: *On the United Government* (April 24, 1945). *Selected Works of Mao Tse-tung*, Volume 3, People's Publishing House, 1991, PP. 1094-1095

The people are to the Party what water is to fish. If the Party does not have a good relationship with people, socialism will be not be possible or consolidated. Mao Zedong: *The Situation of the Summer of 1957* (July 1957); *Mao Zedong's Manuscripts Since the Founding of the People's Republic*, Volume 6, Central Document Publishing House, 1992, P. 547

Water in Geomancy

Geomancy is a metaphysical art with a long history in China, which is coined as Kanyu academically. According to legend, geomancy was founded by Fairy Jiutian Xuan and perfected in the Warring States Period. The core of geomancy is the man-nature harmony. Guo Pu of the Jin Dynasty said in his famous book *On Funeral*: "The funeral bestows vitality on the deceased, who keep traveling along with wind till there are waters ahead. The ancients gather such vitality to prevent it from dispersing and allow it to advance before ceasing the steps. This is how geomancy works, which prioritizes water and attaches the secondary importance to wind."

The ancient Han ethnic group often said, "If a house is compared to a human body, the pattern is body, the spring is blood, the land is flesh, the plant is hair, the bedroom is clothes, and the door is belt. A house as such is an elegant and auspicious one." This analogy of houses indicates that the well-matched pattern is of vital importance to the residence and the people.

Water is the most important in geomantic practice. The so-called water method is to adjust the relationship between building orientation and running water so that the house is in the best position of running water. The "water" in modern geomancy generally refers to all flowing air fields, such as roads and pipes. Waterscape is an extremely important aspect of geomancy. Water follows in mountains and mountains cease to exist when waters are ahead. Obviously, mountains and rivers are inseparable and that mountains and rivers influence human settlements. A good site geomantically

must be embraced by mountains of fertile and dazzling soil and rivers of sweet water, added with good orientation and timing.

Astronomy, geography and human science are the three pillars of geomancy in China, of which the harmony of heaven, earth and man is the highest principle. Ancient Chinese scientists studied astronomy and geography and made full use of everything from near to far. After practice, research, induction and comprehension of five thousand years, they created the world-famous Oriental Science - Chinese geomancy. Geomancy is actually a natural science which integrates geophysics, hydrogeology, cosmic astrology, meteorology, environmental landscape, architecture, ecology and human life informatics. Geomancy is more than a subject. It is also a kind of culture that emphasizes the harmonious coexistence between man and nature.

Water in the Eyes of Literati

Literati refer to the knowledgeable and cultural officials in general. Since ancient times, literati have had an indissoluble bond with mountains and rivers. Perhaps it was their disdain of the secular world and the consequent isolation from it that made literati intoxicated by mountains and rivers. Or perhaps it was the charm of mountains and waters that made these two proper vehicles through which literati and poets expressed their feelings and disseminated their ideas. Mountains and rivers and literati were like a couple in love with each other, most acquainted with each other, and most compatible with each other. Once literati integrated with mountains and rivers, nature was so inseparable with humans that no one could tell their differences.

Zhang Chao, writer of the Qing Dynasty, said in *Dreams of Shadow*: "Landscapes exist in the earth, painting, dreams and human mind." Yuan Hongdao, a scholar of the Ming Dynasty, once said, "My mind has never disconnected from the mountains and rivers for even an instant." Indeed, in the spiritual world of ancient literati, mountains and rivers can be regarded as their religion. In the mountains and waters, you can feast your eyes on the natural beauty of "the clean desert in wild and the bright moon in autumn night", the noble beauty of "the river flowing east, the rocks erecting, the waves lapping the coast, and the piles of snow dancing with wind", and the romance of "turbulent current plummeting down at the height of three thousand feet, as if the Milky Way fell on the earthly world".

In the *Moonlight in the Lotus Pond* by Zhu Ziqing: Under the leaves there are slow flows of water, the colors of which are not seen. The colorlessness makes the leaves more elegant. The moonlight, like running water, falls silently on this leaf and flower. A thin mist floated in the lotus pond. Leaves and flowers seem to have been washed in milk, like a veiled dream. Despite the full moon, there is a thin layer of cloud in the sky that prevents serenity; but I think this fits the best. Sleeping for a long time is indispensable, but a nap brings something different.

The moonlight shines through the trees, and the bushes above lead to uneven patches of ghost-like dark shadow; the sparse and gorgeous shadow of the curved willows is like a painting on lotus leaves. The moonlight in the pond is not evenly distributed, but light and shadow play a harmonious

melody like a famous song played by violin. In all directions of the lotus pond, near and far, there are tall and low trees, among which willows are the most.

Water in Chinese Idioms (literal and free translation)

Like fish in its water/In one's elements

In the Eastern Han Dynasty, although Liu Bei was recognized officially as an imperial relative of Liu Xie, Emperor Xiandi of the Han Dynasty, he was not granted a fixed feudal territory, so he turned to Liu Biao of the same clan. Liu Biao offered him the Xinye area, after which Liu Bei, recommended by Sima Hui, paid three visits to the shelter of Zhuge Liang before Zhuge agreed to serve Liu and helped him defeated Cao Cao utterly in Chibi Battle. Due to this landslide victory, Liu Bei was so proud that he said the assistance of Zhuge Liang made him fish in its water.

Belt-like water (a strip of waters)

During the Northern and Southern Dynasties, the northern Zhou Dynasty and the State of Chen in the south were bounded by the Yangtze River. Yang Jian, the Prime Minister of the Northern Zhou Dynasty, deposed Emperor Jingdi and founded the Sui Dynasty after proclaiming himself as emperor. Yang was so determined to topple the Chen government that he uttered, "I am the parent of the people all over the country. We have to save the people in the South from suffering despite being blocked by the Yangtze River as narrow as a belt, don't we?" Later, people used the phrase of "belt-like" to describe two places close to each other but separated only by a strip of waters.

The end of hills and rivers (At the end of one's tether)

In 1167, Lu You, a great poet of the Southern Song Dynasty, was dismissed from his post for advocating the combat against the Jin invasion, after which he returned to his hometown adjacent to the Shadow Mirror Lake. On a visit to the nearby Shanxi Village, he improvised the poem *A Visit Paid to Shanxi Village*, which is translated as follows: "Please do not mock the wine made by local households, in that it has been reserved for half a year since the first month of the lunar calendar, specially for the guests who eat chicken here. Travelling till the end of mountains and rivers, I supposed there was way ahead. However, passing through the dense willows and bright flowers, I came across another village." This poem expresses Lu's disappointment of his underrated talent. The end of hills and rivers is a metaphor of the despair of going nowhere.

Water, the Gene of Chinese Culture

The written records of "water" are numerous and ubiquitous in historical books of China. "There are thousands of millets in the book, a golden house in the book, and a beautiful jade in the book" (*The Book of Encouragement*), meaning that books are where the mysteries of Chinese culture dwell. What is the secret of Chinese people? It is this secret that has kept the oldest civilization on the planet alive for a long span of millennia.

Descendants of the Yan and Yellow Emperors for generations have set foot on the soil of ancient China. They either trudged westwards or adventured eastwards, or reclaimed the southern heath. Chinese immigrants for generations have travelled abroad, who risk their life to take root and survive all over the world and creating stunning miracles. "Since 221 B.C., China has remained the center of half the world in almost all times." (by Toynbee)

What is the real strength of the Chinese nation? Such strength helps the oldest and most enduring nation to survive and earn their living the harshest natural and social environment, to cultivate land and sow after relentless natural disasters, to regain peace after a string of bloody wars, to play the melodious music after a series of social turmoils that would have ruined most ethnic groups in the world, and to flourish after countless invasions that inflicted bloodshed. Enduring decades of bloody storms and torturing humiliation for over a century, once again, the Chinese nation embarks on the great journey of modern national rejuvenation with solid steps and firm confidence.

The only explanation of such tenacity may be a simple word of "water" and its philosophical wisdom. Water is constantly growing, changing and circulating. The philosophical wisdom of "water" has assisted the Chinese people in surviving, maintaining national unity, carrying forward civilization for thousands of years, and achieving brilliance that leads to rejuvenation in modern history, and to re-enter the road of rejuvenation. The adhesion to the philosophical wisdom of "water" has enabled the Chinese people, like the tenacious grass standing near fences, to revive and prosper after times of social chaos and national decline.

Water is a remarkable symbol that distinguishes the Chinese nation from others in the world. "The way of life developed by the Chinese has been existing for thousands of years. If it could be adopted by the whole world, there would definitely be more joy and peace on earth than now. If we do not learn from the Oriental wisdom that has been long despised, our civilization will have nowhere to go." "China can be the most powerful country in the world as long as its people have the will to do so." (*The Problem of China* by Russell). What Russell advocated was echoed by Toynbee, a British historian, saying "The most well-prepared nation in the world today is the Chinese nation, which has been nurtured by a unique way of thinking over the past two thousand years."

Water, part of heaven and earth, supports the orderly circulation of the whole ecosystem. Despite the changes of seasons and social conditions in the world, the elegance, calmness and eternity of "water" remain intact. Chinese culture is influenced by the quality of "water" so deeply that its nobility has been carved in Chinese people. Having been guided by "water" for 5000 years, the Chinese nation will certainly continue to advance nourished by "water" for another 5000 years or more. Water is the "root", "soul" and "gene" of Chinese culture.

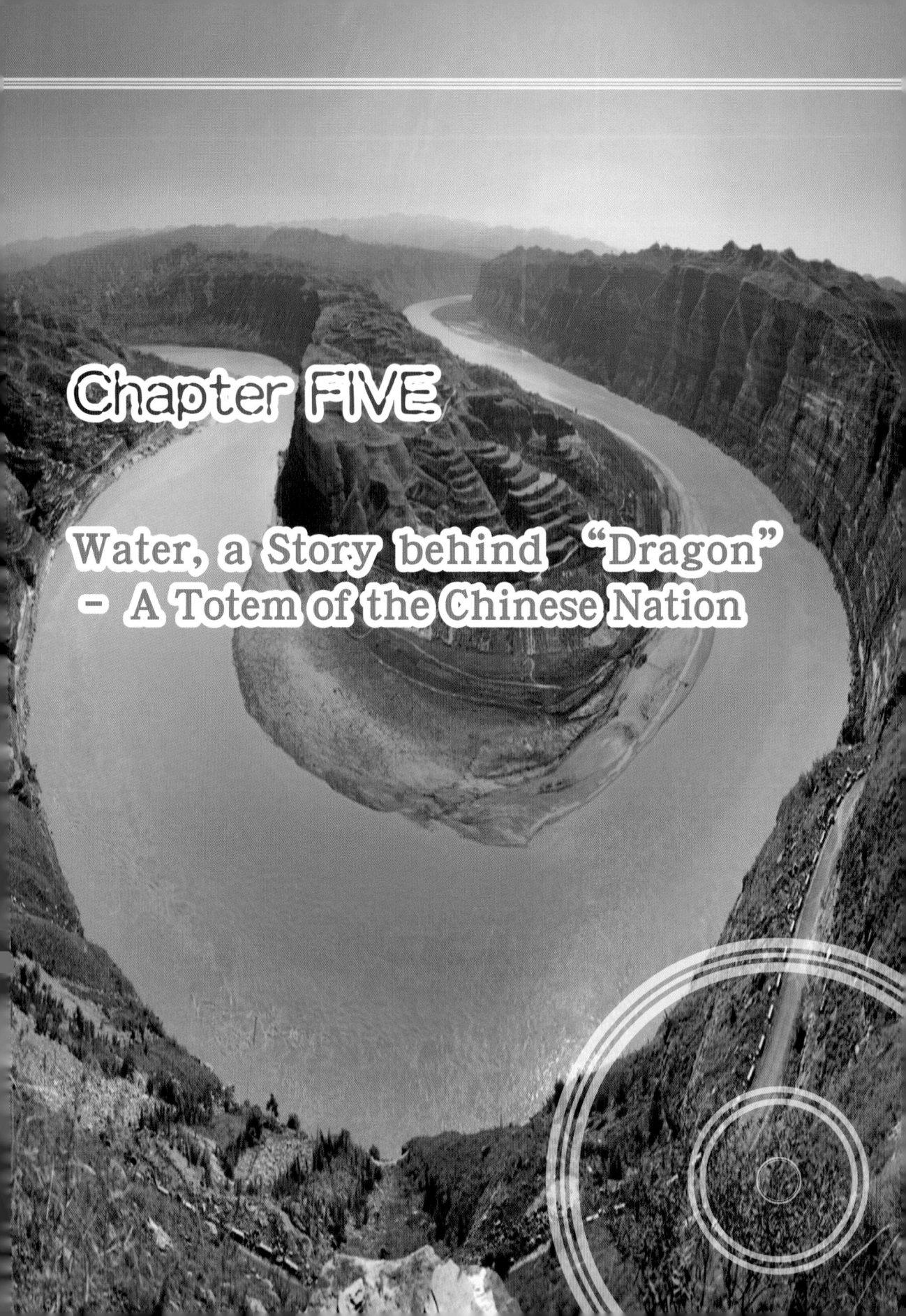

Chapter FIVE

Water, a Story behind "Dragon" – A Totem of the Chinese Nation

Dragon is a totem of the Chinese nation. Dragon is a divine animal in Chinese myths and legends. It has the features of nine animals but does not look like any one of them. As record in *Compendium of Materia Medica*: Wing, "Dragon is the king of all animals with scale. According to the description by Wang Fu, a Chinese politician and thinker in East Han Dynasty, dragon has a cow head, two deer horns, two shrimp eyes, two elephant ears, a snake neck, a snake abdomen, fish scale, two phoenix paws, and two tiger palms. There are eight-one pieces of scale on its back, and eighty-one is a positive number which is the result of nine multiplies nine. It sounds like a strike on a bronze plate. There is beard near its mouth; there is a bright pearl under its jaw; there is reverse scale under its throat. There are horns on its head, with which it cannot fly into the sky. The air it exhales becomes cloud, water and fire.

Its appearance is a combination of several animals. There are many different historical descriptions of its look. Guo Ruoxu in the Song Dynasty (960-1279) also said that "Dragon looks like nine animals": deer horn, horse head, rabbit eyes, snake neck, clam abdomen, fish scale, eagle paws, tiger palm and cow ear. In fact, dragon shows the features of more than nine animals, including, crocodile, lizard, pig, horse, bear, salamander, elephant, dog, goat, silkworm and bird. Moreover, it also has the features of cloud, fog, thunder, lightning, rainbow, tornado, and the fossil of ancient animals.

As a matter of fact, dragon is a divine object created by ancient Chinese people who combined many animals and natural signs. Essentially, it is a natural force that was highly deified by ancestors and spontaneously refined. As a totem, dragon is different from ordinary totems, for it underlines the special emotions and qualities of the Chinese nation. It is a special indicator of the thoughts -- "peace" and "combination".

The earliest god in ancient myths was not human but animal totem. It was difficult for the primitive people to distinguish human from animals. For them, some animal was their ancestor or patron saint. This led to the concept of animal totem. As the sign of a tribe, totem is usually an animal. Once two tribes tried to absorb the other, the winner would eliminate replace its old totem with a new one after winning the battle. The totem of the new tribe was also an animal.

Ancient Chinese people were aware of the essential difference between human and animals and purposely ended the idea of "the weak will stand as an easy prey to the strong." In the creation of the totem of "dragon", they maximized the spirit of "humanity". After each battle ended, the new tribe would comfort, cooperate and care about the clans and tribes that were occupied out of stability, peace and development.

After beating a clan or a tribe, the winner would not erase the loser's spiritual worship or cultural totem; instead, it would incorporate a part of the loser' totem to its own totem to show its generosity and victory. It is obvious that the image of dragon in fact creates an atmosphere featuring the unity of "peace and combination". Aside from revealing the valuable quality and generosity of ancient Chinese people, it conveys Chinese respect to harmony and cooperation for win-win results.

In ancient China, agriculture and farming were completely dependent on favorable weather in different seasons and times. "In case of a draught, people would look forward to seeing cloud". "Rain tastes particular sweet in a severe long-term draught." Loud thunders tend to be the prelude of wind and rain. The Chinese ancestors seemed to rely on water to irrigate their farmland in daily life. When they stood by the farmland which carried their hope for the whole year and gave a helpless look at the withering crops, a thunder from a distant sky and lightening in the thick cloud would become an unforgettable moment in their life, for they knew that a sweet rain was coming.

Since then, Chinese ancestors showed great admiration for thunder. Therefore, it was natural for them to create a visible and audible concept and gave it a name that sounded like thunder as well as dragon. By doing so, they expected thunder and the rain that would follow thunder year after year. After Chinese characters were created, Chinese ancestors creatively developed the character -- " 龍 (dragon)" to signify the concept. In the Chinese language, " 龍 (dragon)" sounds like " 隆 (sound of thunder)".

Apart from having the character " 龍 (dragon)" and the totem of dragon which flies in cloud and controls wind and rain, the Chinese nation purposely used the sound of thunder and lightning before a storm to equip the character with a pronunciation similar to that of " 隆 (sound of thunder)". From this case, we can have an increasingly strong sense of the wisdom of the Chinese ancestors and the ideal they wanted -- an ideal that they were connected with the "truth" of the universe, natural rules and "water". Since ancient times, Chines people have shown faith in the universe, natural rules, the integration of heaven, earth and man, as well as the harmonious combination of universe and human.

In the kingdom of nature, there are heaven, earth and everything. Heaven is high above, and earth is right under, and everything stays between the two. Human has always held a central position on the earth and is the most intelligent group among all living creatures. According to Chinese people's view on the world, the orderly development of the universe follows designated "truth". The "truth" refers to natural rules. Everything in the world is restricted, standardized and dominated by natural rules. The universe gives birth to Yin and Yang." The growth and death or the prosperity and decline of everything in the universe are all influenced by the rules for the change to Yin and Yang. Either "truth" or Yin and Yang theory is something invisible and relatively "mysterious".

By saying that "truth" is "mysterious", it means that "truth" cannot be traced. It cannot be seen, heard, touched, touched or felt, but it exists and is universal. To have a better understanding of natural rules, it is natural for ordinary people to find a concrete reference object to understand natural rules in a specific way.

Laozi, the sage of ancient Chinese philosophy, explained, "Water is good at benefiting everything without vying for any fame or gain. Water is in a place which is despised by the public, but it is the place where one is closest to truth." The supreme goodness is like water in pursuit of perfection; water is good at nourishing all things without competing with them for fame and wealth, stays in undesirable places. Therefore, water is closest to Tao or natural laws. Over 2,000 years old, Laozi told people how to understand and grasp "truth".

Since then, "truth" has no longer been a virtual concept or an illusion. "Water" has become "truth" in the daily life of Chinese people or an incarnation of natural rules. Laozi used "truth" to explain natural rules and creatively compared "natural rules", which are hard to describe and perceive, to "water". Water is colorless and tasteless. It can take the shape of a square or a circle according to situation. It is fluid and can be any shape in nature and reach any place.

Water is of extremely excellence and softness. Sometimes, it flows silently; sometimes, it runs turbulently. It is free from any competition, but at the same time it is inclusive to all. Water can moisten everything. It benefits everything but never contradicts with any of them. It keeps a harmonious, peaceful and inclusive relationship with everything. For that reason, Chinese people are really touched by "truth" and "water". Chinese people respect nature and natural rules, follow the natural rules of the universe, learn from water and obtain wisdom and inspiration from the research on water.

Despite that ancient Chinese people had the aware of perceiving "water" and understood "truth" or "natural rules" which were hard to perceive, it is no easy to create a totem and find common source and spiritual symbol that would be passed down by Chinese people from one generation to another. The totem of a clan or a tribe must be expressive, amazing and appealing, so it is rather difficult to create a water-shaped totem.

Finally, the Chinese nation came up with " 龍 (dragon)", a combination of animals which is interconnected with water and conveys the spirit of "peaceful combination". It was confirmed as a standard totem for all the descendants of Emperors Yan and Huang. According to *Origin of Chinese Characters*, " 龍 (dragon) is the king of all animals with scale. It can become dark and bright, thin and thick, and short and long. In spring, it would fly into sky; in autumn, it would dive into an abyss." " 龍 (dragon)" is almighty and can reach any place, with its amazing tolerance. Even if it lurks itself, its tremendous power remains.

In his *Romance of Three Kingdoms*, Luo Guanzhong described the features of dragon in the name of Cao Cao, "Dragon can become small and big and visible and invisible. It can bring cloud and exhale fog and hide itself. Also, it can fly into the sky and dive into the sea. Now it is deep in spring, dragon changes itself according to the times." In the Chinese myths and legends, dragon is sometimes depicted as a creator that created heaven and earth and shared the same reputation with Pan Gu. Sometimes, it is described as an attendee to the marriage between Fuxi and Nvwa, which led to human beings. Sometimes, it is depicted as a helper for Emperor Huang to win the battles for the union of warring states. Sometimes, it is described as an assistant for Xia and Yu to control floods and thus benefit the people of different generations. Dragon is interconnected, shares the same reputation and move ahead with water. Today, the stories about dragon are actually the ones about "water".

The basic divine features of dragon are "show preference to water", "enjoy flying", "be able to fly into the sky", "be changeable", "bring auspicious things", "predict misfortune", "show authority" and "be dignified". Dragon oversees all creatures as divinity. According to legends, it always lives

in rivers and lakes. Changeable, dragon is a magic animal which enjoys bringing cloud and rain and benefiting all creatures. According to ancient legends, dragon can become invisible and visible, and small and large; it can fly, run and swim; it can fly into sky to touch the moon and dive into the oceans to catch turtles; it can easily control cloud and rain and bring benefits to everything.

In the Chinese culture, dragon is a symbol of luck, authority, nobility and prosperity. Chinese people are the "descendants of dragon". For Chinese people, dragon is a supreme totem of luck. They take pride in calling China an "Oriental Dragon". Dragon is the representation of the Chinese nation as well as a symbol of China.

Westerners, however, have a different opinion on dragon. Before the prevalence of Western Christianity, Western dragon had always been a national symbol of Vikings, Celtics and Saxons. But in the Christian culture, dragon is a ferocious animal and a symbol of evil. It is regarded as a fierce monster and an incarnation of devil. In the Revelation in *New Testament*, a Christian Bible, dragon is depicted as an evil "serpent", "devil" and "Satan". As the Chinese and Western nations have lived in different cultural backgrounds for a long time, they have developed different opinions on the same animal. This is a fact.

Against the backdrop of globalization, it is inevitable for Chinese people to be doubted and even misunderstood and alienated by Westerners when they traveling to Western countries. The stories about China need to be told in an effective way. They need to be interpreted in a language that is understandable to Westerners. It is difficult to understand Chinese characters, and it is even more so to understand the cultural stories through Chinese characters.

Conversely, it is much easier for all people in the world to observe and understand water, for water can be found in every corner of the world. It is a part of our life, so everyone can understand it. If Chinese people share more commonplace and knowledge of the Chinese culture, especially the wisdom about "water", with Westerners after understanding the stories about "water" and "dragon", then Westerners will have a deeper understanding of Oriental values and ideas, the Chinese "dragon" and the Chinese culture.

Water is a global language as well as the source of the culture and wisdom of the Chinese nation. It is accurate, interesting, creative and rigid to regard water as a medium to tell the stories about Chinese people, analyze the cases about China, and sort out Chinese models. In this way, the story tellers will share stories with great interest, and the audience will have strong empathy. Water is closely tied to our daily life. It is something natural and true rather than something pretentious or homiletic. Everything natural will be touching. Telling the stories about the Chinese culture is a process similar to that where water silently benefits everything. When water flows, a channel is formed, and twice as much can be accomplished with half the effort.

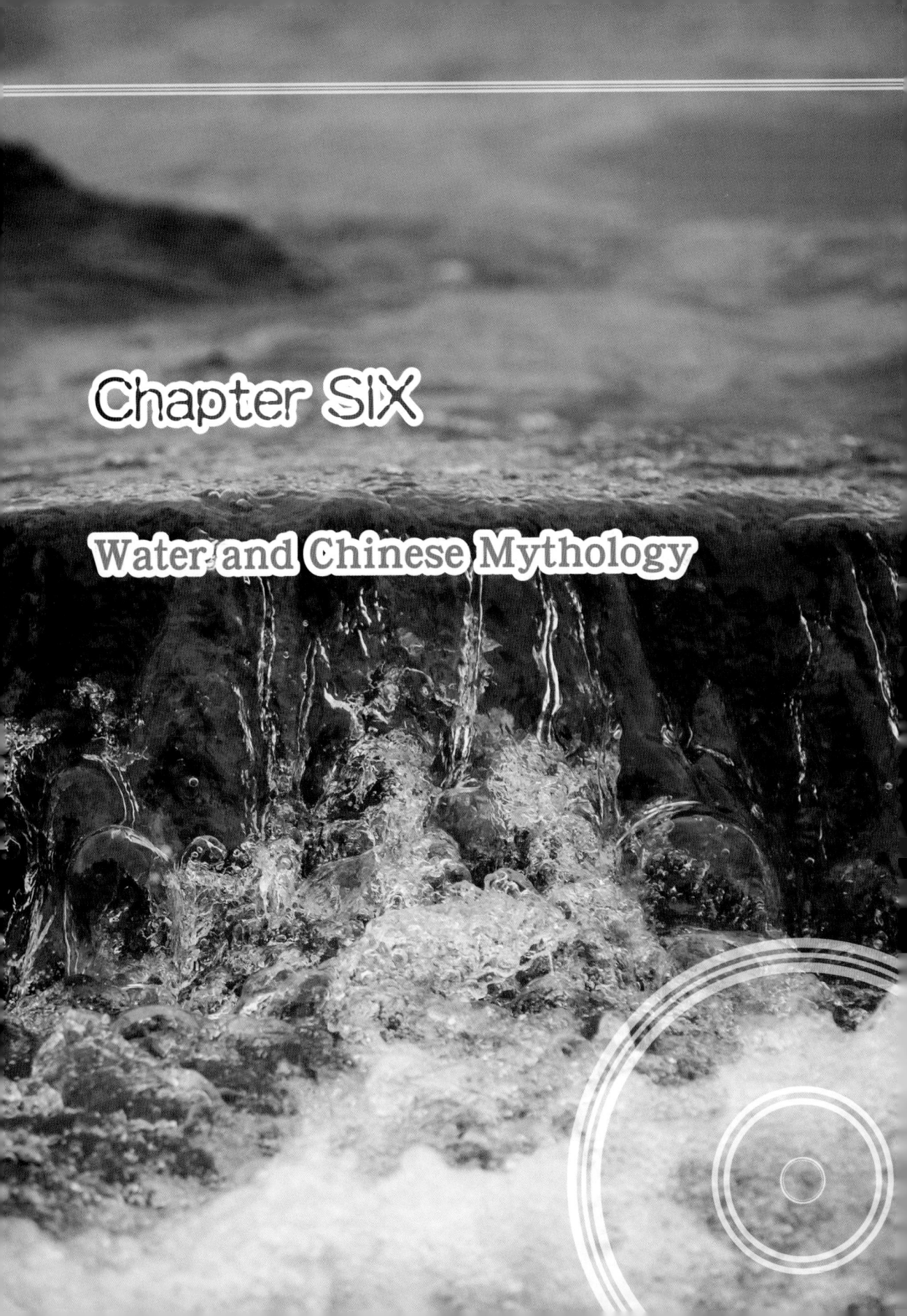

Chapter SIX

Water and Chinese Mythology

Water is one of the most important and key factors for the formation, development, evolution and evolution of Chinese culture, and the importance of water outrides almost any other element.

A secret about the traits of Chinese people that has been haunting the world for years may be discovered, deciphered and deconstructed. Nowadays, the whole world is eager to understand the vastness and depth of Chinese culture and its profound charm, because the Chinese people, Chinese ways of thinking and Chinese behavior patterns are more than being unique and different. They are obviously better than others in practice, which intensifies the world's strong curiosity to decipher and grasp the mystery. To interpret China with Western mentality will lead to a dead end, so a new perspective is indispensable to re-examine and understand the unique quality of Chinese culture.

Water is an objective substance in the universe. Chemically a water molecule consists of two hydrogen atoms and a oxygen atom. Numerous water molecules gather together to form water flow, which aggregates and recycles to form a natural ecosystem. Physically and biochemically, water seems to be as common as other substances with nothing special. It is an ordinary part of the world. A complete natural world would be impossible without any substance.

However, water is not simple. Socially and culturally water is a very distinctive substance. It endows Chinese culture, philosophy and value ethics with considerable intellectual thinking and special quality, which is in stark contrast with Western culture. Able to go anywhere in the world, water is unstoppable as long as it is determined to go and do something.

In other words, water has its own plans and ideas, as well as its own abilities and methods. It either flows with the tide, or concentrates on infiltration, or springing, or overcoming all difficulties and obstacles independently and advancing despite the repeated setbacks. The harsher the external environment, the stronger the water is, and the more determined it will be until it reaches the destination. For water, there is "no insurmountable difficulty".

The quality of water has deeply influenced and molded the traits and quality of the Chinese nation. Believe it or not, you will be surprised to find a large number of ancient myths and legends concerning the Chinese people who are undaunted by hardship and diligent, and who embrace challenges and push their own limits. Faced with natural challenges, the ambitious Chinese people will not surrender themselves and dare to fight. They believe that they can create a new world with their wisdom and hands, and reject to believe the existence of insurmountable difficulties. Diligence and perseverance have already been integrated into the inner of the Chinese nation.

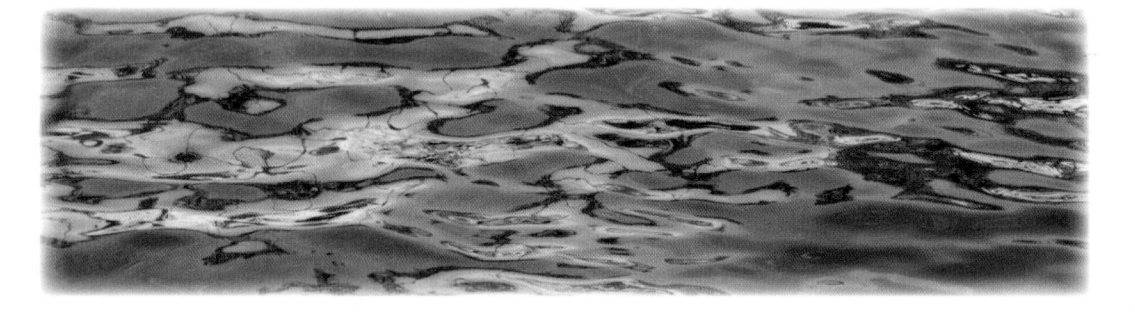

Dayu Harnessed Water

The flood of the Yellow River started in the reign of Yao when the Yellow River Valley was frequently subject to water disaster that drowned farmland, ruined houses and displaced people who led a miserable life. As a result, Yao was determined to exterminate flood. After consulting with all tribal leaders, Yu appointed Gun to control flood. However, being inexperienced in flood control, Gun knew nothing but diking and damming rivers. Consequently, despite Gun's effort to control flood for nine years, flood was not tamed and occurred more frequently inflicting more damages.

After Gun's flood control proved improper, Yu continued the cause, whose first priority was to grasp the causes for the flood in the Yellow River. If water could not be blocked, why not release the water by dredging the river? Longmen Mountain turned out to be the culprit, which blocked the water flow of the river and narrowed the river channels to such an extent that the river overflowed and caused flood.

Once the causes of the flood were found, new methods for water control were determined subsequently. Dayu took the entire landscape of China as a whole to comprehensively harness water. The first target of water harness was Jiuzhou Island: the land of Jizhou, Qingzhou, Xuzhou, Yanzhou, Yangzhou, Liangzhou, Yuzhou, Yongzhou and Jingzhou, which should be dredged and smoothed to turn a considerable number of areas into fertile land; then Dayu harnessed mountains including Qishan Mount, Jingshan Mount, Leishou Mountain, Taiyue Mountain and Taihang Mount, Wangwo Mount, Changshan Mount, Dizhu Mountain, Jieshi Mountain, Taihua Mountain and Dabie Mountain.

The last thing was to dredge the waterway so that water could flow downstream smoothly without blocking the waterway. Longmen Mountain that blocked the waterway would be split. It took Dayu and his people 13 years to break the new path and dig nine canals that finally diverted the Yellow River to the sea. Yu's effort to harness water proved his sharp understanding of water that is inclined to flow downwards and enter the sea. To this end, "drilling high and dredging low" held the key to the successful water harness. Suppressing the flood, Dayu became the first hero to harness the Yellow River in Chinese history, and was honored as "the God of Yu" by future generations.

Kuafu Chased the Sun

In ancient times, there was a splendid mountain rising into the clouds in the wilderness of the north. Deep in the mountains and forests, there was a group of giants with infinite strength. Their leader, Kuafu, was the grandson of Houtu, the God of Hell, so this group earned the name of Kuafu Tribe. They were stout, tall, strong-will and extraordinary. Moreover, they were kind-hearted, hard-working and brave living a peaceful life.

However, the land then was desolate where beasts dominated and people lived miserably. In order to sustain the life of its tribe, Kuafu led his people to fight against flood and beasts every day. One year, it was so hot that the scorching sun burnt crops, withered trees and dried rivers on the earth. The heat was so unbearable that the people of Kuafu tribe died one after another. Saddened by the

death of compatriots, Kuafu looked up at the sun and told his people, "The sun is such evil. I will catch up with the sun and catch it so that it can be commanded by us." On hearing this, the clans tried to persuade Kuafu out of doing so.

Nevertheless, Kuafu was so determined to catch the sun so that it was controlled by people and served them. Looking at the clan of apprehension, Kuafu said, "For the sake of happy life, I must go." When the sun just came out of the sea, Kuafu bade farewell to his people ambitiously. Starting from the East China Sea to the direction of the sun, Kuafu embarked on the journey of chasing the sun with strides. Kuafu crossed mountains and rivers, and finally caught up with that burning red fireball when the sun set.

Kuafu stretched his arms with great joy in an attempt to hold the sun in his arms, but he was thirsty and exhausted. He drank up the Yellow River and the Weihe River in one breath, but thirst remained, so Kuafu ran northwards where there was a huge lake extending for thousands of miles. The lake water was enough for Kuafu. Unfortunately, Kuafu died of hunger and thirst on the way to the lake. When Kuafu died, he was still eager to rid his people of suffering.

Yu Gong Moved Mountains

According to legend, there were two giant mountains in the south of Jizhou and north of Heyang long time ago. One was Taihang Mountain and the other was Wangwu Mountain, both of which were so high that they almost touched the sky. These two mountains covered an area of seven hundred miles. The north of the mountain was inhabited by Yu Gong, an old man in his nineties. His house facing these two mountains, it was very inconvenient for him to go to somewhere else. Thus Yu Gong made up his mind to do away with the two mountains.

One day, he assembled the whole family and told them, "These two mountains have blocked our way out. Let's work together to take it down and break a way to Yuzhou. Will you?" All applauded except his wife, who doubted on where to store the stones and mud dug out from mountains as tall as Taihang and Wangwu. Then the family came up with the idea of dumping the mud and stones on the coast of Bohai Sea where there was large space to pile up stones.

The next day, Yu Gong led the whole family to start digging mountains. An old man living by the Yellow River was so shrewd that he earned the name of the wise old man. Having seen Yu Gong dig mountains and transport mud all year round, he found it ridiculous and tried to persuade Yu Gong out of such futile effort. He said, "You are such a fool. You are so old and your days are numbered. You are too physically weak to outroot the grass on the mountain. How can you move such a huge mountain?"

Yu Gong sighed deeply and said, "You seem smart, but you are stubborn actually. Even no better than widows and children. Yes, I am too old to live long, but when I die my sons will remain, who will have grandsons and grandsons have their sons; descendants for generations come up in an endless stream, but these two mountains will not grow any higher. Of course we can take them down." Hearing what Yu Gong said, the allegedly wise man was stuck for words.

Knowing what Yu Gong had been doing, the God of Mountain feared that Yu Gong would keep digging the mountains down till they disappeared. So he reported what was happening to the heaven, which was touched by Yu Gong's tenacity. The heaven sent two Titans down to earth to carry away two mountains, one moved to the east of Shuofang and the other to the south of Yongzhou. From then on, there were no mountains between the south of Jizhou and the north of Hanshui.

Houyi Shot Suns

According to legend, there were ten suns in the sky in ancient times, which gave off heat like fire balls that burnt the earth and killed many people and animals. The forest was on fire, the river was dried, and all the trees, crops and houses were burnt to ashes. Those people and animals surviving the fire ran around to crazily look for shelters and water and food, praying for the God's mercy.

At this time, there was a young and handsome hero named Houyi, who was a skilled archer. He was summoned by the Emperor of Heaven who assigned him the mission of driving away the suns. Seeing people tortured by fire, Houyi was determined to shoot all the other nine suns to spare people suffering.

To this end, Houyi trudged over ninety-nine mountains, crossed ninety-nine rivers, and travelled across ninety-nine canyons before arriving in the East China Sea, where he overlooked the boundless ocean from the top of a mountain. Houyi targeted on the scorching sun with his arrow of five hundred kilograms, and released it from the bow of five thousand kilograms. The first arrow took the first sun down. Houyi repeated and shot down another two.

With seven suns remaining in the sky, Hou Yi still felt scorching and shot the third with his full strength. The arrow was so powerful that it took down four suns directly, scaring the other suns to tremble. Following such momentum, Hou Yi shot arrows one by one to the sun, all of which hit the target accurately. Nine suns disappeared from the sky.

Houyi did not stop till the last sun remaining in the sky agreed to follow Houyi's instructions and contribute light and heat to the earth and all things. Since then, the sun has risen from the eastern seaside every day, and set on the west, warming the world, preserving all and granting people peace and contentment.

Jingwei Filled up the Sea

According to legend, the Yan Emperor had a daughter named Nvwa, who was so smart, lively and gorgeous that raised the fondness of his father. One day, she went to a small village to have fun with other children and saw an elder child riding a younger one like a horse. The younger one was too exhausted to continue but the elder child refused to stop. Seeing the bully, Nvwa pointed at the elder child and scold angrily, "You are too bad. It is nothing decent to bully a child. If you are capable, just fight tigers and bears. People will admire you as a hero."

The elder child did not take Nvwa seriously at all, who seemed to be little and weak. He jumped off the little child he rode on and went to the girl and said, "I am the son of the Dragon King. Who are you? How dare you to criticize me?" Nvwa responded, "Who is the son of the Dragon King? I'm the daughter of Shennong (God of Agriculture). Don't pee on the land, or I will hang you up to the tree and dry you."

The son of the Dragon King said, "I'll let you know how capable I am. What I do is none of your business." He intended to attack Nvwa as soon as he finished his words. Nvwa had hunted with her father in the mountains since she was young, so she was highly flexible and vigorous. The rudeness and impoliteness of the boy did not scare her. She dodged from the punch thrown by the boy and jumped up to kick the Dragon King's son in his ass. The boy stood up and refused to give in, so he went on throwing punches. However, he ended up with a punch by the girl in the chest. Knowing he could not even hold a candle to Nvwa, the Dragon King's son fled back to the sea upset.

A few days later, Nvwa went swimming in the sea happily, but she was caught by the son of the Dragon King. He swam over and said to the girl, "You took advantage of me on the land that day. Now you are at my door. Just say sorry or I will stir up a storm to drown you to death." Nvwa insisted that she was right and would not confess. Realizing that Nvwa was relentless and did not intend to give in, the son of the Dragon King immediately stirred up the sea and set off a storm. The girl was drowned to death and would never return to the earthly world before she could struggle.

Nvwa was unwilling to die so her soul converted into a bird named Jingwei. Jingwei was outraged by the merciless sea that took away her life and that might kill other young people, so she moved branches and stones from the Xishan Mount continuously to throw them into the sea to fill up the sea. She flied endlessly between the Xishan Mount and the East China Sea, only to find the mockery of the roaring sea, "Forget it, my little bird. Even if you work for millions of years, you can never fill me up."

However, Jingwei soaring in the sky answered with resolution, "I will never stop till I fill you up, even after ten million years or to the end of the world." Jingwei left the sea flying and roaring back to the Xishan Mount, where she assembled stones and branches to thrown into the sea. She has flied back and forth like this without pausing, and still endeavors to fill up the sea till today.

Drilling Wood to Make Fire

In ancient times, people did not know the existence or use of fire. When night loomed, it was dark everywhere. The roar of wild animals came and went, scaring people to huddle because of coldness and fright. Without fire, people could only eat raw food, resulting in the frequent diseases and short life span.

Then there was a god named Fuxi in the heaven. Saddened by the hard life led by mankind on earth, he wanted people to know how to use fire. Thus Fuxi showed his capability to cause a thunderstorm in mountains and forests. As the thunder cracked trees, the forests got burnt and soon burst into a sea of fire.

After the fire, a young man found that the cries of animals that used to haunt the mankind had vanished, so he was thinking about whether beasts were afraid of shining things. So he bravely went to the fire and found himself warm. He summoned everyone excitedly: "Come on, this fire is not horrible at all. It brings us light and warmth." People coming around also smelt the sweet taste of the beasts burned to death. Since then people have begun to realize how valuable fire was.

What was happening on earth was witnessed by Fuxi. He penetrated into the dream of the young man who first discovered the use of fire and told him that he could go to the Suiming State in the far west and bring back the fire there. After waking up, the young man remembered the words of the Fuxi in his dream, so he was determined to go to Suiming State for fire. After crossing mountains, wading rivers and trudging forests, the young man finally arrived in Suiming.

However, sunshine was absent in Suiming, where darkness reigned all the day without fire. The young man was disappointed and took a break under a big tree named Sui Tree. Suddenly, a flash of light was caught by the young man, and then flashes came continuously to illuminate all around. The young man immediately rose to look around for the light source. At that moment, he found some big birds pecking insects with their short and hard beaks on the Sui Tree. As soon as they pecked, the tree sparked brightly.

The young man was inspired by what he had seen. He immediately broke off some branches of the Sui Tree and drilled big branches with smaller ones. The branches sparked but there was no fire. Undaunted, he rubbed the Sui Tree with branches of different tress patiently. Finally, the branches smoked and fire broke out. The young man brought the method of "drilling wood to make fire" back to his hometown. People admired the young man's courage and wisdom so much that they elected him to be the leader and called him "Sui Man", that is, the fireman.

Xing Tian

During the reign of the Yan Emperor, Xing Tian was a prime minister. He was fond of songs all his life, and composed the music *Plow* and poem *Harvest* for the Yan Emperor to celebrate the happy life of the people at that time. Later, the Yan Emperor was defeated by the Yellow Emperor in the battle of Banquan, but the son of Yan and his men would not give in. When Chiyou gathered his troops against the Yellow Emperor, Xing Tian wanted to go to the battlefield, but he was persuaded out of the war by the Yan Emperor.

Chiyou's defeat and death in the battle to the Yellow Emperor triggered the fury of Xing Tian. He secretly left the Heaven Court in the south and went straight to the Central Heaven Court to compete with the Yellow Emperor. He rushed to the palace of the Yellow Emperor with a square bronze shield in his left hand and a huge axe in his right hand. The Yellow Emperor was infuriated by the aggression of Xing Tian and took up the sword to combat him. Their duel erupted inside the palace and was extended to the Changyang Mountain on earth.

The Yellow Emperor was experienced after fighting for years on battlefield. He slashed Xing

Tian in his neck with his sword. Xing Tian could not dodge the attacked and was beheaded. Realizing that the Yellow Emperor had cut off his head, Xing Tian was not discouraged. He rose and waved the axe in his right hand and the shield in his left. Confined to utter darkness, Xing Tian looked with his two nipples and breathed with his navel, and continued to fight against the Yellow Emperor. Although Xing Tian ended up with failure, his being uncompromising inspired future generations.

Unique Charm of Chinese Culture

The myths and legends in traditional Chinese culture, such as "Dayu Harnessed Water", "Kuafu chased the Sun, "Yu Gong Moved Mountains", "Houyi Shot Suns", "Jingwei Filled up the Sea", "Drilling Wood to Make Fire", and "Xingtian", all convey the quality of being "uncompromising" and struggling. That is, to do what is considered impossible. The results are important, so are the uncompromising attitude. Sometimes, attitude, courage and spirit are more important. When problems, conflicts, difficulties or disasters occur, should we pray for God's blessing or solve them on our own? To this question, Chinese people always have their own answers and methods.

Unlike the Chinese mythology, the Western mythology holds that fire is God's gift; in Greek mythology, fire is stolen by Prometheus, but in Chinese mythology, fire was made by drilling wood relentlessly. This is the difference. The Chinese ancestry told these stories to remind their descendants of fighting against nature. "When the doomsday flood occurred, we took refuge in Noah's ark, but in Chinese mythology, their ancestors defeated the floods."

"If there was a mountain in front of your house, would you move to somewhere else or dig a tunnel? Clearly, moving to somewhere else is a better option. In Chinese stories, however, they moved mountains away. Unfortunately, such a spiritual core is absent in our mythology. Our mythology is to follow the God (David Chapman, USA). Westerners usually solve problems by waiting for help, dodging the reality or resorting to existing facilities and resources.

The Chinese mythology is different from the Western one. In the event of an upheaval, the Chinese people tend to be proactive, while the Westerners are relatively passive. "Chinese people grow up with such myths and stories, so the spirit of fighting has become part of their gene, so it is easier to understand why the Chinese people never yield. This explains for their existence till today." (David Chapman, USA)

The Chinese culture and the Western one vary greatly in the response to environment and events. The former resembles water more, which is characterized by "independence and autonomy". They act in accordance with the situation as water flow downwards. They create wealth on the way ahead, challenge external hardship and difficulties and never believe in any God or Savior. So they do not care about God or Savior, and even hold that there is no supernatural power or god. The Chinese people only believe in the human strength. They survive and flourish through their own strength, diligence and struggle. "Heaven will follow the wishes of the people." (*Book, Oath of Tai, I*). That is, the public opinion is so inviolable that even the God will respect it.

"Know thyself" (by Socrates, ancient Greek philosopher). "He who knows others is smart; he who knows himself is wise". It is important for Chinese people to know themselves and their characteristics, and to explain these with the language that the whole world understands, rather than disseminating the image of the Chinese people by the hand of others and the words of foreigners. Frankly speaking, Westerners cannot understand the Chinese people because most of them "know what it is" without "knowing why it is". They can experience and understand the quality of "being uncompromising and resistant" presented by Chinese myths and legends, but they may not be able to recognize the real reason and value that support the spirit of "not yielding".

In a world whose discourse power is dominated by the West, a lot of people naturally misinterpret the Chinese people and Chinese culture. Many people say that the Chinese nation has no religious beliefs, no sense of awe, no sense of responsibility, and no sense of social morality.

In fact, what the Westerners say is imprecise. The question is how many people understand Chinese people and Chinese culture, in that even the Chinese people themselves fail to explain the proposition of "who are the Chinese people". Can a nation without religious beliefs exist uninterruptedly for 5000 years? I am afraid that what the world lacks is a correct explanation or answer.

Indeed, the "unnatural" artificial religion in the West is absent in China, which, however, does not necessarily mean the absence of religion in China. Chinese people have their own "natural" religions, and was the only nation that worship the "God" of nature. The Chinese believe in the universe composed by heaven and earth, in the natural law (Tao) of the universe. In the eyes of the Chinese, water is almost the synonym or byword of the law of nature. Tao is recessive, while water is dominant. To understand and master "Tao", one can learn the characteristics and quality of "water".

The Chinese cultural value system is drastically different from the Western one. The worship of Chinese people is "natural", while that of Westerners is "unnatural". Chinese people like "water" and worship "water", from which they contemplate and gain wisdom. Westerners, however, prefer to be close to the world of animals and plants from which they acquire knowledge and common sense for human life. The mankind can indeed study and acquire a vast amount of knowledge from animals and plants, but it is absolutely impossible to gain wisdom of human civilization, namely equality, fairness and justice. Man is the soul of all things. What humans aspire to and pursue is definitely superior to

that of animals and plants. We should not or cannot learn the great wisdom of human civilization from animals and plants.

Culture is the root and soul of an ethnic group. Different cultures have different roots and souls. To be honest, it is hard to find a culture as unique as the Chinese culture in the world. Chinese culture is so unique that it stands out from the crowd. Of course, the uniqueness of Chinese culture serves for nothing unless the Chinese economy thrives. Without economic prosperity, no one will take Chinese people seriously, at most as an "abnormal" or "freak" that drifts away from the world family, and no one will come to realize that the Chinese civilization system is actually the leading one, more advanced and civilized than the Western civilization.

Only when China develops and revives to such an extent that it leads the world can the West set arrogance aside to listen carefully to the Chinese people telling how the Chinese culture was created and developed. Telling Chinese stories and those successful ones will present the Chinese philosophical thoughts, value ethics and discourse to the world and influence the world like the amazing "Made in China".

Chapter SEVEN

Water, the Prominent Feature of Chinese Model

There are many development models in the world, such as the neoliberal "American model", government-led "Japanese model", and "Rhein model" represented by the German social market economy. These models are similar to and different from each other. Thus a civilized country so great as China, with an uninterrupted history of 5000 years, is supposed to have its own "Chinese Model" that is well-known and well-received.

It is of great benefit for a country to expound clearly their own methods and characteristics of social governance to people from home and abroad, which is also in the interests of other countries. In doing so, people all around the world understand and communicate with each other. This is what a responsible large country should do for the world, especially when China is ready to make greater contribution to the world and top the global list of GDP in the immediate future. Therefore, China should explain itself clearly as soon as possible.

What is a model? A model is an imitable paradigm, a collection of the characteristics of how things develop, and a reflection of the typical characteristics of such things. The model must have two basic elements: one is the unique and distinct characteristics in comparison with the same kind of things; the other is the consistency of these characteristics that forms a stable system.

The development model is an economic and social development system with distinct characteristics, which is created by the interaction and mutual promotion of political, economic and cultural factors. It is the product of the establishment and development of the basic national system under different political, cultural, historical and social frameworks. In the process of economic development, different development systems have emerged as the state-market relationship, government-enterprise relationship and state-society relationship undergo constant adjustment.

The Chinese model is an economic and social development system with distinct characteristics, which is created by the interaction and mutual promotion of political, economic and cultural factors in China. The study on the special nature of the Chinese model is an attempt to find out the invariable structural factors that are deeply embedded in the development model. These factors may be the most core and fundamental elements of the Chinese model.

From the perspective of historical development, we can clearly understand the rationale for the long-term survival of the Chinese model and the advancement of civilization. Although the Chinese model is manifested in different aspects, the key is the political and economic models peculiar to China, which are interrelated, interdependent and mutually reinforcing. Undoubtedly, China had been ranked among the most advanced countries in the world for over one thousand years in the ancient times. China's economy did not go downhill until the Wanli period of the Ming Dynasty; following the Opium War at the twilight of the Qing Dynasty, China's economy declined sharply and even decayed.

After the founding of PRC, China had failed to reach the top ten of the world in terms of GDP. However, by the end of the twentieth century, China's economy has resumed its momentum and kept leaping forward, overtaking Canada, Italy, France, the United Kingdom and Germany and becoming

the third largest economy in the world within a decade; in 2010, China replaced Japan as the second largest economy in the world; if it develops smoothly, China will be expected to surpass the United States and top the world in terms of GDP in around 2035.

This is a rare miracle in human history. Within the 32 years from 1979 to 2011, China's GDP had doubled for four times in a row every eight years. In modern history, it took 58 years for Britain to double its GDP (since 1780), 47 years for the United States (since 1839), 33 years for Japan (since the 1980s), 17 years for Indonesia and 11 years for Korea. Moreover, few countries have been able to double their GDP consecutively, but China has made it and keeps advancing.

If a country fell from the peak of historical development, to an extent that it almost perished, and stood up tenaciously to run as one back to the peak, this country could be said to be creating a miracle. In this world, no country other than China has achieved this miracle. The Chinese people is the only ethnic group that "dares to lead the world" to break a new path and embark on the journey of rejuvenation. Why can the Chinese do that? Why can't other nations? The answer lies in traditional Chinese culture.

The Chinese model has a consistent philosophical basis, that is, the 5000-year state governance model in China is based on a consistent philosophical theoretical basis. Since ancient times, the philosophical and ethical orientation of Chinese people has remained the belief in the natural law of heaven and earth, the obedience of Tao to nature, and the combination of universe and human. The mankind should learn from the nature humbly. The Chinese model is guided by Tao, the natural law of heaven and earth, and by water, which is endowed with the unique characteristic of eternity. Consistency, sustainability and reliability lasting for 5000 years or longer constitute a stable and mature comprehensive system of social governance and social development.

In the natural kingdom, there are natural laws of the heaven and the earth, namely "Tao". Although "Tao" cannot be seen, heard, touched or sensed, it does exist and permeate. Laozi, the sage of ancient Chinese philosophy, explained, "The highest excellence is like water. Water is good at benefiting everything without vying for any fame or gain. Water is in a place which is despised by the public, but it is the place where one is closest to truth." The supreme goodness is like water in pursuit of perfection; water is good at nourishing all things without competing with them for fame and wealth, stays in undesirable places. Therefore, water is closest to Tao or natural laws.

Since then, "water" has become a synonym or byword of "Tao" in the real life of Chinese people, as well as the embodiment of "Tao" in the natural law. Laozi described the natural law with "Tao" and was the first one to use the perceivable "water" to describe and recognize the natural law, which was difficult to perceive. Such description and perception were straightforward, simple and concise. Chinese people are so convinced in Tao and water that they worship water. No matter how the history evolves, the Chinese people adhere to their own traditional beliefs and philosophical ideas. The mode of state governance often reflects the special quality and characteristics of Chinese philosophical thinking.

Characteristics of Chinese Model:

1. Ecology

The water circulation system in nature is a green ecological system with endless movement. Water never stops flowing and circulating. Driven by solar radiation and gravity, water forms a cycle between land and sea. The solar heat evaporates water of the ocean surface to the sky, where vapor in the air forms cloud that moves with the atmospheric circulation to be converted into rain, snow, hail and precipitation on the ground surface. When precipitation falls to the ground, it transforms into groundwater, soil water and surface runoff (rivers and lakes), which eventually passes through an outlet and flows back to the ocean, thus forming a dynamic water circulation system. Various living things thrive nourished by the water circulation system.

Chinese people learn the knowledge of water recycling system, from which they come to realize that the prototype of national governance system is similar to water recycling system featuring unity, sustainability and endless cycle. Since ancient times, the Chinese people have highly recognized the state governance system characterized by the "Great Unity", to which they have adhered for thousands of years. Since the First Emperor of Qin reunified China, the Chinese nation has been adhering to the state governance system of "Great Unity" unswervingly, regardless of the countless times of disintegration of other countries in the world.

The generations of our fathers and grandfathers had their own ideals, their own reasons for perseverance and persistence, and the guidance of traditional wisdom and the protection of real practice. Otherwise, the national governance system of great unity would have soon been eliminated by the historical trend. The reason why such system can survive is self-evident. The recognition and perseverance of the Chinese ancestry were closer to the natural and primitive ecological conditions and conformed to the "Tao" of heaven and earth, rather than human imagination.

The current state governance system in China is also the result of long-term development, gradual improvement and endogenous evolution on the basis of the 5000-year historical inheritance, cultural tradition and economic and social development of the Chinese nation. This system is not the result of the groundless imagination by anyone or any party, so it does not allow for random alteration. Generally speaking, the political stability, economic development, social harmony and national unity of the country are the most fundamental reasons for the ultimate decision to preserve and improve the state governance system of "Great Unity".

The traditional Western culture holds that "government is necessary evil", which is not echoed by the Chinese who advocate that "government is necessary kindness". That is to say, government should speak for and materialize the collective will of the people, and play a primary role in state governance. The Chinese people have a strong sense of "home and state", which permeates books in ancient times. According to the *Great Learning*, "If a person wants to disseminate his virtues in the state, he should first govern the state; to this end he should have a harmonious family, before which he should cultivate his personal quality." "Individual, family, society, state and world" is the unique social ethical value logic of Chinese people.

"Family and state have existed before a person was born, and will remain when the person is dead. No matter how much a person has suffered or how much time has elapsed, he should keep home and state in mind." "Home is the same as state structurally, and these two share the same destiny." Home is a smaller state while state is a bigger home. "A country is big, but in fact, it is also a home." What everyone experiences in life is closely linked with home and state. "Hereditary monarchy" is one of the most essential characteristics of the Chinese tradition. The concept that a person should love his country as deeply as his family and prioritize the interests of country over those of family in times of danger has been integrated into people's mind. At the critical moment of national crisis when the loyalty to country and filial piety for family cannot be both fulfilled, rising to tackle national crisis will be more legendary and heroic than taking good care of families, because country is a big family whose existence is the premise of many smaller families.

2: Stability

The natural water circulation system is a highly "stable" life movement system. Water in nature forms a huge water circulation system consisting of the atmosphere, hydrosphere, lithosphere and biosphere, through a series of processes and links such as evaporation, including plant transpiration, water vapor transport, precipitation, infiltration, surface runoff and groundwater runoff.

No matter how water changes in form, ranging from liquid state to solid state and gaseous state, the total amount of water remains unchanged. Laozi said, "Heaven and earth are permanent, because they do not live for themselves." The reason why heaven lasts long is that it does not exist for itself, and so is the reason for the long existence of earth. The everlasting stability of heaven and earth is deeply rooted in the inner desire of every Chinese.

The Chinese people attaches great importance to a stable environment for internal and external survival and development. Without stability, China's "reform and opening up" would have been a pipe dream; without stability, development would be inapproachable for China. As an old Chinese saying goes, "Crossing the river by groping for the stones in it". To put it more plainly, if a person wants to cross a river without boats or bridges or previous experience that tells him where he should go, he has no alternative but grope for the stones in the river. That is, we should wade through the river after taking a conservative or even primitive approach to figure out the situation.

The reform conducted by China follows a stable and progressive approach by adopting the Oriental "gradual reform" for transformation instead of the Western "shock therapy" reform. Reform is conducted on the premise that the basic social institutional framework (especially the political system) and the dominant ideology remain unchanged, with particular emphasis on self-improvement on the basis of adhering to the fundamental national system and principles.

The economic reform is progressive featuring the gradual adjustment of the respective proportion of public and private ownership, and the priority to the state-led economy. China's reform implements the strategy of "from outside the system to inside the system". Specifically speaking, China's reform first focuses on "what is outside the system" instead of first targeting the state-owned sectors, the most prominent obstacle against smooth reform. Thanks to the policies of rural reform, opening-up, development of non-state-owned economy in some areas, and expansion of regional markets, the economy of pioneer areas of reform, mainly coastal areas, has developed rapidly and thus experience and capital for reform have been piled up. In this way, we can sustain our reform economically and politically, and there is more time and space for further reform.

China's reform is an "item-by-item, partial, incremental and progressive" pilot project. Usually some sites are selected as pilot to which predetermined targets are given for testing. After experience is accumulated, the reform will be gradually extended to a comprehensive level. The reform is from bottom to top and progresses from what is easy to what is difficult, that is from economy to politics. Reform is first conducted in the incremental part, the results of which are used to drive the existing reform. The "bottom-to-top" Chinese-style progressive reform prevents huge social shock, allows seeking truth through trial and error, and delivers remarkable achievements.

The Chinese-style reform is special for the priority to "stability". China does not resort to comprehensive and large-scale privatization, avoiding extreme social polarization and turbulence. Despite the absence of mature theoretical guidance and pre-designed reform blueprint, the reform in China is materialized and well delivered by the Chinese people who fully understand the art of "crossing the river by groping for the stones in it" and break a unique Chinese-style development path. Therefore, the reform in China receives huge success.

3: Openness

The natural water circulation system is an open one embedded in the system composed of "heaven, earth and man", featuring overall independence, open dynamics and ecological cycle. Water remains open-minded to all the creatures it encounters in the cycle, including plants and animals. Water communicates freely and equally with all things and nourish them. Water never refuses to communicate with others. No matter how far you can go, how high you can fly, or how much you want, water will respect you, make friends with you and make you who you are. "He who fishes should know water well, and he who raises birds should plant tress first. Fishes assemble in vast water and birds gather on dense trees."

The Chinese people are keenly aware of what "openness" and "seclusion" would bring about respectively, due to the severe pain caused by "seclusion and the consequent suffering". Considering Qin and Han Dynasty, Tang and Song Dynasty, Yuan and Ming Dynasty to the early Qing Dynasty, and the "40-year reform and opening up" today, the states in Chinese history have all been strong and open.

In the late Qing Dynasty, the government completely closed itself up and excluded foreign cultures and civilizations by imposing stricter sea ban. During the reign of Emperor Kangxi, the controversy of etiquette between the Qing Dynasty and the Roman Church not only restricted Western missionaries in China, but also fundamentally changed the attitude of Qin towards foreign trade. The closed-door policy and arrogance of the Qing Dynasty isolated China from the world outside and severely hindered China's social and economic development.

The strategic decision of "reform at home and opening up to the world" is the first major national policy with the theme of opening up since the founding of New China. This policy has changed China's long-standing seclusion and made China open its door to free trade. The impact of reform and opening up is remarkable, and the achievements are enormous. From 1978 to 2018, the People's Republic of China has transformed from an isolated country with 680 million people living below the poverty line into a strong and prosperous economy with an active market, and has reduced the number of the impoverished in the world by nearly a quarter.

The material and mental life of the Chinese people has also been diversified thanks to the "reform and opening up". According to official data, from 1978 to 2018, China's per capita GNP has rose from $225 to more than $9,000. In 2018, China's foreign exchange reserves exceeded $3 trillion, making it the largest creditor of the United States. In 2018, China's gross domestic product (GDP) surpassed $13 trillion, becoming the second largest economy in the world that nearly triples Japan's GDP.

Today China is more open, confident and hard-working. China is striving for returning to the top of the list of "champion countries" as soon as possible.

4: Integrity

Water in nature is divided into three different forms: gaseous, solid and liquid. Three different forms of water are connected and transformed independently, and comprise a unified and orderly whole. Water in constant motion and changes evaporates through solar transpiration, and the vapor forms cloud and rain after cooling. The rainfall is converted to surface runoff and underground runoff including rivers, glacier, soil water, lakes and groundwater, which return to ocean for a complete cycle. Each independent water body is closely related with and complements each other in terms of energy, quality and quantity, the loss of any of which would paralyze the cycle. Individuals cannot be separated from the whole while the whole would be incomplete without individuals. These two complement each other.

China is one of the oldest ancient civilizations in human history. China remains vital despite the turbulence for thousands of years. Although ancient China suffered setbacks and divisions, the country has never collapsed. On the contrary, it has been moving towards unity and once became the strongest country in the ancient world.

When Toynbee, a famous contemporary British scholar, talked about Chinese history and culture, he once lamented: "For thousands of years, hundreds of millions of Chinese people are more unified politically and culturally than any other nation in the world. Such political and cultural unification demonstrate proves to be unparallelly successful." A distinct "tradition" in Chinese culture is the long-lasting patriotism and collectivism.

The Chinese people boast the whole-oriented, while the West emphasizes the individual-oriented tradition. Chinese people learn the overall structure and consciousness of "water", integrate the macro and micro worlds and treat them as a whole. The importance attached to individuals and the whole is equal, and the planning is well-coordinated as a whole. The aspiration to freedom and democracy must be accompanied by unity and centralization. Individuals is more inclined to freedom and democracy, advocating the freedom followed by unity and the democracy followed by centralization; while collectives emphasize unity and centralization.

The Chinese collectivism is typically shown to the world in the opening ceremony of the 2008 Beijing Olympic Games. China's development needs to be achieved not only by individual means, but also by collectivism. Thousands of Chinese dancers acted, beat drums and danced like one person, and walk in a precise formation without stumbling or bumping. The strength and skills of "collectivism" have been fully demonstrated, and China's miraculous development and rejuvenation have been witnessed by the world.

The society is composed by individuals whose personality of whom should be respected, while the collective is the full collection of individuals and the collective representative of multiple individuals. The individual freedom and democracy are followed by collective unity and centralization so that the front and back echo each other and the whole operates orderly. The advocacy of "collectivism" is by no means the disregard of personal, local and temporary interests.

On the contrary, such emphasis means that individual interests and collective interests, temporary interests and long-term interests are equally important. "Individualism" should not be selfishness that disregards public welfare or even harms others for one's own interest, but should be the equal rights and responsibilities shared by all individuals. Society will not allow any individual to trample on the rights of any other individual for any reason or sacrifice the interests of others to achieve one's own private interests.

5: Inclusiveness

In nature, water has affinity for most substances because water molecules can form hydrated particles with other substances. Water molecule is an inorganic substance formed by the bonding of two hydrogen atoms and one oxygen atom. Water molecule has polarity. Therefore, water itself has the basic conditions to become a source of life. Water in nature does not exist in the form of a single water molecule, but is aggregated by a number of water molecules through hydrogen bonding, which move continuously to form a water cycle.

Since there is a lone pair of electrons with Lewis alkalinity on the oxygen atom of a water molecule, most electrolyte substances can dissolve in water. Therefore, liquid water can dissolve many other substances, and can provide the best medium for the collision and reaction of substances. Water is an omnipotent solvent and an unparalleled solute. China's governance model fully demonstrates the dissolution and fusion of "water".

Traditionally, Chinese people have no strong religious consciousness. The Chinese people's attitude towards life is "moderate" without falling into the extremes of either "asceticism" or "indulgence" and losing the harmony of life. The Chinese people are neither stubborn nor paranoid with foreign religions, stay open-minded, unbiased and appropriate, make good use of what benefits the development of our nation and abandon what harms the development of our nation. The general policy of the state towards foreign religions features respect, openness, inclusiveness, harmony and integration.

Quanzhou, Fujian Province, is a holy place where the secular and gods bathe together, and is known as the World Religious Museum. To describe this place where Buddhism and Confucianism coexisted, Zhu Xi said, "This place was called the Buddhist Kingdom in ancient times where the streets were full of saints". In fact, in the heyday of Quanzhou, Buddhism, Taoism, Christianity, Catholicism, Islam, Hinduism and Japanese religions coexisted in harmony.

In the West Street of the core area of ancient Quanzhou, there were two ancient Hindu stone pillars carved with famous Indian epics *Mahabharata* and *Ramayana* in the center of the corridor behind Ziyun Hall of Kaiyuan Temple, an ancient Buddhist temple. Not far away from Kaiyuan Temple is Quanxi Christian Church, at the door of which there are Shigandan stones put by Taoist believers who hold they can drive evil. Various religious beliefs coexist in harmony in an old street, demonstrating the unparalleled inclusiveness and tolerance in the world.

The Chinese people are self-disciplined and peace-loving advocating "do not impose what you

dislike to others". Major conflicts in daily life are often dealt with as minor ones, and minor ones are even regard as nothing. Chinese people boast strong tolerance and inclusiveness and will not be hostile because of one's beliefs or custom. Moreover, the Chinese are very hospitable and can coexist peacefully with people of other countries. Meanwhile, the Chinese people are very independent and dislike imposing their own ideas on others or accepting the ideas imposed by others. Such unique rational power featuring compatibility, harmony and reason is more likely to assimilate "non-Chinese: things. This is indeed powerful cultural inspiration.

The unique rational and cultural forces of the Chinese nation have influenced and assimilated "non-Chinese cultures" for many times. In today's China, Christianity, Catholicism, Islam, Judaism, Orthodox Eastern Church, Buddhism, Taoism and Confucianism coexist in harmony and prosperity; the former foreign enemies, Khitan, Hun, Xianbei, Tuoba, Qiang, Di, Qi, Jurchen, Nvzhen, Jin, Mongolian and Manchu, have been tightly bound up with the great Han people and become indispensable members of China since they entered the Chinese territory. People of all ethnic groups in China should live in harmony and share weal and woe. The strong cultural power of the Chinese nation to influence and assimilate foreign religions has supported the existence of the Chinese nation for a long time.

6: Harmony

Water circulation system in nature is a coordinated monitoring system of the whole ecosystem and its subsystems. Water connects living things on each link of the biological chain, balances the even development of each independent species, so that the whole ecosystem can follow the existing laws between heaven and earth, and operate orderly and harmoniously. In the ecosystem, one living thing feeds itself on the other, while the other preys on another, constituting a food chain among living things. Green plants in the food chain convert inorganic matters into organic ones, and light energy into chemical energy stored in organic matters through photosynthesis.

The survival of animals depends directly or indirectly on the organic matters produced by green plants. Herbivores depend on plants, carnivores prey on herbivores, and omnivores feed themselves on both plants and animals. Microorganisms such as bacteria and fungi decompose the complex organic matters contained in the corpses, excrements, and debris of animals and plants into simple inorganic matters and return them to the inorganic environment where these inorganic matters are reused by green plants to produce organic matters. In the ecosystem, water is a coordinator of unique importance, responsible for energy flow, material transfer and transformation.

Chinese people advocate the philosophy of "harmony". In the remote ancient times, the *I-Ching* written by Fuxi showed philosophical ideas such as "combination of universe and human", "harmonious coexistence" and "contradiction and unification". Yellow Emperor, Confucianism and Taoism have adhered to the theory of "combination of universe and human", which underpins harmony between man and nature, society and world. This is also where the concept of harmony originated. Confucius also proposed the concept of "harmony" more than 2000 years ago. Chapter 1 of the *Doctrine of the Mean*: Moderateness is the foundation of the world. Harmony is why the world

flourishes. That is, to reach Tao, harmony is moderate without going extreme, in line with the law of development of things.

The coordination and harmony contributed by water to the ecological circulation system make water the ideal object for Chinese people to imitate. The strategy and method of the Chinese state governance are inspired by the wisdom of water. Chinese people strive to act like water in human society, that is to properly and flexibly coordinate the interests of all parties for harmony and inclusive growth. More specifically, Chinese people are making effort to build a "harmonious" society at home and promote a "peaceful" world on the planet.

Over the past 60 years, PRC has provided assistance of nearly RMB400 billion to 166 countries and international organizations in the world, dispatched more than 600,000 aid workers, of which more than 700 Chinese have sacrificed their precious lives for the development of other countries. China has announced seven unconditional exemptions from government interest-free loans due to China by heavily indebted poor countries and least developed countries.

By 2020, China will also provide 600 projects for developing countries, including 100 poverty alleviation projects, 100 agricultural cooperation projects, 100 trade promotion assistance projects, 100 ecological protection and climate change response projects, 100 hospitals and clinics, 100 schools and vocational training centers; China also grant developing countries 120,000 seats of training and scholarship for 150,000 students. China will develop 500,000 technicians for developing countries and establish South-South Cooperation and Development Colleges.

Looking back at China's poverty alleviation and development at home, a total of 680 million people have been lifted out of poverty rapidly in a short span of 40 years from 1978 to 2018, which is known as the "Chinese miracle" in global human history. Poverty is a persistent disease of civilized society. Eradicating poverty is the duty and mission of the ruling party of China. Unlike the non-governmental and small-scale life relief in foreign countries, the Chinese government alleviate poverty in a planned and organized manner with the whole country running as one. The "government-led" poverty alleviation model is the basic prerequisite for rapid poverty reduction in China. Being government-led and people-oriented, the development poverty alleviation featuring social engagement and self-reliance, as well as the path of poverty alleviation and development line with China's national conditions, are splendid in the history of poverty alleviation.

"Harmony" is always on the road. There is no best effort, only better, higher and farther. The "imperial examination" system peculiar to ancient China and the "college entrance examination" system today have pave the way for the social mobility of ordinary people to the core of the national knowledge and management stratum; "all farmers have farmland", "well-shape field system", "harmonious society", "defeating local landlords and giving their farmlands to farmers", "human community of shared destiny", "the Chinese dream", "Belt and Road Initiative", "the Asian Investment and Infrastructure Bank (AIIB)" and "Shanghai Cooperation Organization" (SCC), BRICS, BRICS Bank, New Sino-US Great Power Relation, Candid and Win-win Neighboring Diplomacy, 10+1

China-ASEAN, 10+3 China-Japan-Korea ASEAN, China-Japan-Korea Free Trade Area, "Agricultural Tax Reduction and Exemption", Environmental Pollution Control, "anti-corruption campaign" that cracks down on both high-ranking and low-ranking corrupted officials.

"Meeting between President Xi and Ma Yingjiu (Taiwan leader)", "Military Reform", "UN Peacekeeping", "Boao Asia Forum", "Xiangshan Forum", "China-Asia-Europe Economic Development Cooperation Forum", "China-Europe Cooperation Forum", "China-Africa Cooperation Forum", "China-Arab Cooperation Forum", "China-Small Island Countries Economic Development Cooperation Forum", "National Medical Security System", "National Social Security System". All these initiatives serve as testimony to the government's great importance attached to livelihood and its effort to build ten livelihood security systems covering urban and rural residents, ranging from employment, pension, medical treatment, relief and housing to education, public cultural and sports services, environmental protection, public safety and rights and interests protection. There should be no brake for the effort for "harmony".

Conclusion

Nowadays, people all over the world, including the Chinese themselves, are not sure whether there is a Chinese model or not. The answer is, of course, positive and clear. China has always had a model of national governance suitable for its own development, which has lasted, stabilized and operated for 5,000 years bearing remarkable results. The current Chinese government is still inheriting and adhering to the consistent Chinese model initiated by their forefathers.

Since the traditional Chinese state governance model has existed for 5000 years and proven fully able and effective to nourish the Chinese nation as well as the long-term stability of the country, we have reasons to summarize experience comprehensively and thoroughly and explain clearly the Chinese model from a theoretical perspective. The clear understanding of the internal and external implications of the Chinese model contributes to enlightening China, inspiring other countries and nations in the world, and enhancing China's development influence.

All the rulers in Chinese history, irrespective of ancient emperors, imperial families or any modern political parties, have adhered to a basic principle: observing "Tao" on behalf of the "world". That is, acting on behalf of the interests of all people in the world, unlike the Western political party system where there are only political parties in the interests of minor groups without representing the interests of all the people. In stark contrast, the rulers of any dynasty in China swore to represent the interests of all people. Thus the dynasties in Chinese history were essentially different from the Western political parties focusing on the interests of a few, and the former delivered far better governance than the latter.

To evaluate the merits and demerits of rulers in power and decide on whether they should remain in power or be replaced, China has its own democratic procedures and practices of Chinese characteristics.

The replacement of the ruling power is usually defined and implemented by the replacement of a "dynasty", rather than competition among political parties for ruling in the modern Western society,

where government leaders are elected to power every four or several years. Once the Chinese believe in a rule or a ruling group and choose it to represent the interests of all people to run affairs for the nation, they will generally place the greatest trust in the ruling class. The change of personnel within the ruling class is generally handled by the ruling authorities themselves. In the social division of labor, everyone does what he or she is best at. For instance, the government concentrates on the major affairs of national development; democratic parties are in charge of supervision; people are dedicated to undertakings aiming at personal development independently. The government and the people perform their respective duties and do what they are supposed to do to complement each other.

In terms of political model, since the First Emperor of Qin unified China in 221 BC, he resolutely abandoned the feudal system left by the Zhou Dynasty and implemented the county system nationwide, marking the first endeavor to create a centralized political system. Over the past two thousand years, despite the ups and downs of dynasties, the Chinese people have never changed their own model of political governance. It was a firm fact that the average lifespan of a dynasty in Chinese history was two to three hundred years.

Compared with Western countries, the execution of "democratic procedures" in Chinese-style state governance mode reflects more Chinese philosophical thinking that abides by the natural law and the nature of "water". Considering that the social prosperity and development of society require a lasting, stable, sustained and harmonious external environment, the Chinese model does its best in practice to double its effort to this end.

In terms of economic model, China has been implementing a mixed public-private economic model since the Spring and Autumn Period and the Warring States Period till now. According to historical records, Guan Zhong, Chancellor of the State of Qi, was the first person to propose the idea of "proprietary sale of salt and iron", which was taken by Emperor Wudi of Han Dynasty as a national policy. Since then public or state-owned enterprises have been involved in the national economy for more than 2000 years. China has adopted a typical mixed economic model in which the state and non-state sectors, the government and the market should maintain a proper balance.

There is hardly any economic governance model like China's in the world. Over the past 2000 years, a strong state-owned sector has remained directly guide the key economic fields. Historically, private economy has invariably existed in China. It is absolutely impossible for China to come to the point where private economy dominates the national economy like that of the West.

Neither the full nationalization or full privatization can be the normalcy of China's economy. It is the mixed economic model that marks the normal of China's economy. Generally the proportion of state-owned economy and private economy has been adjusted accordingly in different time periods. Sometimes, the proportion of state-owned economy rises and that of private economy declines, while

there are times when the proportion of state-owned economy drops and that of private economy increases. Such adjustment aims to meet the needs of the national economy in a certain period. Change and adjustment are definitely nothing new to Chinese people.

The "Chinese model" based on the originality is nothing else than a path of survival broken by the Chinese people in the practice for thousands of years, and a path of development created by the Chinese people with hard work and wisdom. The exploration and innovation of the Chinese model is undoubtedly the greatest practice and the most brilliant social system innovation project in human history. The Chinese people are using their political wisdom to perfect a brand-new social governance system and create a new model of social governance for the world. The Chinese model is undoubtedly a new form of human civilization.

The inheritance and implementation of the traditional Chinese-style state governance model is a choice made by China in its historical development. This is a decision that does not allow for the random change by any person or any ruling party. The people are the real "masters" of the country, and what they choose and decide tops anything else. "The world is vast and magnificent. Those who follow the trend flourish, those who go against the trend perish."

There is an invariable driving force in the progress and development of history. Once gaining momentum, this force will be converted into a strong "trend" which will push forward the history long and continuously. It is highly difficult to resist or change this trend, and there is definitely no way to redirect the trend despite the occasional counter-current for a short period of time. The Chinese history has proven and will continue to prove that the Chinese governance model will remain the answer to the Chinese people unless it is out of line with the reality and the ideals and aspirations of the Chinese people.

Chapter EIGHT

Water, the Key to Understanding Chinese People

In today's world, more and more people are eager to understand and comprehend Chinese culture, including Westerners and Chinese themselves. The reason is that China's influence is increasing day by day. The whole world is paying more and more attention to the existence of China. It has shown unprecedented interest in the Chinese model and realized the importance and urgency of understanding China. With China's rapid development, China's comprehensive national strength is approaching that of the United States as the world's top, and it is likely to catch up with and surpass the United States in the near future and replace it as the world's top economy country.

Modern Chinese learn from the West and gradually grow up in this process. However, all the prevailing and universal knowledge and wisdom reserve existing in the West and all the theories and laws suitable for the operation of western society have been unable to explain the development story of China effectively. At the same time, it is rare to clearly explain the Chinese phenomenon and the Chinese people's words and deeds at the cultural level in the world.

Who are the Chinese and what are they thinking about? This is really a bit confusing. If no one can answer this basic question clearly, the whole world will worry about where the Chinese people will take the human society once they become the world's leader in politics and economy. It is undeniable that the Western society represented by the United States has been the first to stand up and fiercely oppose China to take the helm and replace the existing dominant position of the Westerners. How can the Chinese carry the banner of leading the human world? This is probably the fundamental reason why "China Threat Theory" and "China Collapse Theory" are popular all over the world today, and there are still many people who believe and follow them.

"China Threat Theory" and "China Collapse Theory" are intertwined with "Civilization Conflict Theory" and spread widely to the world. Conflicts will inevitably occur between different civilizations. A civilization in its strong period will inevitably colonize, expand and dominate to export its own culture, and use its own culture to eliminate and replace alien cultures. As Huntington said, "Culture almost always follows power. Historically, the expansion of the power of a civilization is usually accompanied by the prosperity of its culture, and this civilization almost always uses its power to promote its values, practices and systems to other societies." Westerners are really very afraid that the future will be out of control in their generation.

Westerners are greatly frightened that the situation will be out of control if the Chinese continue to grow up like this. Westerners have a development path that they have gone through. They believe that they can explain China clearly according to their own historical and cultural knowledge, and they can explain other people with different history, culture, region and thinking mode as well as their behavior patterns. Subjectively, they attempt to incorporate China's transformation and development into the "development stage" that the West had experienced. After demonstrating with the experience and wisdom of Westerners that China's rise and revival, they think China would inevitably colonize, expand and dominate as they did in the past.

Westerners are judging all forms and evolution paths of "civilization" with their own way of

thinking as if there is only one path of development for human civilization, that is, the path that Westerners have already taken. Westerners' judgments are really too simple. They have only a little knowledge, but they are especially stubborn, opinionated and refuse to know and accept new knowledge. They live in a small pocket of their own thoughts. It is an illusion that very difficult to realize that outsiders want to expect Westerners to tell stories of China clearly. The knowledge and wisdom of the West may be too shallow, too simple, too scarce, not enough.

Marco Polo's *Travels of Marco Polo*, Mendoza's *The History of the Great and Mighty Kingdom of Chinaand the Situation Thereof*, Trigault's *De Christiana expeditione apud Sinas*, Louis Le Comte's *Nouveaux Memoires sur L'Etat Present de la Chine*, Anson's *A Voyage round the World*, Du Halde's *Description de la Chine*, Chin Shunshin's *Japanese and Chinese*, Matteo Ricci's *Regni Chinensis Descriptio*, Arthur Smith's *Chinese Characteristics* have all analyzed Chinese people from different aspects and to different degrees and involved some superficial phenomena of Chinese culture, but they have never explained the logic of thinking and philosophical basis behind Chinese words and deeds.

Of course, the Chinese themselves should face the wall and reflect on themselves, and they will also get angry. So far, no Chinese have stood out to explain the unique characteristics and features of Chinese culture. Yan Fu, Lin Yutang, Lu Xun, Bo Yang, Jin Ziqian and other Chinese scholars have also tried to describe the national character of the Chinese people, but there are always doubts from the outside. The world still does not understand China, or does not understand China enough.

The world's "incomprehension" of China is not necessarily a negative "misunderstanding", but that "negative misreading" of China still exists for a long time, but the more common phenomenon is that the world still lacks a comprehensive and correct understanding of China. Not many people in the world understand China, and the Chinese people will also doubt what they have and how they can lead the human world unless you make it clear and explain it clearly so as to convince people.

It is a great challenge to explain clearly the thinking mode and group behavior of Chinese people. To be fair, it has never been easy to explain and interpret Chinese people accurately, and it is even more difficult to fully understand Chinese culture. In the past, no one talked about or understood Chinese people. The problem was not very serious. After all, it was not easy for Chinese people to go out or to welcome others in because they were surrounded by their geographical environment. Even if there was contact with the outside world, it was not too much, and its scale and scope of influence are limited.

For thousands of years, the Chinese people have been living their own lives. As long as you follow the books, rules, and the footprints of your predecessors and develop yourself in a relatively closed natural environment, you will be satisfied with yourself. However, in today's globalization situation, if no one tells about or understands the Chinese, the problem will be very prominent, very troublesome, and even some conflicts will be intensified and escalated, because many people around the world do not know or understand and thus doubt the reasonable expectations of the future of mankind.

At present, the biggest misunderstanding of westerners about China is that they subjectively believe that there is no unified national religion in China, which is too terrible for them. Looking around the rest of the world, most countries have a mainstream religion. European and American countries believe in Christianity, Judaism or Catholicism, while Islam is widely believed in countries of Central Asia, West Asia and North Africa.

Thailand, Myanmar, Sri Lanka and other Southeast Asian and South Asian countries believe in Buddhism. Most Japanese people believe in Shintoism. Only Chinese people believe in have all kinds of religious beliefs. They believe in whatever they meet, and believe in everything is equivalent to believing nothing. If a nation does not have its own religious belief, the soul of the nation will not be bound by religious disciplines, and they are easy to be possessed by evil spirits and commit unimaginable bad acts, which eventually lead to man-made disasters.

As the saying goes, "there are mountains outside the mountains and buildings outside the buildings". Westerners may be less knowledgeable and worry too much. In fact, Chinese people never lack religious beliefs, but the belief worshiped by the Chinese is different from that of Westerners. Westerners have never really walked into the hearts of Chinese people and understood Chinese culture. They have never realized that the specific target groups in Chinese people's study of nature are completely different from those in the West.

Human beings live on the earth. There are many sources of knowledge and wisdom in the ecosystem, including biological chain (food chain) system, water circulation system, wave circulation system, light circulation system and magnetic field energy system. Faced with many targets to be referred to and imitated, the Chinese people mainly tend to learn knowledge from the water circulation system, obtain the wisdom inspiration of their traditional culture, and extract the essence of philosophy and ethics. At the same time, Chinese also learn the knowledge of survival and reproduction from animals and plants and various technical means to improve efficiency.

Chinese people speak of water, worship water as their teacher, and are serious in learning. When describing the natural law of "Dao", Laozi, the sage of Chinese philosophy, described it as, "The highest excellence is like water. Water is good at benefiting everything without vying for any fame or gain. Water is in a place which is despised by the public, but it is the place where one is closest to truth." (*Chapter VIII of The Book of the Way* by Laozi) The supreme goodness is like water in pursuit of perfection; water is good at nourishing all things without competing with them for fame and wealth, stays in undesirable places. Hence, water is closest to "truth."

In Chinese people's cognition, the natural law "Dao" is no longer a nihilistic conceptual illusion. "Water" has become the embodiment of great "Dao" or natural law in the real life of Chinese people. Laozi described the law of nature with "Dao" and creatively described and recognized the law that are difficult to perceive of nature with perceptive water. All the people in the world should understand the fact that in the hearts of the Chinese people, there has always been their own consistent insistence, devoutly believing that "water is the origin of everything" and "water is closest to truth."

Water is the religious belief of Chinese people. Dao is the religious belief of the Chinese people. The integration of all laws in the natural world is the true religious belief of the Chinese people. The Chinese people are sincerely obedient to "Dao" and to "water". They respect the nature and laws of nature. They worship water as their teacher and are inspired by learning, researching and exploring the virtue and character of water. The Chinese nation has been imitating, studying and practicing water constantly for generations for 5,000 years. They are the people who have grown up under the guidance of "water".

Chinese people's group behavior

1: Like water that travels everywhere, Chinese people have settled down all over the world.

The Chinese are born such a group of people who love making a living away from home, making friends, and experiencing life. They are willing to travel all over the world. At present, you can find Chinese people everywhere around the Nile River, the Aegean Sea, the Alps, the Amazon River, the Great Barrier Reef, the Norwegian Fjord, the Central Rocky Mountains, and Antarctica and the Arctic. As long as you can get a foothold in the outside world and have a successful career and family, you are all good and worthy of the family's praise. You will be able to return to your hometown gloriously and honor your ancestors.

In the summer of 2004, Mr. Li, a journalist friend of mine, along with two other Xinhua journalists, traveled on the Chinese scientific research vessel, "Xue Long", to explore Antarctica and passed through Coari, the second largest city of the Amazon in Brazil. According to their professional habits, the journalists agreed to go ashore together to find Internet cafes to publish their articles.

Under the guidance of local enthusiasts, they finally found a small Internet cafe. The Internet café was a nightmare. The speed of the Internet was incredibly slow, and they were disconnected from time to time. Just as they were surfing the Internet, a strong Asian man appeared and went straight to a machine to surf the Internet quietly. Mr. Li casually said, "Here comes a Japanese." Unexpectedly, the man raised his head and said, "I'm Chinese" in Chinese.

This Mr. Deng is from Taiwan and has been in Coari for 10 months and was in São Paulo before. Their family came to Brazil from Taiwan very early to make a living, and all of them were doctors. Ten months ago, Mr. Deng and his wife and two children came to Coari to work as surgeons in a public hospital. He introduced that there were only five Asians in the city. Besides their family of four, there was also a Japanese.

The three reporters were very surprised and talked with Mr. Deng for a long time. They all marveled at the pioneering and survival ability of the Chinese people, because many indigenous people along the Amazon had moved to cities because they could not stand the harsh natural conditions and mosquito bites. However, the Chinese people were still marching deep inland. Mr.

Deng liked the tranquility and simplicity of Coari, as well as the current situation of life and work. When they parted, they said good-bye to each other and wished all the best. This is a true response to the old saying that where there are people, there are Chinese people, I did not expect to meet people from my hometown in such a remote place.

In nature, water can go anywhere it wants to and penetrate anywhere it wants to. The whole world has such a surprising discovery that where there is water, there are Chinese people. The whole world has seen the footprints of Chinese people settling down.

2. Like water that nurtures everything, Chinese people are keen to make money.

The Chinese are born such a group of people who instinctively like wealth, desperately make money and love saving money. No matter how good or bad the living environment is, they always believe that making money is the most basic and the first important thing in life. They always put earning money and supporting their families in the first place in their lives, while other things can be put aside or even ignored. The absolute importance of having money outweighs everything else. Over the past 5,000 years, Chinese people have worked hard with their own hands to create wealth, accumulate wealth and pass on wealth from generation to generation with their hard work and hands-on efforts.

In November 2009, Lee Kuan Yew, Minister Mentor of Singapore, attended the APEC CEO Summit. In an exchange with Michael Eliade, editor of the International Edition of *Times* magazine from the U.S., Lee Kuan Yew complained that the West did not know anything about the East or China when he talked about Western criticism against China that "it is not a democratic system". He said that the Chinese wanted better lives rather than votes. China may not have a democratic system, but the Chinese are more interested in improving their living standards than in voting and freedom of speech.

Lee Kuan Yew said, "Chinese people are not interested in democracy." He explained that in the process of Chinese trying hard to catch up with the world, their main concern was to achieve the standard of living they saw in the more developed economies of Asia. He further said, "You have your democracy activists, but are the Chinese worried about their right to vote and freedom of speech? They want to live the life they saw in Hong Kong, Singapore and Taiwan before the financial crisis."

Lee Kuan Yew was equally impressed by the vision of the Chinese leadership. When he was asked if he agreed with Larry Summers, Head of the US National Economic Council, that China is planning for 20 years from now, Lee Kuan Yew said, "It is further than 20 years. They are planning for the next generation." He pointed out that China already had candidates for the next generation of leaders. "This is not a random choice made at the whim of voters, but is formed under the strict supervision of an institution they call the CPC Central Commission for Discipline Inspection (CCDI).

"This is an impressive system." What Mr. Lee Kuan Yew said is true and appropriate. His subtext is that Chinese people are most concerned about making money, not other things. They are devoting themselves diligently to planning for long-term and super-long-term economic development plans and accelerating wealth accumulation. Chinese people can do any kind of work, as long as they

can make money. Chinese people are reluctant to handle works with no money. The vast majority of Chinese people are busy making money day and night for only one purpose, to obtain a more abundant material basis of life.

In nature, everything cannot grow without water. In human life, the company and support of money are indispensable at all times. The function of wealth in the world is as important and indispensable as that of water in nature. The world has such a wonderful discovery that Chinese people particularly like money, can make money and love saving money.

3. Like water that circulates in cycle, Chinese people are especially homesick.

In the world, every one of every nation loves his/her hometown and country. However, no nation can be as homesick as the Chinese people, who yearn for their birthplace and country of origin so passionately and enthusiastically. The Chinese are born such a group of people who spend their whole lives missing home. "Wanderers long to go back home as leaves come back to their roots, and they want to return home gloriously after loaded with honors." This is the deepest, strongest and most sincere complex in the heart of our Chinese people. It is this kind of homesickness complex that haunts the nerves of homesickness of generations of travelers and wanderers.

In April 1956, faced with Mao Zedong's outspoken admonition that "Be patriotic and united regardless of order. Meet sincerely. Come and go freely" and the "Four Cans" opinion that "Mr. Li can come back and settle in his motherland. He can come back or go to the United States. He can stay in Europe for a period of time and then decide. He can go out again after he comes back, and he can come back again if he still wants to come back. In short, there is no restriction on freedom of movement." the former Vice President of the Republic of China, Mr. Li Zongren, said categorically, "We can no longer be like kites with broken lines, floating around like duckweeds and wandering everywhere. Even for trees thousands of feet tall, the leaves still fall to their roots. I am a Chinese, so I must go back to China and find my final destination on the land of my motherland."

"I can't leave my old bones in a foreign country. People in old ages miss their motherland even more. Chiang Kai-shek's so-called China would never appear in my life. It is too late for me to regret now. My biggest mistake was to break up with Chiang Kai-shek too late. A moment of hesitation made me miss the good opportunity and result in eternal hatred. Zongren is old, but I still want to go back to my motherland. Now there are still years before my death to make up for my mistake and do something helpful." At 0:30 on July 18, 1965, a Boeing 707 took off from Karachi, Pakistan, broke through the long night and flew to the motherland carrying Li Zongren's patriotic heart.

At midnight on January 30, 1969, at the moment just before his death, Li Zongren insisted on dictating a letter to Mao Zedong and Zhou Enlai, "I resolutely returned to my motherland from abroad in 1965 and I took the right path. In this great era, I deeply feel that it is a great honor to be a member of the Chinese people. At the last moment of my death, I am still deeply concerned about the future of the Kuomintang and all patriotic intellectuals who remain in Taiwan and abroad. There is only one way for them, that is, to return to their motherland, just like me."

Water, no matter how far or how long it flows away, it will always return to its starting point without hesitation to its home and departure place, and then gather again and start a new cycle. In reality, Chinese people love water deeply and are infatuated with it. Their feelings of homesickness are often more profound and lasting than those of other ethnic groups in other countries. The whole world has such a surprising discovery that Chinese people particularly miss and love their hometown and they especially love their country.

4. Like water that is humble and friendly, Chinese people love to keep a low profile.

The Chinese are born such a group of people who have been taught by their elders from an early age earnestly and tirelessly, "To be humble and keep a low profile. People are afraid of being famous and pigs are afraid of being fat. The bird takes the lead will be shot." We should keep a low profile and be tolerate and quiet. Mountain do not explain its height, but this do not affect its towering into the clouds. Sea do not explain its depth, but this do not affect its capacity to accommodate all rivers. Land do not explain its thicknesses, but still no one can replace its status as the bearer of all things. People don't flatter their gifts and talents, but this does not affect the real dignity that humans are at the top of the biological chain.

In response to the global heated debate on the phenomenon of *China's Megatrends* by American futurologist John Naisbitt in 2009 and *When China Rules the World* by British scholar Martin Jacques in 2010, Mr. Li Zhaoxing, the Foreign Minister of China at the time, calmly commented, "It is not necessary to talk about the rise of big powers all the time, but to keep a low profile and do our jobs." The purpose is to remind the Chinese people not only to see our achievements in development, but also to face up to our current situation. We should be firm and confident, but not blindly arrogant.

On the topic of "China's Rise", we cannot stop others from saying good things. The key lies in how we treat and evaluate ourselves. It is not a very good phenomenon that, after listening to these flatteries from abroad, some people in China are really naive and childish and become arrogant and self-conceited. Even the rise of our country is not enough for us to be arrogant and proud. This is true both economically and militarily. If we compare ourselves with ourselves, our economic, national defense and scientific and technological strength have indeed made considerable progress, but there is still a long way to go compared with developed capitalist countries, especially with the United States.

If we really rise to a strong position, some neighboring countries or even small countries will not dare to occupy our territory and islands and will not rely on a superpower to engage in militarism in front of our doorstep. The Chinese people should always keep a sober mind, prepare for danger in times of peace and speed up development so that we can realize the real "rise of the great power" and "national rejuvenation" in safeguarding world peace, safeguarding territorial integrity and promoting the great cause of the reunification of our motherland. Li Zhaoxing's remarks expressed the aspirations of the Chinese people.

Water remains at lower places and avoids competing with others. Water has the character of nourishing all things. Water graces all things calmly and helps all living things to thrive. However, it

never competes for fame and fortune or care for returns. It just devotes its heart silently and selflessly. Contribution with a low profile is the supreme character of "water". The whole world has such a novel discovery that the Chinese people are particularly appreciative and worship low profile.

5. Like water that refuses to stay the same, Chinese people appreciate changes.

The Chinese are born such a group of people who never fear changes, but face them calmly, accept them readily, and grasp them skillfully in the palm of their hands. Water flows according to the terrain, while victorious army adapt its strategies that vary from one enemy to another. Use the static to control the dynamic and vice versa and use this static or dynamic to check and balance that static or dynamic. "Where there are policies from superiors, there are countermeasures by inferiors." "Take one step at a time." "Soldiers will block enemies when they come, and soil will be used to keep flood out if it comes". No matter what kind of changes happen in the outside world and what means are used by the other party, the Chinese people will always find appropriate countermeasures to solve the problem.

Mr. He Yingjie, chairman of the board of directors of the Hong Kong Tobacco Company and a famous philanthropist, who is known as "He Bo", has kept a low profile and been mysterious for his entire life. His true face has been little known. He Bo, whose ancestral home is Wuxi, Jiangsu Province, had a strong interest in machinery in his childhood. He entered school at the age of 9 but dropped out at the age of 14 and entered the printing factory of his family as an apprentice. With the energy of young people, in just two years, he learned the whole set of techniques such as stone painting, typesetting, printing and so on. At the age of 16, he became the manager of the family printing factory.

Diligence and eagerness to learn were the basis for his success. He got married at the age of 18 and started his own business at the age of 20 with 2,000 yuan and founded Shanghai Xinya Printing Factory. During the Anti-Japanese War, most people fled for safety, and there was a large shortage of workers and technicians. However, he persisted and made Xinya Printing Factory the only open printing factory in Shanghai at that time, and its operating profit also increased by 10 times. In just one year, He Bo made a great fortune in paper business alone. By that time, he had had his own investment strategy and intended to set up a cigarette factory.

In 1942, He Bo founded a cigarette factory in Shanghai. The first brand "Gao Le" was very popular, so he continued to expand his investment scale and other business fields. After World War II, the 36-year-old man went to Britain to order advanced cigarette machines. He arrived in Hong Kong in 1949 and formally established his Hong Kong Tobacco Company. Over the past half century, He Bo's business has developed from printing to paper, from paper to cigarettes, from cigarettes to financial investment, covering Hong Kong and the United States and Canada.

Water in nature is the most changeable substance. "It passes on just like this, not ceasing day or night!" Water is the best at following the trend and adapting to the situation and to the changes in the external environment. Water is flexible and changeable. It either hides under the ground without revealing it or gushes up into a clear spring. When there is less water, it will please itself with tinkling. When there is more water, it will gallop bravely.

Water is located between heaven and earth in both dynamic and static forms. It goes into the mountains into springs, streams and rivers. It flows into depressions into pools, lakes and seas. Water is soft and friendly, combining hardness and softness, controlling rigidity with softness, and very changeable. The world has such a special discovery that Chinese people are particularly good at change, happy to study and adapt to the ever-changing world.

6. Like water that is grateful and appreciative, Chinese people try their best to practice loyalty and filial piety.

The Chinese are born such a group of people who are loyal to their country and filial to support their families. The thought of loyalty and filial piety has dominated the Chinese people for thousands of years. It is an indispensable link to maintain the country and families, and it is the unique wisdom of living of the Chinese nation. In Chinese cultural thinking, people not only have blood kinship, but also have the moral kinship inherited from heaven, which is the philosophical basis of mutual love, loyalty and harmonious coexistence. On the basis of loyalty and filial piety, the extended values of benevolence and loyalty have constructed the moral framework of the super-stable mechanism of China's "Great Unity" society.

Every year, there is an important festival in China – the Qingming Festival. The Qingming Festival is a day that embodies the spirit of life of the Chinese nation. It reflects the national spirit of the descendants of Yan and Huang (Chinese people) who respect their ancestors and admire the ancient sages. The Qingming Festival reminds us all that we have common ancestors, and the same blood is flowing in our blood vessels.

Qingming Festival began in the Zhou Dynasty and has a history of more than 2500 years. Since the reign of Tang Dezong (790 A.D.), there has been a system of holiday and worship on Qingming Festival, presenting a grand occasion of common celebration among officials and common folks. Qingming Festival embodies the significance of gratitude for the source of present benefit, cohesion of ethnic groups, doing fitness and caring for nature. Its contents mainly include tomb worship, eating Qingtuan, putting jujubes together on poplar and willow branches, going out to plant trees, wearing willow branches and enjoying flowers, flying kites, swinging, farming, writing poetry and prose, etc.

During the Qingming Festival, the Chinese people spare no effort to return to their hometown to pay tribute to their ancestors and remember their ancestors. In the solemn sacrificial activities, the chain of life and blood relationship was linked by living individual lives and family life to the deceased family and clan life, forming the bond of the Chinese nation's recognition of ancestors and sense of belonging and precipitating into the important foundation of personal moral education, family and family unity and national unity. Therefore, Qingming Festival is another life theme reflected by Chinese people through offering sacrifices to their ancestors, worshipping the sages and remembering the martyrs: remembering and thanksgiving.

"A drizzling rain falls endlessly like tears on Qingming Day; The mourners' hearts are going to break on their ways. I ask a local person where the restaurant is; The shepherd boy pointed to

the Xinghua Village." This poem, *Qijue Qingming*, by Du Mu, a poet in the Tang Dynasty, depicts a beautiful ink painting of spring rain, shepherd boy and restaurant. The poet's hasty steps lead the poetic sentiment of Qingming Festival. Today's Qingming Festival still occupies an important position in people's daily life. We pay gratitude to our predecessors, commemorate our ancestors, cautiously pursue the days past and look forward to the future.

Water in the nature comes and goes. It moves constantly. The cycle of water goes on eternally. It is a typical example of being loyal to one's duty and performing "loyalty and filial piety" in nature. Wherever water exists in the world or whatever form it is in, it will always return to the earth in the form of precipitation, return to the place where it selflessly devotes its efforts and nourish the earth and all things. It never complains. It never slacks off. The whole world has such a unique discovery that Chinese people particularly respect and adhere to loyalty and filial piety.

7. Like water that travels together in company, Chinese people like to gather together to have fun.

Chinese people are born such a group of people who especially like joy and excitement. They like to gather together and have fun together happily and freely. Usually, when Chinese people attend banquets, activities, or travels, they always prefer companions. They look for familiar companions and quickly gather together to form a small group, so that they can have a sense of security and talk and laugh freely. Otherwise they will feel nervous, lonely, bored and uncomfortable.

Wang Zhujie, who emigrated to Canada in 1984, spent six years in "immigration prison" there, and then went to Hong Kong after "being released". He then moved back to Beijing and never returned to Canada. Speaking of the experience of "rebirth" in Beijing, Wang cheerfully claimed that Chinese people are gregarious, who like to gather together in lively groups. The Chinese pay attention to family and social relations and advocate four generations living together and their children around their knees.

Westerners are independent and have their own way of doing things. They live their own lives independently from each other. It seems that they lack the human touch of the Chinese people, which we Chinese can never be used to it. In Beijing, there are many relatives and friends. There are dinners several times a week. We may either treat others or be treated by others. We eat and drink in a lively and bustling atmosphere and talk about trivial gossips and laugh together. Chinese people always like to find a reason to invite guests to have a dinner party, or a reason to let others have a dinner party and be invited. They are always thinking about who owes whom a meal, or an appointment, and asking for an opportunity to get together.

Eating is a major cultural phenomenon in China. This national hobby of eating and drinking collectively among Chinese people is not only to satisfy their appetite, but also to create an opportunity for everyone to gather together and talk and laugh. While eating-and-chatting is one of the greatest pleasures in life. Besides having dinner together, Chinese people love visiting each other's home as well. You come to my house tonight and I'll find a reason to pay a return visit tomorrow. This is Chinese people. When they have leisure, they always visit others, gather together, chat, have fun, communicate and deepen their feelings for each other.

Westerners, on the other hand, pay more attention to personal solitude. They would rather read at home, surf the Internet, meditate and watch TV than go out to eat, drink and talk with others. Chinese people are a people who like to live in groups and are fond of lively activities. The habitual life style left over thousands of years is hard to change, and of course, there is no need to change it.

Since water in nature has fallen to the ground in the form of precipitation, it has been scattered freely in any corner of the earth in an independent form and nourishes all things with pleasure. However, water is never satisfied with the present situation. It needs to do more. Only when water gathers together to form a scale can it possibly does great things.

Water is distributed and scattered everywhere, but always focuses on the same goal. With thousands of streamlets, it converges and flows into rivers and lakes and heads east straight to the sea. It becomes greater and stronger all the way and forms scale efficiency. The whole world has such a discovery that Chinese people especially maintain "gathering" and like "collectivism" from the bottom of their hearts.

8. Like water that is impartial and neutral, Chinese people believe in the doctrine of the Mean.

The Chinese are born such a group of people who like to occupy the middle position. Compared to up and down, left and right, front and back, east and west, north and south, the middle position is the safest, most reliable and most flexible, and it has the shortest distance to any direction. It has both offensive and defensive capabilities and basis for advance and retreat, which can comprehensively and reasonably control the overall situation and career process.

The Chinese people stick to the doctrine of the Mean and maintain moderation temperately to prevent the two non-ideal states of "too much" and "too little". The doctrine of the Mean is to avoid the extremes of "too much" and "too little", to supplement the "too little" and to remove the "too much" so as to make things impartial and appropriate. The doctrine of the Mean emphasizes the peaceful nature of things, the appropriateness of the way of doing things, and the flexibility that must be possessed when using this method.

One day, Zi Xia, a disciple of Confucius, asked the teacher, "What kind of person is Yan Hui?" Confucius said, "Yan Hui, he surpasses me in integrity." Zi Xia asked again, "What about Zi Gong?" Confucius answered, "Zi Gong surpasses me in agility." Zi Xia asked again, "What about Zi Lu?" Confucius answered, "Zi Lu surpasses me in bravery." Zi Xia asked again, "What about Zi Zhang?" Confucius answered, "Zi Zhang surpasses me in solemnity." Zi Xia stood up and asked Confucius, "Then why do all four of them worship you as a teacher?"

Confucius said, "Sit down, I tell you. Yan Hui is honest, but he doesn't know that there are still times when he can't be honest; Zi Gong is agile, but he doesn't know that there are still times when he can't speak too smartly; Zi Lu is brave, but he doesn't know that there are still times when he should be afraid; Zi Zhang is solemn, but he doesn't know that there are times when he should be humorous and intimate. That's why they recognize me as a teacher!"

Therefore, it is the right way to avoid extreme paths and stick to the middle path.

In the process of movement and circulation, water in nature upholds the principles of fairness, neutrality and integrity. It never shows partiality to or takes sides with any party in nature. It always treats all things in the world and nurtures and nourishes all things to help them grow. Water forms solid ice at or below zero degree, which is an extreme of water. Water evaporates into gas at or above 100 degrees, which is another extreme of water. Between 0 and 100 degrees, water is in its normal state as liquid, which is the middle and upright position of water.

Water, at normal temperature, maintains a liquid state in the middle to nourish the earth and nurture all things in the world selflessly to the greatest extent. The world has such a unique discovery that Chinese people are particularly good at the "the doctrine of the Mean" to be impartial, neutral, compromise and to avoid extremes.

9. Like water that is sleepless and restless, Chinese people love hard work.

The Chinese are born such a group of people who love working and enjoy working. The enthusiasm of the Chinese people for their hard work is by no means imaginable by other nationalities or comparable with others. It is no exaggeration to say that the Chinese people are the most industrious and frugal and have the spirit of enduring hardship. And the spirit of getting rich through hard work is one of the most widely respected virtues in the world today.

"Chinese employees are the world champions in industriousness". According to German media reports, GfK, a well-known market research institute, once conducted a survey of 8,000 employees in Germany and seven other countries with the title of "Which country's employees are the most industrious". The results show that Chinese employees are generally recognized as the most industrious. "You Chinese are really hard-working!" A foreign friend said. "How do you see that?" One Chinese asked curiously. The foreigner said earnestly, "I have observed that some people even work busily at 5 or 6 o'clock in the street, but you don't think it's early enough. Even in the breakfast places every day, there are signs set up to urge people to eat breakfast quickly."

Although it is a joke, the diligence of the Chinese people is not boastful. "Diligence is the essence of all business" and "all kinds of maladies come from laziness" always alert Chinese people not to be lazy live their lives in vain. Diligence is already an eye-catching label that distinguishes Chinese people from others, and even a "gene" that is integrated into the blood of Chinese people. The industriousness of the Chinese people is well known all over the world.

The Chinese seem to be a race born for hard work and happy for work. The diligence of the Chinese is the oldest "plant", which not only sends forth wonderful fragrance with the passage of time from ancient times to the present, but also blooms out magical lights in exotic places with the footsteps of the Chinese people from China to the rest of the world. Every nation in the world is industrious, but the industriousness of the Chinese nation is undoubtedly superior to that of other nationalities.

Many races in the world are diligent, but the diligence of Chinese people is unparalleled in intensity and length, geographical distribution and inheritance from generation to generation. The world agrees that unparalleled tenacity and incomparable diligence are the unique noble virtues of the Chinese people.

In nature, water cycle is a dynamic system that never stops. Under the action of the sun, water on the ocean surface evaporates into the atmosphere to form water vapor. Water vapor moves with the atmospheric circulation, part of which enters the sky and forms rain and snow under certain conditions. After the atmospheric precipitation reaches the ground, it is transformed into groundwater, soil water and surface runoff. Underground runoff and surface runoff eventually return to the ocean, thus forming a dynamic cycle of freshwater, which circulates cycle after cycle and runs constantly day and night.

10. Like water that is equal, Chinese people advocate respecting each other.

The Chinese are born such a group of people who are devoted to each other's courtesy and respect. "Do not do what you don't want to others" has been a conscious claim and self-demand of Chinese people for thousands of years. Don't expect or intend to force others to do what you don't want to do, what you can't do and what cannot be done. When doing anything, one should consider others in one's own place, feel for others, do not force others to suffer, let alone cause harm to others. We should insist on respecting others and treating others equally in interpersonal communication.

The Five Principles of Peaceful Coexistence were put forward by the Chinese Government and jointly advocated by the governments of India and Myanmar. They are the basic principles that should be followed in establishing normal relations and conducting exchanges and cooperation among countries.

On June 25, 1954, Premier Zhou Enlai of China paid a visit to India and Myanmar. During his visit to India, he held talks with Indian Prime Minister Nehru. The Prime Ministers of the two countries issued a joint statement reiterating the five principles of the relationship between the two countries stipulated in the *Agreement on Trade and Transportation between China's Tibet Region and India*: mutual respect for territorial sovereignty; non-aggression against each other; non-interference in each other's internal affairs; equality and mutual benefit; and peaceful coexistence. The statement stated that these principles are applicable not only to the relations between China and India, but also to general international relations issues. The Prime Ministers of the two countries are particularly keen to apply these principles to solve the problem of Indochina issue.

From 28 to 29 June, Zhou Enlai visited Myanmar, held talks with Prime Minister Wu Nu of the Union of Myanmar, and issued a joint statement agreeing that the five principles of peaceful coexistence are also the guiding principles of Sino-Myanmar relations. The historic talks and the joint statements of the Prime Ministers of China, India and Myanmar have been praised by the people of Asia and the world.

Every nation and country in the world has such a consensus and expectation to respect and to be respected, to understand and to be understood. Countries and countries, nations and nations should treat each other equally and respectfully, instead of treating each other with discrimination due to

different sizes, strengths or wealth. Therefore, the world has found that Chinese people spare no effort to advocate "respecting each other" and maintain and promote the diversity of world culture.

Water in nature is humble, calm, peaceful, intellectual, and free. It does not put on airs or make a scene. Although water is the source of all living things, it created the world and created thousands of living things. Water has never planned to be proud of its merits, to make indiscreet remarks or criticisms on others, or to command others or to be arrogant. Water, always with humility and gratitude, treats all living things equally and serves all living things in the world.

11. Like water that combines hardness and softness, Chinese people advocate the combination of both hard and soft.

The Chinese are born such a group of people who never forget to have all kinds of methods that combine hard and soft strategies while adopting the "the Mean". The hard and soft methods should be both implemented equally. Sometimes the soft is softer, the hard is harder. The hard and the soft should be used at the right time. The two alternately help each other. It is quite effective to use the soft and hard methods appropriately to achieve the ideal "the Mean" effect.

Vietnam has invested heavily in purchasing advanced weapons such as warplanes and submarines to confront China on the South China Sea issue. Vietnam believes that its advantage in the South China Sea dispute is to fight at home. Vietnam's missile-equipped warships and submarines could return to their bases after attacking, while Chinese fleets coming from afar might be caught in a dilemma that it is both difficult for them to attack or retreat. Vietnam does not have to compete one-to-one with Chinese warships, but could took its guerrilla tactics freely used skillfully in Vietnam war to the sea to possibly gain an advantage in potential conflicts with China.

Modern warfare is a three-dimensional war. If the South China Sea War broke out between China and Vietnam, how could it be such a trifle as guerrilla warfare? At the beginning of the war, Vietnam's airports, ports, waterpower, electricity and military bases would be destroyed by saturated attacks from air and sea from the other side, which would completely paralyze Vietnam's air force and navy. Furthermore, China would seize a large number of oil wells illegally exploited by Vietnam and recover 29 South China Sea islands illegally occupied by Vietnam. Vietnam intends to play "tough" hooliganism in the South China Sea, and China would respond in an even tougher way.

Chinese people learn the two characteristics: hard and soft of water and imitate and absorb It and apply flexibly. The soft and the hard each have its effects and characteristics. To implement soft and hard methods, we should adopt appropriate measures to solve the problems according to different times, different environments and different situations. There is no fixed right and wrong measures, and the final result must meet the target requirements. The whole world has found that Chinese people do not make troubles and are not afraid of troubles. The Chinese are not fond of wars but are not afraid of war. The Chinese are strong, but not arbitrary. The Chinese advocate the establishment of a high-pressure and strong position to "defeat the enemy without war".

Water is a combination of hardness and softness. Hardness and softness coexist in one object. With zero degree as the boundary, above zero degree, water presents a soft and friendly side, which is warm and happy and friendly; below zero degree, water presents another side of firmness and toughness, which is calm and decisive. Water is both soft and hard. Softness and hardness integrate and work together. Softness will eventually control hardness. The two interact and transform with infinite changes.

12. Like water that is natural and original, Chinese people like purity and innocence.

The Chinese are born such a group of people who like originality and simple and real things. They love lands and houses most. An object should be exactly what it looks like originally. Chinese people like the natural and original appearance. Since it is a natural thing, there is a proper reason for its existence. There is no need to try to stop or change it, but only to actively adapt to and respect and cherish it. Original nature has always been a kind of simplicity, a kind of reality, and a kind of actual existence.

Westerners generally find it difficult to understand the enthusiasm of Chinese buyers for houses. In Chinese people's view, they can only have roots after having houses, and everything is about ownership. Lee Shau Kee, chairman of Hong Kong Henderson Land Group, once used the phrase of "women buy handbags" to describe the mentality of mainland Chinese customers when they came to Hong Kong to buy houses, "Generous customers only buy expensive, beautiful and famous houses, which is just like women buy handbags that they can only be happy if they buy handbags worthy of hundreds of thousands, and those worthy of hundreds are not worth paying attention to at all!"

According to statistics from Jones Lang LaSalle (JLL), a multinational real estate and capital management company, 20% of Hong Kong's luxury houses worth 10 million Hong Kong dollars are bought by wealthy people in the Mainland; 30% of the luxury houses worth 20 million Hong Kong dollars are bought by mainland buyers; 40% of the luxury houses worth 50 million Hong Kong dollars are bought by mainland buyers, and 70% of the luxury houses worth more than 100 million Hong Kong dollars are bought by wealthy people in the Mainland. Shih Wing Ching, the owner of the Centralline Property, a Hong Kong real estate agency, lamented that "Hong Kong's real estate market is no longer a market of 7 million people, but a market of 1.3 billion people nationwide."

Chinese people prefer clothes made of pure wool, pure linen, pure silk, pure cotton and pure velvet. They prefer houses to be owned by themselves. They prefer gold and silver to be 100% pure. The Chinese also like the complete and original image. The food served on the table emphasizes the word "whole", such as the whole sheep, the whole pig, the whole fish, the whole shrimp, the whole chicken, the whole duck, the goose, which means having both a beginning and an ending.

What's more, the Chinese people are also fond of the natural, and somewhat precious things. They are keen on collecting gold and silver, jade, aloes, oracle bones, mahogany, emerald, tree roots, porcelain, and even walnuts, which are handed down from generation to generation. The whole world has come to realize that Chinese people have a natural affection for the original, authentic and natural things.

Water molecules in nature are small and simple in structure. Two hydrogen atoms and one oxygen atom bond together to form a water molecule, which is so simple that it cannot be simpler. However, the original natural function of water is not simple, practical, versatile, complex and irreplaceable.

Water is the most abundant substance in the earth and our bodies. 70% of an adult's body is water, while 90% of a baby's weight is water. For the human body, water participates in the movement of life, eliminates harmful toxins, helps metabolism, maintains aerobic breathing, and maintains body temperature. The function of water is the most primitive and basic. It is a unique substance.

13. Like water that follows each other, Chinese people adopt following others to go forward.

The Chinese are naturally a group of risk-averse people who generally more conservative and do not like high-profile and risks. The Chinese are willing to take the strategy of following others running ahead to go forward and imitate others rather than to innovate or explore. In a collective, the individual is required to keep consistent with the collective. If there is inconsistency, the individual is required to adjust the individual's behavior in order to comply with the will and interests of the whole. Therefore, the collective always requires all its members by uniform standards.

It is said that in the TIRSO DE MOLINA market in downtown Madrid, there are at least five shops of the same type with a Chinese shop as the center and in an area with a radius of 20 meters. If the goods can be differentiated after they are categorized, there may be still some profitable business. However, the problem is that the goods are identical, the business models are identical, and even the layouts are identical, all of which lead to the current situation of everybody's dismal operation. In the past, people flocked together to make money in group. Now, they are flocking together to compete for business. They all sell the same goods, and the market is getting smaller and smaller.

A Chinese boss who ran a restaurant in TIRSO DE MOLINA said, "Now this Chinese wholesale street is no longer competitive. Almost all businesses with no deep foundation have withdrawn from this area. Most of them who can stick to it are Chinese businessmen with strength and capital. TIRSO DE MOLINA Chinese Wholesale Street has long lost its former prosperity. It used to be a crowded place but now it is nearly deserted. The business now is really miserable.

The Chinese people especially like to use others' strength to help their own strength to make things happen with less effort. According to the principle of mechanics, the resistance borne by the leader is much greater than that borne by the runners who follow the leader closely behind. The follower obviously takes advantage of the leading runner. It is relatively time-saving and labor-saving to follow the trend. "The back waves of the Yangtze River push the front waves, and the front waves die on the beach."

Most Chinese would rather follow than lead. They prefer to be average among the top group rather than be the top among the average group. Moreover, relevant figures show that the success rate of original innovation is 26%, while that of imitative innovation is 90%, which is the latecomer advantage

in the subconscious of Chinese people. Adopting follow-up strategy can not only ensure the safety of life to the greatest extent, but also easily obtain follow-up bonuses. Why not? The whole world has come to realize that the Chinese are particularly fond of following up and then making steady profits.

The water in nature is free, comfortable, relaxed, independent and joyful in the upstream water source. Once it is ready to set off for a long-distance journey, it will voluntarily abandon itself and join forces in the embrace of the river. Starting from the upstream, it will go all the way down following the leaders. The river continuously attracts new entrants along the way. It flows freely in a big crowd, rushing thousands of miles to the sea. It does not take much effort to follow.

14. Like water that flows endlessly, Chinese people attach importance to long-term planning.

The Chinese are born with such a group of people who like to make long-term plans. Chinese people have a very mature and sophisticated set of methods for finding and solving problems. Chinese people obey the ancestor's precepts in all things, "The art of war is of vital importance to the State. It is a matter of life and death, a road either to safety or to ruin. Hence it is a subject of inquiry which can on no account be neglected." and do things carefully. Be cautious and prudent. Be careful that one careless move will lead to the loss of the game. When things happen, the Chinese tend to formulate a long-term plan to solve the problem. They are more willing to work patiently and steadily, and push it forward bit by bit. They are better at strategy and making long-term planning and implementing them to the end.

China is now working on a long-term plan to defeat foreign enemy naval offenders by missiles, focusing on guarding against the potential threat of destruction by foreign powers in the region, and on provoking unreasonable incidents and fishing in troubled waters. China does not have the capability to compete directly with Western powers in terms of quantity of aircraft carrier battle groups, destroyers and fighter planes, but it is seriously considering plans to have hundreds, thousands of long-range ballistic missiles and anti-ship cruise missiles as a direct deterrent to foreign enemy surface vessels operating within about 1,000 kilometers of China's coastline.

Meanwhile, China is trying to establish an increasingly sophisticated network of radar, sonar and reconnaissance satellites to track foreign naval forces and restrict their mobility in the Western Pacific. Avoid weaknesses and foster strengths. You aim at your target and I aim at mine. I will fight if I can win, and I will not fight if I cannot win. We change the way we fight and wrestle with our opponents. Without a complete confidence of victory, the PLA is not prepared to compete with powerful countries in terms of the quality of aircraft carriers, ships or aircraft, but is careful to concentrate its resources on missile development and procurement in order to gain a unique advantage over enemy naval and air forces in the Western Pacific. When the time is ripe, we shall strive for the overwhelming superiority of military comprehensiveness.

The water in nature flows from the high mountains to the valleys, and converges into small streams at the valleys between the mountains. Hundreds of small streams gather into large rivers,

rushing down the plain and rushing to the sea endlessly. Water circulation system itself has a set of supervision and inspection mechanism to timely replenish water supply in water source areas according to seasonal changes, forming a long-term effective mechanism to supply freshwater resources to the earth and nourish living creatures.

The Chinese are inspired by the water cycle system. Once the direction is set, the target is identified, and a major route through the overall progress and retreat is defined, an executable medium- and long-term action plan will be implemented. Subsequently, it is to persevere in the implementation, revise if necessary, and then re-implement until the results are harvested. The world has finally found out that the Chinese love to make long-term plans, operate steadily and make steady progress.

15. Like water that mirrors the moon, Chinese people care a lot about face issues.

The Chinese are born such a group of people who like to pay attention to face issues. Face-saving is one of the important psychological characteristics of Chinese people. People have faces and trees have barks. Men live on their faces and trees live on their barks. Driving Mercedes means higher status ("more face-saving") than driving Audi. Driving Audi means higher status than driving Santana. Living in villas with mountains and rivers means higher status than living in apartments in cities. Living in apartments in cities means higher status than in courtyards. Playing golf means higher status than playing table tennis. People living in this world are trying to leave a "noble" impression to others and to let people look up to and remember.

During the Lantern Festival in the Sixth Year of Daye in the Sui Dynasty, in order to receive the chiefs and businessmen from various countries in the Western Regions and to fully display the prestige of the Sui Dynasty, "There are all kinds of entertainment shows in Duanmen Street (in Luoyang, the East Capital) and there are 18,000 people playing instruments, which can be heard from tens of miles. From dusk to dawn, lights and candles light up the sky. The event lasts for a whole month and costs a lot of money."

The imperial court also ordered the decoration of the city's appearance, requiring the eaves and roofs to be unified, precious goods to be filled and accumulated, the curtains and flags to be hung up in shops, people to wear beautiful costumes, the place where vegetables were sold to be covered with mats woven with asparagus grass, and the trees on both sides of the street to be covered with silk and satin, so as to make them colorful. When the guests pass by, the restaurant owner shall invite them to have dinner. "The guests have a wonderful meal and leave, and the dinner is totally free of charge." They will also lie that, "China is rich, and all meals are free of charge."

According to history books, during the first month of the lunar calendar which coincides with the freezing season in the north. Emperor Yangdi of the Sui Dynasty ordered people to wrap silk around trees, telling visitors who did not know the truth that this was "the place of heaven". During Sui Dynasty, China was strong and wealthy enough at that time. It was much better than foreign small countries and it did not need to decorate its facade at all. However, it was different from what Emperor Yangdi wanted to show the foreigners. Therefore, there was the "face" project of Emperor Yangdi of Sui Dynasty.

Chinese people love "face" particularly. "Domestic shame should not be made public. Try to satisfy one's vanity when one cannot really afford to do so puffy face. Beat a person without hitting in the face and expose a person without disclosing the shortcomings." However, face cannot be clearly interpreted to foreigners and cannot be accurately defined. It seems to be an honor, but not entirely an honor. It seems to be wealth, but not exactly wealth. However, it is more precious than any secular property.

Sometimes, face is more powerful than fate and favor, and it is more respected than laws and disciplines. The Chinese just believe in this kind of vanity which supports all aspects of life, and they pay attention to "face" for a lifetime. The world has finally found that Chinese people are so obsessed with relationships, human relationships, and faces.

Water is colorless, tasteless, clear and quiet, just like a mirror reflecting the nature of the world. A lake is surrounded by green hills and decorated with willows. The greenness is vigorous and the bamboos are kissing the waves. Lakeside peaks stand still quietly, which is reflected in the water. In this scene, the mountain is the support of water and the water is the interpretation of the mountain. The never-ending water-scape reflection is the most beautiful and charming, which vividly and smoothly demonstrates the static and dynamic beauty of the water. It is also with water that everything around becomes lively and vivid, and it makes us feel lost and intoxicated and amazed.

16. Like water that stays behind and does not compete, Chinese people stick to the principle of "gaining mastery by striking only after the enemy has struck".

The Chinese are born such a group of people who are accustomed to defending first, courtesy before force, catching others off guard, and gaining mastery by striking only after the enemy has struck. Wise people need great wisdom to survive. When using wisdom, others start from a small place and I look from a big place. Others look from a close place, I look from far away. The more restless and chaotic others are, the calmer and steadier I am, and things can return to normal. When others are helpless, I handle problems with ease.

China strikes back Vietnam due to its making troubles out of nothing in the South China Sea. Vietnam insists on attempting to strengthen its legal claim to China's Xisha and Nansha Islands with Ocean Law, and Vietnam's provocation happens first. In response, the Ministry of Civil Affairs of China announced that the State Council approved the establishment of prefecture-level Sansha City to strengthen the administration and development and construction of the islands and reefs of Xisha Islands, Zhongsha Islands and Nansha Islands and their sea areas.

China National Offshore Oil Corporation (CNOOC) announced that it would open nine offshore blocks in the South China Sea near the "Nine-dashed Lines" for exploration and development in cooperation with foreign companies. Hainan Province also announced that four areas of the Xisha Islands would be designated as cultural heritage reserves. The formation of China's maritime surveillance vessels and fishery administration vessels have set sail to the South China Sea in time to safeguard the rights and enforce the law in the jurisdictional sea areas claimed by our country, and regular cruising is more powerful.

At the same time, China and ASEAN countries have further strengthened high-level exchanges and friendly cooperation, properly handled differences with relevant countries, broken and disintegrated individual countries' attempts to use the Cambodia - ASEAN Series Conferences, Shangri-La Dialogue and other international occasions to hype the South China Sea issue and interfere with the overall cooperation between China and ASEAN.

China's later punches really reflect the rationality, advantage and restraint, turning passivity into initiative, so as to both safeguard both rights and maintain stability. The reason of China's punches is to hope that all parties in the South China Sea will be alerted and return to the correct track of dialogue and cooperation rather than blindly infringe upon rights and misinterpret China's restraint and tolerance as weakness and concession. China does not seek to compete with other countries on the South China Sea issue to see whose fist is tougher, but to pursue a peaceful and stable surrounding environment in which countries in a region can concentrate their efforts on developing cooperation.

Water in nature has always shown its courtesy and gentleness to people, "It is because he is thus free from striving that therefore no one in the world is able to strive with him." Water does not compete for profit or merit and does not seek for fame or wealth. The only thing it does is to dedicate silently. Water always stays at the lowest place, always stays where others do not want to stay, and helps others wholeheartedly, so it is widely respected. Nothing in the world can match it, and nothing can compete with water for the status of "the highest excellence".

Chinese people use courtesy before force, and gain mastery by striking only after the enemy has struck. When confronted with confrontations and conflicts that are difficult to reconcile, the Chinese people do not attack first or provoke arbitrarily, or shoot the first bullet. The Chinese always put negotiation and understanding first to be benevolent and righteous. If "courtesy" does not work, then "force" will be used. The purpose of military use is not to conquer others by force and violence, but to completely stop and eliminate disputes and conflicts. Since then, the whole world has finally understood that the Chinese people stick to the traditional wisdom of courtesy before force and gaining mastery by striking only after the enemy has struck.

17. Like water that avails itself in every hole, Chinese people lack border awareness.

The Chinese are such a group of people who lack of the concept of public boundary, difficult to abide by public rules, and lack the awareness of rules. In public, they don't know much about what they should do. They don't know much about their duties and responsibilities they should shoulder for public affairs. They only care about their own convenience, regardless of how others feel.

When in a foreign country, respecting the local traditions and customs can not only effectively help one integrate into the country and bring convenience to travel, but also avoid frictions and save unnecessary troubles. However, some Chinese tourists do not seem to understand these principles. In Egypt, a Middle Eastern country, locals complain that some Chinese women tourists dressed in miniskirts and suspenders "wear too little". For Muslims who believe in Islam, women should dress in public modestly and try to avoid exposing too much skin. Foreign friends hope that tourists can

respect local customs as much as possible, and do not wear miniskirts and mini shorts, especially when visiting mosques.

When some Chinese tourists visit churches, palaces, museums and theatres, they dress too casually and even make phone calls while visiting. These are all extremely disrespectful to cultures and arts of other countries, which easily arouse local people's resentment. However, facing other people's strange looks, Chinese tourists seem to be unconscious and still go their own way. These impolite acts that ignore the customs and habits of their countries often become the excuses and triggers of the "clash of civilizations".

Water moves between the ocean and the land. In the course of water movement, it presents various forms. Sometimes it stays in one place in solid form and sometime moves in liquid form. Sometimes it transpires upwards, sometimes it permeates downwards, and more often it drifts parallel. Water can move in all directions at one time: up and down, back and forth, left and right. There is no definite boundary for water flow movement. There are few rules to follow.

Chinese people are especially casual. They are accustomed to irregular movements and avails themselves in every loophole and naturally lack border awareness. Chinese people have little sense of public boundary, little sense of social rules, and even less sense of the concept and norms of public order. Chinese people are fearless, dare to say anything, dare to do anything, and dare to be the first in the world. The whole world has realized that Chinese people are so special and so conspicuous. They have a set of game rules in their minds that outsiders may not understand and only belong to their own. It is easy for the Chinese to cause others' dislike and displeasure.

18. Like water that hides itself, Chinese people are used to not revealing all the things but hiding some.

The Chinese are born such a group of people who regard "hiding without revealing" as a virtue and do not advocate the outward expression of emotions and feelings. The Chinese are reserved and implicit and their moods are not visible. It is a skill to hide something deeply without reveal. Deep concealment should be a mature, modest and prudent side, and has a deeper meaning of shrewdness.

Chinese people advocate "ignorance is a rare blessing" and would rather appear foolish than too smart; would rather be restrained than to show too much sharpness; would rather be easy-going than arrogant; would rather be modest rather than too radical. Chinese people encourage handling affairs properly and smoothly, because the circle has the smallest pressure, the largest tension, and the strongest plasticity, so it is the most safe and reliable.

How big is China's national defense force? The answer given by the U.S. Department of Defense to this question is interesting, "No one knows how big China's real national defense force is, and this is terrible." In its 2012 edition of the *Defense Authorization Act*, the U.S. Department of Defense wrote that China is not only committed to developing sophisticated weapons, but also to investing extensively in space combat effectiveness.

The report also mentioned for the first time the operational configuration of China's latest anti-ship missile Dongfeng-21D. The Dongfeng-21D, known as the "carrier killer", has a range of 1,500 kilometers and is considered a major threat to U.S. operations in the Western Pacific. U.S. military experts also generally believe that Dongfeng-21D has the ability to attack the U.S. nuclear-powered aircraft carrier "George Washington" operating in the region.

The report also contained many questions that the United States could not answer immediately. That is to say, because China attaches great importance to internal confidentiality in the military field, the United States cannot accurately analyze China's military situation. "China is not only hiding its military capabilities, but also hiding its strategic objectives and decision-making process, which is becoming the cause of insecurity among the countries in the region." China's military power will grow stronger and stronger, which is very terrible.

The part of precipitation that falls on the land surface in nature is mostly hidden deep underground and forms groundwater and underground runoff except for the ice and snow that condenses on the mountains, the water used by human beings, animals and plants, and the surface runoff. Usually, no one knows the flow rate, velocity and depth of underground runoff accurately. Water often hides itself deeply. Understand and master the state of laws of nature which is partly hidden and partly visible and know how to hide ourselves and how to hide the good in the bad.

Everything is obvious there. Everything is a plan and there is no conspiracy. Transparency depends on how good you are. You cannot expect others to tell you the whole truth, because the world is not completely transparent, and ambiguity is a normal and common state. The whole world is beginning to understand that the Chinese people are playing with the strategy to "hide one's capacities and bide one's time" skillfully in such a way of that they hide deeply, accumulate richly and break forth vastly.

19. Like water that coexists homogeneously, Chinese people do not show each other respect.

The Chinese seem to be born such a group of people who are not good at unity and are constantly fighting each other. They pay attention to the theory of "Yin and Yang". The sky is Yang and the earth is Yin. The upper is Yang and the lower is Yin. Male is Yang and female is Yin. Single is Yang and double is Yin. Yin and Yang are interconnected. They are both independent from each other and transformative between each other.

Yin is Yang, and Yang is Yin. You can always say it positively or negatively. No one can convince anyone. Finally, there is no right or wrong, no conclusion, and it will always end in a tie. Wherever Chinese people gather, infighting is inevitable. In Chinese idioms, there are: a mountain cannot be shared by two tigers; fratricidal strife, fight against each other, scheme against each other, brothers fight against each other, friends turn into enemies, literati treat each other lightly, and peers are enemies. Moreover, it is probably the Chinese themselves, not foreigners, who are the best in trying every possible method to cause harm to Chinese people.

The aggression of the Chinese is confined to infighting. In the 1920s, Chiang Kai-shek led his troops to fight against warlords in the north. He was provoked by the Japanese when he passed through Shandong. He was afraid of causing friction, and did not dare to make it public. Instead, he continued to go north to fight the Chinese. In 1931, during the 9.18 incident, 200,000 troops in Northeast China refused to resist and lost the three northeastern provinces. Chiang did not respond positively and suppressed the people's fighting against Japan. However, this Chiang Kai-shek, who retreats step by step in the face of strong enemies, repeatedly encircled and suppressed the brothers of the Red Army who even did not have salt to eat. He would rather kill one thousand people than miss one and hopes to put them to death and as quickly as possible.

He beautified it as "if you want to solve exterior problems, you must first settle the interior issues". In fact, he just wanted to fight against his brothers. Without the Soviet Red Army's attack on the Northeast and the two nuclear bombs dropped by the United States, Chiang Kai-shek would probably have to hide in Chongqing's air defense shelters for several more years. Chiang Kai-shek was crazy about infighting and lose his mind. Just like Cixi's words that "rather contribute to the neighboring countries than contribute to domestic inferiors", he ignored the Japanese invaders and devoted himself to slaughtering his brothers.

Water molecules on the earth are composed of two hydrogen atoms and one oxygen atom, which is simple and practical. Water molecules are extremely easy to separate, and they are also extremely easy to recombine together. Moreover, water molecule is a universal solvent, which can dissolve and combine with almost all other substances except oil to produce new substances. Water molecule and water molecule are homologous. They neither owe each other not influence each other. You can leave me, and I can leave you. You and I have exactly the same value, equal status and function.

The Chinese are very good at dealing with foreign countries and making friends widely whether they go out or invite others in. The Chinese even have enough courage and toughness to assimilate foreign invaders and turn enemies into friends many times. However, among the Chinese people, it is common to see "the Chinese look down on each other". You despise me and I despise you. Everyone refuses to show respect to others, which leads to hurting each other secretly and endless infighting.

One Chinese is a dragon, three Chinese are worms, "One monk carries water to eat, two monks carry water to eat, while three monks do not have water to eat", and "a dish of loose sand (lacking spirit of cooperation)" has become prominent marks of the Chinese people. The whole world seems to have realized that there is no unity among the Chinese, and that "infighting" is a common thing among the peers.

20. Like water, the Chinese people have always been tolerant of adversity and submission.

The Chinese are born such a group of people who are resigned to adversity and bear humiliation and heavy burden. The unparalleled endurance of the Chinese nation must be used to accomplish a lofty mission. They have to endure grievances, misunderstandings, even being exploited to be ill, or even be taken of their lives.

However, there is a day when the Chinese people are forced into a corner and when they cannot bear it or retreat further, they will burst in this silence and fight back with their overwhelming force to throw you off your position with a life-and-death struggle and fight to death.

One day, a reporter interviewed Japanese veterans. Some of them spoke dialect, and the reporter could not understand and had no choice but to find his Japanese friends to translate. That Japanese friend translated very fluently at the beginning, but later he heard these veterans telling how to beat the Chinese people and kill the Chinese people. The crueller the story was, the more painful the Japanese friend became.

The next day, the reporter received a call from the Japanese friend early in the morning. He thought about it all night and felt that he had to make the call. He went on to say that the relationship between China and Japan is quite good now and asked the reporter to consider the friendship between China and Japan and not to disclose these facts to the Chinese people and not to affect the relationship between the two countries. He said that if the Chinese knew what the Japanese army had done, they would definitely hate Japan.

The reporter held the phone for a long time and could not speak a word. Finally, the reporter said, "Do you know? The whole world knows about this history, and it's only you Japanese who don't know it!" After hearing this, the Japanese friend was shocked and said, "Ah, you Chinese all know that!" It is extremely tolerant and generous of you to treat Japan like this since you already know it.

Among the obedient and faithful Chinese people, for thousands of years, brutal emperors, greedy bureaucrats, cruel officials, heavy military service, arduous labor, harsh laws, strict system, rigorous ethical codes, rigid hierarchy, aggressions by tyrants, looting by bandits, harassment by hooligans, oppressions by clansmen, authority of the elders, wills of the officers, suppression by the strong, attacks by the weak, jealousy from peers, hostility from friends, rebellion from comrades, suspicion from old people, brutality of men, envy of women, and so on are all exercises of the capacity of "tolerance" of Chinese people.

Water in nature changes with the changes of the environment. It resigns itself to adversity, flows with the trend, and never cares or complains about unfair treatment. When water is in the cup, it is in the shape of the cup. When water is in the pool, it is in the shape of the pool. When water flows and rolls in rivers, it varies with its surrounding environment and in all kinds of shapes. However, in terms of the nature of water, its functions remain unchanged and will not be affected by any changes in the external environment.

Water has no constant state and no fixed form, but can adapt to any environment. The whole world is amazed to find that the Chinese people have exceptional endurance of hardship, which are the best in the world.

21. Like water that is independent and neutral, Chinese tend to care for own business.

The Chinese are born such a group of people whose minds are full of the concept of "human relations". Chinese traditional culture stresses the relationship between monarch and minister, father and son, husband and wife, brothers and friends. Simply speaking, it is to take one's own life as the center of the circle and draw a radius to expand outward and it out in circles. When doing something, Chinese people often have to consider its relationship with ourselves before deciding whether to do it or not and how to do it. Most Chinese people care about their blood relatives first, and then others. Sometimes, they show unusual selfishness and indifference to the suffering of others, and generally lack care for public affairs.

On New Year's Eve, I went to a party with a group of friends in Sanlitun, Beijing. Just as we were enjoying the wonderful moments of New Year's Eve, an unexpected event brought our laughter to an abrupt halt. My American fellow Jack and I walked about 100 meters ahead of other friends. We first saw about twenty or thirty people gathered at the roadside. A young girl was lying on the ground twitching. Her whole body was shaking, and her head was constantly bumping against the concrete floor with the shaking of her body.

The person nearest to her was only about two meters away, but no one reached out to help her, and no one took any action at all. According to the number of bystanders around her, the girl should have been lying on the ground for at least three minutes. Jack and I blurted out, "Doctor! Doctor!" But no one responded. People just looked at us in silence, and the atmosphere was terrible.

Chinese people are accustomed to taking care of themselves in all things, but do not care about others' business. They are devoted to a life style of "independent development". They do not ask or seldom ask for others' help in troubles. They think that asking for help from oneself in better than asking from others. They advocate good management of internal affairs and do not like to take the lead and do not like alliances. Over time, the world has been left with the impression that "everyone sweeps the snow in front of their own doors, regardless of the frost on others roofs". The world has found that Chinese people like to take care of their own business. Their ears do not listen to things outside the window but wholeheartedly devote themselves to reading books of sages and virtues, which has a sense of "good for oneself".

The water circulation system in nature is an independent and neutral operation system. Independence means that the water system itself can circulate independently and complete the round trip cycle independently without the support and cooperation of other ecosystems. Neutrality means that the water system never forcibly aligns itself with others, but treats things in a neutral way.

22. Like water that is freely separated by people, Chinese people lack a sense of security.

The Chinese are born such a group of people who always have an inexplicable anxiety and worry in their hearts. They are restless and uneasy and getting more and more perplexed and hesitant

day by day. Nowadays, the whole society is generally inclined to make fast money. The amount of money and wealth seems to be the only value indicator of success. The poor make money to change their lives, while the rich make money to pass it on for generations. Those who cannot make money are anxious. Those who cannot make much money are worried. Those who make a lot of money are even more anxious, because they have to make more painstaking efforts to preserve and increase the value of their wealth. There is no end to the story of money, so there is no peace, happiness and security in our hearts.

Taking a bus in China is like taking part in a hand-to-hand combat. Whenever a bus comes, people will never stay in line and go onto the bus with order, but everyone is in a mad rush to be the first. As soon as the door opens, all passengers swarm in. Everyone tries their best to squeeze into the carriage to occupy a seat, lest they should be the last one left on the platform.

Every time I took the train, it is like reviewing the modern history of China of losing power and being humiliated. Before tickets were checked in the waiting room, a large crowd of people crowded in front. They preferred to stretching their heads and necks to look around and pushing back and forth to fight for a place. When the staff began to check the tickets, the crowd became agitated and went to surround the staff with no order. The waiting room was crowded so tightly that no one can move. They just want to rush out of the gate.

You may have good luck occasionally when you meet the situation of queuing, but from time to time there are people who jump in the queue and turn a blind eye to the queue already formed. They do not care about the first-come-first-served social order. They trample on the social morality known to all ages under their feet. With a kind of unremitting overbearing spirit, they march forward with their heads held high, and use all kinds of tricks to detour around the queue to see if there is a place to jump in. They will not give up even if being accused and will not retreat even if they meet setbacks.

Water is quiet and plain, honest and humble. When you need it, the water waits carefully to serve at any time and anywhere. When you don't need it, the water stays quietly in the low-lying place and is ready at any time. If you put water in a cup, the water will be in the shape of a cup. If you put water in a basin, the water will be in the shape of a basin. If you put water in a bucket, the water will be in the shape of a bucket. If you put water in a pool, the water will be in the shape of a pool. Water never complains. To be fair, water is allowed to be placed and played with by others, and there is no "safety" guarantee.

Chinese people often have a natural sense of insecurity in their hearts. There are a lot of uncertainties in the social environment. Any uncertainty leads to the unstable state which often brings people many unsafe shocks. In an era of drastic change, people are easily trapped by external forces and will be left behind if they make a slight mistake in response to them, so the sense of security tends to weaken.

23. Like water that flows in large scale, Chinese people are good at mass movements.

The Chinese are born such a group of people who have a special interest in mass movements and are familiar with crowd tactics. Chinese people have always advocated that when we do great things, we should "concentrate our strength" to break through difficulties and obstacles and to smash them one by one because "cutting off one finger is more effective than hurting all ten fingers". Chinese people love "mass movement", are good at "mass movement", and have an extraordinary ability of organizing and mobilizing. In the memory of the Chinese people, it is not uncommon for the people to participate directly in the mass movement with great scale and momentum. There are both the joy of success and the lessons of failure.

Zhang Yimou, chief director of the opening ceremony of the 2008 Beijing Olympic Games, described the design ideas of the opening ceremony as that "This is the greatest festival of the Chinese people. We want to make people all over the world feel the passion and romance of the Chinese people." The opening ceremony used a lot of high-tech technology, "and I absolutely did not ignore human nature. If the traditional crowd tactics are old ideas, we are using a combination of crowd tactics and new media. This one plus one is definitely not simply equal to two. It is a new force."

The opening ceremony of the Olympic Games was highly praised by foreign friends. The *New York Times* commented: "If this amazing opening ceremony expressed the highest respect for the ancient Chinese civilization and tried to inspire the pride of an ancient nation, it also sent a signal to foreign countries full of doubts: Don't be afraid, we have no malice." The *Guardian* commented: "Zhang Yimou did his best and cleared all the obstacles to match the performance with everything around it, and well interpret the intention that China is a modern country rising on the basis of ancient civilization."

When water vapor in nature meets cold air in the sky and falls to land, it will gather at one place and flow in a specific direction. It flows all the way downward. In the downward gathering and flowing process, water forms a scale effect gradually and ultimately constitutes a strong water potential and water energy. Water flows and gathers downwards from high places. The larger the area covered by water flows through is, the larger the scale of water is, and the greater the contribution of efficiency is.

The Chinese have always been familiar with the "whole nation system" and using mass movements. Mass movement is the heirloom and magic weapon for Chinese people to defeat their enemies and win victory. With this magic weapon, they have won all over the world. All the people work together. The rich contribute their money and the strong contribute their strength. The fire flame is high when all people gather firewood together. If all people work together, even Mount Tai could be moved. Take the whole country's efforts and lead the whole nation to operate on a large scale, and concentrate the superior forces to break through difficulties one by one. The whole world has come to realize that the Chinese people are so keen on "mass movements" that they have achieved remarkable results.

24. Like water that flows constantly, Chinese people practice lasting fights.

The Chinese are born such a group of people who have known the magic of "lasting" since childhood. "Drops of water pierce through the rock." The water drops from high above gently rush to the bleak chest of the rock, kissing and wetting the rough stone. In this way, with the passage of time, a drop of water finally pierces through the rock one day before everyone notice it. The two roles of water and stone have deduced a philosophy in the long run: when a track of movement persists in a righteous way, even if it moves forward with the weakest force, the world will eventually give way to it.

In May 1938, Mao Zedong wrote *On Protracted War*. Chairman Mao Zedong made his entire plan for the Anti-Japanese War clear and plain to the public. As a result, China's Anti-Japanese War just began and ended in this way. It means that Japan, the belligerent country, must faithfully abide by this plan after reading it.

Chairman Mao Zedong's *On Protracted War* is a pre-written history. This is the only time in human history that the war plan has been made public and carried out according to this plan, and the enemy have to cooperate with it. As a result, the three stages of the plan, namely, strategic defense, strategic stalemate and strategic counter-offensive, have been realized.

Japan is a small country. It has few lands, few goods, few people and few soldiers. It cannot stand a long war. Moreover, in the international arena, the enemy is unjust and helpless, while we have a lot of lands, goods and people, and we are on the just side and thus receive much help. This is determined by the nature of war. These characteristics stipulate all political policies and military strategies and tactics of the two sides, and determine the durability of the war and that the final victory belongs to China, not Japan.

The earth rotates and revolves around the sun. Water is always in a state of motion. Persistent and continuous movement is a normal and regular form of activity conforming to natural laws. However, the stillness or pause of visual perception is only an illusion caused by the relative static of the reference object. The living and flowing water nourishes all living creatures on earth and make them grow and flourish.

During the Warring States period, Hsun-Tzu said in his article *Encouraging Learning*, "Therefore, unless you accumulate little steps, you can never journey a thousand mile; unless you accumulate tiny streams, you can never form rivers and seas. The finest thoroughbred cannot travel ten paces in one step, but the sorriest nag can go a ten days' journey because it does not give up.", which is also an interpretation of this truth. If you persevere, you will achieve your ambition. The world is amazed to find that the Chinese people have the ability to handle affairs with endurance and patience, to conquer the hard with the soft, to defeat the strong by the weak, to accumulate small victories to great triumphs, and to exchange time for space of development and progress.

25. Like water that flows freely, Chinese people like to muddle along.

The Chinese are born such a group of people who always do things casually and carelessly. Most of them have developed the habit of being content with the status quo and not eager to make progress. They are just muddling along like "being a monk for a day strikes the clock for a day". Chinese people do not take things seriously and do not pursue precision. Almost is enough. This is just like the *Biography of Mr. About-the-Same* written by Mr. Hu Shi at that time. Most of the Chinese people are descendants of Mr. About-the-Same. They always treat rights and wrong with a casual attitude that it is OK to be just fine.

Wang Binggang, a specialist in the 863 Project of the Ministry of Science and Technology of China, visited the Great Wall Automobile Factory a few days ago and carefully learned about the situation of their independently developed in-cylinder direct injection turbocharged 2-liter gasoline engine. He found that many of the key components integrated into the Great Wall engine were products of foreign companies: the electronic injection system was Delphi's, the supercharger and chain were Bergwarner's, and the variable valve timing (VVT) was INA's, which was still understandable.

However, even some simple accessories were bought from foreign countries: the valve was Eaton's, the valve seat was Tiebertz's, the piston and bush were Federal Mogul's, the piston ring was ATG's, the pump belt was Gates's, the spark plug was Bosch's, the belt tensioner was Litens's, the booster pressure control valve was Pilberg's, and even the cylinder cover was supplied by a foreign company called Bologne. How can the Chinese be so unproductive and live on the technology of foreigners to?

The destination of water flowing in nature is only the lowest depression. Nothing can prevent water from flowing into the lower depression. Water wants to be its real self and to get rid of shackles and break through fetters to wantonly rush to the field. It loves casualness and freedom and hates limitations and restraints. It is stubborn and persistent but smart and clever. It is brave and resourceful on its way forward without being entangled with trivial matters or losing time as long as it can make its way through.

In China, there is a Mr. About-the-Same. Everybody knows his name, and he leaves his name everywhere. You must have met him, known him, or heard others talk about him. The name of Mr. About-the-Same is often referred to in the Chinese people's mouths every day. "Whatever we do, it's OK to be just about right." The world is afraid of the word "serious". It is the most difficult to be serious with the Chinese people. The whole world has come to realize that the bad habit that the Chinese people have always been doing things carelessly and they think all things are just about the same.

26. Like water that is everywhere, Chinese people advocate territorial advantages.

The Chinese are born such a group of people who like to own territories and win control of territories with people's hearts. "Under the whole heaven, every spot is the sovereign's ground; To the borders of the land, every individual is the sovereign's minister." Although the Chinese believe

that it is important to occupy territory, it is even more important to win the hearts of the people by strategies. If you lose the hearts of the people, you will lose the original territory easily, and vice versa. Therefore, it is not necessary to conquer the "barbarian lands" if one wins the hearts of the people, and the best policy is to win over the hearts of foreigners and pagans.

One night in October 1962, Mao Zedong summoned his political and military generals in Zhongnanhai. At the foot of the Himalayas thousands of miles in the west, the Chinese and Indian armies are confronting each other in the bitter cold. The dispute took place on a controversial border. India insisted on the McMahon Line drawn by British colonists, while China recognized only the borders of the pre-Qing Dynasty. The disputed area is a region defined by the so-called McMahon Line at the foot of the Himalayas of 125,000 square kilometers, equivalent to the entire state of Pennsylvania in the United States.

Mao Zedong decided to "knock" India this time to get them back to the negotiation table. However, we need to exercise restraint and just teach the Indians a lesson. The military deployment was arranged in accordance with Mao Zedong's thinking. A few weeks later, the Chinese army dealt a heavy and devastating blow to the Indian army. However, after the victory, China went back to the former actual control areas, and even returned all the heavy weapons captured from the Indian Army.

China is a legendary country. Its civilization, which has lasted for thousands of years, contains rich strategies and policies for governing the country. The Chinese people pay attention to territory, but they do not emphasize the small gains and losses, such as one city or one place. They can both advance or retreat. They advocate slowly accumulating strength, winning by trend, and letting their opponents submit and surrender obediently.

Water in nature can be seen everywhere. It is one of the most widely distributed substances in the world. Since it landed on the ground, water first permeates into the ground and becomes part of the groundwater and underground runoff. It is keen to camp and distribute in every corner of the land, forming an absolute advantage. Unless the earth is saturated and persuades water to leave, the water can flow away at any time if it is willing to. It can retreat to other areas, or gather into the ground runoff and run down towards the sea to continue to participate in the next cycle.

When people go somewhere, their influence will be naturally brought there. Chinese people have always liked enclosing and occupying fields to establish geographical advantages. They are faithful implementers of strategies of strength. They occupy land first in a first-come-first-serve order and then form a circle, joining ground and underground as a whole, cultivating patiently and accumulating comparative advantages. Wide occupation of territory often means to gain tangible and substantive benefits and accumulate small victories to great triumphs. Chinese people are infatuated with the charm of water. Inspired by water, they know how to win by "trend", master superb wisdom and strategy, implement effective strategic encirclement and seize the precious fields.

By virtue of the flexible skills of controlling water energy and water potential, the Chinese are skilled in the art of "strategic encirclement". In mobile warfare, they often adopt the strategy

of circuitous encirclement to divide and encircle their enemies. The Chinese can contend with their enemies patiently and persistently and respond to changes flexibly. They often mobilize their enemies to attack as much as possible, thus causing them to lose their ground. After consuming their enemies' vital strength to the greatest extent, they can force their enemies to retreat and give up the land occupied. The Chinese can win the hearts of the people to "defeat the enemy without fighting" and ultimately to completely win the victory. The world is finally beginning to understand how the Chinese people win the hearts of the whole world and seize its territories.

27. Like water that does things fairly, Chinese people pursue a world of great harmony!

The Chinese are born such a group of people who are always pursuing their dreams whether prosperous or declining, rich or weak. The Chinese are unremittingly pursuing the "Chinese Dream" and constantly pursuing the dreams of "the whole world as one community" and "the world is a great harmony". Nowadays, 239 countries and regions, thousands of nationalities and 7 billion people coexist on the same planet, Earth and coexist in the same world, which is a Community of Shared Future for Mankind. The "Great Harmony World" is not only the needs and dreams of the Chinese people themselves, but also the common aspirations and dreams of the peoples of the world.

The ideal society in Confucius's thoughts is that, "When the Grand course was pursued, a public and common spirit ruled all under the sky; they chose men of talents, virtue, and ability; their words were sincere, and what they cultivated was harmony. Thus men did not love their parents only, nor treat as children only their own sons. A competent provision was secured for the aged till their death, employment for the able-bodied, and the means of growing up to the young. They showed kindness and compassion to widows, orphans, childless men, and those who were disabled by disease, so that they were all sufficiently maintained. Males had their proper work, and females had their homes. (They accumulated) articles (of value), disliking that they should be thrown away upon the ground, but not wishing to keep them for their own gratification. (They labored) with their strength, disliking that it should not be exerted, but not exerting it (only) with a view to their own advantage. In this way (selfish) schemings were repressed and found no development. Robbers, filchers, and rebellious traitors did not show themselves, and hence the outer doors remained open, and were not shut. This was (the period of) what we call the Grand Union."

When the Grand course was pursued, a public and common spirit ruled all under the sky. They chose men of talents, virtue, and ability; their words were sincere, and what they cultivated was harmony. Thus men did not love their parents only, nor treat as children only their own sons. A competent provision was secured for the aged till their death, employment for the able-bodied, and the means of growing up to the young. They showed kindness and compassion to widows, orphans, childless men, and those who were disabled by disease, so that they were all sufficiently maintained. Males had their proper work, and females had their homes. (They accumulated) articles (of value), disliking that they should be thrown away upon the ground, but not wishing to keep them for their own gratification. (They labored) with their strength, disliking that it should not be exerted, but not exerting it (only) with a view to their own advantage. In this way (selfish) schemings were repressed and found

no development. Robbers, filchers, and rebellious traitors did not show themselves, and hence the outer doors remained open, and were not shut. This was (the period of) what we call the Grand Union.

In *Tai Gong Liu Tao*, Jiang Tai Gong once explained that "the world is not one person's world, but a world of all people". (*Tai Gong Liu Tao*) When Mencius talked about the position of king, he said, "He caused him to preside over the sacrifices, and all the spirits were well pleased with them; thus Heaven accepted him. He caused him to preside over the conduct of affairs, and affairs were well administered, so that the people reposed under him; thus the people accepted him."

The "Great Harmony World" should be a society that practices democratic governing in politics and sharing in economics. In the Great Harmony World, human nature has developed to a perfect state. Not only can we share social materials harmoniously, but also we can live a life with human dignity and respect each other. Therefore, the vision of the Great Harmony World is "the world is one community". The ideal of "Great Harmony World" in the hearts of the Chinese people is not to rule the world by force.

The ideal of "Great Harmony World" of the Chinese people is by no means an expansion of territory. "Peace" is the ideal pursued by Chinese politics at all times. The "flourishing age" of the Chinese people such as the "rule of Emperor Wendi and Jingdi" in the Western Han Dynasty, the "rule of Zhenguan" in the Tang Dynasty and the "prosperous age of Kang Xi and Qian Long" in the Qing Dynasty are all times of peace, happiness and prosperity. China's territory has been expanding continuously since the Xia Dynasty, which relies on peaceful cultural integration rather than military conquest by war.

Water in nature has never been ambiguous about the principle of fairness, justice and openness, and it has been strictly and conscientiously implemented. No matter who it meets, strong or weak, rich or poor, water treats them all equally and fairly. Water is absolutely free from any prejudice or bias. It never prefers or bullies any other living substance. If the water is uneven, it will overflow; if people are unfair, they will express it. If water cannot keep balance and stability, it will not be able to stop, stand steadily or stay, and it will flow down and overflow.

Chinese people have always yearned for the pursuit of a world of great harmony and a world as a community and advocated that "The superior man is affable, but not adulatory". "I am sick of inequality between the rich and the poor, and now I have made it equal." Chinese people can tolerate not being "rich" in life, but they absolutely do not accept the social status quo of not being "unequal". Do things fairly and justly like water. Treat others fairly and honesty like ice. The world finally knows and understands the reasons why Chinese people have been pursuing the "Great Harmony World" for generations.

28. Like water that is kind and friendly to all creatures, Chinese people advocate peace and harmony.

The Chinese people are born such a group of people who have always advocated kindness, harmony and peace of individuals, families, communities, societies, human beings, and the whole

world. From the beginning to the end, Chinese culture takes "harmony" as the ultimate value of pursuit. "Harmony" is widely used in families, countries and the world. Confucius put forward that "harmony is precious" and affirmed the role of "harmony" from the perspective of governing the country.

Confucius also proposed the idea of "harmony but difference" and believed that the essence of "harmony" lies in the unity and coordination of the differences among various factors. Hsun-Tzu put forward "harmony is unity, unity means force" and believed that if people in an organization can get along harmoniously, they can achieve unanimity and their strength will increase. Mencius put forward that "Opportunities of time vouchsafed by Heaven are not equal to advantages of situation afforded by the Earth, and advantages of situation afforded by the Earth are not equal to the union arising from the accord of Men." He believed that as long as there is internal harmony and the upper and lower levels work together, we can be invincible.

More than two thousand years ago, the Chinese people had already carried out business and trade with other countries around the world through the two Silk Roads of land and sea. From Zhang Qian's mission to the Western Regions more than 2100 years ago to Zheng He's voyages to the west seas more than 600 years ago, the two silk roads of land and sea brought China's silk, tea and porcelain to all countries along the way and brought civilization and friendship as well, which won the praise and affection of the people of all countries.

At present, The Belt and Road Initiative focuses both on sea and land approaches and goes both to the north and the south. It is the "China wisdom" and "China plan" that China has contributed to the world. Xi Jinping, on behalf of China, put forward the top-level strategic conception of building the New Silk Road Economic Belt and the Twenty-First Century Maritime Silk Road in September and October 2013 respectively, and stressed that all countries concerned should create a "community of interests" of mutual benefits and the "community of destiny" of common development and prosperity.

The Belt and Road Initiative, the longest economic corridor in the world, is originated in China and links Central Asia, Southeast Asia, South Asia, West Asia and some parts of Europe. It leads the Asia-Pacific Economic Circle to the east and the European Economic Circle to the west. It is the most potential economic zone in the world. The future and destiny of the countries along it have never been so closely linked and related. The grand conception of the Belt and Road Initiative spans time and space. It comes from the depths of history, integrates the past and the present, connects China and foreign countries and conforms to the trend of peace, development, cooperation and win-win. It carries the dream of prosperity of all countries along the Silk Road, and gives the ancient Silk Road a brand-new connotation of the times.

Water in nature treats all lives in the world equally. Water is not satisfied with wealth and does not complain about poverty. Whether placed in pottery bowls or gold bowls, water always treat things equally and friendly. Water is still water. It does not change its attitudes with the change of the objects it touches. The container may be skew, but the water always keeps horizontal. Therefore, water is related to "standard" and is friendly to everyone. If it encounters unfair evil acts of bullying the weak and deceiving others, the water will rush and roar and the so-called "exclaim against injustice".

Chinese people are well aware that military force, physical strength and material resources cannot conquer the hearts of the people. Those who can conquer the hearts of the people use the way of fairness and the trend of harmony and peace. "Good deeds" are derived from the fairness of water. When dealing with people, we should be friendly both to the strong and the weak. We should respect the strong and understand and help the weak. The attitude you use to treat others with be the same attitude that others treat you with. If you treat the strong and the weak equally with no prejudice, you will be able to win the support of all people and to achieve and win everything.

Chinese people hold the same quality of peace and affinity as "water". They value harmony the most precious in everything. They live in this world by virtue of the affinity and tenderness like water, the silent dedication to nourish all things, the harmony and friendly to dissolve other things and generosity and compatibility. The Chinese nation adheres to a path of peaceful rise which is different from that of the Western powers that rely on war to complete their development. The world has finally begun to understand that the Chinese people are so obsessed with peace and harmony and regard harmony as the most precious.

On "Who on earth are the Chinese?"

To answer the question of "Who on earth are the Chinese?", we try to sort out the group behaviors of some Chinese people, which are only a small part definitely, and the thinking logic, philosophical thinking, and cultural context behind these group behavior patterns. There is no doubt that there is a clear "positive correlation" between Chinese people's group behaviors and "water" in nature. This may be a new perspective to understand and understand Chinese culture and Chinese people.

Even only with this group of Chinese people's group behaviors as a model, the world may be still able to accurately judge that how Chinese people think, what they say, what they do, how they treat people, as well as their lifestyles, ethics, morals and values are totally different from those of other countries and nationalities in the world. The culture of China and the ultimate belief of Chinese people have their own heights and breadth. They are unique.

Lu Xun, a Chinese writer, once said, "China is deeply rooted in Taoism. If one wants to understand the history and culture of China, one must understand Taoism first. Lin Yutang, a great figure of Chinese culture, said, "The Chinese are Taoist in nature and Confucian in culture, but their Taoist thoughts are even more than Confucian thoughts."

Laozi, the sage of Chinese philosophy and the founder of Taoism, said, "The Dao produced One; One produced Two; Two produced Three; Three produced All things." (*Chapter 42 of The Book of the Way*). The Dao produced One, and One is Tai Chi. Two produced Three, and Two is Yin and Yang. Two produced Three, and Three is the coordination of Yin and Yang. Three produced All things. Dao is the natural law, which is unique. Dao itself contains Yin and Yang, which intersect to form a proper state - harmony, in which everything comes into being. All things back Yin and face Yang, and form new bodies of harmony in the agitation between the two Qis of Yin and Yang - everything.

The target of belief of Chinese people is essentially different from that of Westerners. Westerners believe in a fabricated religion under the subjective consciousness of human beings. Religion sets up a God or theocracy system with great power, strength and moral status to force people to revere, to rely on, and to make people dare not disobey or betray, or even to make people dare not think about or question this absolute authority.

Those who believe in religion go to heaven for eternal life; while those who do not believe in religion go to hell. Religious theocracy under high pressure and majesty often has a set of philosophical and theoretical system, which gives people spiritual and practical guidance. What can be explained belong to God, and what cannot be explained also belong to God. It is simple, high-oppression and powerful.

Compared with Western religions, Chinese people's religious views are much more relaxed and natural. Believers naturally grow their worships out of their hearts freely and casually. Laozi said, "In the universe there are four that are great, and the (sage) king is one of them. Man takes his law from the Earth; the Earth takes its law from Heaven; Heaven takes its law from the Dao. The law of the Dao is its being what it is." There are four that are great in the universe, and the living creatures represented by human is also one of them. Man follows the law of the earth, earth follows the law of the heaven, heaven follows the law of Tao,

Tao follows the law of nature, and the law of nature is the dominant of everything. Whether you believe or not, or what you believe, is your freedom. Heaven, earth and nature will not interfere with you, hinder you. You can do what you want to do, believe in any target you want to believe in. Whether to go to heaven or go to hell is your personal choice. Only the will of heaven and earth can never be violated. Only natural laws can never be defied or resisted. No matter how talented people are, it is impossible for them to surpass natural laws. Obedience to natural laws is the right path.

The law of nature "Tao" has no trace. It cannot be seen, heard, touched, or felt, but it really exists everywhere in the world. However, natural phenomena are obvious. They can be seen, heard, felt, so they are tangible. Therefore, all kinds of things and phenomena in nature have become a reasonable way to observe and understand Tao. Starting from natural phenomena, we can observe Tao and explore the essence, core and nature of Tao.

There are heaven and earth in the natural world, and also the law of nature "Tao". Heaven is above, earth is below, and "water" represents the law of nature governing all other substances. Water is the origin of everything and the foundation of all living beings. Similarly, taking natural objects as models for reference and imitation, there are great differences between China and the West in their choice. The philosophical concepts ultimately formed are totally different.

Westerners focus on finding and digging targets for learning in the biological chain (food chain). They focus on efficiency, material and money. They mostly learn knowledge and acquire wisdom from animals and plants that are less intelligent than human beings. On the other hand, Chinese people have a wider range of interests and concerns. They are better at finding and digging targets

for learning and reference in the two systems of biological chain and water cycle. While learning and acquiring the technologies and skills of human survival and development in the biological chain circle, Chinese people also seek knowledge from the water circle which is higher than human intelligence, and obtain the inspiration for human ethics, morality and philosophical wisdom.

The clever Chinese fully recognize the limitations and shortcomings of human species, and strive to expand their own realm and vision upward and outward to seek knowledge and learn further and deeper outside the circle. They humbly seek knowledge and human wisdom from the water circulation system, instead of just burying themselves in the biological chain and looking downward and inward for reference objects as Westerners do. The uniqueness of Chinese culture lies in its standing position, which is much higher than that of the West. The level of Chinese philosophy is much higher than that of the West.

British historian Toynbee believed that, if the world would have a future, the future world would depend on China. Why? He believed that China was the only country with the feelings for the whole world. Since Darwinism became prevalent, the concepts of "the law of the jungle", "survival of the fittest", "jungle doctrine" and "national nationalism" have swept across Europe. They have only an "ego" nation-state, while the Chinese have a broad mind of "peace in the world", which is a kind of feeling of accommodating the world.

Leibniz, Germany's most important scientist and philosopher, wrote in the introduction to *Das Neueste von China*, "We never believed in the existence of a nation that is more advanced than our ethics and more progressive in our ways of conducting oneself in society. Now China in the East gives us a big awakening!" He praised China for "the highest level of human culture and the most advanced technical civilization. If a wise man is elected to decide which nation is the most outstanding, rather than deciding which goddess is the most beautiful, then he will hand over the golden apple to the Chinese."

More than 400 years ago, Italian missionary Matteo Ricci traveled thousands of miles to China. With the question of "why the powerful Chinese Empire did not colonize the weak nations around it", he began to devote himself to the study of Chinese civilization. He found a totally different historical and cultural tradition from the West, and found a country that was not a militarist but a pacifist. Therefore, in his famous *Answer to China*, Matteo Ricci expressed his sincere exclamation, "Although China has a well-equipped army, his people never thought of launching an aggressive war and never had the ambition to conquer." The concept of harmony has long been deeply embedded in the cultural tradition and national character of the Chinese nation and rooted in the historical practice of the Chinese nation for thousands of years.

Russell, a great thinker, believed that "The Chinese nation is one of the best nations in the world that I have ever met." For such a wonderful country "being abused like this, I would like to make a more serious condemnation to every powerful country in the world". He is deeply aware of the importance of China, "China issue, even if it has no impact on anyone outside China, is still of far-reaching importance, because China's population accounts for about a quarter of the total human population.

However, in fact, the whole world will be greatly affected by the progress of China's affairs. For better or worse, the progress of China's affairs will be a decisive factor in the next two centuries."

Russell saw the value of Chinese civilization wisely, "After Chinese traditional culture is supplemented with new excellent elements from the West, the new civilization produced in the future may be better than all kinds of civilizations ever produced in the West." A Westerner is still aware of the value of Chinese culture, the Chinese themselves should know and understand the unique nature and essence of Chinese culture in the East.

In the cosmic ecosystem, the law of nature is the supreme, and the "water" is the supreme. Whether you believe it or not, like it or not, for both theists and atheists, Chinese or Westerners can hardly disobey the orders of heaven and earth or resist the destiny of nature. Within the scope of the human world, the Chinese have been learning from "water" with no stop for 5000 years, and will continue to study "water" for another 5000 years or more in the future and to practice "water" and move forward.

The Chinese nation position itself to play the role of "water" in human society to treat others like water and live in harmony with other countries and nations for common prosperity. China's new discourse right strongly advocates respect, inclusiveness, equality, mutual understanding, mutual assistance, mutual benefit, win-win cooperation, harmony and peace. It standardizes the world leader's demeanor with the conduct of "the excellence of water appears in its benefiting all things without contending". The Chinese people behave in a "no-contending" manner to treat people and things and make achievements.

The spirit of water gives birth to Chinese philosophy and culture, ethics and values, as well as manners.

Chapter NINE

Thoughts after reading

The Chinese nation is a nation with its own religious faith. It has faith in the universe and natural rules or "Tao" and believes that nature is the sole deity. The Chinese people are purely theists, rather than atheists as widely recognized by foreign people.

The only reason why the Chinese people are regarded as atheists is that their religious faith in "nature" is inconsistent with the standards for the religious faith in "unnatural" things in the Western world. As a result, they are mistakenly seen as special atheists.

There is significant difference in the view on the world and in values between the Oriental and Western countries. In most cases, the Oriental countries show a view on the world and values which are opposite to that of the Western ones. For instance, the Oriental countries appreciate "collectivism", while the Western ones advocate "individualism"; the former attach equal importance to "freedom, centralization, democracy and unity", while the latter emphasize absolute "freedom and democracy"; the former regard the government as a problem-solver, while the latter deem the government as a trouble maker.

With faith in natural rules or "Tao", the Chinese nation believes in water which is "closest to Tao". Their behaviors and moral systems are all modeled after water. Then, what did the Westerners follow or imitate in their growth? Or how did they grow in a completely independent and separated way? What is certain is that the influence of water is rarely seen in the Western culture and philosophy.

The persons or things that have the highest excellence are just like water, and the wisdom of water is supreme. Theoretically, it is impossible that the Chinese nation, which has followed and revered the quality and virtue of water in the past 5,000 years, would lag behind any nation in the Western world in terms of philosophy and culture. Nor should it. It should have a discourse system featuring special Oriental wisdom.

Water is good at benefiting everything without vying for any fame or gain. A Chinese nation which has followed and imitated water in conduct would instinctively free itself from hegemony and power even if it has not thrived or has thrived and become powerful. Therefore, "Theory on a Dangerous China", "Theory of the Collapse of China" and "Thucydides Trap" cannot hold water. They are groundless in theory and are hard to be supported in practice.

For 5,000 years, the Chinese nation has been doing one thing persistently and attentively -- providing most people in the world with a fairer and more harmonious, justifiable and civilized social organization. The Chinese people are creative in that they focus on and operate a natural mechanism that follows and imitates the water cycle. It aims to establish a human society according to the requirement that "humanity" should be consistent with "natural rules".

If one understands water, he/she would have a chance to understand the essence of the Chinese culture and philosophy and realize that China is no longer a mysterious country and the Chinese people are no longer a special people that separates itself from other peoples. He/she can be a Chinese

or a foreigner. Nevertheless, the Chinese culture remains extensive and profound, has a long history and creates endless wonderful things.

China lacks partners? The Chinese nation likes and admires water, and few countries or nations in the world equates it in this regard. As an increasing number of countries and nations have become aware of the wisdom of water, it is inevitable that China's partners will be found all over the world.

Water is universal in every corner of the world. Different countries and nations share similar understanding of the physical attributes and functions of water. But they differ from each other in the social and cultural attributes reflected by water and in the understanding of the spiritual world. Nonetheless, it doesn't necessarily mean that water has lost its universal value; it just shows that different groups of people differ from each other in the understanding of water. Water has unique and supreme "universal value".